INDUSTRIAL PROGRESS IN
POLAND, CZECHOSLOVAKIA, AND
EAST GERMANY
1937-1962

Industrial Progress in Poland, Czechoslovakia, and East Germany

1937-1962

BY

ALFRED ZAUBERMAN

Lecturer, London School of Economics

Issued under the auspices of the
Royal Institute of International Affairs

OXFORD UNIVERSITY PRESS

LONDON NEW YORK TORONTO

1964

Oxford University Press, Amen House, London E.C.4

GLASGOW NEW YORK TORONTO MELBOURNE WELLINGTON
BOMBAY CALCUTTA MADRAS KARACHI LAHORE DACCA
CAPE TOWN SALISBURY NAIROBI IBADAN ACCRA
KUALA LUMPUR HONG KONG

Printed in Great Britain by
The Camelot Press Ltd., London and Southampton

TO MY WIFE

PREFACE

OWING to what is probably something more than a whim of fate, the collectivist, centrally planned 'model' based on Marxian socialism first established itself in an economic milieu which was in radical contrast with its doctrinal premises. It came to be regarded as the model of the industrial development of retarded areas. This corresponded to the realities of the part of the Euro-Asiatic continent under its sway, with one exception which is more often than not forgotten: Central Europe. Here, and here only, Marxian socialism came into its own in its doctrinally postulated environment as the successor of a mature capitalism. (The forces which brought it into operation need not be considered here.)

This exceptional characteristic gives the post-war industrial experience of Central Europe a singular interest. It may also justify the apparently artificial delimitation of the area under study. Two of the countries—Czechoslovakia and East Germany —rank indisputably among the industrially mature countries of the world. The inclusion of the third may seem more questionable. Semi-industrial Poland, however, forms in some respects the very centre of industrial Central Europe. This is due partly to her size and geographical position, partly to the highly industrialized 'islands' contained within her present boundaries, but above all to her control over by far the greater part of Silesia, the industrial heart of the area, sometimes referred to as the Ruhr of Central Europe.

The sponsor of this study, the Royal Institute of International Affairs, originally gave it two specific terms of reference. One was to concentrate on industrial growth rather than on the overall economic development of the area. The other was to analyse the position of the area and its progress against the European background. As time went by emphasis on the second of these was relaxed.

The inevitable point of departure in an inquiry into industrial growth was an examination of the economic strategy pursued and the mechanism applied to promote it. It was, however, the sponsor's express wish that this study should be addressed to the general reader rather than the specialist, and this, as well as the limitations of space, did not permit full justice being done to these rather technical matters. I have, therefore, confined myself to some rudiments and propose to return later to a fuller and more rigorous treatment of problems of Soviet-type systems.

A point which inevitably called for a good deal of attention was quantification of growth, the more so as the validity of official claims in this respect has been, to say the least, controversial. In anticipation of further argument it may be stressed that no absolute 'truth' as to the 'real' pace of growth is conceivable. But—if only to give more meaning to comparability—an attempt has been made to measure the three countries' industrial progress by the use of concepts and conventions accepted in the West. As far as the area goes this has been partly a pioneering effort; of its weakness the author is only too conscious. Results covering the first two post-war decades have already been published. The study has since been both expanded and brought up to the early 1960's, and it is proposed to publish the new version in a not too distant future, together with an appraisal of the growth of national products and changes in their composition. Hence, on the sponsor's initiative, no more than a short summary of findings has been included in the present book. As against this, the two factors contributing to growth have been accorded a somewhat lengthier discussion. One is capital formation—its size, composition, and sources—the other is manpower.

The reasons for concentrating on at least three principal 'growth' industries—those supplying energy, metal, and chemicals—are self-evident. The countries' foreign economic relations also receive attention. The relevance of foreign trade to industrial growth has been recognized now, if somewhat belatedly, in the area. It is against this background that the problems of the integration of industrial Central Europe into the wider economic framework of the Soviet sphere of influence have been analysed.

The construction of this study on such patterns has given it a primarily descriptive character. Moreover it has almost turned it into a monographic collection of case studies, which has its obvious disadvantages as well as advantages. The writer had in mind that some admirable studies covering various countries of the area, various periods, and specific problems were available to the reader, to mention only the works of Dr Alton, Professors Douglas, Taylor, Marczewski, Montias, Gleitze, and the publications of the Deutsches Institut für Wirtschaftswissenschaft. Their excellence has been recognized by references in these pages.

In conclusion I would wish to convey my warmest thanks to all from whom I have received help and encouragement: particularly to the Royal Institute of International Affairs, under whose auspices the book is being published, to its Research Secretary, Mr A. S. B. Olver, and Miss Katharine Duff, who prepared the book for press with great patience and ingenuity; further, to Mr E. F. Jackson, who kindly discussed some part of it with me; also to Mr Hugh McCormick of the British Iron and Steel Foundation and Mr L. F. Haber of Imperial Chemical Industries. To my wife, whose help included the typing of a difficult manuscript and the compiling of the indexes, a special debt of gratitude is due.

A. Z.

May 1963

ABBREVIATIONS

Amer. Econ. R.	*American Economic Review* (Amer. Econ. Assoc.).
Biul. Stat.	*Biuletyn Statystyczny* (Poland, Min. of Finance).
BNLQR	Banca Nazionale del Lavoro (Rome), *Quarterly Review.*
CSR	Czechoslovakia.
Dtsch. Inst. Wirtsch.–Forsch.	Deutsches Institut für Wirtschaftsforschung (Institut für Konjunkturforschung).
ECE, *Bulletin*	ECE, *Bulletin for Europe.*
—— *Survey*	—— *Economic Survey of Europe.*
Econ. J.	*Economic Journal* (Royal Econ. Soc.).
Ekon.	*Ekonomista* (Polish Econ. Soc.).
Gosp. Plan.	*Gospodarka Planowa* (Poland, State Planning Commission).
Hosp. Nov.	*Hospodarske Noviny* (CSR, Nat. Planning Office).
Int. Lab. R.	*International Labour Review* (ILO).
Maly rocz. stat.	*Maly rocznik statystyczny* (Poland, State Planning Commission).
Peaceful Uses of Atomic Energy	U.N., Int. Conf. on the Peaceful Uses of Atomic Energy, *Proceedings* (N.Y., 1955–6).
Plan. Hosp.	*Planovane Hospodarstvi* (CSR, Nat. Planning Office).
Plan. Khoz.	*Planovoe Khozyaistvo* (USSR, Gosplan).
Pol. Ekon.	*Politicka Ekonomie* (Czechoslovak Academy of Sciences).
Przeglad Stat.	*Przeglad Statystyczny* (Polish Econ. Soc.).
Przeglad Zag. Spol.	*Przeglad Zagadnien Spolecznich* (Poland).
Quart. J. Econ.	*Quarterly Journal of Economics* (Harvard).
R. Econ. Stat.	*Review of Economics and Statistics* (Harvard Univ. and Econ. Soc.).
R. Econ. Stud.	*Review of Economic Studies* (Cambridge).
Rocz. pol. i gosp.	*Rocznik polityczny i gospodarczy* (Poland).
Rocz. stat.	*Rocznik statystyczny* (Poland, Central Statistical Office).
Rolnik Ekon.	*Rolnik Ekonomista* (Poland).
Sov. Stud.	*Soviet Studies* (Glasgow Univ., Dept. for Study of Soc. and Econ. Institutions of USSR).
Stat. Jb.	*Statistisches Jahrbuch* (GDR, Statistisches Zentralamt).

Stat. Jb. (FR)	*Statistisches Jahrbuch für der Bundesrepublik Deutschland.* (Statistisches Bundesamt).
Stat. Obzor	*Statisticky Obzor* (CSR, State Statistical Office).
Stat. Prax.	*Statistische Praxis* (GDR, Stat. Zentralamt).
Stat. roc.	*Statisticka rocenka* (CSR, State Statistical Office).
Stat. Zpravy	*Statisticke Zpravy* (CSR, State Statistical Office).
Vjh.	*Vierteljahrshefte.*
Vopr. Ekon.	*Voprosy Ekonomiki* (Academy of Sciences, USSR, Institute of Economics).
Wber.	*Wochenbericht.*
Wiad. Stat.	*Wiadomosci Statystyczne* (Poland, Central Statistical Office).
Wirtsch. und Stat.	*Wirtschaft und Statistik* (Germany (FR), Stat. Zentralamt).
Ww.	*Wirtschaftswissenschaft.*
Yb. Lab. Stat.	*Yearbook of Labour Statistics* (ILO).
Z. Gosp.	*Zycie Gospodarcze* (Poland).
Z. Warsz.	*Zycie Warszawy* (Poland).
Zagad. Ekon. Rol.	*Zagadnienia Ekonomiki Rolnej* (Poland).

CONTENTS

CHAPTER I

The Economic Mechanism and the Strategy of Industrial Growth

THE effect of the economic mechanism can scarcely be isolated with any degree of precision from that of other influences on post-war industrial progress in Central Europe. As there can, however, be but little doubt that its impact was considerable, at least a few words should, perhaps, be said on this subject in the opening pages of this study.

THE INTRODUCTION OF CENTRALIZED PLANNING AND CONTROL

A collectivist, centrally-planning system came to the Central European economy as a result of its incorporation into the Soviet sphere of political and ideological influences. A direct and far-reaching engagement of the state in economic life had, however, strong historical roots in the area. Inter-war Poland had a distinct inclination towards *étatisme*, partly due to the lack of a vigorous, capitalist middle class.[1] To fill the vacuum the state took upon itself the role of pioneer and entrepreneur in many fields of the economy. As elsewhere, once it had entered the economic stage it tended to expand its domain of control. Roughly half the bank credits flowed from government banks and agencies. Some of the leading sectors of the economy were almost completely owned and managed by the state.

In her part of the world Poland was far from being an exception. Germany and Czechoslovakia profoundly differed from Poland in their pre-war social and economic structures, yet in both the state had the tradition of an active initiator, supporter, controller, and entrepreneur. The Great Depression set in motion

[1] F. Zweig, *Poland between Two Wars* (London, 1944), pp. 106ff.

a 'cold socialization'—the assumption of control over key concerns by the governments which came to their rescue. The high degree of vertical and horizontal concentration of capital and enterprise in industry facilitated state penetration. The Third Reich and its *Wehrwirtschaft* strengthened the public hand in the economy, both at home and in the Czech Protectorate.[2] Massive wartime investments—because of their scale and character—worked in the same direction. Two world wars provided experience and a training school for central planning.

The ideological climate which spread during the war in the two Slav countries of Central Europe favoured a still more active role on the part of the state. The programme of the Underground State of Poland foreshadowed a new era in which public authority would assume greater responsibilities in economic life, and planning was seen as an antidote for many of the ills of the inter-war period. Czechoslovak policy developed along the same lines. 'Our state', declared Dr Benes in 1944, 'will carry out a number of economic and social changes, and will adopt the principle of a planned political and economic policy.'[3] The Kosice Programme (April 1945) foreshadowed a wide sector of public ownership in industry and effective central planning.

Out of the chaos into which Central Europe was plunged in the first post-war days, something like a mixed system grew up more or less spontaneously. The state took over the predominant part of industry. A nucleus of planning machinery was created. But the more or less traditional tools of economic policy were still used by the governments. Markets retained a relatively wide sphere of operation, though—no less than in the West—dislocations called for a resort to direct controls and to rationing by card rather than by pocket. Profit was still largely accepted as the prime engine of economic life.[4] Initial short-term plans were in the nature of broad statements of policy and guidance.

There was more than a grain of truth in the saying that Poland's economy looked towards Marx with one eye and towards Keynes with the other;[5] but even by the time that the remark appeared in print this tendency to squint was diminishing.

[2] Cf. W. Guillebaud, *The Economic Recovery of Germany* (London, 1939), p. 104 and *passim*.
[3] P. D. Henderson and D. Seers, in *Bull. Oxf. Inst. Stat.*, ix (Nov. 1947) and no. 11, 1950, p. 357.
[4] Ibid. pp. 358ff.   [5] S. E. Harris ed., *Economic Planning* (N.Y., 1949), p. 433.

Before the end of the 1940's state enterprise covered almost the whole of the industry of the three countries. East Germany stood out as an exception in a double sense: first, because much of industry was controlled and run as a Soviet economic enclave through the Sowjetische Aktiengesellschaften (SAGs); secondly, because for various reasons a residual private sector remained, and was to persist for some time longer.[6] Comprehensive, centralized planning and control came in the wake of the extinction of private property and enterprise. The principle of the uniqueness of the road towards a socialist society—vigorously asserted throughout the area at the beginning of the 1950's—was soon also understood to embrace Soviet experience in this field as an integral part of the construction of socialism. Accordingly Soviet concepts, methods, and techniques of planning and running the economy were transplanted, and Soviet industrial organization was copied.

The degree of approximation to the Soviet example has varied from period to period and from country to country. The minutiae of the borrowed institutional framework and planning methods will not be described here; space allows us to deal only with the fundamentals.

The central plan defines quantitatively the basic macro-economic proportions, rates, and directions, such as the rate of growth of national product and its components, its basic uses, the rate and components of capital formation, and the size, and partly the composition, of public and private consumption.[7] It determines the size and pattern of productive capacities and of outputs. The plan is drawn up on two inter-related planes: in a 'real', physical-term version and a money-term one. By definition

---

[6] By 1947 the socialist sector in Polish industry accounted for 99·5% of total gross output (*Rocz. stat., 1949*, p. 29). In East Germany the SAGs and the nationalized and co-operative enterprises represented 77·6%, and the private sector 22·4%, of gross output in 1950. By 1956 private enterprise accounted for 12·3% of industrial gross output in current prices, excluding construction and handicrafts. The percentage for construction was 43·9. Moreover, by mid-1957, the state was partner in about 500 industrial enterprises, in which it owned 45% of stock capital. Cf. R. Lukas, *Zehn Jahre Sowjetische Besatzungszone* (Mainz–Gonseheim, 1955), p. 167; *Stat. Jb., 1956*, p. 5; *Neues Deutschland*, 30 Aug., 1957.

The share of the socialist sector in Czechoslovak industrial output was 75, 95, and 99% in 1946, 1948, and 1951 respectively. Cf. *Deset let rozvoje narodniho hospodarstvi a kultury Ceskoslovenske Republiky* (Prague, 1956), p. 67.

[7] For a brief and excellent outline of planning in socialist countries, see Oskar Lange, 'Les fondements de la planification économique', *Cahiers de l'Inst. de Sci. Écon. Appliquée*, no. 49, 1957.

both mirror two facets of the same phenomena and processes. Logically the method would call for harmonized correlation of flows of equipment, of raw and intermediate materials, and of labour in both versions. More on this later.

Plan-building is supposed to be based on a two-way flow of information and co-ordination. On this basis output goals are set to meet the postulated final demands with corresponding requirements in productive capacities. In practice they form a rather mixed bag of targets for key commodities, intermediate as well as 'final'. Their coherence is conceptually secured by means of 'material balances'. In planning procedures borrowed from Soviet methodology these are the principal vehicle for co-ordinating requirements and supplies: a material balance sets in physical quantities the requirements of a given commodity against expected availabilities from production and stocks, with due allowance for foreign trade. In this way, for instance, the balance of steel links up the steel-making and steel-using sectors of industry, with allowance for imports and exports involved. Material balances are constructed with reference to a system of input coefficients. (This is also true of manpower balances, which are akin to them.) These are derived from technological practice and possibly corrected for technical advance, usually in the light of experience of advanced plant at home or abroad. The planner works his way towards consistency—towards equilibrium—through successive adjustments. He will expect this iterative process to bring him eventually somewhere near the efficient (optimal) solution: it is worthy of emphasis that the mechanism as such does not verify optimality.

A plan thus arrived at is conveyed down the administrative ladder. At the bottom, enterprises receive their orders, stating their targets and the implied technological methods. The watch over the discipline of 'norms'—coefficients of material and labour inputs—is one of the essential tasks of the economic administration at all levels. Physical-term goals converted into money terms are then consolidated in the overall financial plan, correlated with the balances of social product, of the state budget, and of the population's income and expenditure. The core of the latter is the national wage bill and estimates of the peasants' incomes.

What has been sketched here is, however, only a broad idealized scheme of the methodology. Life has revealed its limitations.

We may safely refer the reader here to the experience of Poland, because this is both typical and the best documented.[8]

The underlying assumption of the 'material-balance' system is a high degree of comprehensiveness, homogeneity, and precision. Neither of these two premisses has proved sufficiently realistic. First, there is a handicap of 'circularity' in the build-up of balances, none of the supply-branches being able to commit itself as regards its 'material-balance' proposal before it is told about the others' possibilities and programmes. Furthermore, the central planner is engaged in a losing battle against time. The whole conception of a system of balances depends on 'the principle of simultaneity'. To be consistent it must be homogeneous, that is, it must correspond to the same 'plan variant'. This requirement stands little chance of being met in actual life. The computational burden of an adequately expanded system of balances corresponding to each plan variant is so heavy that by the time calculations are completed it is already out of date,[9] in the sense that the planner has moved to a next-stage variant; and time would hardly allow for it to be brought up to date by repeating the procedure: hence the planner has to put up with rough correctives. Precision has proved as often as not quite 'illusory'.

As technical difficulties came to be realized, the range of items covered by the system of 'material balances' was cut down to include only commodities of key importance, lending themselves to physical-term aggregates—usually those individually treated in the national plan. Thus the premiss of comprehensiveness has been dropped. 'Material balances' have become no more than fragmentary estimates; they have failed to form an integrated system.

One of the fundamental weaknesses of the 'material-balance' method is that the underlying technical production coefficients mirror only direct—'first order'—interdependencies in the economy. They do not inform the planner of wider implications of his choices: for instance, he will know how much coal is used in steel-works per ton of steel produced but not the quantities needed at preceding stages throughout the system. In still other words, the direct 'norms' leave the planner in the dark as to the

---

[8] See an illuminating analysis in *Prace i materialy Zakladu Badan Ekonomicznych*, (research papers of the Planning Commission of the Polish Council of Ministers), no. 11, Apr. 1958, especially pp. 31ff.

[9] Ibid. p. 34. On Soviet experience see A. Yefimov, *Perestroyka upravleniya promyshlennstyu i stroitelstvom v SSSR* (Moscow, 1957).

full range and size of capacities needed to support his targets. The resulting lack of integration reveals itself—as the plan is being implemented—in bottlenecks, strains, and stresses. The lack of coherence reduces *pro tanto* the chances of *optimal* choices. In reality the planner gropes for them in a hit-and-miss fashion. A Soviet authority has convincingly argued that what by now is a traditional method results in accidental choices with best solutions only rarely adopted; that planning is quantitative rather than qualitative; and that it does not keep pace with the rhythm of economic life.[10]

It is clear from our sketch that, in the system described, the role of value-term indicators in resource allocation is subordinate. Indeed, it is not too sweeping a generalization to say that the second half of the 1940's and the first of the 1950's saw throughout Central Europe a gradual atrophy of value-term planning and controlling. The connexion between the set of 'material balances' and national money-term accounting was becoming increasingly loose. This also corresponds to Soviet experience. Academician Strumilin pointed out that in practice the Gosplan concerned itself primarily with 'material balances' of individual commodities, such as ores, coal, iron, and so on, and 'far less often with economic balances such as those of consumption and accumulation of national income or of the population's incomes and expenditures, and apparently not at all with general balances of national economy . . .'.[11]

It is a sufficiently safe generalization to say that by the early 1950's the mechanism, transplanted from the Soviet Union, imparted to the economies of the area a high degree of dynamism: it indeed 'institutionalized' growth. But at the same time it revealed its shortcomings. In agreement with its logic, growingly centralized planning and controls, relying primarily on physical-term calculations, tended to hold a grip on details down to the level of enterprises beyond the administrative machinery's ability to cope with them. Further, it proved to be tilted towards quantity at the expense of quality. Thirty years of Soviet experience have signally failed to produce an effective system of qualitative checks and controls. It is very probable that the shortcomings of

[10] L. V. Kantorovich, *Ekonomicheski raschet nailuchshego ispolzovaniya resursov* (Moscow, 1960).

[11] S. G. Strumilin, *Ocherki sotsialisticheskoy ekonomiki SSSR* (Moscow, 1959), p. 144.

the mechanism manifested themselves with greater force in the highly complex environment of Central Europe than in the Soviet Union herself, at least in the earlier period of her planning era. It will be suggested further on that, by its very nature, Soviet policy for economic development is of the shock-strategy—unbalancing strategy—kind, at least for the period of the gathering momentum of growth. Seen from this angle the unbalancing effect of the mechanism should probably be treated as a part of the price paid for expansion. Whether the price is fair would probably depend on given circumstances.

One could hardly apportion the root causes of the severe strains and stresses which affected Central European economies, especially those of Poland and East Germany in the early 1950's, as between the consequences of the strategy for growth pursued and the shortcomings of the mechanism operated. However, around the mid-1950's, an acute awareness of its defects influenced thinking in Central Europe. In a celebrated essay Oskar Lange[12] likened the economic system to that of a war economy. He also emphasized the increasingly adverse psychological impact of this system and blamed it for a prevailing apathy and 'nihilistic' attitude to which excessive centralization in planning and control had contributed. The second half of the decade, in contrast to the first, saw a trend towards devolution in management and—as the Polish Economic Council pointed out in its theses on the economic mechanism[13]—towards the primacy of economic 'levers'.

THE REFORMS OF THE LATE 1950'S AND THE 1960'S

The reforms of industrial organization and management carried out in Central Europe towards the end of the 1950's were to a certain extent inspired by contemporary events in the USSR. They displayed, however, a considerable variation of approach. While the Soviet reforms—those of a huge country—tended to transfer responsibility on territorial lines, devolution in the much smaller countries of Central Europe was mainly on a vertical basis. East Germany, however, abolished most of her industrial ministries, especially those in charge of such key industries as iron and steel, coal, power, heavy machinery, and general engineering. Most of their powers were transferred to the State Planning

[12] *Z. Gosp.*, no. 40, 1956.
[13] Ibid. no. 22, 1957. The Polish post-1956 'model' is discussed in J. M. Montias, *Central Planning in Poland* (1962), published after this book was completed.

Commission, which thus now unites the functions of management with those of planning. Territorial planning agencies serve as the Commission's executive organs; and so also, to all intents and purposes, do the 'associations' of enterprises (VVB). By now they have a wide sphere of decision on the patterning of output, labour and wages, and investment. Some of the largest firms, however, come directly under the Commission. Over small-scale, local industries the Commission exercises its authority through the Economic Councils (*Wirtschaftsräte*). The East German reforms are thus the nearest to the Soviet prototype.

Though both Czechoslovakia and Poland have retained a wide range of ministries, their 'reformed models' also find a place for 'associations' of enterprises, to which all but the largest units are required to belong. The proportion of exempted enterprises is smaller in Poland than in Czechoslovakia. In the latter country the concentration of industry has been carried further than in any other Central European country. By 1959 the 1,417 industrial firms existing in 1948 had been merged into 929, but only 487 of these had been grouped, into 67 associations. The Czechoslovak associations, however, differ considerably from the VVB, in principle at least, in that they are designed to act as clearing-houses, coordinators, and links between the central administration and the enterprises.

The most recent Polish view is that an association represents the collective interest of the enterprises *vis-à-vis* the ministry. Its 'college of directors' (*kolegium dyrektorow*) is accordingly constituted as a forum and a consultative body. Conversely, the association is expected to 'represent' the ministry *vis-à-vis* the enterprises. It does, however, also possess some executive and controlling powers. Among other functions it coordinates enterprises' activities, redistributes their profits, allocates investment funds, and helps to administer reserve funds.

In all three countries enterprises, and their associations and/or territorial authorities, have much more freedom than before to pattern supplies and to some extent output and sales policy as well; and the lower ranks of industrial administration, from the enterprise unit upwards, may now exercise more initiative in planning output and capacity. Everywhere much less is now prescribed in the way of centrally fixed targets and planning 'indices'.

Managers throughout the area have been given more scope for initiative and for making decisions with regard to product-mix, technology, internal organization and, to a lesser extent, the expansion of capacity. Freedom of manœuvre has been particularly wide in the Polish 'experimental' enterprises, which are expressly set aside for the empirical working out of suitable forms of organization, for instance in inter-industrial planning, organizing supplies, marketing, and calculating prices and costs. Any appraisal of the actual degree of autonomy at intermediate and lower levels should, however, allow for disparities between schemes on paper and in actual working.[14]

Czechoslovak enterprises are encouraged to enter into mutual long-term transactions stabilizing their sales and purchases; and such arrangements are to form the basis of long-term plans. Czechoslovakia has also gone further than the other countries in decentralizing new capital formation as well as replacement. Poland has tried to follow her example: direct central control—apart from new projects—is only to apply to major technological reconstruction or expansion of plants, other decision-making being left to firms or associations. The Czechoslovaks have, however, discovered that decentralization in investment has tended to result in building-material bottlenecks and to slow down the pace of construction in other ways as well. Some checks have proved to be inevitable.

In the incentive system emphasis has shifted from gross output to profit performance. As early as 1957 Professor Michal Kalecki[15] proposed a 'new system of stimuli and command' based on four 'elements': value-added as the principal index of a firm's activities; its wage-bill component; the rate of increase of profits as a basis for premium-type remuneration; and non-repayable interest-bearing investment credits. A proportion of amortization allowance would also remain with the firm. Mechanisms actually devised have borrowed a good deal from this scheme—in varying degrees and different combinations in individual countries. The Czechoslovak model is probably the most consistent in building up its system of incentives for enterprises and labour as a basis for decentralization. It relies on a set of norms which determine the

---

[14] On the status of the Polish industrial associations see J. L. Töplitz, in Z. *Gosp.*, 20 Nov. 1960, on their status in East Germany, *Die Einheit*, no. 6, 1963.
[15] Z. *Gosp.* no. 29, 1957.

firm's share in profit and profit-increment, and in wear-and-tear allowances; and which put aside part of the retained profits for the firm's employees.

The crudity of the Soviet-type 'gross-gross' output index[16] as a planning and control device and as a measurement of success and reward has been widely recognized. The Polish 'theses' on planning of 1960 vindicate it as the 'fundamental' value index of production, 'since in most cases it forms the only (feasible) basis for the planning of the wage bill, employment, capital accumulation, and so on, . . . [and also because] a departure from it would be impossible from the angle of international and inter-temporal comparability'.[17] It is hoped that distortions of the operational picture due to this index will be mitigated by the use of more rational prices and by adequate recording of (and allowance for) transactions inside industry. Besides this, however, an index 'approximating net-output' has been recommended for certain industries, those, for instance, with a high fabrication component in cost-structure; and for certain special purposes, such as assessing labour-productivity and relating it to wages.

Demand is to have a more immediate influence on Polish planning of outputs. In Czechoslovakia it is directly to guide production (which incidentally reduces the importance of the gross-gross output index). Here enterprises are given scope for adjusting their product-mix to their marketing possibilities. (See V. P. Miroshnichenko ed., *Sovershenstvovanie form upravleniya promyshlennostyu* (Moscow, 1961).)

The dichotomy on which the reforms of the late 1950's rest—devolution in administration and management combined under a command system with disciplined central planning—raises the question of providing the central planner with a box of effective tools for the implementation of his policy. There is at least a *prima facie* link between decentralization and the operation of value parameters. (Qualifications of this statement will be made later in our argument.) It seems logical *prima facie* that once detailed, direct guidance is abandoned or circumscribed this alternative has to be resorted to. It is therefore understandable that ever since the mid-1950's the role of the price mechanism, and the form this should take, should have focused attention in

---

[16] On the working of this index see below, pp. 110f.
[17] Cf. *Z. Gosp.*, no. 24, 1960.

economic theory and practice in Central Europe as well as in the Soviet Union. The fundamental question at issue was whether value relations (the 'law of value') can have any place at all in a socialist system: that is to say whether goods can be considered as 'commodities' under socialism.[18] In the course of twenty-five years Soviet economic thought has veered from a complete rejection of the 'law' (which would follow from Marx's view), to first a partial and then a full, if qualified, recognition of its survival under socialism. The mode of its operation under socialism has been the label under which the problem of value-terms instrument for a collectivist command system has been treated since the mid-1950's in the Central European discussions on a new re-formed 'model'.

To be sure—except for period of emergency—value-instruments (wages and retail prices) have been in use for decades in the Soviet-type system in the sphere of consumption as the principal tools for allocation and for the distribution of incomes. The retail price is devised so as to broadly equilibrate supply and demand. By contrast, what is adopted for intra-industrial use is a cost-plus price. As in the Soviet Union, this is conceived in Central Europe as an average branch cost of materials, wear-and-tear, and labour —reducible to wages cost—with a small profit margin related to it. The retail price is in fact completely insulated from it by means of differentiated surcharge of profit-cum-purchase-tax calculated so as to clear the market. This surcharge is seen as 'surplus product' feeding investment and public consumption. By definition price is not a scarcity measure—it is not an opportunity cost price.[19] In actual fact, for most of its period of operation, in both the Soviet Union and Central Europe, prevailing price relations have deviated widely from its schema. In this sense and, as we shall point out, in the sense of the use that has been made of them, they have been largely 'irrational' or 'illogical'. It is a defensible tenet that any harm arising from this 'irrationality' or 'illogicality' has been mitigated by the nature of their function. Indeed it is arguable that a system of quite random price relations

---

[18] See this writer's discussion in *R. Econ. Stud.*, xvi/39 (1948–9), no. 39 and 'The Soviet Debate on the Law of Value and Price Formation', in G. Grossman ed., *Value and Plan* (Berkeley, Calif., 1960).

[19] I have discussed the subject in 'Principles and Methods of Price-Formation for Producer-Goods', in the forthcoming Osteuropa Institut, Freie Universität Berlin, *Probleme der Wirtschaftsplanung im sowjetischen Wirtschaftssystem*. See also A. Nove, *The Soviet Economy* (1961), pp. 218ff.

is by itself tolerable so long as this function is essentially one of aggregation and recording, as it is conceptually in the Soviet-type planning method, based on physical-term calculation.

The matter is more tricky in so far as price is used—with not too much concern for conceptual tidiness—as a steering instrument as well as a planning tool.[20] We have seen that the planner's macro-balances are compiled, of necessity, in value terms and some macro-allocative decisions, such as decisions concerning the uses of national income, are also made in these terms. Further on, we will show that choices in capital formation—and the inter-connected choices in foreign trade—increasingly rely on value-term calculations. For these and other reasons, decisions which basically rest on physical-term calculations, are affected by the price relations adopted. It appears, in fact, that even the technological norms applied in these calculations are themselves to some extent affected by price calculus—they are being corrected in this way especially to allow for relative shortages (although the prices are not devised as scarcity measures).[21]

Even stronger is the influence of the inter-industry price on the firm's behaviour. While broad targets are conveyed to the firm in physical-terms both with regard to its inputs and outputs, the manager has a certain freedom of manœuvre within these limits. To this extent, and increasingly in recent times throughout the area, prices perform the function of stimuli in guiding the firm's management towards the goals pursued by the central planner (in support of physical-term orders). In actual fact they form one of the components of complicated and, indeed, multi-angled systems of incentives and disincentives related to various money and quantity indicators that have been evolved by practice in Central Europe.[22] It is certain that these systems have failed to provide

[20] For an excellent discussion on the uses of price for these two purposes in Soviet-type economies see M. Bornstein, in *Amer. Econ. R.*, Mar. 1962.

[21] See above, p. 71.

[22] The following set of indicators laid down by the Czechoslovak Ministry of General Engineering for subordinated firms may be considered representative.

Output and marketing

Rate of growth of gross output: in the last year of the current five year plan as compared with that of the previous plan	F
Value of commodities produced	Y
Tasks for production of specified commodities, in quantity terms—by years	F. Y
Gross output	Y
Value of commodities marketed	F. Y

[*Continued on opposite page.*]

homogeneous and consistent frameworks of guidance. As often as not they push and pull in conflicting directions.

The question of intrinsically conflicting—'quarrelling'—systems of incentives has raised a more fundamental issue of the yard-sticks of success which verges on that of means and ends in a planned economy.[23] (Profit guidance raises, however, we think, some valid objections, one of which can be formulated broadly on these lines. In Central Europe, as in the Soviet Union, proposals for adopting profit as the single yardstick of industrial performance envisage it as being applicable to the lower tiers,

---

Output and marketing—cont.

Value of commodities for export	F. Y
Value of commodities for capital construction	F. Y

Capital Construction (centralized)

Capacities put in operation	F. Y
Purchase of machinery and equipment not included in the construction budget	F
Volume and structure of centralized investment	Y
Total value of projects completed	Y
Time-limits for the completion of contracted projects	Y
Total construction started, by years	Y
Volume of centralized investment over the five year plan	F

Labour

Limit of number of employees in the last year of the five year plan	F
Total number of employees	Y
Ratio of growth rates of labour productivity and average wages	F
Norms of formation of the premium fund	F
Total wage fund	Y

Material and technical supplies

Limits of consumption of specified ('funded') materials by years	F. Y
Limits of imports	F. Y

Technological progress

Technological-economic parameters for individual tasks: performance, amount, weight, reliability, &c.	F

Finance and costs

Depreciation	F
Incremental rate of profits	F
Profits transferred	Y
Taxes	Y
Percentage reduction of costs in the last year of the five year plan as compared with that of the previous plan	F

Source: mainly from *Czechoslovak Economic Papers*, no. 2, 1962.

F = targets set over five-year-plan period. Y = targets set annually.

---

[23] The problem of indicators of success is discussed by A. Nove, in *Economica*, Feb. 1958, pp. 1ff.

in the first place to the enterprise, only. But profit is rejected as the exclusive, or even the primary criterion for the planner's decisions, guided as he must be by his view of the 'ultimate ends'. Thus in their decision-making the manager of the firm and the planner would be guided by different criteria; as often as not this would result in conflicting choices.)[24] Generally, in recent thinking profit—gross or net—and value-added have undoubtedly been gaining increasing recognition as a 'synthesized' index of success. (It is also believed that more mature economies lend themselves better to such a synthesized approach.) As in the Soviet Union, however, the question has been raised in Central Europe whether this is compatible with the social and economic basis of a system where profit motive is not the propelling force. There is now a tendency, especially in Poland, to answer this question in the affirmative; and the argument is that while by their very nature ultimate goals, and the motives behind them, are extra-economic, any rational economy must aim at economizing the cost of achieving these goals, and thereby—which is merely the obverse of this postulate—must aim at maximizing profit.

This line of reasoning has influenced, if not always consistently, the thinking on planning and control parameters other than prices. An important domain is that of time discount in patterning investment: the reader will find a brief discussion on the subject of investment-efficiency coefficients in the context of capital formation. Soviet practice has partly overcome its inhibitions in regard to this tool, although it appears to disagree with the labour theory of value. Yet though it stems from the same source, the inhibition on the use of interest is still strong. But we have seen that Kalecki included it in his schema for 'a new system of stimuli and command' devised as early as the mid-1950's; the value of assets assigned to an enterprise would be treated as a non-repayable, interest-bearing credit obtained from the state; the charge would be then a means of disciplining the use of capital by managers who are at present little concerned about economizing assets which they get free. Interest would be charged, according to these proposals, in addition to allowances for wear and tear and obsolescence, hitherto rather neglected in Central European

[24] See A. Zauberman, 'Liberman's Rules of the Game for Soviet Industry', *Slavic Review* (Washington Univ.), Dec. 1963.

practice.[25] Since then these ideas have acclimatized themselves throughout the region: probably the Czechoslovaks have gone furthest in relating rewards for the enterprise and its staff to net product.

As to the price structures, reforms carried out since the second half of the 1950's in Czechoslovakia and East Germany have relied on the traditional price-schema. As in the USSR, theoretical controversy in those two countries has largely centred on how to charge the profit margin on the cost component of the price. The Czechoslovak general revision of prices—to be spread over a period of years up to the mid-1960's—has revealed that about one-quarter of inter-industrial transfer prices were inefficient in the sense that they were more or less arbitrary and necessitated large budgetary subsidies: in some branches, such as heavy engineering, the proportion of the contribution from the treasury to revenue was as high as half the total. The deficits have been eliminated or reduced, and in this way price structure has been at least brought closer to its own logic. In Poland the general overhaul carried out in 1960–1 broadly followed the same line, though with less rigid adherence to principle. Thus in ferrous metallurgy prices were set at the full cost at older plants rather than at the branch average level; in branches where obsolete equipment predominates, such as, for instance, cotton spinning, costs of inferior plants were adopted as the price-basis instead of the average. All in all, in order to eliminate deficits, the money value of industrial output was raised by about one-quarter; in iron and steel it was increased by one-half, and in fuels, it was even doubled.

More important still, the methodology of pricing itself is no longer considered in Poland to be definitive. In this respect Polish thinking is less wedded to dogma than it is in other countries of the area. The search for a rational price has been given the green light ever since the Polish State Economic Commission formulated its theses.[26] These suggested a 'peg' of price relations on world markets through basing prices of principal exportable raw materials on those prevailing in world trade. They would be related to these prices by means of a realistic rate of exchange.[27] In manufacturing, the 'price of departure' on which price relations would rest would correspond to the average cost of the

---

[25] Kalecki, in *Z. Gosp.*, no. 29, 1957.   [26] See above, p. 7.
[27] J. Struminski, in *Gosp. Plan.*, no. 1, 1962; J. Kowalski, ibid.

marginal producer in the relevant group of plants in a given branch—relevant, that is, from the point of view of meeting posited requirements; and it would be supplemented by a proportionally charged margin for overheads. Indeed, the view has gained ground in Poland that where bottlenecks in capacities form the ceiling of supply, short-term prices should, as a rule express scarcities. A strong school of thought has evolved in Poland which cogently argues that optimization of choices logically implies a price structure corresponding to equality of marginal rates of substitution and transformation.

Marxist tradition[28] militates against the marginalist approach in pricing. Traditionalism apart, it has been opposed on more rational grounds, especially on the ground that a marginalist price is static and thereby hampers growth. We shall not enlarge here on these matters but confine ourselves to the suggestion that while setting prices corresponding to tomorrow's equilibrium is, for many reasons (if only because of the uncertainties to be coped with) more difficult than setting them for to-day, such difficulties do not invalidate the logic of the 'marginalist' price as a condition of optimality.

THE NEW PLANNING TECHNIQUES

Since the end of the 1950's new vistas have been opened to centralist planning through the assimilation of certain econometric techniques. It is too early to attempt an answer to the question whither (to use Academician Nemchinov's words) the 'invasion [of planning offices] by mathematics and machines' may ultimately lead. But it may be fair to say that at least the 'novelties' do give the planner a better insight into the problems of economic life which confront him; and that the combined effect of advance in the techniques of quantitative analysis and decision-making and in the efficiency of calculating equipment (greater speeds, larger memories) does hold out a promise of a gradual improvement in the traditional crude practice.

Polish and East German experiments suggest that input-output techniques can be usefully applied at least at two stages of plan-construction: at the initial stage to help formulate a tightly aggregated, broad variant of departure; and later for a scrutiny

---

[28] The influence of Marxian doctrine on practice is brilliantly discussed by P. J. de la F. Wiles in *The Political Economy of Communism* (Oxford, 1962), published after the completion of this book.

of consistence of individual 'material balances'. *Ex post facto* overall 'balances' of the economy were compiled in the early 1960's in Poland and, in a less expanded form, in East Germany. Consolidated excerpts from the two in the following tables may give an idea of their structure and the usefulness of the double-entry *tableau économique* in portraying inter-sectoral relationships.

Contributions of Product Groups to Material Consumption of Industrial Branches, East Germany (Percentages)

The industrial branch of.... uses up / Supplies from the product group of....	Energy	Mining	Metallurgy	Chemicals	Building materials	Metal working	Timber	Textiles	Food	Total industry	Total industry & building
	1	2	3	4	5	6–13	14	15	20		
1 Energy	**45·0**	11·5	3·1	3·6	6·6	.	1·1	0·9	0·4	3·5	3·4
2 Mining	41·3	**22·9**	25·7	11·7	21·7	.	1·3	2·3	1·1	6·9	6·6
3 Metallurgy	1·9	9·0	**54·0**	2·9	9·5	.	3·8	0·2	0·2	12·2	11·9
4 Chemicals	1·9	15·1	2·2	**52·2**	11·8	.	9·3	21·6	1·2	13·7	13·5
5 Building materials	0·6	1·5	3·0	1·2	**29·7**	.	0·4	0·1	0·1	1·2	3·9
6–13 Engineering & metal working	5·8	28·2	5·4	6·8	8·7	.	9·3	1·7	0·6	22·4	21·5
14 Timber	1·4	3·2	0·2	0·9	1·5		**38·8**	0·4	0·3	2·3	2·7
15 Textiles	0·1	1·4	0·2	4·9	1·3	.	7·0	**66·0**	0·3	10·0	9·5
20 Food	0·1	0·7	0·1	3·3	0·4	.	0·2	0·1	**53·0**	11·8	11·2
Agriculture & forestry	0·0	2·3	0·1	0·7	2·3	.	24·0	2·3	38·8	9·9	9·5
Other sectors of material production	0·3	0·9	5·5	0·7	1·2	.	0·6	0·9	0·3	1·0	1·0
Total	100	100	100	100	100		100	100	100	100	100

Note: Based on data for 1959. Only covers state-owned enterprises (VVB's). Excerpt for 8 industrial branches out of 20 included in the original. Elements along the diagonal in bold figures show the use-up by industrial branches of their own products.
Source: Werner Karbstein, in *Stat. Prax.*, no. 6, 1962, p. 142.

Disposal of Industrial Gross Production: Poland (Percentages)

	Industry (1)	Electric & thermal energy (2)	Fuels & coking (3)	Iron and steel (4)	Non-ferrous metallurgy (5)	Machine construction & metal working (6)	Chemicals (7)	Textiles (11)	Food processing (14)	Material production total (22)	Material consumption — Household (23)	Material consumption — Other (24)	Accumulation — Investment & capital repairs (25)	Accumulation — Addition to stocks (26)	Exports (27)	Total distributed (28)	Differences unaccounted for (29)	Gross production and imports — Total (30)	Gross production (31)	Imports (32)
1	**39·1**	0·3	2·5	3·4	1·1	6·6	2·5	6·3	8·5	49·1	34·2	2·5	5·7	4·5	5·8	101·8	−1·8	100	92·3	7·7
2	67·1	**0·6**	15·9	7·7	4·9	13·1	6·2	3·2	6·2	81·6	17·1	12·2	—	0·4	0·2	111·5	−11·5	100	98·5	1·5
3	50·0	5·1	**22·3**	10·6	0·6	2·4	2·2	0·7	2·2	64·5	8·2	10·8	—	3·6	11·6	98·7	1·3	100	87·4	12·6
4	79·7	0·1	1·3	**40·5**	0·7	33·8	1·8	0·1	0·3	92·1	0·0	1·3	—	7·4	6·7	107·5	−7·5	100	90·6	9·4
5	98·0	0·1	0·4	2·0	**49·4**	37·2	6·8	0·2	0·1	100·7	0·0	1·0	—	0·7	9·7	112·1	−12·1	100	83·9	16·1
6	24·6	0·1	2·5	0·8	0·1	**17·8**	0·7	0·4	0·8	37·6	10·7	3·8	37·3	9·4	6·9	105·7	−5·7	100	85·6	14·4
7	47·1	0·1	3·6	0·8	0·4	5·5	**20·2**	9·4	2·2	60·3	23·0	3·7	—	8·5	4·6	100·1	−0·1	100	82·8	17·2
11	58·0	0·0	0·1	0·0	0·0	0·6	0·9	**38·5**	0·3	59·1	31·6	0·8	—	0·7	6·0	98·2	1·8	100	91·2	10·4
14	25·2	0·0	0·0	0·0	0·0	0·0	0·5	0·0	**24·0**	29·4	60·8	0·0	—	2·3	6·3	98·8	1·2	100	97·5	2·5
22	33·2	0·2	1·7	2·2	0·7	4·1	1·7	4·0	12·4	50·8	30·3	1·9	10·6	3·3	4·0	100·9	0·9	100	94·6	5·4

Note: Based on data for 1957 and 1958 expressed in ex-factory prices (largely estimates). Except for 8 industrial branches out of 20 branches of material production included in the original table.
Elements along the diagonal in bold figures show the use-up of a branch's gross production by its own enterprises.

The East German tabulation shows the share of individual product groups in the material consumption of individual branches of industry. The Polish one observes the flows from another angle and describes the disposals of gross material production. The rows show what happened with the output of each of the tabulated branches and sectors, i.e. the use-up at intermediate stages of production and the channeling of the residuum into 'final' uses, that is, consumption, capital formation, and exports. Each column tells what proportion of the output of other sectors is absorbed by that depicted in this column.

A Polish-built matrix for ninety-five commodity groups yields about 300 input coefficients describing their inter-dependencies: each of the coefficients, of the a_{ij} type, shows the quantity of one (the i-th) commodity group required for the production of a unit of another, the j-th, group. (In the same way another matrix shows requirements in capital, in money terms, involved in an additional unit of capacity.)[29] The high degree of aggregation inevitably restricts the picture of inter-industrial dependencies. (The right degree of aggregation is one of the pitfalls of the exercise: too little of it defeats the purpose, too much makes the picture unwieldy.) Nor has the amount and quality of data currently available to central planning offices proved sufficient to feed expanded matrices adequately. But they point to the practicable way of perfecting the 'material balances' borrowed from Soviet methodology. We have noted earlier the losing battle a planner has to fight against time when working with these 'balances'. The Leontief-type treatment does at least provide him with an effective means of calculating cumulative input coefficients technically (by means of the 'inversion' of the Leontief technological

---

[29] For the original Polish matrix see *Prace i materialy Zakladu Badan Ekonomicznych*, no. 10, Apr. 1960, and for the discussion of some points of methodology, ibid. no. 11, Apr. 1958.

The matrix of full coefficients of output related to final demand is the 'inverse'
$$[I - A - 'J]^{-1}$$
where I stands for identity (unit) matrix, A for matrix of the a_{ij} coefficients of direct consumption of i-th material per unit of j-th product, and J for diagonal matrix of coefficients relating imports of a given material to domestic production.

The matrix of full capital coefficients is the product
$$[b] . [I - A - 'J]^{-1} = [B]$$
where b stands for diagonal matrix of direct capital coefficients.

The matrix of full import coefficients is the product
$$['J] . [I - A - 'J]^{-1} = [J]$$
Investment programme is thus the product of full capital coefficients and the vector of postulated increments in the final bill of goods.

matrix). In this way total requirements of a given commodity in the production of a unit of a 'final good' can be established—for instance, the total quantity of metal used in manufacturing a machine-tool both directly and in all the branches that support it throughout the economy. The table below illustrates the relevance of such calculations in planning: it shows Polish-calculated full requirements in materials and investment cost connected with expansion of consumption of finished steel. (Cumulative labour-input coefficients have been adopted in E. German industry as a substitute for piece-cost calculation.)

Total Requirements Involved in Expanding Consumption of Finished-steel Products by 200,000 tons

Materials (000 tons)		Investment capital (mill. zloty)	
Iron casts	11	Iron casting	32
Rolled steel	23	Steel casting	2
Crude steel	28	Rolling mills	549
Pig-iron	155	Steel furnaces	437
Scrap	171	Blast-furnaces	468
Ore—domestic	45	Iron-ore mines	269
Ore—imported	130	Coking plants	95
Coke	198		
		Total	1,852

Source: Cf. J. Pajestka, K. Porwit, and W. Slawin, in *Gosp. Plan.*, no. 5, 1960.

It is in this way that the planner obtains fuller information as to the implications of his choices. Eventually such techniques may help to rationalize the general course of planning. We have said that at present the Soviet-type procedure starts from an assortment of goals which is due partly at least to the roughness of the instruments at hand. This factor apart, it may be a legacy from the period when production of any materials—particularly of 'growth' materials such as fuels or metals or building materials— was almost an end in itself. The new, more sophisticated instruments would permit starting construction of the plan from the

'final bill of goods' that is, targets for private and public consumption, capital accumulation, and exports; in other words they
would permit shifting the basis of planning from gross output to
national income.[30] The immediate virtue of the matrix formulation
of 'material balances' is an inbuilt check on consistency. The use
of cumulative coefficients provides a scrutiny of capacities which
are necessary to support goals against resources which are at the
planners' disposal, as in the example for finished steel we have
just cited. It thus points to the direction of adjustments which
would make the plan more effective as well as internally coherent.

This brings us back to the way the planners' choices can be
made efficient (optimal). As has been mentioned before, in the
traditional Soviet-type methods in use in Central Europe this is
being done by a sequence of trial-and-error rounds till what would
appear to be the best fit has been 'hit'. While the input-output
method does help in this quest for the 'best fit'[31] it does not provide
a systematic procedure serving this purpose. Efficient choices—
especially choices of efficient technology—have to be made, as it
were, behind the stage of the matrix.

Contemporary econometrics has evolved some methods of
making an explicit, systematic selection of the efficient (the
optimal) from among the feasible, consistent alternatives. Very
broadly speaking it provides a technique by which a formulated
criterion of performance, the 'objective function', can be maxi-
mized subject to given conditions, in a computational process
which simulates an ideally competitive market; the conditions,
'the constraints', describe the limitations of available resources or
policy aims: say, preserving certain minimum levels of living
standards. At present these techniques of 'programming' can deal
with less complex situations—chiefly those where magnitudes
involved are related in a 'linear' way. To mention one important
limitation of linear programming, returns to scale are assumed to
be constant, which is hardly realistic.

For some time past the planners in the area, especially the Polish

[30] I have discussed these problems in *Sov. Stud.*, July 1962.

[31] Professor J. M. Montias identifies the Polish method as a Gauss–Seidel iterative
procedure. He himself, in fact, independently elaborated an interesting iterative
model for securing consistent solutions in planning with Soviet-type 'material
balances': the pattern of his model would appear to be quite close to the actual
Polish procedures. (See J. M. Montias in *Amer. Econ. R.*, Dec. 1959, and his contribution to the *Bulletin of the Association for the Study of Soviet-Type Economies*, Nov. 1960,
mimeo.)

planners, have also looked to these techniques for relief in their task of choice-making. However, the immense volume and quality of data required, the numbers of decision-variables involved in planning the real economic life of a country make these techniques hardly applicable as yet in practice on the scale of an overall plan. The time dimension involved in perspective dynamic planning adds to the formidable difficulties. The techniques are being resorted to in Poland for a solution of sectoral tasks including those at the enterprise level; but it is safe to say that they have not driven out the ghosts of innumerable equations with which the planner on the all-national scale has to cope.

REAPPRAISAL IN THE 1960's

However, the interest in these techniques and experiments with them have helped to make planning thought conscious that efficient value parameters—rents, prices, rates of interest—can only be derived from an overall efficient programme. (In programming these appear as coefficients, the 'dual' of the technologically best solution.) They have also helped to make it conscious of the fact that the average cost-plus prices, as used in the countries of Central and Eastern Europe, are not efficiency prices: that they cannot lead to optimal choices whether employed in the planning offices (that is, applied as accounting prices), or as actual, 'operational' intra-industrial transfer prices. It is the realization of this fact—combined with the conviction that at the present state of technique the planner is unable to provide the economy with efficient value parameters—that has given rise to the view that it may be safer to rely consistently on physical-terms planning and conveying orders down the administrative ladder: that is, it may be safer to make prices as 'passive' as possible in order to avoid the tug-of-war between them and physical-term calculation.[32] We are now back at the matter from which we started this discussion. Experience in the area (and also as a matter of fact in the Soviet Union) since the later 1950's, the disappointments in the attempts to widen the scope of decision-making by lower echelons and, on parallel lines, that of industrial guidance by means of value instruments, which led since the early 1960's to

[32] There is an interesting discussion of this point by A. Wakar and J. G. Zielinski, in *Ekon.*, no. 1, 1961, and J. G. Zielinski, *Rachunek gospodarczy w socjalizmie* (Warsaw, 1961).

a discernible tendency for re-centralization, seems to make a *prima facie* case in support of such views. It is arguable, we think, that this tendency has revealed the inherent conflict between the decentralization demanded by the growing complexity of industrial economies and the instruments which a planner in a command economy can find in his 'box of tools'. Tensions in the economies of Czechoslovakia and East Germany which resulted in deceleration of growth and the abandoning of their plans in the 1960's may, at least, be partly attributable to this conflict. Indeed the Central European test case seems to provide a *prima facie* support for the hypothesis that once the initial break-through phase of industrial expansion is completed it becomes increasingly difficult to plan and run a highly industrialized economy with the mechanism designed for the Soviet-type environment of four decades ago.[33]

The problem of an alternative mechanism becomes, therefore, something more than a mere intellectual exercise. As we have already remarked, when established in Central Europe, the Soviet-type mechanism for a centrally planned and managed economy was seen as the only one compatible with Marxian socialism, indeed identified with it: to be fair, it was the only one empirically tested. Since then the Yugoslav experiment has been developed as at least a potentially significant variant. In Central Europe the ideas of a 'competitive socialism' model gained currency since the mid-1950's; to some extent they have been influenced by Yugoslav concepts and practice.

In East Germany these ideas hinged upon some fundamental issues of political philosophy as well as economics. During a rather short-lived *Sturm und Drang periode* in East German economic thinking in the mid-1950's it was argued that, once the dictatorship of the proletariat had been firmly established, a conscious shift away from state intervention towards a market guided by a system of economic 'levers' belonged to the logical dialectics of development; that it would make part and parcel of the withering away of the state postulated by Marxian teaching; that the failure to comply with these inexorable dialectics accounts for observable,

---

[33] In 1962 the rates of growth of net material product were 3% in E. Germany and Poland, half the planned rate in the latter, and $\frac{1}{2}$% in Czechoslovakia.

Official analyses have stressed faulty planning organization and management as major factors contributing to the continuing strains in the economies. Cf. in particular *Z. Gosp.* no. 37, 1963 and *Hosp. Nov.*, 12 July 1963.

dangerous contradiction and tensions. Such ideas, very much out of step with the political attitudes of the East German régime, were strongly resisted by the official doctrine.[34] The less articulate rumblings in Czechoslovakia fared no better.[35]

For a time developments in Polish industry appeared to tend towards a 'real' market model. The emergence in the mid-1950's of workers' councils seemed to strengthen the tendency towards a rather syndicalist, an 'atomistic' structure of industry resting on the enterprise as the basic unit largely controlled by its personnel. These councils sprang up more or less spontaneously as organs of industrial management but have subsequently been diluted by extraneous elements; their authority has been curtailed through reassertion of undivided powers of state administration.

However the scope for a market solution continues to be explored in Poland. (It is still rejected on *a priori* ideological grounds as incompatible with socialism by Soviet doctrine which has full sway in Czechoslovakia and East Germany.) In Poland it is being argued that 'Marxist theoretical thought has not rid itself fully of the view—erroneous for a socialist economy—that the use of a market mechanism surrenders [the system] to an unconditional rule of the law of value, and opens the doors to elemental forces'; and that 'It is a profound misunderstanding . . . to think of [the market mechanism] . . . as synonymous with an economy based on micro-economic impulses [of activity] where macro-economic processes are only their derivative. . . .'[36] In the view of this school of thought an intra-industry market is neutral from the angle of social and political philosophy: the choice of the organizational 'model' and allocational mechanism would be a matter of expediency; market mechanism—and decentralization as its corollary—would be preferable for higher stages of maturity of

---

[34] See in particular P. A. Benary's paper in *Ww.*, no. 1, 1956, and F. Behrens, in 'Zur ökonomischen Theorie und Politik der Übergangsperiode' *Ww.* (1957), *Sonderheft*, no. 3. For further development of the debate which ensued see Behrens's contribution in *Ww.*, no. 1, 1958, pp. 31ff. and also an article by K. Richter and K. Zieschang, ibid. pp. 39ff. and an editorial, ibid. pp. 22ff. For a reaction to the views of Behrens and Benary, see also the official organ of the Soviet Communist Party, *Kommunist*, no. 9, 1957, pp. 39ff., where both are charged with suggesting the abandonment of economic planning. See also criticism by W. Ulbricht in his address to the Central Committee of the East German Party, in *Einheit*, no. 6, 1957.

[35] For a reference to the ideological legacy of 'Socialist democratic opportunism and its anarchistic counterparts', see J. Dolansky's report to the Central Committee of the Party, 27 Feb. 1957.

[36] W. Brus, *Problemy Funkcjonowania Gospodarki Socjalistycznej* (Warsaw, 1961), pp. 241 a nd 240.

the economic environment and for phases of smoother development, rather than for underdeveloped economies and periods of rapid social and economic reshaping.[37] It is further argued with equally good logic that a decentralized organization does not, *per se*, prejudge the degree of the firms' freedom in decision-making; and assuming that value parameters for the firms provided by the central planner are perfect, a market mechanism could in fact be operated in a command economy as effectively as one resting on physical-terms fiats.

When looked upon in this way the issue has still two facets. One is that of hierarchy of preferences in setting ends and therefore, ordering the use of means. As time passed, concern for the consumer's choices has undoubtedly increased in the region—more attention has been paid to his needs: undoubtedly the economies are more responsive to signals from the consumer's market than they were even a decade ago—in the period of stormy growth. But there is no question of an abdication of 'sovereignty' by the planner in favour of the consumer. The individual's myopia is still seen as the great menace to growth. The planner's attitude has been well described figuratively as that of a manager of a joint-stock company whose shareholders are future generations.[38] This is true *a fortiori* in a non-acquisitive society. Hence in such a society the dynamics of the system—the volume of saving—must be left to the planner's discretion. Growth is, in this sense, his paramount aim: there is some analogy to wartime planning in non-socialist countries with its paramount objectives. (The rationale has been suggested by Professor Devons in his analysis of wartime economics: if the community attempts to act as a single individual it must leave to the government the decision as to how its paramount objective can best be achieved.)[39] This, in fact, involves the whole of the scale of preferences if its consistency is to be safeguarded.

The rank of growth as a policy aim is indeed such that hardly anybody is prepared to leave the strategic elements of capital formation out of the sphere of *direct* control exercised by the central planner: this entails *direct* patterning of strategically important capacities and mobilizing of resources to support them. But, we think, it is far from certain that the 'growth' and 'non-growth' areas of an economy can be separated in a satisfactory way,

[37] Ibid: see also review article by this writer in *Economica*, Nov. 1962.
[38] A. K. Cairncross, *Factors in Economic Development* (London, 1962).
[39] E. Devons, *Essays in Economics* (London, 1961), p. 65.

especially in a complex industrial economy of the Central European type. Assuming that they can be so separated, there still remains the risk of particularist interests. Without sharing the view that, in any case, decentralization must 'burst the economy'[40] one can yet agree that there is, in the socialist market model, a serious risk of monopolistic and oligopolistic tendencies in conflict with the central planner's preferences. This has been borne out by Yugoslav experience; and, again, a mature industrial economy of the Central European kind may have still greater difficulty in coping with such tendencies than one at the Yugoslav level of development. When the market mechanism was first mooted by the Polish State Economic Council it declared unequivocally that the level and structure of prices cannot be determined in automatic processes of the market; and that the state's social preferences must shape price relations. But this throws us back to the question of the central planner's limited ability to shape efficiency parameters.

THE STRATEGY OF GROWTH

Space will allow for only a very brief exposition of the strategy for growth. It is prescribed in a set of rules claimed to stem from the Marxist–Leninist analysis of 'expanded reproduction'. The contributing factor has been the experience of a country exceptionally rich in natural resources and—through economic as well as political circumstances—gravitating towards self-sufficiency. The rules are seen, at least in Soviet doctrine, as immutable and of universal validity. As actually applied they may appear, in historical perspective, somewhat less rigid than the doctrine would suggest. Indeed, as our discussion proceeds, varying nuances—through time and space—will be noted.

The strategy is usually summed up as the 'law' of 'proportionate' development. The sense of the adjective is anything but precise unless it expresses a tautology. It is usually meant, however, to convey something more—an idea of smooth or balanced growth. The law is, in fact, antithetic to what, at least in Western writings, is usually understood as the balanced-growth doctrine (as expounded in particular by Scitovsky, Rosenstein-Rodan, and Nurkse).[41] Indeed, as practised, the strategy can be properly

---

[40] B. Minc, in *Gosp. Plan.*, no. 6, 1960.

[41] P. N. Rosenstein-Rodan, in *Econ. J.*, June–Sept. 1943; Tibor Scitovsky in *J. of Polit. Econ.*, Apr. 1954; Ragnar Nurkse, *Problems of Capital Formation in Underdeveloped Countries* (Oxford, 1953).

described as one of moving through a sequence of disequilibria consciously generated—and of consequential bottlenecks put up with—each of them acting as an impulse to the next growth phase. In a sense, the path prescribed is then akin to the conception of a 'chain of disequilibria' elaborated as a growth-policy for underdeveloped countries by Hirschman.[42] Such a meaning would be particularly applicable to the Soviet-type shock strategy pursued at the early stages both of industrialization and of restarting industrial expansion after the war.

PREFERENTIAL GROWTH IN CAPITAL-GOODS INDUSTRIES

The strategy subscribed to is understood to imply two principal postulates. One identifies optimum with an achievable maximum pace of industrial growth, and the second requires that production of producer goods should continuously outpace that of consumer goods: the latter is what is usually termed—the 'law' of preferential expansion of the 'Department I', in Marx's conceptual frame and terminology. It rests ultimately on the assumption of what Marx defined in the first volume of *Capital* as the rising 'organic composition of capital', which means an upward trend of the material flows—for the value of plant and materials employed in production—as against wages (in other words, for Marx innovation has a labour-saving bias). From Marx's model of growth, as reformulated by Lenin, the latter derived the following rule for movement for the system: '. . . growth in the production of means of production as means of production is the most rapid, then comes the production of means of production as means of consumption'.[43] Although the rule is, in Marxist–Leninist analysis, connected with the mode of operation of capitalism, it has been interpreted in the Soviet doctrine as independent of the social and economic structure.[44] In the last instance the 'law' implies a preferential increase in the production of capital goods (on the historically tenable assumption that, over time, inputs of raw and

---

[42] Albert O. Hirschman, *The Strategy of Economic Development* (New Haven, 1958), pp. 65ff.
  With regard to the Soviet Union see also an interesting discussion in A. Nove, *The Soviet Economy* (London, 1961).

[43] V. I. Lenin, *On the So-called Market Question*. English translation in vol. 1 of Collected Works (Moscow, 1960), pp. 79ff.

[44] For a more rigorous discussion see Zauberman, 'Le centenaire du modèle marx-iste de la réproduction: le réexamen soviétique de ses aspects stratégiques', *Bulletin* of Centre d'Etude des Pays de l'Est, Université Libre de Bruxelles, 1963, pp. 27ff.

intermediate materials in the manufacturing of capital goods tend to decline, or at least to remain constant). Consequently—with qualifications we shall suggest later—this 'law' can also be reduced to a postulate of a more rapid rate of increase in capital formation than in consumption, or, alternatively, of a more rapid growth of investment than of national income. It is in such a frame of reasoning that the two precepts would follow from the same postulate: indeed, not only does the second principle aim at a fast pace, but it entails a continuously accelerating rhythm of capital formation.

Translated into concrete tactics for industrial growth, the strategic 'law'—alternatively understood as preferential growth of producer-goods or heavy branches—is implemented through a strong emphasis on a few key industries, the 'leading links'. These are the heavy industrial branches, providing the economy with energy, metals, chemicals, building materials, and engineering. In this hierarchy the latter forms the apex, being the industry which provides the economy directly with equipment. As the principal supplier of basic material for engineering, metallurgy— particularly the iron-and-steel industry—is considered (or at least was considered until the late 1950's) as *the* growth industry *par excellence.*

A stereotyped application throughout the area of the rule of the 'leading links' in growth has sometimes entailed a disregard of the specific conditions of a given national economy and has resulted in some rigidities and waste: a case in point was the drive to expand pig-iron production in East Germany.[45] Valid criticism has pointed out that it was in any case questionable in a complex, highly diversified economy such as that which existed already at the start of the era in industrially advanced parts of Central Europe: in Czechoslovakia, East Germany, and even to some extent in Poland.

It would lead us too far away from our central subject were we to try to retell the history of the debate about the 'law' which started in the Soviet Union in the early 1920's.[46] It is enough to point out that in the area under survey the argument was revived amid the critical tensions which developed in the economies around the mid-1950's. Even towards the end of the 1950's a

[45] See below, p. 182.
[46] See the present writer in *R. Econ. Stud.*, xvi (1948–9), no. 39.

debate continued on this point between the Polish economists and those of the Soviet Union, where the principle was officially reasserted after the fall of the Malenkov Administration. It is not without significance that in this debate the universal validity of the law has been challenged in Poland even by the school of thought which has otherwise been far from any doctrinal heterodoxy.

Professor Bronislaw Minc[47] contended that, since it was not feasible to go on raising the share of capital accumulation in the national income year in year out and *ad infinitum*, a faster tempo of the 'first department' of industry could be regarded only as a tendency peculiar to some phases of industrial development: that it applied in fact primarily to periods of profound industrial metamorphoses. When the law was conceived by Lenin in Tsarist Russia in the beginning of this century, technological progress consisted chiefly in the substitution of machines for labour. In contrast, so the argument continues, in the subsequent period the predominant characteristic of progress has been the substitution of perfected machines for less advanced ones. The conclusion is that what was wrongly generalized as 'the law' is, in fact, at present an anachronism as a rule of economic strategy for industrial growth. Stress has been put in this argument on the experience of Britain, a typically mature industrial country, where consumer goods represent a broadly stable proportion of industrial output, about half of the total.

It has been argued then, in Poland, that there were no valid general rules as to the relative dynamics of investment and national income: that the planner's decision as to which of them should rise faster must depend on the prevailing type of technological progress as well as, among other things, on the assumed shape of the consumption curve and the state of labour resources.[48] Polish economists have contended that advance in techniques was accompanied by secular trends of rising capital intensity and productivity of labour, but was either capital saving, or capital

---

[47] *Ekon.*, no. 5, 1956, pp. 54–56. See also his *Zagadnienia teorii socjalizmu* (Warsaw, 1957), p. 269 and *passim*. Minc argues that the actual cause of development is co-determined by at least four variables: (*a*) the net to gross ratio in output; (*b*) the ratio of capital formation to national income; (*c*) the relative proportions of producer and consumer goods in capital formation; (*d*) the structure of foreign trade. Minc's contention was emphatically condemned by Soviet authoritative economic writing. (See A. Pashkov's critique in *Vopr. Ekon.*, no. 6, 1958, pp. 49ff.)

[48] Kalecki, in *Ekon.*, no. 5, 1956, pp. 61ff.

absorptive, or from this angle, neutral; and that it was the latter aspect that was decisive for the relative growth rates of the production and consumption spheres of the economy.

If an empiricist attitude is taken up, no assessment of the strategy actually pursued for industrial growth in Central Europe can afford to overlook—we believe—some long-range directions of change observable in industrially advanced countries. Thus one must bear in mind that, over the first half of the century, the representative 'heavy' industries—metal-processing and chemicals—between them increased their share in Western European manufactures from about one-fifth to close on one-half. Over that time the share of typical light industries was reversed.[49] This bears out Hoffman's findings on the role of capital-goods industries.[50]

For the world as a whole a recent United Nations inquiry brought out some phenomena which are relevant for the point discussed here. (1) Generally speaking, the higher the degree of industrialization the greater the proportion of manufacturing employment and output in heavy industries; these also rank higher in productivity per person than light industries. (2) Over the two decades 1938–58 the heavy-goods industries made the greatest gains in output among all the manufacturing industries. The volume of production of heavy manfacturing expanded twice as fast as that of light manufacturing, i.e. food, textiles, leather, rubber and related products, and printing and publishing.[51] While comparative data in this field are rather treacherous (if only because of differences in definitions and classifications) it would seem that over most of the 1950's—when reduced to a comparable basis—the relative pace of growth of heavy industry in the area was broadly similar to that in the world at large and in the advanced industrial countries of Western Europe.[52]

The case of the classical 'light' branch deserves special attention because of its relevance for developments in the area. Textiles have become *the* problem industry of Europe. It is increasingly difficult for Europe to compete in this particular field with countries cursed with extremely low living standards and blessed with an easy access to textile raw materials. Between the outbreak

[49] Paretti and Bloch, in *BNLQR*, no. 39, 1956, p. 205.
[50] W. G. Hoffmann, *The Growth of Industrial Economies* (Manchester, 1958).
[51] U.N., *Patterns of Industrial Growth, 1953–1958* (N.Y., 1960).
[52] E. Rychlewski, in *Gosp. Plan.*, no. 1–2, 1959, pp. 64ff.

of the First World War and the end of the 1950's the weaving and spinning equipment of British cotton industry was reduced by one-half in terms of spindles and looms:[53] in Continental Western

Heavy versus Light Industries in Western Europe, 1901–55

	1901	*1955*
Basic metals	7	9
Metal products & chemicals	21	48
Textiles & food processing	47	21

Source: Paretti and Bloch, in *BNLQR*, no. 39, 1956, p. 205.

Europe it shrank by nearly two-fifths. It seems right to say that the 'relative importance of textile industries declines in proportion as industrialization progresses'.[54]

The causes behind the phenomenal *élan* of West Germany's economic expansion since the Second World War are numerous and complex. (One of the major causes is no doubt that her initial recovery was assisted by a supply of foreign capital; whereas East Germany was heavily decapitalized owing to Soviet exactions.) It hardly lends itself to an interpretation in terms of industrial patterns only. But an illuminating analysis plausibly stresses as an important contributor to West Germany's economic 'miracle' the traditional preponderance of heavy branches in her industrial structure, a preponderance which has been accentuated in the post-war period. This—it is convincingly argued—has helped in reconstruction and expansion, and in taking advantage of the behaviour of world markets.[55]

The trends and tendencies which we have just mentioned are a significant background to developments in the area. The case of Czechoslovakia is illuminating. Light industries formed an obstinate sphere of depression in that country's industrial life between the wars. As we shall see, by 1937 more hard coal was mined in Czechoslovakia than before the First World War, the

[53] R. Robson, *The Cotton Industry in Britain* (London, 1957); OEEC, *The Future of the European Cotton Industry* (Paris, 1957).
[54] Paretti and Bloch, in *BNLQR*, no. 39, 1956, p. 212.
[55] H. C. Wallich, *Mainsprings of the German Revival* (Yale U.P., 1955), pp. 195ff., 200ff.

output of pig-iron was larger by more than one-quarter than in 1913, and steel production had nearly doubled over a quarter of a century. This contrasted strongly with what happened in light industries, which never recovered from the effects of the Great Depression. Between 1920 and 1937 the number of cotton spindles fell by about one-third and that of cotton looms by about one-half; and the reduced equipment of industry was under-employed. Luxury and semi-luxury light industries fared no better, some of them even worse: the famous Czechoslovak chinaware industry regained only three-fifths of its pre-First World War output in the boom years of 1928–9; and between that date and the mid-1930's its output shrank by about two-thirds. By 1937 production of sugar and beer was lower by about one-half and one-third respectively than in 1912–13.[56] Policy-makers had to face the problem of the adverse trend in Czechoslovak light industries when decisions were made as to the lines of the initial post-Second World War reconstruction. The strong concentration of the light branches in the Sudeten area, depopulated in the course of the post-war migration, complicated the problem. The dilemma was whether to re-equip the decaying industries up to modern technological standards, which would involve a substantial investment and the tieing up of a large labour force, or to cut the losses in this sector and concentrate on the heavier branches.[57] The second alternative was chosen, which is defensible.

A policy of preferential expansion of the heavier branches of industry was inaugurated at an early stage in what is now East Germany, when the country became the centre of the *Luftkriegs-wirtschaft*. Indeed the very impressive expansion of East German engineering during the Second World War was such as not only to secure sufficient equipment for the home economy, but also to add to that of some of the dependent areas under German control.[58]

Before these remarks are concluded, a point worth making is that the 'law' of an absolute rule of preferential growth of heavy or capital-goods industries rests on a tacit assumption of a closed economy. Once this is removed and comparative advantage is

[56] Cf. F. Hertz, *The Economic Problem of the Danubian States* (London, 1947), pp. 173ff.; E. Zaleski, *Les courants commerciaux au cours de la première moitié du xxᵉ siècle* (Paris, 1952), pp. 119ff.
[57] Cf. the discussion of this dilemma in W. Diamond, *Czechoslovakia between East and West* (London, 1947), pp. 96ff.
[58] ECE, *Econ. Survey of Europe since the War* (1952), p. 2.

brought in, the universality of the law breaks down. However, the fallacy of the dogmatic approach is in a sense shared—though *à rebours*—by some of the Western critics of the post-war economic

Development of East German Industries, 1933–44[1]
(gross output, 1936 = 100)

	1933	*1939*	*1944*
Total	64	138	168
Mining	58	138	166
Iron, steel, & non-ferrous metals	31	113	155
Chemicals	58	172	211
Machine, vehicle, & steel construction	38	193	332
Electrical equipment	68	245	324
Precision & optical instruments	48	138	326
Consumer goods	85	131	117

[1] Figures rounded.

Source: Compiled from B. Gleitze, *Ostdeutsche Wirtschaft* (Berlin, 1956), pp. 170ff. This table refers to gross output in current prices. In constant prices the index for total net output stood in 1944 at 145, for investment goods at 186, and for consumer goods at 100 (p. 173). Adjustments for price changes (p. 169) would suggest that gross output amounted in 1944 (as a percentage of the 1936 level) to about 165 in mining; 178 in chemicals; 114 in iron, steel, and non-ferrous metals; 265 in machine, vehicle, and steel construction; 258 in electrical equipment; 259 in precision and optical instruments.

strategy pursued in the two industrial countries of Central Europe. As often as not they are inclined to confuse the issue with that of living standards. Clearly, under an assumption of a reasonably open economy, a country's pattern of industrial production does not, *per se*, determine supplies for, and thus the levels of, consumption. In a word, criticism of the preferential growth of heavy industries tends to overlook the fact that it is the countries' handicaps in their foreign trade, or rather more generally in their foreign-payments position (this includes the impact of substantial transfers of capital to the Soviet Union during the early post-war period), that is the villain of the piece, rather than the structural lines of post-war industrial growth taken *per se*.

To avoid a misunderstanding, two points may be worth

stressing. First, that preferential growth of heavy industries may include some sectors of consumer-goods production, i.e. goods serving household and public consumption, in the latter case specifically armaments. In the Soviet doctrine the 'law' of preferential growth of the producer-goods sphere is in fact confused with that of priority of development of heavy industries. Indeed, the pronounced secular trend in Western Europe away from light industries to the manufacture of chemicals and engineering products veils a rising proportion of consumer goods in their output. In particular, durable consumer goods represent a growing share of heavy metal-processing in Western Europe (and, though to a far smaller degree, since the mid-1950's in Central Europe as well). Secondly, the acceptance of preferential growth of heavy industries as a valid line of economic strategy does not prejudge the answer to the question of what should be the specific branch pattern of heavy industry. The answer depends, among other things, on the general line of technological progress as well as on the conditions of a given economy.

The argument holds thus far, mainly with regard to the two industrial countries of Central Europe. Poland's case may call for special qualifications. True, neither in her case is there any ground for subscribing to the view that preferential expansion of light industries would necessarily bring about an optimum progress. On the contrary such progress presumably requires a general direction in broad agreement with the main secular line of development in the highly industrialized world. A pragmatic approach to Poland's economic strategy cannot, however, afford to ignore her specific economic background, particularly the very important demographic differences between her and her two neighbours. These differences would inevitably influence the shaping of the relative factor proportion in a different fashion.

In his theory of investment in a socialist economy[59] Professor B. Minc has systematized the types of growth policies with regard to technological levels and consequently capital intensity, under these three headings: (1) a policy of 'thinning out' investment, with high levels of employment and productivity of labour; (2) a policy of 'concentrated' investment, known in East European literature as that of 'block investment', relying on

---

[59] Minc, in *Ekon.*, no. 3, 1960, p. 469. Some of the issues involved were discussed by me in *International Affairs*, July 1962, pp. 339–52.

advanced technology and high labour productivity; and (3) the Chinese 'walking on two legs'—a policy which earmarks the bulk of centralized outlays preferentially for high-level technology, but channels the rest of investment to plant of lower technique and lower productivity. He places Poland in the second category and this invites comment.

This point will also be referred to in our chapter dealing with manpower, where it will be suggested that Poland sees herself induced to build up certain highly capital-intensive industries with very advanced labour-saving technology in apparent conflict with her factor position. Her dilemma in this respect is not unlike that treated in the literature on underdeveloped countries as one of 'dualistic development'.[60]

The analogy is of course less close when reference is made to countries whose economic growth is still in its infancy. But it is much more in evidence in the case of Italy, where capital for industrial expansion is at the same time abundant and scarce, depending on the sector of industry. As in Poland the Italian 'dualism' in growth appears in both structural and geographical planes, as is pointed out in an illuminating study on the problem of Luigi Spaventa.[61] Italy too, especially fast-developing Sicily, belongs to the intermediate class of countries of a certain demographic type whose particular growth problems differ in some respects from those of both economically underdeveloped and industrially well-advanced nations. (Analytically relevant for these problems is Professor Eckhaus's argument[62] on limits to full employment, as defined by him, under given technological conditions and demand/supply factor position.) It would seem that planners in Poland are compelled to impart specific development patterns more or less of the kind which elsewhere the free-enterprise mechanism brings about automatically.

In so far as light industries are, as a rule, relatively more labour-intensive, there is more room for them in Poland's industrial structure than in that either of Czechoslovakia or East Germany. So long as a rapid transfer of Polish labour to industries of higher productivity is obstructed by deficiency of capital, a *pis aller* has to be adopted.

[60] See *i.a.* J. H. Boeke, *Economics and Economic Policy of Dual Societies* (N.Y., 1953).
[61] In *BNLQR*, no. 51, Dec. 1959. See also Vera Lutz, *Italy: a Study in Economic Development* (London, RIIA, 1962).
[62] R. S. Eckhaus, in *Amer. Econ. R.*, Sept. 1955.

The same point, relative productivity of factors, in the given environment, may also form (*mutatis mutandis*) one of the criteria for the appraisal of economic strategy in regard to agriculture, as against industry. Policies which since the war have shaped in the area the type, the scale, the institutional framework and organization, and the output pattern of agriculture have, undoubtedly, been influenced to a high degree by various *extra*-economic considerations. On the other hand criticism of the policies pursued tends sometimes to overlook the demand/supply position of factors and the relative productivity of agriculture and industry.

Here again a pragmatic approach cannot ignore specific conditions prevailing in one country as against another. Deep structural differences between Poland and the two other countries form a very illuminating general case militating against a stereotyped treatment of these problems, which was characteristic of official policies over a good part of the 1950's. Poland's handicap, which results from the narrow scope for transfer of an agricultural surplus population to industrial employment, carries important implications for general economic and industrial strategy: a handicap superimposed on the general one affecting all late-comers to industrialization. It is a well defensible contention that for nations which passed through industrial revolution in the eighteenth and nineteenth centuries, the withdrawal of factors from agriculture was largely determined by higher productivity in industry. For nations which started industrialization, or whose industrialization acquired momentum, only in the present century, the additional co-determining element is the lower productivity of their new industries as compared with the level of efficiency in the old industrial countries.[63] This creates a problem of compensation for outlets for the new industries, and sharpens the balance-of-payments difficulties and the dilemma of financing industrial development. The difficulties which arise are superimposed by the direction of the trend of terms of trade for products of agriculture as against those of industry. Over a comparatively long period after the last war the persistence of a long-run trend in favour of agricultural prices was widely believed to be predictable, on the assumption that the process of industrialization would

---

[63] See discussion on this point by J. Marczewski, 'Quelques considérations générales sur le probleme agricole des démocraties populaires', which appeared as a preface to J. Poniatowski, *Productivité, capital et travail dans l'agriculture polonaise d'après-guerre* (Paris, 1955), pp. i, xxiii.

embrace the most populous areas of the world, an assumption which proved correct. Yet the predicted trend failed to materialize. The resumption of the movement of terms of trade in the opposite direction, i.e. against agricultural prices, distinctly noticeable towards the end of the 1950's would by itself not leave unaffected the economic strategy of the countries of the area. However, general foreign trade and foreign-payment position would be no less relevant for practical policies than the direction of movement of terms of trade.[64]

As to the quantitative aspect of capital accumulation, the paradox has been noticed (by Dr Gregory Grossman) that Soviet economic theory, despite its unique concentration on the problems of capital formation, has had very little to say as to how the size of investment can be determined beforehand for a given period.[65] Practice has evolved some crude rules of thumb. These have been transplanted to other collectivist economies, among others to the countries of Central Europe. (We shall note that Polish thought has endeavoured to lend them some sophistication.)

The extent of reliance on the planner's intuitive judgement signally transpires from Professor B. Minc's[66] discussion of the maximum and minimum limits of the investment called for. While insisting that these limits cannot be arbitrarily fixed, he at the same time argues that it is subjectively as well as objectively conditioned; that elements which have to be taken into account are: the state of material resources; the goal of full employment; the efficiency of capital at various levels of investment; the degree to which needs can be met over short-run periods; international competition; the population's natural growth and its age structure; and—on the subjective side—society's readiness to bear sacrifices. Since these elements are not reducible to a common denominator, the argument leaves the rate of capital formation indeterminate. While we would hesitate to subscribe to some of the conclusions drawn from this reasoning (it was evolved in the context of an attempted refutation of the applicability of the rate of interest), we are inclined to agree that regulating the intensity of capital formation in a

---

[64] Representative of this school of thought was Dr Colin Clark's *The Economics of 1960* (London, 1962). On trends and fluctuations in terms of trade see Sir S. Caine, *Prices for Primary Producers* (London, 1963), esp. p. 10.
[65] Grossman, 'Suggestions for a Soviet Investment Planning', in *Investment Criteria and Economic Growth* (Berkeley, Calif., 1956), p. 91.
[66] *Ekon.*, no. 3, 1960, p. 466.

centrally planned system is a matter of art rather than knowledge.

It is arguable on the whole that the planners' thinking has tended to be characterized by a double single-mindedness. First, there is the noticeable tendency, at least over a long period, to place a rather one-sided emphasis on the expansion of society's stock of capital. While undoubtedly the nexus between it and economic growth is very intimate indeed, the planners have been rather apt to underestimate other interacting elements and in particular extra-economic imponderables.[67] Secondly, and this is an interconnected point, the central planner whose eyes are directed towards the paramount objective of a very rapid growth is inclined to treat living standards as a much more manœuvrable variable of his equations than it is in real life. This, plus the rules of thumb to which we have referred, may help to account for the striking fact that, throughout the group of European planned economies over long periods, ratios of capital formation have not reflected the substantial differentials in per capita national products of its member nations.

The planner's attitude with regard to growth versus welfare creates an issue which has been admirably stated in an ECE analysis.

In a pure capitalist system the limiting factor on the expansion of output is at times the morale of entrepreneurs: if it can be raised, the investment multiplier [of national product] comes into operation. In an economic system in transition to socialism the raising of the morale of workers and peasants may sometimes bring a 'consumption multiplier' less powerful but not negligible into operation. . . . More generally, it would probably now be agreed in all eastern European countries that if consumption had been allowed to increase in the years 1951–1953 faster than actually happened, more, rather than less, investment could have been accomplished during the long-term plans, and progress would have been more regular.[68]

In a word, while theoretically it may be contended that a dynamic equilibrium can be imparted to an economic system at any level of capital accumulation, even the most exacting,[69]

---

[67] See for discussion *i.a.* K. Mandelbaum, assisted by J. R. L. Schneider, *The Industrialisation of Backward Areas* (Oxford, 1956), p. ix., also P. T. Bauer and B. S. Yamey, *The Economics of Underdeveloped Countries* (Chicago, 1957).

The 'place of capital in economic progress' is a subject of A. K. Cairncross's very illuminating analysis, in his contribution under that title to L. H. Duprez ed., *Economic Progress* (Louvain, 1955).

[68] ECE, *Survey, 1955*, p. 231.

[69] Joan Robinson, *The Accumulation of Capital*, (1956); see also K. Laski, in *Gosp. Plan.*, no. 3, 1959.

the post-war economic history of the area suggests that, in real life, the planner's possibilities are rather narrowly circumscribed. Nor has his freedom of manœuvre proved to be as wide as was expected: *ex post* corrections of any miscalculations have shown themselves difficult to carry out once resources were committed in a given direction. Biases built into programmes have tended to perpetuate, and indeed to accentuate, themselves, as it were in spirals beyond the planner's intention.

THE PACE OF CAPITAL FORMATION

The actual course and intensity of capital formation—and the measure of sacrifices it has entailed—are, through a combination of causes, only inadequately reflected in official and semi-official assessments.[70] They fail in any case to provide a satisfactory

Accumulation and Gross Fixed Investment as Percentage of National Income

	Accumulation	Gross fixed investment
Czechoslovakia		
1953 in prices of		
1949	31	27
1953	25	17
1957 in prices of		
1949		30
1953		18
1957		21
,, turnover tax excluded		29
Poland		
1953 in prices of		
1950	38	26
1953	25	17
1957 in prices of		
1950	32	23
1953	21	15
1957	23	21
,, turnover tax excluded		24

Source: UN, *World Econ. Survey, 1959,* ch. iii, p. 53.

[70] Summarized in the table on p. 43.

framework for comparisons with the West. This is partly due to conceptual differences in measuring social products (in particular in the treatment of 'non-material' services). Major distortions stem from the method adopted for price-weighting of investment goods —and producer goods generally—as against consumer goods: during the early 1950's as capital formation was gaining momentum, prices of investment goods were held down while those of consumer goods were rising. Heavy indirect taxation, almost exclusively burdening consumption, tended to overstate the share of this in national income, as against capital formation: this effect was further strengthened owing to a policy of keeping investment-goods prices, over long periods, well below cost levels by means of budgetary subsidies to industrial enterprises. A United Nations

Gross Capital Formation as Percentage of Gross National Product, 1950's
(recalculation on Western method)

	Early 1950's	Mid- 1950's	End of 1950's
Czechoslovakia	44	36	
East Germany	26 (?)	26	24
Poland	48	38	35
Western Europe	18	20	
France	19	18	
Western Germany	22	26	
Greece	21	15	
Italy	19	22	
Netherlands	28	24	
Norway	29	30	
Sweden	18	22	
Turkey	9	14	
United Kingdom	11	16	

Sources: Early 1950's, for Czechoslovakia, East Germany, and Poland, refer to 1953; mid-1950's to 1956; for Western Europe early and mid-1950's refer to 1950 and 1956, respectively. Late 1950's = 1959 for Poland, 1958 for East Germany. Western share data from OEEC, *Statistics of National Product and Expenditure*, no. 2, 1938 and 1947 to 1955 (Paris, 1957). Overall Western share data: for OEEC as a whole expressed in U.S. $ at 1954 exchange rates; for individual countries in national currency at price levels of various dates.

Study clearly illustrates the effect of applying a different price basis for measuring the burden of capital formation in the same year.

Our own inquiry into post-war developments in the area's national products and capital accumulation (relegated to a study to be published separately) has attempted to assess the burden, if only approximately, by the use of Western statistical conventions. The results of what approximates to a factor-cost, current-price calculation of Gross National Products, is summarized on p. 40.

For a variety of reasons the pressure of domestic capital accumulation made itself less heavily felt—at least on the psychological plane—in the initial post-war stages of reconstruction. In Poland and Czechoslovakia the massive aid from UNRRA of nearly $750 million[71] added directly to capital formation in well-selected key branches such as mining, transport, and food production; it assisted consumption and thus set free a relatively larger proportion of home-produced national incomes for capital formation. Further, in that period comparatively small amounts of capital sufficed to bring back to fruition capacities paralysed through war damage. In the special case of Poland, the injection of comparatively little capital could and did result in large gains in output, thanks to her territorial acquisitions, even if one allowed for the very heavy destruction from which the new territories suffered. The shift of manpower from branches of lower efficiency to those of higher efficiency—especially from agriculture to industry—enhanced as it was by the territorial changes, helped to speed recovery.

Broadly speaking by the turn of the 1940's the national incomes of both Poland and Czechoslovakia—but not of East Germany— returned to their pre-war levels. In both countries this implied *per*

[71]   *UNRRA Assistance*
                              ($ *mill.*)

	to Poland	to Czechoslovakia
Food	202	107
Clothing, textiles, footwear	44	29
Medical supplies	21	27
Agricultural rehabilitation	76	33
Industrial rehabilitation (incl. transport)	134	74
Total	476	270

Cf. *UNRRA*, Operational Analysis Papers, nos. 16, p. 34 and 45, p. 6.

capita magnitudes higher—in Poland considerably higher—than those prevailing before the war.

By that time the intensive capital formation had acquired impetus: expansion tended to self-perpetuation, as did stagnation in the past. Compared with the past the change was particularly drastic in the case of Poland, which before the war was among the countries with a moderate or low ratio of accumulation—amounting to about 14 per cent in 1938. This refers to gross capital formation: over a considerable span of the inter-war period,—which, of course, included the Great Depression—there had, in fact, been considerable net disinvestment.[72] The successes of the initial post-war period added to the self-confidence of the planners. Ambitious development programmes were embarked upon. Larger proportions of national incomes were devoted to capital formation. Simultaneously heavy military commitments added to pressure on consumption. The returns from the effort tended to decline. As was pointed out, falling living standards affected the morale of the populations and their efficiency. Bottlenecks and imbalances became acute.[73] To use Professor Lipinski's term, investment which was too sharply tilted in some directions at the expense of others created 'foci of deceleration'. Rapid additions to capital stocks in some domains were accompanied by actual disinvestment in others, undermining the balance and handicapping

---

[72] Net accumulation as a percentage of Polish national income has been estimated as follows for the 1929–38 decade.

1929	1930	1931	1932 to 1935	1936	1938
5·5	3·2	0·6	negative	nil	6·8

See K. Laski, in *Ekon.*, no. 4, 1955, p. 50, based on estimates by M. Kalecki and L. Landau, '*Szacunek dochodu spolecnego w r. 1929*', and '*Dochod spoleczny z r. 1933*', and Cz. Klarner's *Dochod spoleczny wsi i miast w okresie przesilenia gospodarczego 1929–1936* (Lwow, 1937); with the assumption that depreciation of fixed capital stock would amount to about 700 mill. zl. K. Secomski, in *Polish Perspectives*, no. 2, 1958, p. 21, relates pre-war capital expenditure to post-war as follows (1955 prices).

	1938	1946	1949	1955	1957
Total	100	107	209	437	534
Per capita	100	153	296	615	656

[73] Difficulties were bound to grow, and returns on investment to decline, as a rising proportion of it was taken up by new projects. K. Secomski, in *Gosp. Plan.*, no. 7, 1954, draws attention to this factor. The share of new projects in investment rose from 7 to 42 and to 62%, in the rehabilitation period, the start of the first five year plan, and 1953 respectively.

expansion; under conditions of full employment of resources, shifts to such sectors as armament industries created illusory acceleration.[74]

Expansion of Capital Formation
(p.a. percentage increases (rounded) in gross fixed investment)

	1949–53	*1953–8*	*1956–60*	*1961–3* *(plans)*
Czechoslovakia	15	9	14	8
Poland	21	6	8	7
	1950–3	*1953–8*	*1956–60*	*1959–65* *(plans)*
East Germany	20	18	17	10

On the whole the stepping-up of capital formation was, in the 1950's, both faster and smoother in East Germany than in the two other countries. It must, however, be borne in mind that East Germany's national product was burdened—very heavily over the early post-war years—with the load of occupation costs and reparations. (Reliable authorities suggest that as late as the early 1950's, reparations, plus Soviet demands on uranium mining, and occupation costs amounted to rather more than one-fifth of the net national product, at factor cost.)[75] As these external obligations were reduced, East German investment could be steeply expanded over a considerable part of the 1950's without earmarking for it a correspondingly greater proportion of national product. In the second part of the 1950's the curve of capital accumulation again showed an upward swing in both Poland and Czechoslovakia—though it was weaker in the former than in the latter; both countries programme the pace of increase more cautiously in the

[74] Edward Lipinski, in *Nowe Drogi*, nos. 11–12, 1956. Cf. also Lange, in *Z. Gosp.*, no. 40, 1956 (quoted on p. 7).

[75] 'Germanicus', in *Economia Internazionale*, ix/2, estimates the cost of reparations, uranium mining, and occupation expenditure at around 3,300 mill. RM., in 1936 prices, yearly for 1950–3. In 1951 this amounted to 22% of NNP at factor costs.

For 1946–7, E. Wolf, 'Aufwendungen für die Besatzungsmächte öffentliche Haushalte und Sozialprodukt in den einzelnen Zonen', in *Wirtschaftsprobleme der Besatzungszonen* (Berlin, 1948), pp. 120, 136, estimated occupation costs and other Soviet receipts debited to current production at 26·1% of national product as against 15·9 and 12·7, respectively, in the American and British zones.

1960's, and East Germany's programmes for the 1960's envisage a marked drop, narrowing the disparity between her and the two other countries.

Even in the late 1950's, after the ratio of capital formation to national income had been reduced and stabilized under the social and economic strains, about one-third of the national product was still currently accumulated in Poland. The Czechoslovak proportion was probably of the same order. Only the East German ratio was at that time substantially lower—about one-quarter (on our own recalculation,[76] based on Western conventions and methodologies). The overall West European (OEEC) ratio, oscillating in the 1950's around one-fifth, may provide a yardstick for an appraisal.

Understandably, bringing the different valuations to a common denominator is an extremely tricky task. Hence no more than a broad illustration may be expected from estimates such as the Polish calculation which suggests that, on a per head basis, capital cost of overall economic and industrial expansion is between three-quarters and four-fifths as high again in Czechoslovakia as it is in Poland: clearly differences in income make the same cost disproportionately higher to a Pole than to a Czechoslovak. On all counts the income of the average East German is still mortaged with the comparatively smallest burden.

Relative Cost of Investment Per Head of Population, 1956–60

	All investment	Industrial investment
Poland	100	100
Czechoslovakia	180	174
East Germany	95	about 90

Source: Derived and partly estimated on the basis of calculations by B. Zielinska, in *Gosp. Plan.*, no. 3, 1961.

Very probably developments across the Elbe added to the East German population's sensitivity to pressures on its living standards, and restrained East German policy makers: at the end of the 1950's East and Western Germany were more or less on a par with

---

[76] To be published separately.

regard to the intensity of investment. It may be presumed, however, that it was in the poorest of the three countries that the sacrifices involved were felt to be relatively heaviest: CMEA calculations suggest that Polish national income, at the beginning of the 1960's, equalled 98 per cent of the average for East European planned economies, and that the figures were 144 and 143 per cent for Czechoslavakia and East Germany respectively.[77]

As we have noted it was in Poland, under conditions of greater freedom for public debate on matters of economic strategy, that the fundamental problems of optimal tempi of capital formation came to be investigated and discussed. When the very long-term or 'perspective' programme of Polish economic development, extending into the mid-1970's, came to be formulated, two schools of thought began to argue on the classical lines of to-day's sacrifices versus the benefits to be reaped tomorrow. One stressed the imperative needs of high rates of accumulation during the transitional 'period of manœuvre' for the sake of higher living standards by the end of the perspective plan. It argued[78] that even a high rate of increase in capital formation—say starting from 7 per cent a year, reaching 10 per cent after a decade and dropping down to $6\frac{1}{2}$ per cent—would secure to Poland only a very modest level of development compared with the West. The fact, this school argued further, that Poland's population is growing very fast calls for exacting rates of saving: capital accumulation rising at a rate of about 5–6 per cent a year would imply a race of at least half a century to catch up with Western living standards, rising as these are by about 3–4 per cent. The precept of this school is then to speed up the spiral of capital accumulation over one or one and a half decades, and thereafter to relax. Its opponents[79] question the validity of treating the increase in national income as the exclusive effect of investment; they—Pajestka in particular—have emphasized the 'non-investment' element which may be counted upon to come into play in promoting expansion. However, Pajestka's own subsequent investigations were to show that, in Polish experience, its actual contribution to the country's

---

[77] Note that, according to US Dept. of State calculations, average GNP *per capita* for the same group of economies (Albania, Bulgaria, Czechoslovakia, East Germany, Hungary, Poland, Rumania), at market prices, converted at purchasing-power equivalents amounted in 1962 to $1,002. (Corresponding magnitudes for the USA and USSR would be $2,974 and 1,145 respectively.)

[78] M. Rakowski, in *Gosp. Plan.*, no. 12, 1957, and no. 1, 1958.   [79] Ibid.

economic progress was strikingly insignificant.[80] The problem would thus turn on the question whether there is a valid expectation that the role of 'non-investment' does rise at advanced stages of industrial development, and one wonders if there is a unique empirical answer to this question.

The battle has not come to an end. The official vision of the development of the Polish economy has not become crystallized. Judging from the first variant of the twenty-year programme (1956–75) drafted by a planning body under Professor Kalecki, it seemed that a middle-of-the-road view would prevail.[81] Even then national income would be heavily mortgaged for half a generation. As is shown below, the intended rate of investment would be about one-third. When indirect taxation and subsidies were evenly spread in investment and consumer-goods prices the planned ratio of gross capital formation to national income would be nearly two-fifths.[82]

More recently, however, the somewhat more impatient school seems to have been winning the day. At least in part this may perhaps be ascribed to the influence of Soviet strategic thinking and the accent on the coordination of the 1980 plans throughout the whole CMEA area. The Polish 1980 plan, as it now stands, is closer than the original Kalecki variant to the Soviet plan of reaching 'the threshold of Communism' in respect of the pace of growth of income and gross investment, but there is considerable discrepancy in the assumed trend of increase in consumption.

General Strategy of Polish, Czechoslovak, and Soviet Very-Long-Term Plans

(average rates of increase—per cent per annum)

	Kalecki variant 1961–75	1960–80 Programmes		
		Polish	Czechoslovak	Soviet
National income	6·5	7·5	±7	8·5
Industrial output (gross)	.	8·9	±8·5	9·7
Industrial productivity of labour	.	7·8	±7·5	7·2–7·7
Gross investment	±6·9	±8	±8·4	9
Consumption—per head	4·4	4·5	.	6·4
Share of investment in national income	31·5	.	.	.

---

[80] Pajestka, ibid. no. 12, 1957.   [81] See p. 64.
[82] Zielinska, in *Gosp. Plan.*, no. 3, 1961.

Very little has been revealed about the Czechoslovak and nothing as yet about the East German 1980 programmes.[83] What is known of Czechoslovak targets tentatively set shows a striking similarity to their Polish counterpart. To achieve broadly similar rates of expansion of national income the two nations would go ahead with their capital formation at roughly the same pace. They would also in this way achieve the same speed in their industrial development, which would imply a perpetuation of the disparity of their respective status on a per head basis. A noteworthy point is, further, that, in spite of the differences in the potential supply of labour, the Poles expect the same relative contribution of rising productivity to industrial output as do the Czechoslovaks. *Prima facie*, at least, there is no reason for questioning the consistency of either of the two programmes.

Compared with these the Soviet programme is bolder in planning the growth of both national income and industrial output. (The proposed rate of growth of industrial productivity, broadly the same as in Poland and Czechoslovakia, would suggest that the USSR is relying on a more intensive transfer of manpower from farms to factories.) It is also more exacting than the plans of either country in setting the rate of growth of investment. One may wonder, therefore, how realistic is the expectation of a rise in consumption per head at a rate half again as fast as the proposed Polish one. (The Czechoslovak programme in so far as revealed does not commit itself on this point of strategy.) However, the Poles are patently reluctant to proclaim 1980, as does the Soviet Union, as the threshold to the era of plenty identified with full Communism. The architects of the Polish programme seem also to be more sober in appraising the significance of economic programmes for twenty years ahead. They are more ready to admit the uncertainties with regard to extra-economic and economic factors on which the validity of the programme depends. They are, indeed, inclined to look upon their 1980 plan as an attempt at a very broad vision rather than a programme in the sense in which the authors of the Soviet plan do, or at least profess to do.

[83] Tentative East German plans for 1964–70 envisage a marked slow-down of growth, to 7 and $4\frac{1}{2}\%$ respectively for national income and industrial output.

THE PATTERN OF CAPITAL FORMATION

Capital formation is essentially patterned in non-value terms, but Soviet-type planning does resort to value criteria of efficiency within a certain area of choice-making.[84] The instrument is the limiting 'recoupment' period—the period over which reduction in annual operating cost 'pays off' the initial capital outlay, or its reciprocal, the rate of investment efficiency. Planners set the normative rates for the use in screening acceptable solutions. The investment alternative selected on this count will be the one for which—with given outputs—initial capital cost, 'discounted' at the normative rate, plus current cost and depreciation, is the lowest. In other words, in substance the coefficient of efficiency sets the minimum rate of profit to be 'earned' on capital: it has also some technical affinities with the rate of interest.[85]

Of course the coefficient of minimum efficiency is not the only choice-criterion. Additional yardsticks used are various physical-term indicators of performance, such as output per unit of equipment or per man, or related to inputs. But, other things being equal, the test by means of the coefficient of efficiency is decisive.

The Polish methodology of investment-efficiency measuring, evolved by the Kalecki–Rakowski school[86] adopts the principle of a single rate for the economy as a whole. The Czechoslovak approach is closer to the Soviet, inasmuch as it accepts differentiated branch rates.[87] Hence essentially the Czechoslovak tool can be applied only for intra-branch choices of project alternatives: this narrows the operational scope of the instrument. It cannot be applied in the sphere of substitution across traditional branch frontiers, although contemporary technology continuously widens this sphere, especially in fuels and power, natural and synthetic materials, and so on. (The use of the Polish rate for the whole

[84] The subject is discussed with greater rigour by the present writer in *Sov. Stud.*, Ap. 1950; *Quart. J. Econ.*, Aug. 1955 and *Economica*, Aug. 1962. See also literature quoted in these sources.

[85] There is inconsistency, we believe, in applying a quasi-rate of interest in investment choices and its rejection in pricing (see above, p. 14). The conflict is, however, denied by some students of the subject; in the West, in particular by Mrs Joan Robinson, see her article on the 'philosophy of price' in *Ekon.*, no. 3, 1960 (in Polish), p. 530.

[86] See in particular Kalecki and Rakowski, in *Gosp. Plan.*, no. 11, 1959; J. Czarnek, Z. Knyziak, and Rakowski, in *Ekon.*, no. 3, 1961; Rakowski, in *Gosp. Plan.*, no. 3, 1962.

[87] For Czechoslovak approach see in particular J. Hon, 'Rozbor effektivnosti technickeho rozvoje v socjalismu', in J. Hon. ed., *Effektivnost technickeho rozvoje* (Prague, 1962), ch. ii.

economy has had some influence on its construction: we shall not enlarge on this and other technical aspects.)

The usual objection against a single rate is that it would distort the planner's preferences, since, so it is argued, such preferences must be expressed in appropriately differentiated performance requirements; and that in any case there is no room for such a rate in a socialist planning system, where no automatic forces equalize returns of capital throughout the economy as they do under capitalism. The reasoning is hardly convincing. The rationale of the value-based yardstick is to rank decision-alternatives according to their comparative efficiency in terms of value. The wider, then, the range of comparison the more dependable are the choices; and greater width of the range does not by itself preclude reaching a decision on another basis. This disposes also of the argument as to the lack of a profit-equalisation mechanism in a non-market system. For, in so far as value-term efficiency is measured and taken into consideration by the planner, he must refer himself to some weighted, overall averages.

Weak as the objections against a single rate of investment efficiency are, they reflect the conceptual difficulties which the measuring of efficiency of investment in value-terms (that is, in substance, basing choices in investment on the minimization of cost or, what amounts to the same thing, on the maximization of profit) encounters where profit is rejected as the economic motive and the price of capital is alien to the theory of value adhered to. In the area we are interested in, resistance against the value-criteria for choices in capital formation seems to be at its strongest in East German thinking: the view prevails that even the purely economic effect of investment cannot be fully quantified.[88]

As to the computational aspect of the time-discount, the defensible view gains ground that a fully satisfactory way of setting it would be only to derive it from the technologically optimal programme: a programme which maps out the efficient path of growth of the economy over the plan's time-horizon (the planner imitating in his calculus a competitive capital market). While the theoretical basis of the conception has been by now well developed, especially in Poland, the solution is still far beyond the realm of practicable techniques.

[88] On the general problem of consistency of choices, based on physical-term and price parameters, see above, p. 14.

In Polish methodology the rate of minimum efficiency of capital to be invested is conceived as broadly reflecting some optimum correlation of the two primary factors—labour and capital. It is based on the postulate of a labour-market equilibrium corresponding to full employment; this is a rather ambiguous concept, since, on the one hand, full employment would determine the choice of technology, and on the other, the technological levels adopted would in turn determine the sense of the full employment. But the Polish conception is logical in relating the norm (the price) for capital to the planned relative factor position, that is, to levels of capital intensity and thereby to the planned pace of capital formation.

Choices in investment may involve those in foreign trade— hence the measuring of the efficiency of the two is interrelated.[89] In practice, however, as it has developed in Central Europe (the Soviet contribution in this field is rather limited) the test of foreign-trade efficiency has been of a static nature; it assumes, that is, existing capacities. In its most refined form the tool used—the coefficient of efficiency of foreign trade—assesses net currency earning from 'pure' manufacturing. On this principle ranks of export-worthiness of specific commodities are determined: in Czechoslovakia and East Germany it serves for intra-branch comparisons of this 'worthiness' only, but in Poland it has a wider, inter-branch application as well. Until recently the test of foreign-trade efficiency has largely been confined to exports: imports have been left, as it were, to take care of themselves—their need is determined from 'material balances',[90] and the rule is that they should in any case be limited to the minimum of what is necessary. In more recent times efforts have been made to widen the test of profitability of foreign trade by dropping the assumption of constant capacities: bringing in a time-dimension naturally widens the choices. The tool evolved for this purpose is the marginal capital/net-foreign-exchange output ratio. It brings into the efficiency calculation export-stimulating and import-saving investment. By its use foreign-exchange—revenue or alternatively foreign-exchange saving on imports to be cut—is related, over a given time-horizon, to the total cost of production in question, account

---

[89] This subject is discussed in my 'Note on the Criterion of Efficiency of Foreign Trade in Soviet-type Economies', *Economica*, Feb. 1964.
[90] See above, p. 4.

being taken of investment. Total cost means here current cost plus initial capital outlay discounted at the adopted quasi-rate of interest, that is, at the coefficient of efficiency of investment (clearly, meaningful inferences can be drawn from such calculations only where a single rate for the whole economy of investment-efficiency is in application).[91] While their logic is defensible these calculations add to the difficulties and pitfalls of measuring the efficiency of both capital formation and foreign commerce, for a non-market system.

One or two preliminary remarks may usefully precede our more detailed discussion of the shapes capital-formation takes in the area. Both concern elements of considerable impact on its productivity. One of them is the relation between additions to fixed and other shapes of investment. A high marginal ratio of inventories to fixed capital formation has been a signal characteristic of the Polish economy: for most of the period under survey it was of the order of 1 : 4 as against something like 1 : 10 prevailing in Western Europe.[92]

The build-up of reserves throughout the area in the early phase of forceful industrial expansion might be partly ascribed to the need to replenish exhausted stocks, but continuing excessive stock accumulation has become a serious handicap in the 1960's. High inventory ratio has something to do with the working of the economic mechanism itself: when supply channels are unreliable, managers tend to insure themselves by maintaining larger stocks (which raises the cost of capital).

The other noteworthy element is a strikingly low ratio—about 5 per cent—of replacement to national product, partly reflecting the high proportion of new—'young'—fixed capital, but partly, also the deliberate disregard for wear and tear and obsolescence. Accounting methods with regard to capital repairs have tended somewhat to underrate actual amortization.[93] On the other hand,

[91] Recently more ambitious attempts have been made at devising models which build foreign trade into general optimization programmes. The questions to which answers are sought are: what should be produced, what should be imported (and whence) and what exported (and whither) to meet posited final-demand targets, with domestic currency cost at minimum and net foreign-exchange gain at maximum. Cf. in particular W. Trzeciakowski, in *Gosp. Plan.*, nos. 4 and 5, 1961, and *Przeglad Stat.*, no. 2, 1962.

[92] This is roughly the 1955 ratio for the OEEC countries. Cf. OEEC, *Statistics of National Product and Expenditure*, no. 2, *1938* and *1947 to 1955*, p. 39.

[93] In Polish conditions the actual fall-out of assets through wear and tear corresponds to about 1·5% of the value of productive capital stock and to about 15% of that of current investment (W. Lissowski, in *Gosp. Plan.*, no. 4, 1958, p. 60).

maximum utilization of capacities installed has undoubtedly been pursued as a point of policy, the non-competitive system permitting the operation of plants with vast efficiency differentials. It must be borne in mind, especially when inter-country comparisons of net investment are made, that not only does capital injected under this heading replace wear and tear, but, as often as not, it brings more up-to-date technology into the economy.[94] Another factor with obvious relevance for capital efficiency is the length of the investment-'maturation' period. There has been a good deal of criticism on this count: the abnormally long averages are connected with the straining and dispersion—'wide front'—of the investment effort, which in turn is undoubtedly influenced by the economic mechanism. Last but not least the productivity of capital is influenced by the respective shares borne by equipment and construction in relation to total outlay.[95]

Share of Equipment in Investment

(*percentages*)

	Poland	Czechoslovakia	14 Western countries	Britain	Western Germany
1936–56:					
Manufacturing				69–80[1]	64–69[2]
1950–56:					
All investment	30	30	48		
Industry	41		70–80		
1957 or 1958:					
All investment	33				
Industry	38	40			
1961–5:					
All investment	29	33			

[1] Min. and max. for the period. [2] All industry.

Sources: Lissowski, as quoted in *Gosp. Plan.*, no. 2, 1958, p. 13; *Hosp. Nov.*, 17 Apr. 1959; *Rocz. stat.*, 1959, p. 66; ECE, *Survey, 1959*, ch. iii, p. 22; T. Barna, in *Vjh. Wirtsch-Forsch*, no. 2, 1957.

The two-fifths ratio recorded for equipment over long periods in the area's industrial investment is strikingly below what is usual in Western economies, even allowing for the difficulty of comparing the data available, owing to differences in the type of investment, and methods of cost recording, &c. In physical terms the volume of buildings per unit of industrial capacity is between one-half and

[94] A very interesting discussion of the implications of this point for the growth process in dynamic economies will be found in E. Domar, *Econ. J.*, lxiii/249.
[95] See below, p. 66.

four-fifths as large again as it is in industrially advanced Western European countries.[96] The continuous effort made to improve the ratio has been rewarded with little visible success.

On the other hand the proportion of equipment in total outlay, as distinct from industrial capital, obviously depends in its distribution between directly productive and non-productive investment. High priority for immediately productive, as against nonproductive, fixed capital formation—in the accepted terminology the latter has a wider coverage than social or welfare 'overheads' since it includes those services which are considered 'nonproductive' in Marxian terms—stems from the basic strategy already discussed. So does priority accorded to industry within the 'productive' sphere, and to heavy branches, including construction, within industry.

Various authorities have suggested various optimal patterns of fixed investment. The well-known study by Professor Lewis, for instance, suggests a 'typical' programme in which housing would take about one-quarter, public works and utilities rather more than one-third, and manufacturing and agriculture rather less than one-third, with a remaining tenth going to 'other commerce'. The actual pattern of Western European fixed investment (gross) in the first five years of the 1950's may provide another standard for an analysis.

Distribution of Fixed Investment in OEEC Member Countries, by Main Sectors. 1951

(per cent: rounded figures)

Manufacturing (incl. iron-ore mining, & construction)	24·0
Energy	10·5
Transport (excl. roads)	12·7
Agriculture	8·5
Services	11·0
Housing	24·0
Roads, schools, public administration	9·7
	100·0

Source: OEEC, *Europe To-day and in 1960* (Paris, 1957), ii, 67.

[96] Rychlewski, in *Ekon.*, no. 1, 1959, p. 139. The ratio of construction seems to be somewhat lower in the total investment of East Germany: G. Kohlmey gives it at 58% for the 1951–5 period, *Vopr. Ekon.*, no. 11, 1956, p. 56.

Differences in classification interfere with a satisfactory comparison, but it is doubtless 'welfare' investment that has consistently been given more attention in Western than in Central Europe; it will be noted, however, that a comparison within the area will also reveal substantial variations, and no less substantial fluctuations of national patterns in accordance with trends already mentioned.

It can be broadly said that in Western Europe industrial investment in a wider sense—including energy generation and construction—takes about one-third of the total. The proportion was not much different in the area on the eve of the post-war development era; later it rose to as much as one-half. (At least one student of the subject noted an empirical rule that to approach —and still more to surpass—50 per cent spells tension in the economy).[97] Subsequently, towards the end of the 1950's, industrial investment came down nearer two-fifths, or about seven-tenths of the whole investment defined as 'productive'; it has been planned at approximately the same level for the first half of the 1960's.[98]

Within the industrial total, light industries have accounted for no more than between one-eighth and one-seventh. If light industry is bracketed together with agriculture, housing, and trade as a broad 'welfare sector' and juxtaposed to the 'heavy sector' covering heavy industry only, a striking similarity of pattern appears for Czechoslovakia and Poland: in both cases the years

[97] Marczewski, in *Revue Économique*, no. 2, 1956, p. 192.
[98] See table on p. 55.

According to the Czechoslovak national inventory, by the end of the 1950's overall fixed capital stock increased—as compared with the end of the post-war reconstruction period—by about two-fifths; 'productive' capital stock by one-half; industrial capital stock by two-thirds; while the stock of installed industrial machinery and equipment doubled.

Fixed Capital Stock, Czechoslovakia, 1958
(per cent increase over 1948)

Total	Productive	Industrial	Industrial equipment
41	54	68	98

Source: *Stat. roc.*, *1959*, p. 39: valued in 1955 prices, no allowance made for wear and tear and obsolescence. The valuation seems rather precarious. Data on changes in the fixed capital stocks in the two remaining countries are even less reliable.

Gross Fixed Investment. Distribution by Selected Sectors

(*per cent: rounded figures*)

	Industry[1]	Agriculture & forestry	Transport & communications	Housing[2]
Czechoslovakia				
1949 (a)	50	6	14	15
(b)	55	6	16	10
1953 (a)	42	12	15	13
(b)	47	5	17	11
1951–5 (a)	45	12	12	14
(b)	51	5	15	12
1956–60 (a)	33	13	8	
(b)	49	7	12	11
1961–5 (Plan) (a)	39	13	9	
1961 (a)	41	17	10	14
East Germany				
1950	42	6	6	13
1953	50	10	8	17
1961 (b)	57	10	16	
1951–5 (b)	49	10	13	11
1956–60	53	9		
1959–65 (Plan)	42	10	10	21
Poland				
1946 (a)	28	16	43	
1950 (a)	37	13	15	12
1953 (a)	48	8	12	11
1961 (a)	40	12	11	19
1956–60 (a)	39	13	9	18
1961–5 (Plan) (a)	39	18½	12	9 (5)

(a) All investment. (b) State investment.

[1] Industrial investment does not as a rule cover the building industry, as is generally the case with Western data. Building investment in the three countries normally amounts to 2–3% of total investment, e.g. 3% for Czechoslovakia, and an average of 2·5% over the years 1956–60 for Poland.
[2] Polish data only cover urban housing; figures in brackets refer to rural housing.

Sources:
Czechoslovakia
  (a) (b) *Stat. roc., 1958; 1959; 1962.* In 1957 prices for all years except 1958 (1959 prices); 1961—in 1961 prices.

East Germany

1950 and 1953: (*b*) ECE, *Survey, 1955*, ch. viii, pp. 229, 242 (1950 prices).

1951–5: (*a*) ibid. 1956, ch. ii, p. 4 and Table XXII; (*b*) H. Herr, in *Stat. Prax.*, no. 6.

1956–60: (*a*) ECE, *Survey, 1957*, ch. i, p. 30.

1961–5: terms of reference uncertain.

1961: *Stat. Jb., 1962* (1961 prices); industry here includes construction.

Poland

Rocz. stat., 1961; in 1961 prices.

Data for 1946 refer to investment in the 'socialist sector' of the economy amounting to rather more than two-thirds of the total investment of the country.

1952–3 make a watershed dividing a low from a rising allocation to 'welfare' in the sense defined here.

Just as East Germany's expansion in capital formation in the 1950's was smoother than that of the two other countries, her distribution of investment also showed more stability: the share of heavy industries remained almost unchanged after 1953. It will, however, be remembered that her post-war industrial development was differently phased. Correctives have been carried out

'Heavy' versus Welfare Sectors in Gross Fixed Investment

(*per cent of total*)

	1949	*1952*	*1958*
Czechoslovakia			
Heavy sectors	43	44[2]	38
Welfare sectors	15	16[2]	26
East Germany			
Heavy sectors	34[1]	44	43
Welfare sectors	16[1]	18	22
Poland			
Heavy sectors	32	46	34
Welfare sectors	24	17	30

[1] 1950 for East Germany. [2] 1952 for Czechoslovakia.

Source: UN, *World Economic Survey, 1959*, ch. iii, p. 62. 'Heavy' and welfare sectors as defined on p. 54 above. Owing to differences in classification and valuation the percentages do not always agree with those in the table on p. 55 above.

since the second half of the 1950's in favour of 'welfare' sectors. By the early 1960's 'non-productive' investment was taking—on a comparable basis—about one-third of the total in both Poland and Czechoslovakia, and rather more—nearer to two-fifths—in East Germany.[99]

Housing in particular obtained a more generous allocation of capital; its share rose in Poland to one-fifth, or one-quarter if rural housing is added. Both Poland and Czechoslovakia are among the European nations with the highest population densities per room. Larger transfers of rural population to Poland's growing towns made the housing drive especially urgent. Housing throughout the area, and in Poland agriculture and small-scale industry as well, have become, from the late 1950's onwards, the domain of relatively substantial private investment. In the late 1950's the rate of housing construction in the area amounted to about 4 household units per 1,000 of population. This was stepped up in the 1960's to about $7\frac{1}{2}$ units in Poland, $6\frac{1}{2}$ in East Germany, and 5 in Czechoslovakia.[100]

INDUSTRY VERSUS AGRICULTURE

From the point of view of allocational strategy, the participation by the two main producing sectors of the economy—industry and farming—in factor endowment and investment may be conveniently noted as a digression in this context.

Industry versus Agriculture: Capital, Manpower and Investment, Beginning of the 1960's

(per cent)

	Czechoslovakia	East Germany	Poland
Industry			
Gross fixed investment	39	42	39
Fixed capital	30		28
Manpower	43	40	28
Agriculture			
Gross fixed investment	15	10	19
Fixed capital	9	.	19
Manpower	31	21	56

[99] A. Bodnar in *Gosp. Plan.*, no. 5, 1961, p. 42.   [100] Ibid.

The heavy labour-intensity of agriculture, whether in relation to its stock or its current supply of capital, is brought out into very strong relief here in the case of Poland. It is also a feature—to a lesser degree—of the other two economies.

At the time to which this table refers, the pro-industrial bias of investment policies was accompanied by (and facilitated) transfers of labour force from agriculture to sectors of higher productivity. On parallel lines the share of industry in national products rose considerably. The measuring of inter-sectoral shift in the latter is inevitably affected by statistical methods and—very obviously—by the relative prices adopted. The effects of valuing consumption of farm products on the farm in one way rather than another is, *inter alia*, a factor of considerable importance where economies with a strong peasant element are concerned. For instance, when Polish consumption on the farm is valued at the average realized prices of marketed production, the share of agriculture in GNP will be around one-quarter, as will be seen in a moment: but it would go up to nearly one-third if retail prices were adopted as the yardstick.[101] Another source of distortion when comparisons over time or space are aimed at are differences in the classification of the various branches of economy. Our recomputation (to be published separately), based broadly on methodology and conventions applied in the West and on pre-war pricing, would indicate that, soon after 1955, the relative share of agriculture dropped, throughout the area, by about two-fifths.

Perhaps a somewhat safer yardstick (even if less satisfactory in principle) for inter-temporal as well as inter-spatial comparisons is provided by aggregates of contributions to national products from commodity sectors only.

[101] The following table of the percentage share of agriculture in Polish national income shows the effect of changes of price weighting.

	1937	*1947*	*1950*	*1955*
At 1937 prices	45	23		27
At 1950 prices			29	22
At current prices	45	38		26

Cf. *Do hod Narodowy Polski* (Warsaw, 1949), p. 16; ibid. (1957), p. 3; ECE, *Bulletin*, ix/3, p. 22.

At current prices, in 1959, the share of agriculture in national income was 27% (forestry included); and the share of industry with handicrafts was 4%, and 58% when construction is added. Cf. *Dochod Narodowy Polski 1957 i 1958* (Warsaw, 1960), p. 133.

It has sometimes been argued that the status of an economy is determined by its proportion of 'service' industries. A more convincing view, based on more recent analyses, is that, on the

Shifts in National Products: Industry versus Agriculture
(percentage contribution to national products)

	Czechoslovakia	East Germany	Poland
Pre-war			
Agriculture	23	16	41
Industry	(53)	49	29
1961			
Agriculture	14	11	24
Industry	(74)	75	56

Note: Czechoslovak figures for industry are bracketed to indicate that there is no adequate way of separating contribution of handicrafts. Construction is included in industry. 1961 data taken from official estimates which are not fully comparable with our pre-war figures.

contrary, the heterogeneity of what is lumped together under the heading of services—private and public—blurs the distinction on this score between countries rich and poor, industrially developed and undeveloped.[102]

The dynamics of change within the commodity sphere, and the position reached by the three countries are shown in the table on page 60, against the background of selected Western European countries.

A glance at this table suggests that (with only one exception—which is Britain, the country with the lowest share of agriculture in commodity production) the same unmistakable trend is at work everywhere. It continuously reduces agriculture's contribution in favour of industry, although at a pace which varies from one country to another. As is only to be expected, the pace is more rapid in the agricultural and semi-agricultural countries than in those industrially advanced.

This regularity, however, has no universal validity. Indeed, in the area we are interested in, it is (somewhat unexpectedly)

[102] E. F. Jackson, 'Social Accounting in Eastern Europe', *Income and Wealth*, series iv, p. 250n.

Czechoslovakia which shows the quickest decline: agriculture's share in commodity output dropped within two decades by two-fifths in Czechoslovakia, in East Germany by one-quarter, in

Agriculture, Industry, and Construction: Percentages of Commodity Output, Pre-War to Late 1950's

(per cent)

	Year	Agriculture	Industry	Construction
Czechoslovakia	1937	28	63	9
	1956	17	73	10
East Germany	1936	22	67	11
	1956	16	70	14
Poland	1938	54	36	6
	1956	37	52	11
United Kingdom	1937	9	75	16
	1955	10	80	10
Western Germany	1936	22	69	9
	1955	15	75	10
Netherlands	1950	25	65	10
France	1938	35	59	6
	1954	30	60	10
Denmark	1938	38	53	9
	1954	36	52	12
Italy	1938	49	47	4
	1955	36	56	8

Source: Percentage shares for the three countries above the line are taken from the author's series of national products, to be published separately. Those below the line are from ECE, *Survey, 1956*, ch. vii, p. 13. All data are taken from commodity outputs at constant prices. (Differences in weighting may account for some discrepancies.) Industry in each case includes handicrafts.

Poland by one-third. The comparatively modest decline in the last case hides, in fact, an exaggeration, if the post-war position is compared with that of pre-war Poland, which comprised the predominantly agricultural areas annexed by the Soviet Union. In the West several countries experienced a comparable or even more rapid fall in the share of agriculture. Finland and Italy are notable examples: in particular the drop in the latter's agricultural 'over-weight' has been more drastic than in Poland.

There is a very close parallel between developments in the two parts of Germany: the striking similarity between both the east and the west of the country observable under such very different social and economic mechanisms and policies strongly suggests that the forces which produce these changes are not entirely dependent on the socio-economic system.

Both parts of Germany belong to the small group of countries where agriculture contributes less than one-fifth to the overall material national product. (Czechoslovakia too is, on this score, a member of the highly industrialized group. In Poland the share of agriculture is close to that in Denmark, Finland, and Italy.)

In the most industrial countries industry proper (that is, excluding construction) makes up 70 per cent or more of the non-agricultural total. Only very few nations—notably Britain and Western Germany—have reached or passed this mark. Both Czechoslovakia and East Germany belong to this most highly industrialized 'club'. Poland, where the proportion increased over the last two decades or so from two-fifths to about one-half, belongs, in company with Denmark, Finland, and Italy, to the middle group where the share of industry is from one-half to three-fifths. As one would expect in each of the three countries, the forceful investment drive has expressed itself in a rising proportion of building; this has doubled in Poland.

Such broad groupings are adequate only for a rather crude classification. Closer scrutiny would discern differences and shifts in the scale of production closely linked with technological levels as well as with capital intensity. From this angle the industrialization push in the countries under review has no doubt been stronger than is suggested by data so far analysed: particularly in Czechoslovakia and Poland, where larger-scale industries swallowed up much of the handicraft. In Czechoslovakia the contribution of handicraft has, in fact, fallen from rather more than one-quarter of that of industry (in the narrower sense) before the war to a mere 2 per cent.

ALLOCATION OF INVESTMENT BETWEEN BRANCHES OF
INDUSTRY

Analysis over periods of time would suggest that, within both the heavy and the light branches, the allocation of development capital has been shifting in response to several—partly conflicting —pulls. The policy of each country has inevitably been shaped by its natural resources, but each government has also shown an obvious preference for pushing rapidly ahead with the high-fabrication branches.[103] This has called, however, for a correspondingly rapid development of the basic infrastructure—of basic industries supplying power and raw materials, and of the lower (or 'base') stages of manufacturing. The unreliability of foreign trade as a provider of the lower-stage products—to say nothing of the accepted rules of strategy—has made this line of development all the more imperative. Broadly speaking, during the 1950's fuels and metals—mining plus ferrous and non-ferrous metallurgy —accounted between them for two-fifths of the gross fixed investment allotted to heavy industry, or nearly one-quarter of that absorbed by all productive sectors.

Percentage Distribution of Gross Fixed Investment in Polish Industry,
1956–60

Heavy industry	70	Engineering	14
Power	11	Chemicals	13
Fuel & coking	20	Building materials	9
Ores & metallurgy	13	Textiles	4
		Food & other light industries	15

Sources: Rocz. stat., 1959, in 1956 prices; *Gosp. Plan.,* no. 3, 1962, p. 50.

By or about the mid-1950's investment in East Germany was re-routed in favour of the basic industries, because the power shortage was seriously threatening the manufacturing branches. During the rest of the decade nearly one-half of all industrial investment was directed to the energy-supplying branches, coal

[103] This agrees with the general trend in the highly industrialized countries of the world. The UN inquiry on *The Patterns of Industrial Growth in 1938–58* (p. 19) brings into strong relief the fact that, in these countries, efforts after 1938 to expand industrial production were focused on manufacturing.

alone taking almost three-tenths. As a result the margin left for processing was severely curtailed.

Poland's allocational preferences, on the other hand, were gradually shifting towards higher-stage manufacturing, though the development of her coal resources necessarily ties up much of her capital: roughly one-third of the industrial total is channelled into fuel and power.

These trends have persisted in the present decade, but with certain important correctives. On the one hand East Germany has been able to cut down her outlay on coal because the USSR has made herself responsible for providing her—and the area in general—with substantial quantities of industrial energy, especially in the form of oil. Poland, on the other hand, to preserve the balance of growth, has been compelled once more to channel an increasing proportion of investment to basic industries. In contrast to this, engineering has received a below-the-average allocation, and its output has been planned on the assumption that existing capacity would be more intensively employed. Certain new factors, moreover, are now superimposing themselves: for instance the high priority accorded to the expansion of chemicals, especially petrochemicals.

Allocation of Industrial Investment. First Half of 1960's
(*percentage increase*)

	E. Germany[1]	Poland[2]	E. Germany[3]	Poland[4]
Coal	−13	63	13	32
Power generation	90		25	
Metallurgy (incl. mining)	36	49	10	
Metal processing	17	42	12	
Chemicals	75	58	20	14
Light industries:	37		7	11
textiles & clothing		50		

[1] 1956–60 = 100.   [2] 1961–5 over 1956–60.
[3] Rough estimate based on data from *Einheit*, no. 11, 1959, for 1965.
[4] 1961–5. The comparability of juxtaposed data is uncertain.

The discussion of the way investment is being patterned brings us back to the question of the planners' area of manœuvre.

Experience has shown that this perhaps amounts to no more than setting the relative tempi of income and investment; it is certainly more circumscribed than was generally assumed in the earlier periods of the planning era in Central Europe: indeed, as we have pointed out, the two problems are but two facets of one wider dilemma. Here again we may be referred to certain illuminating inferences from attempts at the very-long-range 'perspective planning'. (If nothing else, these inferences may prove valuable and lasting fruit of these attempts; in Poland, fortunately, the empirical exercise has been performed by an eminent theoretician, which has helped to articulate and generalize them.)

To put it briefly the lesson can be summarized as one of a sequence of encountered 'ceilings'.[104] As the plans were evolved they 'bumped up' time and again against *sectoral* obstacles, blocking overall development. To be more specific, the Polish Kalecki programme for the mid-1970's was found to be checked by both technological and organizational barriers in individual branches of industry—fuels, ferrous and non-ferrous metallurgy, and chemicals—and in agriculture, as well as in the supply of skilled manpower sufficient in quantity and quality to construct and to run the required capacities. In chemicals technical ceilings were found to set the limit to substitution of synthetic for 'natural' materials. Higher yields in agriculture were found to be limited by organizational as well as technological factors. Technical feasibilities were found to form ceilings in coal, steel, and chemicals. One of the most significant of these ceilings proved to be, in this planning experiment, the adverse impact of dispersion of investment to which Soviet-type planning is prone: beyond a certain point the rise in the number of construction sites appeared to extend intolerably the period of maturation of investment and thereby its effectiveness. Plan-'bottlenecks' in these sectors directed the planner to engineering and animal husbandry (the latter based to a substantial degree on imported fodder), as being the fields which, on the face of it, could provide potential dynamic support for necessary exports. But expanding capacities in these fields were found to involve unreasonable risk as to outlets. Generally, as a rule, overall growth was discovered to be accompanied by exacting import requirements and more than

---

[104] See Kalecki, 'Z zagadnien teorii dynamiki gospodarki socjalistycznej', in *Zagadnienia Ekonomii Politycznej Socjalizmu* (Warsaw, 1959), pp. 145ff.

proportionately rising difficulty in paying for them by expanded exports. In this way barriers closing 'thoroughfares' of development would be connected with each other; and in so far as they would stem from, or affect, foreign trade they would push the planner into a policy of self-sufficiency. In turn this policy would entail additional investment: to be more precise, investment with yields declining more than proportionately, which, by itself, would curtail the overall pace of growth. (Our discussion of the growth sectors of industry will provide a fuller background to the problem of inter-connected ceilings.)

Understandably such sobering lessons could be evolved in the smaller countries of Central Europe, restrained by poorer natural endowment, rather than in the Soviet Union. Hence, they may be thought to carry more general significance.

NOTE ON PRODUCTIVITY OF INVESTMENT

A few words only will be said on capital cost as related to output. Insecure and scarce data make inferences risky, but one or two points may be made with a sufficient degree of safety. All available information indicates that, in terms of capital, expansion in industry has been less costly than in agriculture. A Polish estimate for the mid-1950's, by K. Porwit, suggests that the agricultural capital-output ratio would be about two-and-a-half times as high again as the industrial.[105] Nor is it surprising to find from a United Nations calculation for 1953–8 that the cost of expansion in terms of capital per unit of output in Polish heavy industry was about six times as high as in light branches.[106] Industrial inter-branch comparison for the particular period is probably affected by various distorting elements, but the broad order of magnitudes is plausibly reflected: incremental capital cost per unit of gross output in engineering was about one-third below the average for industry as a whole; it was well above the average for metallurgy, construction materials, and chemicals (between two-and-a-half and three-and-a-half times the average) and particularly high in fuels (about seven times the average).[107]

Even more precarious are inter-temporal, and above all international, comparisons of overall yields from capital. One has also

[105] K. Porwit, 'O zaleznosciach miedzy inwestycjami a wzrostem produkcji', in Lange, *Wstep do ekonometrii* (2nd ed., Warsaw, 1961), p. 396.
[106] UN, *World Econ. Survey, 1959*, p. 129.   [107] Ibid. and Porwit, in Lange, ibid.

to bear in mind—particularly with regard to inter-country data—
the various factors which co-influence them in conflicting
directions, such as various sectoral and branch patterns of
investment (even where productive capital formation only is
compared), different distribution of gross investment as between
replacement of wear and tear and new capacities which normally
embody more advanced technologies, different 'cycles' of
investment-maturation, different proportions of outlay on construction and equipment, different degrees of utilization of
capacities and so on. However, the close similarity of the incremental capital-output ratios in the later 1950's for the countries of
our areas and for France and Italy may carry some meaning.

Incremental Capital-Output Ratios, 1950's

	Productive investment	Industry
Czechoslovakia (1950–3)	2·1	2·2
(1954–8)	2·5	2·0
East Germany (1950–3)	0·8	0·7
(1954–8)	2·4	1·7
Poland (1950–3)	1·8	1·3
(1954–8)	2·3	2·1
Britain ⎫	4·5	
West Germany ⎬ (1950–8)	1·7	
France ⎪	2·7	
Italy ⎭	2·3	

Source: UN, *World Econ. Survey*, pp. 34 and 128. East German
figures adjusted for comparability. Note also in this
context Pajestka's finding on the doubling of the Polish
incremental capital-output ratio between 1950 and
1960, see p. 67.

Whatever data are available seem broadly to bear out a
supposition that more could be achieved with the same amount of
capital in the earlier than in the later post-war phases. The case
of Germany is particularly illuminating. Both West and East
German incremental ratios, for the early 1950's, are exceptionally
low, a phenomenon largely attributable no doubt to the comparatively late start in post-war rehabilitation. On the other hand

the fall in Czechoslovakia's ratios in the early 1950's may have something to do with the comparatively smaller wartime dislocation of her economy and with the differences in the post-war revival.

The reader should be reminded that the ratio with which we are dealing here is of a one-sided nature in so far as, by definition, it relates economic effects to one primary factor only. It does not apportion changes in productivity as between capital and labour (in this it is analogous to the productivity-of-labour yardstick). An attempt has been made by Pajestka to assess the contribution of a 'non-investment' element—a trend of autonomous technological progress—to Polish economic growth over the 1950's.[108] The most significant conclusion of this inquiry is that this 'independent' rise in productivity through time, rather vaguely attributable to improvement in skills and generally in know-how, was negligible. Virtually the whole of the increase in output (gross national product) between 1950 and 1960 would be accounted for by the increase in the 'technical equipment' of labour—by 'means of labour' in Marxian terminology—or net addition to the stock of commissioned fixed productive assets. The model is methodologically interesting. It rests inevitably on various more or less hypothetical assumptions: the basic one concerns the character of functional relationship between increments in capital stock and labour productivity. But the quantitative findings would seem to be broadly plausible, particularly when the whole productive investment in national economy rather than industrial capital formation only is considered.

No doubt splitting the changes in capital-output into those in capital-labour and output-labour, while conceptually tempting, is somewhat evasive in empirical analysis. A broad observation would seem to suggest, however, that in the recent past, all three were rising in the Central European area as they also did in Western Europe. (In Pajestka's inquiry, on his definitions, in 1960 the incremental capital-output ratio was twice as high and

[108] Cf. J. Pajestka, *Ekon.*, no. 1, 1960. Pajestka's model, a Cobb–Douglas type function, is $P = T^\epsilon Z^{1-\epsilon} e^{\delta t}$. The notation is: P, T, and Z increments in gross national product, stock of commissioned fixed productive assets, and productive employment, respectively; e—productivity of 'means of production': the parameter ϵ relates change in output-labour to output-capital: and parameter δt denotes the 'autonomous' trend in labour productivity. The latter has been found to be, over the period investigated, -0.37% p.a. The numerical shape of the function of growth out then appeared as $P = 2.39 \, T^{0.54} \, Z^{0.46} e^{-0.0037}$.

incremental output-labour ratio three times as high as in 1950.) There is every reason to predict that, in future, the securing of continuous industrial growth—particularly in the two countries which are economically developed and acutely short of labour, Czechoslovakia and East Germany—will entail a more rapid rise in capital intensity, in capital-per-man, than in the output-per-man ratio.[109] This is the assumption of their plans for the 1960's with a steep rise in their industrial capital-output ratios—by as much as about two-fifths, compared with about one-eighth for Poland.

Once again a warning may not be out of place as to the relative 'truthfulness' of calculations to which we have referred here, if only because of the flaws in the value-framework, quite apart from the intrinsic conceptual precariousness. But an increasingly labour-saving character of investment and a trend marked by the growing cost of expansion in terms of capital agree with the economic environment of the area and especially of its highly industrialized core.

[109] The tentative E. German plan for 1964–70 shows a considerable decline in the expected output per unit of capital invested.

For a discussion of empirical evidence on the relationship between incremental capital-output ratios and economic growth, see S. Kuznets's pioneering analysis in *Economic Development and Cultural Change*, July 1961.

CHAPTER II

The Labour Force

POPULATION TRENDS

So far our discussion of the three countries' industrial growth has singled out capital formation as its basic propelling element. The picture can hardly be complete, however, unless the other prime factor—labour—is brought in. This we shall do in the present section, which will open with a few remarks on the three countries' demography over the past thirty years.

Natural Increase of Population: Pre-War and Post-War Rates of Growth

(per 000 inhabitants)

	1930–4	*1935–9*	*1950*	*1961*[1]
Czechoslovakia				
Births	19·7	17·1	23·3	15·9
Deaths	13·7	13·2	11·5	9·2
Surplus	6·0	3·9	11·8	6·7
East Germany				
Births	(16·3)	(19·4)	16·5	17·0
Deaths	(11·0)	(11·9)	11·9	13·5
Surplus	(5·3)	(7·5)	4·6	3·5
Poland				
Births	29·0	25·3	30·7	20·7
Deaths	15·0	14·1	11·6	7·6
Surplus	14·0	11·2	19·1	13·1

[1] Czechoslovak data refer to 1960.

As the accompanying table shows, by the early 1960's the population of Poland was thus increasing almost twice as fast as that of Czechoslovakia, which in turn had a rate of growth nearly twice that of East Germany. The demographic development of the first two countries has been strongly influenced by the more or less continuous decline in mortality, corresponding to their own secular trend as well as to that for Europe as a whole. Poland's crude death-rate is now roughly half what it was in the early 1930's; for persons under thirty-five it is only between one-quarter and one-half.

Before 1939 the population within the present territory of Czechoslovakia was growing by less than $\frac{1}{2}$ per cent a year, after a more or less steady decline over a long period. After the Second World War a spectacular increase in the birth-rate gave rise to the view that, in a socialist society, this trend had been definitely reversed. In the 1950's, however, it reasserted itself, though later than in the West: the birth-rate curve flattened out, and had returned to its pre-war contour by the end of the decade. The higher net increase as compared with before the war is due to the considerably lower death-rate. The steady decline in the birth-rate has become a major concern of the policy makers. It is Bohemia and Moravia that justify their anxiety; Slovakia's natural increase is still among the highest in Europe.

Poland's post-war population development makes an interesting case in demographic history. In the 1920's the rate of growth oscillated around $1\frac{1}{2}$ per cent per annum: on the eve of the Second World War it stood at about 1 per cent. After the war it rose to about 2 per cent, the highest figure since population statistics were first recorded at the end of the nineteenth century. At the turn of the 1950's it was still about $1\frac{1}{2}$ per cent, displaying, however, once more a mildly downward inclination. The forces behind the prolonged upturn in the Polish birth-rate still await a full analysis. Opportunities offered by resettlement in the newly acquired lands in the West were no doubt a contributing factor; the net increase in these territories—about 3 per cent per annum—reached heights which bear comparison with only a very few areas in the world. The flow of peasantry to the towns presumably imparted, at least for a time, the peasant demographic type to urban populations. A Polish survey has shown that persons between 14 and 39 years old make up about two-fifths of the total Polish urban population, but nearly three-quarters of the migrants.[1] A significant long-term tendency is the levelling-out of demographic characteristics between town and country. By the early 1960's the rate of natural

---

[1] *Przeglad Zagadnien Spolecznych*, nos. 8–9, 1954.

growth in the country was only one-fifth higher than in the towns: thirty years ago the rural rate was double the urban.

No doubt government policies of the earlier post-war period favouring large families have also contributed to the demographic development. These were reversed in the second half of the 1950's.

As things stand now, East Germany's rate of natural increase—not much over one-third per cent a year—is below that prevailing in any industrially developed Western European nation. Moreover, unlike such nations, she experienced a heavy drain on population through emigration, the *Republiksflucht*. In recent years the exodus from East into Western Germany was one of about a quarter of a million a year: three times East Germany's net natural increase of population. By August 1961, when the erection of the Berlin wall reduced it to a trickle, net emigration since the end of the war totalled about $3\frac{1}{2}$ million, twice the influx from the east in the earlier post-war period. The outward stream varied in response to changes in political as well as economic conditions, but its economically important feature has always been the drain on the most active part of manpower: persons between 14 and 39

Population. Pre-War, Post-War, and Projections to 1975

(million)

| | 1939 | 1946 | 1962 | Projections[1] | | |
				1965	1970	1975
Czechoslovakia	14·7[2]	12·5	13·8	14·2	15·0	15·2
East Germany[3]	16·7	18·5	17·1	18·2	18·4	.
Poland	32·1[2]	23·9	30·2	32·5	35·0	37·7
	34·8[4]					

[1] Projections made in the late 1950's assume continuation of trends of that decade.
[2] Pre-war territory.   [3] Includes East Berlin.   [4] Post-war territory.

years old made up well over one-half of the emigrants to the Federal Republic against one-third in the total population of East Germany[2] (over the 1950's the population of working age declined

[2] *Wirtsch. und Stat.*, no. 6, 1957; *Stat. Jb.*, 1955, p. 20.

by about 8 per cent, somewhat more than the rate for the total population). In this respect there is an economically important contrast between this migration wave and that in the opposite direction from the east in the early post-war years. Both Czechoslovakia and Poland, however, are likely to regain their pre-war size of population (pre-war territory) about the beginning of the 1970's.

THE SIZE OF THE ACTIVE POPULATION

What demographic developments imply in terms of potential employability can be judged from the following table.

Adult Population: Age Structure, Pre-War to 1970

(*per cent of total population*)

	1939	*1956*	*1970*	*1975*
Czechoslovakia				
Aged 15–59	64	60	57	
Aged 60 and over	10	12	15	
East Germany				
Aged 15–59	65	61	54	
Aged 60 and over	13	18	22	
Poland				
Aged 15–59	60	60	57	56
Aged 60 and over	8	9	11	9

Source: ECE, *Survey, 1959.* Pre-war for Czechoslovakia refers to 1930. *Biul. Stat.*, no. 10, 1957, p. 6.

Czechoslovakia, and to a still greater extent East Germany, will share with most of the economically developed countries of Europe an increasing burden of population too old to work; whereas the Polish rate of dependency will be affected—at least over a long period—rather by the number of those too young to work. The continuous fall in East Germany's working population seriously impairs her economic prospects. But whereas East Germany has to face, in the first half of the 1960's, a decline in her adult population of over half a million, Poland (which experienced a substantial cut during the previous half-decade, reflecting the wartime drop in births) expects a sharp increase of about $1\frac{1}{4}$ million. Her current rate of addition to the working-age population is almost twice that of Czechoslovakia.

The employable 'potential' does not in itself determine the actual size of the labour force, influenced as this is by a complex combination of factors. This includes government policy, which, in all these countries over most of the post-war period, aimed at expanding both the labour force and the proportion of it employed in industry as far as possible.

THE EMPLOYMENT OF WOMEN

In the initial stages of post-war reconstruction labour forces could be enlarged and redeployed by making use of some existing reserves. These consisted of pre-war unemployment as well as of some groups of workers, e.g. domestic servants, that could be switched to other sectors of the economy. A vital element in employment policies has been the energetic recruitment of female labour. Generally speaking, where alternative sources of labour have been available, transfer of rural manpower to factories has been considered less advantageous than the tapping of urban reserves, since this necessitates smaller overhead expenditure.

Of the three countries, Czechoslovakia, and even to a greater extent East Germany (because of the sex composition of the population) have had to rely more than Poland on the female-labour 'reservoir' for the expansion of non-agricultural labour. During the first period of intensive post-war economic growth women accounted for about four-fifths and two-thirds respectively of the East German and Czechoslovak additions to manpower, and the proportion has tended to rise in subsequent periods. In Poland, on the other hand, the overall proportion of women in total manpower outside agriculture has remained broadly static.

Post-war changes within the female labour forces have been no less significant than changes in their size. No substantial discrepancies exist between the Western and Central European countries as far as overall female participation in non-agricultural work goes. Differences between branches of industry are more pronounced: the countries under survey have, on the whole, a higher ratio of female employment in mining, certain heavier branches of manufacturing, and building.

The trend towards greater participation of women in gainful

work has been more or less universal and continuous throughout Europe. It has been accentuated since the last war, partly because of acute shortages of manpower in wartime economies. But it has

Female Employment outside Agriculture, Pre-War and 1956

(per cent of total manpower)

	Pre-war (*1934*)	*1960*
Czechoslovakia	28·4	39·1
Industry	23·7	32·6
Building		8·9
East Germany	29·7	48·0
Industry	26·1	40·3
Poland	32·5	33·0
Industry	22·9	31·0
Building	3·0	10·0

Sources: Stat. roc., 1957, p. 68; *1961,* p. 107; *Stat. Jb., 1956,* p. 196; *Rocz. stat., 1959,* p. 50; and ECE, *Survey, 1957,* ch. vi, p. 13. Post-war for Poland = socialist sector.

come up in the West against strong obstacles of traditionalism and established social habits. The trade union movement has not been lending it an unqualified blessing. Such inhibitions could be overcome with comparatively greater ease in centrally controlled economies.

THE MOVEMENT AWAY FROM AGRICULTURE

Large movements of manpower away from agriculture to sectors of higher productivity are in more than one sense the very core of the process of industrialization. The process reflects the fact that as societies become better off they devote less of their resources to the growing of food.

What has actually happened in the three countries since the last war (and partly in the last pre-war years) is far from clear. Data are incoherent and vague, and their terms of reference as often as not ambiguous. Only a broad outline will therefore be given here.

Total and Agricultural Active Population

	Pre-war		Early 1950's		Early 1960's	
	Mill.	*%*	*Mill.*	*%*	*Mill.*	*%*
Czechoslovakia						
Total	6·60	100	5·58	100	6·06	100
Agriculture[1]	2·99	37	2·16	39	1·57	26
East Germany						
Total	8·53	100	7·85	100	8·10	100
Agriculture[1]	1·71	20	1·70	22	1·40	17

[1] Includes forestry.

Sources:

    Czechoslovakia: pre-war data (1930) from *Ann. stat. de la République tchécoslovaque, 1938*, pp. 11, 20. This gives a total active population of 6,537,000 plus 1,071,000 assistant family members—corresponding figures for agriculture 1,590,000 and 1 mill. Early 1950's = 1950. Post-war data from *Stat. roc., 1957*, p. 68; *1958*, p. 89; *1961*, p. 106. *Stat. roc., 1957*, p. 16, provides the following data on persons 'permanently active in agriculture' (mill.): 1937 3·34; 1953 1·67; 1956 1·76. The relation between the respective definitions has not been stated.

    East Germany: pre-war data (1936) based on Gleitze, *Ostdeutsche Wirtschaft*. Early 1950's = 1952, late 1950's = 1958. Post-war data from *Stat. Jb., 1956*, p. 166; *1960/61*, p. 187.

Our table suggests that, over the three decades since 1930, agricultural manpower in Czechoslovakia was nearly halved.[3] This was the combined effect of the expulsion of Sudeten German

[3] J. Vrany, in *Stat. Obzor*, no. 11, 1960, by using criteria defined in his own study, arrives at a substantially different magnitude of decline for the three post-1930 decades:

Agriculturally Active Population
(million)

	Permanently active	Permanently assisting family members	Total active
1930	1·95	1·68	3·63
1960	1·46	1·28	2·74
Decline (rounded)	0·5	0·4	0·9

farmers, the loss of the agricultural areas of Sub-Carpathia after the war, and the exodus from the farms in the years which followed. To put it in other terms, agriculture provided the 'reserve' which partly compensated for the fall in overall national labour force.

The result of immediate post-war migrations on East German agriculture was the reverse of that experienced in Czechoslovakia (partly owing to the time-lag in industrial revival). Agriculture's share of national manpower rose. Decline only began in the 1950's.

The shrinkage of Central European agricultural labour can be seen, in fact, as an expression of a secular trend common to almost the whole of industrial Europe, independently of institutional structure though socialization has enhanced the process. (In Western Europe it is, in the first place, the hired labour of larger units that has been drained away from farming since the last war.)

Agricultural Active Population in Some
European Countries, 1880–1950[1]
(1950 = 100)

	1880	*1920*
Czechoslovakia		136
East Germany[2]	116	112
Poland		113
Western Germany[2]	126	122
Britain	156	126
France	146	130
Italy	93	
Sweden	175	147

[1] Males only.   [2] Linked with the all-Germany index for the pre-World War II period.

Source: FAO, *European Agriculture* (1954).

Nor is the Czechoslovak intensity of the process since the last war without parallel in West European free-enterprise economies. Western Germany is one of the cases in point.

Some interesting facts emerge from a comparison of developments on either side of the Elbe. Pre-war West German agriculture was traditionally more intensive than that of East Germany. This was partly because large estates played a greater part in the East than in the West. The West German ratio of agricultural to total labour force was higher. By the early 1950's the relative positions were reversed. Western Germany now contrives to run her agriculture successfully with a labour force reduced in relative—as well as absolute—numbers, while East Germany's agriculture struggles with considerable difficulties.

Agricultural Labour Force as Percentage of Total Active Population

	1939	*1956*	*1960*
East Germany	20	21	17
Western Germany	25	18	14

This comparison shows the scope for the transfer of labour provided that adequate investment in agriculture compensates for the drain on its human resources, as has been the case in Western Germany.

Opportunities for transfer to non-agricultural work have been far greater in Poland than in her neighbour countries. This has been due to the migrations which followed the redrawing of

Population of Poland: Dependent on Agriculture, Active in Agriculture, Urban

	1931	*1946*	*1950*	*1960*	*1975 (plan)*	*1980 (plan)*
Total population (mill.)	31·9	23·9	24·6	29·4		38·6
Dependent on agriculture (mill.)	19·3	12·6	11·6	11·2		9·2
per cent of total	*60·9*	*50·3*	*47·1*	*38·2*		*26*
Urban (mill.)	8·7	7·5	9·2	14·3		22·9
per cent of total	*27*	*31*	*37*	*50*		*59*
Active (working) pop. (mill.)	15·0	...	13·2		(17·8)	
of which						
in agriculture (mill.)	9·6	...	7·0		(7·3)	
per cent of total active:						
in agriculture	*70*	*...*	*53*	*48*	*41*	
in industry & building	*13*	*...*	*23*	*28*		

Sources: Rocz. stat., 1957, and 1962; Maly rocz. stat., 1939, p. 18; Gosp. Plan., no. 9, 1958, p. 24. Pre-war (1931) data refer to those yielded by the last pre-war census. The original data for active population were readjusted to make them comparable with the series (allowance being made in particular for pre-war unemployment). Bracketed figures as adopted in the assumption for the long-range plans: 'Zalozenia do szczegolowych prac nad planem perspektywicznym' quoted in *Gosp. Plan.*, no. 3, 1959, p. 14.

Poland's frontiers—especially the resettlement of the western territories largely by farmers evacuated from the eastern part annexed by the Soviet Union—as well as to the industrialization drive. The contribution of either of these factors to the overall process would be impossible to disentangle.

One of the main features which tends to blur the occupational picture is the spectacular development in post-war Poland of the intermediate class of 'peasant workers'. In a large sector of Polish peasant agriculture, the family is not fully occupied in the cultivation of its holding; it has always been looking for some additional sources of income. The expansion of industries, particularly in the areas of severe underemployment, provided new opportunities. Permanent emigration to towns has, however, been held back over most of the period by housing shortages, by the scarcity of food in towns, and, in fact, by wage policies.[4] The ECE survey[5] points out the double effect of the mass phenomenon of 'peasant workers' on the non-agricultural labour market: the existence of a large reservoir of easily tapped manpower (especially for building and mining), and, on the qualitative side, the low skill of the labour provided by this reservoir, as well as the instability which it has brought into the industrial labour force.

Depending on labour-market conditions in different parts of the country, the proportions of households which provide peasant workers varies between one-tenth and one-quarter.[6] Estimates of the size of this fluctuating labour force vary widely—between 400,000 and 1,200,000.[7] (Note the effect on the statistical picture. A 1960 survey brought out a curious phenomenon: it revealed villages actively engaged in farming with no 'statistical' agricultural population at all.)

With all the reservations justified by statistical uncertainties, at least one or two broad conclusions emerge from what is known about Polish occupational and dependency structures. One is an appreciable decline in the proportion of agricultural to total labour. While employment has been increasing rapidly in the rest of the economy, in farming it has remained more or less stationary. To be more precise, the agricultural labour force decreased for a time, but made up for its losses towards the end of the 1950's, when

---

[4] See I. Kowalska, in *Zagadnienia Ekon. Rolnej*, no. 4, 1957, pp. 66ff.
[5] ECE, *Survey, 1957*, ch. vii, p. 23.
[6] Kowalska, ibid.   [7] *Z. Gosp.*, no. 9, 1957.

employment opportunities in industry decreased, and official policy tended to discourage mass migration. Broadly speaking, over the last twenty-five years the proportion of those 'active' in Polish agriculture fell from two-thirds of the total population to about one-half.

Within the area bounded by the present frontiers of Poland, however, the proportion of the population dependent on agriculture has not changed much. Estimates suggest a proportion, before the last war, of about 47 per cent. Thus, by 1950, the fall in dependency on agriculture no more than restored the pre-war ratios between the agricultural and non-agricultural population. The change came during the 1950's, when the share of those depending on agriculture dropped below two-fifths, while absolute numbers remained almost unaffected. This implies that over that period some $2\frac{1}{2}$ million people, corresponding to the natural increment of the agricultural population of the country, were absorbed into the non-agricultural community.

Population Dependent on Agriculture in Pre-War and Post-War Territory, Poland

Territory	% of total
Pre-war Poland, 1931	60
Post-war Poland, *c.* 1931	47
'Old territories' of Poland, *c.* 1931	54
Western territories, 1939	29
Territories annexed by USSR, 1931	76
Post-war Poland, 1950	47
1960	38

Sources: Table on p. 77 and W. Parker Mauldin and Donald S. Akers, *The Population of Poland* (Washington, 1954), p. 96.

It should be borne in mind that, over the first few years after the war, between 2 and $2\frac{1}{2}$ million peasants were settled in the Western territories, where they took over the tilling of about 6 million hectares of arable land.

The net effect of the processes discussed has been no doubt a considerable relief of the perennial pressure of Polish population on land. Whereas the pre-war density amounted to some 76 people dependent on agriculture per 100 hectares of agricultural land, the ratio was only 58 by the end of the 1950's.

It may at this point be useful to compare the transformation of the economies of the three countries from the point of view both of labour force and of output structure, since an inherent connexion clearly exists between the two. Some insight may be gained from the following table.

Share of Agriculture in National Product and Labour Force

(*per cent*)

	Pre-war		Second half of 1950's	
	National product	*Labour force*	*National product*	*Labour force*
Czechoslovakia	23	37	14	31
East Germany	16	20	10	19
Poland	41	70	27	53

Sources: Shares of national income taken from the author's series (pre-war prices) to be published separately.

In Czechoslovakia and Poland agriculture's share of both output and manpower declined; in East Germany output declined while manpower remained static—a striking expression of a decline, both absolute and relative, in the productivity of her farmers.

As has already been pointed out, in most countries, including Poland and Czechoslovakia, the process can be seen as a continuous transfer of manpower from sectors of low to those of higher per-man productivity. This in itself tends automatically to raise the per-man productivity of agriculture in countries such as Poland where it suffers from disguised unemployment. Much, in fact, of the overall growth of Poland's national income is only a consequence of this transfer.

The actual relative productivities of agricultural as against non-agricultural pursuits show quite substantial differences as from one country to another. But, with the exception of Britain, farmers' productivity is everywhere below the national average. In each of the three countries, by our estimates, it is now, broadly speaking, between two-fifths and one-half of that average. In this our estimates agree with official calculations for two countries. These show that at current prices output per man corresponded in the early 1960's to about 40 per cent of the overall figure in Czechoslovakia, and to about 50 per cent in Poland. However, the relative productivity in agriculture—some 70 per cent of the overall national average—as deduced from official statistics, would be substantially higher than our figure. In this context one may note parenthetically the differences in agricultural productivity as related to farm acreage: output per hectare at comparable prices is more or less equal in Czechoslovakia and Poland, but in East Germany it is three-fifths higher.

Per-Man Productivity in Agriculture
(overall national output per man = 1)

	Pre-war	*mid-1950's*
Czechoslovakia	0·62	0·42
East Germany	0·80	0·48
Poland	0·64	0·48[1]

	Around 1950
United Kingdom	1·13
Western Germany	0·51
Netherlands	0·92
France	0·57
Denmark	0·76
Italy	0·68

[1] There is no conflict between our ratio based on the national average and Rzendowski's estimate that product per person in agriculture equals 34% of that in industry (see p. 84n.).

Sources: Per-man productivity data are based on national income figures from our series to be published. Western data from ECE, *Survey, 1956*, p. 23.

DISGUISED AGRICULTURAL UNEMPLOYMENT IN POLAND

The reader will have noticed that in our reasoning we have assumed throughout the existence of disguised unemployment in Poland. But is there any—and what is its scale? The answer is clearly of paramount relevance in any analysis of Poland's industrialization and programmes.

Almost at the start of the first development period, that is, at the beginning of the 1950's, it became the official tenet that post-war socio-economic policies—agrarian reform plus industrialization—and the resettlement of the Western territories completely eliminated the structural malaise of the countryside. Policies at the later stage rested, in fact, on the assumption that there was an actual overall manpower deficit in farming.[8]

There are no fully satisfactory ways of measuring manpower needs in farming. The usual criteria, such as standard population densities related to agricultural area or arable area; an optimum of 'carrying powers' of land in respect of total or active population; value-volumes of output per person engaged in farming, and so forth: all these have only limited validity. The types and sizes of farms, soil and climatic conditions, the state of equipment and technology have a decisive influence on labour requirements. There is, of course, a good deal of possible substitution as between the two prime factors—capital and labour. Nor can habits and conventions be disregarded.

What is certain is that Poland no longer has an agricultural surplus comparable with that of the inter-war period, when it was estimated that up to one-half of the agricultural population could be removed from the land without any harm to output.[9] But there

[8] The tenet has been subsequently toned down to claim that rural disguised unemployment has been eliminated 'to a decisive degree'. (See resolution of the Third Congress of the Polish United Workers' Party, *Nowe Drogi*, no. 4, 1959.)

[9] W. E. Moore, *Economic Demography of Eastern and Southern Europe* (Geneva, 1945), calculated the Polish surplus before the Second World War on two assumptions. On the assumption of the prevailing level of output and European productivity (that is, European average per capita output) the surplus was found to amount to 51·3% of the population engaged in agriculture in about 1930; on the alternative assumption, i.e. that of the French level of output per hectare, and European average level of per capita output, the surplus would be one of 29·4%.
Another study, by J. Poniatowski, *Przeludnienie wsi i rolnictwa* (Warsaw, 1935), comparing densities in Poland and Denmark, yielded a surplus of 8–9 mill. of those dependent on agriculture. Some other authorities have agreed that the pre-war surplus was between three-fifths and one-half of the total farming population.
Taking the agricultural active population at the beginning of 1934 to be 12·9 mill., J. Piekalkiewicz, in *Rol. Ekon.*, no. 10, 1934, estimated potential labour supply at

is evidence that a surplus still persists and that this is substantial, even if relative in many senses, although there is a deficit in larger farming units. Net surplus is estimated at between 1,600,000 and 2,300,000 'active' farm population. On certain assumptions as to feasible techniques some students of the subject maintain that the surplus still corresponds to about half the agricultural manpower.[10] All such estimates, owing to their nature, provide no more than a very rough indication of the scale of the problem. They have been built up on various assumptions which qualify their meaning. But they undoubtedly strongly support the view that the transfer of the agricultural surplus population and its absorption into industry remain, in the foreseeable future, the heart of Polish economic policy.

The proportion of manpower engaged in food production is

3,800 mill. man-days (295 working days per person) and the actual labour demand at 2,505 mill., or 65·9% of the supply. On this basis some 8·5 mill. persons could be usefully employed.

A post-war source, K. Secomski, *Podstawowe zagadnienia plana* (Warsaw, 1950), put the rural surplus at 2·2 mill. in 1949, and forecast one of 1·2 mill. by the end of the first plan period (1955). This, considering the author's position, may be taken as the official view at an early stage. A somewhat later attitude is reflected in A. Rajkiewicz, *Zestyty Naukowe Skoly Glownej Planowania i Statystyki* (Warsaw, 1953), i. 189, which states, on the authority of a 1952 survey, that potential manpower made up 63% of total agricultural population, of which 90·5% was actually at work. These latter findings have little significance, no dividing line being drawn between actual and potential work.

A major study on this subject, by I. Kowalska, in *Zagad. Ekon. Rol.*, no. 1, 1957, p. 29, is based on a potential and actual labour input in terms of labour days. It estimates potential input at 6·6 mill. active in agriculture × 250 days = 1,650 mill. days per year. Actual input, varying for different size-groups of farms between 170 and 189 labour days a year per person, is put at 1,090 mill. labour-days a year, roughly one-third below the potential. A detailed check yielded a surplus of 1,345,000 'active' farmers in smaller and medium-size farm groups and a deficit of 200,000 in larger units. Overall unemployment is estimated here at about 1,500,000 able-bodied persons. While some of the criticisms of errors and methodological deficiencies in this study by E. Bialski, in *Zagad. Ekon. Rol.*, no. 3, 1957, seem to be justified, Kowalska's findings may serve as a valuable indication of the magnitudes involved. Considering that, since 1950, the Polish agricultural labour force has actually increased, her findings are probably still valid.

A study by A. Brzoza, in *Ekon.*, no. 3, 1957, based on standard requirements of labour related to output measured in terms of value, calculated surpluses and deficits in active population on peasant farms of various size categories. On the basis of her figures, the surplus would amount to 2,600,000 'actives', assuming the existing structure and output levels of peasant farming, but to 3,000,800 at an assumed optimum output (ibid. p. 43).

In the discussion on the Polish perspective (1975) plan held in November 1958 in the Economics Institute of the Academy of Sciences (*Ekon.*, no. 1, 1959), Rakowski argued that the agricultural labour surplus amounts to at least one-half *under existing productive techniques*, a phrase which calls for more precision to make the estimate meaningful.

[10] See contributions to discussion in the Economics Institute of the Academy of Sciences, in *Ekon.*, no. 1, 1959.

higher by far in Poland than in any well-developed European economy: roughly corresponding to such economically retarded countries as Spain or Portugal. Assuming that the vision of the authors of the Polish 'perspective' long-range plan materializes, the proportion in 1975 will still be one-quarter higher than at present in Czechoslovakia and twice that of East Germany. It will then be equal to that of the mid-1950's ratio of overpopulated Italy.

Manpower Engaged in Agriculture, 1960

(*per cent of total*)

Czechoslovakia	26	Spain	50
East Germany	17	France	26
Poland	48	Italy	41
planned for 1975	41	Netherlands	20
		United Kingdom	5
Western Germany	14	Sweden	21
Austria	33	Portugal	47
Belgium	13	Greece	54

Sources: Int. Lab. R. (ILO), lxxiii/5 (1956); OEEC, *Agricultural Policies in Europe and North America* (Paris, 1957). For the three countries and West Germany, as on p. 77. Planned Polish ratio for 1975 referred to in *Gos. Plan.*, no. 3, 1959, p. 14. All Western data refer to the first half of the 1950's except Belgium and Holland, for which 1947 data are given.

The Polish long-range plan assumes that farming manpower will remain stabilized until the mid-1970's at about 7 million, more or less what it was a quarter of a century earlier.[11] In other words, the hypothesis rests on the premise that other sectors of the economy will absorb the whole increase in employable non-agricultural population plus a migration from agriculture amounting to its

[11] Another school of thought, in particular Professor Minc, postulates a decline of the agriculturally 'active' population to 5 million, but his premises do not seem realistic.

At the November 1958 session of the Economics Institute of the Academy of Sciences, the Chairman of the Statistical Office, Leon Rzendowski, made the interesting point that the 1970's would witness increasingly rising relative costs in Polish agriculture. (The assumption being that agricultural product per person employed will decline between 1955 and 1975 from 34 to 14 per cent of the corresponding figure for industry.) For the discussion see *Z prac Zakladu Nauk Ekonomicznych Polskiej Akademii Nauk*, Dec. 1958.

whole increment. Even allowing for a lower activity rate of urbanized population, this would entail finding employment, over the fifteen years between 1960 and 1975, for about 3½ million net. A still more exacting goal is set in a variant of the programme for 1980. It suggests that by that date three-quarters of Poland's population would be dependent on pursuits other than farming and that during the two preceding decades its size would actually shrink by over 2 million. It is not, however, clear how the authors of the target correlated it with the programme of capital formation to support it.

An interesting point made by some Polish students is that even on the assumption of agriculture's share in national manpower, it will be an increasingly burdensome sector in the economy (burdensome in a specific, defined sense). By the mid-1970's the net contribution to national product of seven farmers would equal that of one person employed in industry.

DISTRIBUTION OF THE NON-AGRICULTURAL LABOUR FORCE

One fact which seems to emerge at this stage is the relative stability—in the two industrialized countries—of the broad pattern of the industrial labour force. The proportions in which non-agricultural manpower falls into the three major sub-divisions —industry in its wider sense (including handicraft and building), distribution, and 'services'—have remained more or less unchanged in Czechoslovakia and East Germany. Collectivization— in both the production and consumption spheres—inevitably results in the expansion of some services. On the other hand the guiding philosophy has a bias against 'unproductive' work, defined as that not employed directly in 'material' production.

There have, in actual fact, been changes of emphasis in allocational policies, influenced, among other things, by the state of the labour markets. These have followed the general line of social and economic policies, which until the early 1950's had less consideration for welfare than towards the end of the decade. Catering and personal services by that time were given somewhat higher priority. Yet, as appears from the table on page 86, the resulting changes have been rather marginal. The impact of deliberate policies has apparently been counteracted by factors stemming from the general level of economic development, habit, &c.

Neither, presumably, has deliberate policy had any decisive influence on Polish patterns. The somewhat deeper changes in that country bear witness in the first place to the metamorphosis in its

Working Population outside Agriculture, Pre-War to 1958

(*per cent*)

	Industry	Distribution	Other services
Czechoslovakia			
Pre-war	61	18	20
1958	61	19	19
East Germany			
Pre-war	61	22	17
1958	60	22	18
Poland			
Pre-war excl. unemployed	50	27	22
1958	59	20	21

Note: Pre-war refers to the last census before the Second World War, i.e. 1930, 1939, and 1931 for Czechoslovakia, East Germany, and Poland respectively.

geography and population. The virtual extermination of the Jewish population, in particular, has had an inevitably profound effect, considering the pre-war size of that community and the peculiarities of its occupational distribution.

All three countries considerably increased their manpower employed in industry proper (factory labour). The increase is very spectacular in Poland, where by the early 1960's the figure was about three and a half times that of before the war. But throughout the area much of the increase was nominal in the sense that it was due to artisan and cottage workshops being absorbed into the industrial framework. There has been virtually no change in Czechoslovakia's and East Germany's industrial labour in the wider sense, that is, building and handicraft included. There has been a substantial shift in the geographical pattern of the former's labour force connected with the forceful industrialization of Slovakia. At the beginning of this decade

Slovak industrial manpower exceeded 400,000—nearly one-sixth of the Republic's total. In contrast, in Poland the numbers were almost doubled as compared with those of a quarter of a

Industrial Manpower

(*million*)

	Pre-war	1948	1950	1955	1961
Czechoslovakia					
(a)	[1·30]	1·54	1·67	1·98	2·36
(b)	.	1·74	.	2·29	2·80
(c)	2·52	2·43	.	2·51	2·60
East Germany					
(a)	[1·95]	.	2·62	2·70	2·92
(b)	[1·97]	.	3·10	3·20	3·29
(c)	[4·10]	.	3·72	3·79	3·79
Poland					
(a)	0·86	1·62	2·05	2·70	3·02
(b)	0·91	1·93	2·55	3·43	3·81
(c)	2·10	2·23	.	3·67	4·10

Note: (a) industry; (b) industry incl. building; (c) industry incl. building and handicraft.

Sources: Comparability of pre-war and post-war data is very precarious, especially where pre-war figures are bracketed.

Czechoslovakia: Stat. roc., 1935, 1936, 1962; Stat. Zpravy, no. 5, 1960. Pre-war data refer to 1930 census: bracketed figure refers to gainfully occupied in larger enterprises, the criterion being a minimum of employment varying in individual branches from five to eighteen persons.

East Germany: Stat. Jb., 1956, 1957, 1962; Stat. Jb. (Bundesrepublik), 1956, p. 542; Gleitze, *Die deutsche Industrie,* pp. 174ff.; *Stat. Prax.,* no. 12, 1948; no. 12, 1959; no. 6, 1960. East German pre-war (a) and (b) data, derived from Gleitze, presumably refer to personnel occupied (*Beschäftigte*) in industry in the narrower sense; (c) = 1939 census figure of gainfully occupied (*Erwerbspersonen*). In each case we have allowed for the estimated size of manpower in East Berlin.

Poland: Maly rocz. stat., 1939; Rocz. stat., 1962; Biul. Stat., no. 12, 1959; no. 6, 1960. Pre-war (a) and (b) figures refer to 1937; (c) = rough estimate based on 1931 census data for industry and on handicraft licences issued in 1937.

century earlier (comparisons with pre-war are precarious in each case). The Polish and East German totals of industrial manpower by the end of the 1950's—i.e. including building and handicraft—were almost exactly equal in absolute size. This, of course, implies a lower *pro-rata* of Polish population, corresponding to the lower degree of industrialization.

To some extent the two highly industrialized countries provide a telling contrast. Forceful recruitment made good the substantial losses in Czechoslovakia's industrial labour force (using the term in its broadest sense) caused by the elimination of the Sudeten Germans. On the other hand—in spite of the increase in the size of her population—East Germany has experienced difficulties in expanding her industrial manpower no less acute than those of Czechoslovakia: demographic elements, differences in age and sex composition and growth, as well as the westward migration, combine to account for them. Virtually no additions are expected for East German industry in the coming years.

It is indicative of the decline in the absorptive powers of Polish industry for labour that, during the second half of the 1950's, the rate of addition to its manpower was no greater than in Czechoslovakia. Nor is Polish industry expected to increase its manpower in the near future very much more rapidly than Czechoslovak, in spite of the great demographic differences between the two countries.

Throughout the area handicrafts were drastically curtailed, reorganized, and to a large extent, socialized in state-controlled co-operatives. This shift from workshop to factory was no doubt in line with the general trend of progress in industrial organization and technology. But in Poland—and perhaps even in Czechoslovakia—it went beyond what was justified by existing conditions. It reduced the scope for useful employment of a substantial sector of the population which otherwise could hardly be made productive at all. At the same time it reduced supplies of some consumer goods which, traditionally, were provided by small-scale enterprise. The lack of discrimination in such policies aggravated the problem of the decaying small towns in Poland, where some remedial action was taken in the latter part of the 1950's.

STRUCTURAL CHANGES IN THE INDUSTRIAL LABOUR FORCE

Structural shifts within the industrial labour force have been at least as significant—from both the social and the economic point of view—as changes in its size. First, post-war nationalizations shifted nearly all of it from the private to the socialized sector by the end of the 1940's; though the process was somewhat more prolonged in East Germany, where the private and 'semi-state' sectors were still responsible, at the end of the 1950's, for nearly one-sixth of total industrial manpower. Secondly, socialization was accompanied by amalgamation.

The concentration drive was most forceful in Czechoslovakia. During the second half of the 1950's the number of industrial enterprises was cut, but three-fifths of the industrial labour force is employed in enterprises with over a thousand on the pay-roll, as against about one-half in the two remaining countries. At the other end of the scale, units with less than 500 employees employed only a little over one-tenth of the Czechoslovak labour force, as against nearly two-fifths in East Germany and Poland.

Parallel with these changes, redeployment policies tended to shape the structure of industrial employment in accordance with the orders of priority adopted. The broad trend has been a redistribution of labour in favour of the heavy and producer-goods branches. A more detailed scrutiny would single out the years 1952 and 1953 as an important milestone.

The table on page 90 gives an idea of the final effect of these changes on the distribution of manpower among the branches of industry. The general impression is one of quite considerable resistance to change: it is easier to mould a country where industry is still in its formative stage. Hence it is not surprising that the impact of change was at its strongest in Poland, while at the other extreme—in East Germany—it was little more than marginal. The avowed aim of East German policy was to re-pattern the industrial structure so as to raise its 'skill-intensity', that is, to reshape it in a way which will bring about relatively smaller inputs of materials (especially important materials) as against skilled labour. The meagreness of actual change in this direction well testifies to the force of the obstacles encountered.

After post-war rehabilitation the share of mining in Poland's industrial employment fell somewhat during the 1950's, but it is still the highest in the area. Of the remaining basic industries, chemicals in East Germany have a record ratio—about twice that

Distribution Patterns of Industrial Manpower, 1960

Building as % of total industrial manpower		% of industrial manpower (excl. building)					
		Fuels	Metal-lurgy	Chem-icals	Engin-eering	Tex-tiles	Food
Czechoslovakia							
1949	14	9	6	3	18	14	9
1960	18	9	8	4	32	11	8
East Germany							
1950	13	8	3	9	33	14	8
1960	11	7	4	9	37	13	7
Poland							
1950	15	13	7	5	18	17	11
1960	21	11	6	5	25	12	12

prevailing in the two other countires. On the other hand East Germany has by far the lowest, and Czechoslovakia the highest, proportion in ferrous and non-ferrous metallurgy, while the share of East German engineering is ahead of that of Czechoslovakia.

Engineering is the branch which gained most over the reconstruction period in both Czechoslovakia and Poland. Its labour force nearly doubled in the former and increased by one-third in the latter. Differences in the rate of growth are presumably partly to be accounted for by changes in classification and organization. By the mid-1950's engineering had established itself in all three countries as the branch with the highest proportion of labour absorbed. By the early 1960's engineering manpower in the area as a whole was approaching the $2\frac{1}{2}$ million mark and making up about one-third of the total Czechoslovak labour force, and close on two-fifths of the East German; in Poland it now employs about one-quarter of the industrial labour, and engineering's share of manpower is still growing throughout the area.

In a sense the change in the status of engineering as measured by its rate of employment per head of population reflects the

industrial metamorphosis of Poland. Over the post-1937 quarter
of a century it increased fivefold. Amounting to about 25 per
thousand of population, it roughly corresponds to that of France,
which is rather less than half the level prevailing in East Germany
and Britain (62 and 61 per thousand respectively; the Czechoslovak rate is 41 per thousand). A common feature of changes in
employment composition is the increase in the share of building
in the overall industrial total, especially in Poland, where in the
mid-1950's it accounted for nearly one-quarter of the labour
force. (This might have something to do with the comparatively
low productivity of building as compared with some other
industries.) Since then the difference on this score between
Poland's industrial employment structure and that of other
countries has tended to narrow. So have differences between
countries as regards employment in consumer-goods industries.
Poland has still the highest proportion of manpower engaged in
food processing, but in the other typical branch of her consumer-
goods group, textiles, the fall has been very sharp; it was more
moderate in Czechoslovakia, *nil* in East Germany. (Most of the
decline in these countries occurred during the previous reconversion.)

To sum up, the overall effect of the changes has been a distinct
levelling-out of disparities in industrial employment structures.
Czechoslovakia has acquired the patterns established in the
Western industrial countries, and Poland has come closer to them.

Industrial employment patterns, let it be noted, are a convenient indicator of industrial development, provided not too much
is read into them. As has been pointed out already, they are
influenced by various factors, not all of which depend on the stage
of industrial maturity reached. Inevitably, for instance, the share
of primary industries is a function of natural wealth. Polish coal-
mining and, to some extent, East German chemicals are cases in
point. Again, statistical classifications can hardly do justice to the
type of industries they cover. Impressions gained from mere
numerical developments in the labour force of such heterogeneous
branches as engineering and chemicals may very often be mis-
leading as to the economic and technological characteristics of the
industry concerned. Relative labour and capital intensity is a case
in point. One need only consider the statistical effect on industrial
manpower structures of a switch from a predominance of small

Structure of the Manufacturing Labour Force: Selected Pre- and Post-War Years

(*per cent of labour force in manufacturing*)

	Metal-making & processing	Textiles, leather (& connected branches), & food processing
Czechoslovakia		
1937	25	48
1958	44	31
East Germany		
1936	38	32
1958	43	30
Poland		
1937	[17]	[34]
1958	33	37
Western Germany		
1936	45	31
1956	45	31
United Kingdom		
1911	30	50
1951	49	31
France		
1906	15	48
1954	37	34

Sources: For pre-war Czechoslovakia, *Ann. stat. de la République tchécoslovaque, 1938*, p. 11, 21; East Germany from Gleitze, *Ostdeutsche Wirtschaft*; for Poland, *Maly rocz. stat., 1939*, pp. 134ff.

The Polish pre-war figures refer to 'medium' and 'large-scale' industries. This exaggerates, in comparison with other countries, the proportion of the metal group, and understates that of light industry. Post-war Czechoslovak, East German, and Polish data derived from *Stat. roc., 1959*, p. 150, *Stat. Jb., 1959*, pp. 278ff., and *Rocz. stat., 1959*, p. 103. Western countries from *Int. Lab. R.*, lxxiii/5 (1956), p. 514.

artisan-type metal-processing workshops to a highly mechanized and automated engineering. This is what actually happened in the area under survey.

Such elements must be present in the mind when changes in industrial labour distribution are followed up on a wider inter-temporal and international scale, very broadly reflected in the table on page 92.

WAGES AND LABOUR COSTS

Forming one of the principal parameters of the cost calculus and indeed of industrial planning in general (and an essential link between the spheres of production and consumption), the price of labour is being centrally determined. In the conceptual blue-print wages are intimately correlated to labour productivity standards (norms), which in turn calls for a comparatively high degree of reliance both on performance-pay and on strong incentives built into the centrally shaped system of rewards.

However, owing to a variety of causes, both social and economic, the operation of a system consistent with the working of the economy has been coming up against strong obstacles. Under the continuously prevailing conditions of full employment, workers' resistance has tended to freeze standards of productivity. Nor have the planners been fully successful in their policy of preserving the discipline of wages. (The blueprint of the system assumes stability of wage levels—falling prices rather than rising earnings being the principal vehicle for transferring to the workers the benefits of growing efficiency.) Inflation has been the inseparable companion of the three economies during the periods of their most dynamic expansion. Indeed it has been one of the instruments by means of which the state has been able to enforce the share of the working class in the cost of industrial growth. For obvious reasons the problem has been particularly acute in Poland, which has been con-fronted with a dilemma similar to that which the USSR solved at a comparable stage of industrialization. It will be argued, however, by this writer (in the part of this study to be published separately) that, unlike the Soviet Union, in Poland the brunt of intensive forced saving has been carried by industrial workers rather than by the peasantry: this has been so because the preservation of indivi-dual farming stiffened the peasants' resistance to the pressure for centralized capital accumulation. It is also arguable that, logically, the shift of the pressure in capital formation was a corollary of the industrial underemployment of the urbanized peasants.

It is only since about the second half of the 1950's that the planners in the area have shown more determination in encountering inflationary pressure by consistent wage/price policies. However, while prices have been kept stable or lowered, inflationary disequilibria have continued to manifest themselves in endemic shortages in all the three countries.

Inflationary inclinations are in fact built into the system. At the enterprise level, faced with the choice of either overspending the allotted 'wage fund' or under-fulfilling output targets, the plant management and supervising authorities would understandably follow the alternative which safeguarded production. Real overall manpower shortages in East Germany and Czechoslovakia, and artificial sectoral scarcities of labour and deficiencies in certain skills in Poland have caused a good deal of bidding between enterprises and between branches, thus distorting the programmed patterns of employment. Policy makers have found out that in a collective system, too, the worker is more sensitive to the behaviour of his nominal than of his real wages. They have thus acquired over some periods an interest in sustaining the 'money illusion'.

On the other hand their experience had taught them that too strong a pressure for higher efforts built into the wage mechanism defeats its purpose and tends to yield decreasing returns. Wage reforms initiated since the second half of the 1950's have mitigated the exaggerations of the existing systems; the situation of the lowest-paid groups has been improved (minimum wages have been introduced); on the other hand, wage-rate differentials have been widened; the main weight has been shifted back from performance to time rates; high-tension incentives (and coercion) have been relaxed, but the process has not always been continuous and consistent.

There is hardly any satisfactory way of mirroring the post-war history of real wages in the area. The violence of fluctuations, divergences in the behaviour of earnings for various sections of the industrial working class, changes in the availability and quality of consumer goods, successive rationings and de-rationings of basic consumer goods, all these and other factors rob any statistical series of real wages of a good deal of its meaning. With this warning the reader is offered the statistical picture in the table annexed.

Real Earnings of Industrial Workers

	Pre-war[1]	1950	1953	1955	1961
Czechoslovakia					
Average monthly earnings, kcs.	860	912	1,160	1,272	1,448
1937 = 100	100	106	135	148	173
Cost of living 1937 = 100	100	111	161	137	117
Real earnings 1937 = 100[3]	100	96	84	108	154
East Germany					
Average monthly earnings, RM/DM gross	100	265	344	386	567[2]
„ net of tax & social insurance contribution	160	225	300	335	
„ 1936 = 100	100	141	187	209	
Cost of living 1936 = 100	100	307	211	192	
Real earnings 1936 = 100[3]	100	46	89	109	154
Poland					
Average monthly earnings, zl.	156		1,051	1,183	1,875
1938 = 100	100		674	755	1,202
Cost of living 1938 = 100	100	500	916	949	1,072
Real earnings 1938 = 100[3]	100	85	72	80	112

[1] Czechoslovakia 1937; East Germany 1936; Poland 1938.
[2] 1960; a new method of computation was employed, see note below.
[3] During 1962 Czechoslovak wages declined by about 1%; Polish and East German remained unchanged.

Notes:

Czechoslovakia

Pre-war earnings estimate, based on the average hourly rate of 4·32 kcs.—from *Yb. Lab. Stat., 1940;* post-war earnings from *Stat. roc., 1957,* p. 90; *1958,* p. 19; *1959,* p. 149; *Hosp. Nov.,* no. 13, 1960. Cost-of-living index, ibid. p. 387, Plan Fulfilment Report for 1959.

Our findings for real earnings in 1953 agree with the estimate of ECE, *Bulletin,* v/2, p. 7, in that average real wages of that year were roughly equal to those of before the war.

Hosp. Nov., nos. 51–52, 1959, gives the following computation of average earnings for the 45 years between 1914 and 1959:

	1914	1937	1953	1959
Average earnings p. hour (kcs.)	0·45	3·80	5·80	6·70
Total real earnings	100	. . . .		177
		100	. . . . . .	148
			100	146

According to *Stat. Zpravy*, no. 4, 1960, between 1937 and 1959 the average worker's monthly earnings for all branches of the economy rose from 764 to 1,302 kcs., i.e. by 70%, the cost of living by 18%, and real earnings by 45%.

East Germany

Pre-war monthly average taken from the all-German industrial average in *Stat. Jb.* (*Bundesrepublik*), *1952* as hourly average of 0·80 RM × 200 = 160 DM. Average budget of 'typical' worker's family given in the *Yb. Lab. Stat.*, *1940* as 2,163 RM, of which earnings of the head of the family 84%. That would yield a monthly average of about 152 RM.

Post-war yearly averages (gross) from *Stat. Jb.*, *1956*, p. 195; and *1959*, p. 213. Gross adjusted net of tax and social-insurance contribution on the basis of *Stat. Jb.*, *1956*, p. 202.

Cost-of-living series from ibid. p. 231, based on expenditures of an industrial worker's family of four, with medium-bracket earnings.

Dr G. Abeken pointedly remarked in *Vjh. Wirtsch-Forsch.*, no. 4, 1956 that the official cost-of-living index stood in 1955 at only 204, while that of retail prices stood at 316, with 1936 = 100. This may perhaps justify some doubts. But it may be noted that the index for services stood in 1955 at only 142.

W. Riege, in *Ww.*, no. 5, 1956, pp. 744ff., compiled a series at variance with the official one. This shows a steeper rise in living-costs, but yields higher real earnings throughout: in 1955 about 24% above pre-war.

Stat. Jb., *1956*, p. 202, gives a series of net real earnings of all workers and employees with 233 for 1956 (1950 = 100).

Poland

Pre-war average monthly earnings based on hourly average for large and medium industry, 0·78 zl. × 200 = 156 zl. Cf. *Maly rocz. stat.*, *1939*, p. 272. Post-war average earnings in centrally-planned industries from *Rocz. Stat.*, *1959*, p. 331.

Cost-of-living index for 1950–6 based on ECE estimates in *Bulletin*, ix/3, p. 36. On this the source has this to say: 'in default of any better alternative the index of retail prices shown in the table has been calculated by using as weights the expenditure pattern of a pre-war working-class family, as slightly modified in 1947. . . . Such an out-of-date system of weights is, of course, objectionable; but allowing for the fact that consumption was confined to little more than basic necessities up to about 1955, the estimate of changes in real wages in the earlier years is probably not a significant distortion of the actual trend' (ibid. p. 34 n.).

Cost-of-living index for 1955–9 from *Rocz. stat.*, *1959*, p. 358; cf. *Biul. Stat.*, 1957, no. 2, and Plan Fulfilment Report for 1959.

Link in the cost of living with pre-war (1938) has been established in the following way. 'Typical' budget for a working-class family of four, i.e. of 3·15 'consumption units', was found to amount to about

2,100 zloty for 1927 (cf. *Maly rocz. stat.*, *1939*, p. 281), or 666 zl. p.a. per 'consumption unit'. Corrected for changes in living costs over 1927–38 (ibid. p. 3), this yields 666 × 61% = 406 zl. The 1956 expenditure per 'consumption unit' was found to amount to about 4,160 zloty per annum by Z. Morecka, in *Z̆. Gosp.*, no. 11, 1956, p. 5, on the basis of a similarly constructed 'typical' working-class budget (*Wiad. Stat.*, no. 111, 1947, special issue). These two magnitudes produce the zloty purchasing-power ratio of 10·2 : 1 for 1956 : 1938.

It will be noticed that our 1950 index numbers thus arrived at, i.e. 500 (1938 = 100) agree with the rough estimate made some time ago by the ECE that the 1950 level was about 5 times that of before the war (*Survey, 1953*, p. 64 n.).

A real-wages index with 1956 = 100 was produced in ECE, *Bulletin*, ix/3, p. 35, for all workers.

1950	1953	1955	1956
100	82	91	101

Though it differs in coverage it does not substantially diverge from our series. Our 1950 and 1953 index numbers have been interpolated on its basis.

The real-earnings series would change substantially were the official 1949–55 cost-of-living series used instead. As slightly readjusted by A. Machnowski, in *Wiad. Stat.*, July–Aug. 1956, p. 10, it reads:

	1950	1953	1955
Money earnings	100	169	181
Cost-of-living (prices of goods & services purchased by population)	100	183	168
Index of real wages	100	92	111

It will be noted that, according to these series, the real wages of 1950 were below those of 1955. The reverse is true according to our own series.

The official index has been a subject of very widespread criticism during and after the political events of the autumn of 1956. Its revised version seems to have been discarded: it does not appear in the official statistical yearbooks for recent years.

A few points of substance stand out in this picture.[12] First: the

[12] The actual post-war situation of the working class has, in fact, been distinctly more favourable than our findings suggest. This is because the pre-war basis-data do not allow for the incidence of short-time working and unemployment, which were substantial in both Czechoslovakia and Poland, amounting respectively to about 12 and 8% of industrial manpower before the last war. The employment position was more satisfactory in East Germany, where the armament drive was already gaining momentum. Furthermore the mere averages do not reflect the rise in real incomes of families due to a steep fall of the rate of dependency. It has been stated that on the average there are now 1·5 incomes per Czechoslovak household, whereas before the war there was only 1 (*Rude Pravo*, 29 Aug. 1958). It is claimed that between 1931 and 1952 the average number of dependants per worker outside agriculture fell in Poland from 1·77 to 1·2 (W. F. Blinowski, *Walka panstwa ludowego o dobrobyt mas praculacych* (Warsaw, 1952), p. 30). Blinowski's terms of reference are not quite clear; the pre-war rate presumably allows for the incidence of unemployment.

depth of the decline in East German real wages. As late as the early 1950's, these stood at less than half their pre-war level—a fact which is perhaps not surprising when it is viewed against the over-all political and economic background of the country at the time. The second point is the setback in the initial post-war recovery of Polish and Czechoslovak real wages, at the peak of the intensive industrial and armament drive, between 1950 and 1953. The third is the advantage which the Czechoslovak industrial worker had over his colleagues in the other two countries at the beginning of the present decade and the strides made by East German earnings towards the end of it. By that time both the Czechoslovak and the East German workers were earning, in real terms, about one-quarter more than before the last war, while the Polish worker was merely as well off as he was twenty years earlier.

It would be tempting to conclude these few remarks by trying to obtain an idea of the relative unit-cost of labour in the area. A recent Polish calculation, based on the purchasing-power parities of national currencies (for consumption) seems to point to a strikingly high cost in Poland and a comparatively low one in East Germany.

Industrial Workers' Hourly Earnings

(in zloty, late 1950's)

Czechoslovakia	East Germany	Poland
9·45	8·80	8·32

Note: Computations based on Polish expenditure structures and carried out for 1958 by the staff of the Narodowy Bank Polski (see A. Zwass, in *Gosp. Plan.*, no. 10, 1959, p. 36) yielded the following purchasing power of the zloty for food, industrial goods, and services—against the Czechoslovak korona 0·743, 0·606, and 1·629, and against the East German mark 0·209, 0·199, 0·611. By applying 'weights' of the three items in Polish family budgets, i.e. 59, 29, and 12% respectively, we arrived at a purchasing power 1 zl. = 0·78 kcs. = 0·24 DM (E). Month taken equals 200 work hours.

To give a fuller meaning to labour unit-costs one would have to place them beside relative productivities.[13] It seems to us that even if allowance is made for certain exaggerations of the relative Polish labour-cost estimate, as against those of the other two countries (which we suspect would be justified),[14] it will still appear rather high in relation to efficiency.

THE MECHANISM OF THE LABOUR MARKET

How far have the mechanism of the labour market and the assumptions and policies behind it withstood the test of experiences?

The far-reaching contrasts in manpower-resources would lead us to expect correspondingly different approaches in the three countries. The striking feature, on which once again stress must be laid, is their inflexibility and uniformity, at least over the first post-war decade, in widely varied environments.

Deliberately chosen lines of policy tended to aggravate labour scarcities in both Czechoslovakia and East Germany. The in-adequacy of compensatory capital inputs in agriculture, which had reduced the scope for a transfer of labour to other occupations, is a case in point. It is true that, in the particular case of East Ger-many, the continuous—and selective—westward migration has contributed to labour shortages (though on the other hand it must be borne in mind that East Germany, unlike Czechoslovakia, has had at her disposal a larger potentially active population than before the war.) But, these elements apart, real scarcities of human resources are inherently characteristic of both economies. Real— particularly in the sense that the capital/labour ratios at which they have to work are set by the supply of capital. Far more than Poland, both countries have had to rely in their industrial growth on steeply rising productivity—more or less to the same extent as in most Western industrial societies.

Whatever the quantitative optimum, the post-war economic history of both East Germany and Czechoslovakia appears to

[13] A recent computation of relative levels of industrial productivities yielded this picture: Czechoslovakia 100; East Germany 95; Poland 80; USSR 97. (*Plan. Hosp.*, no. 11, 1959, p. 869.) The source does not give any indication of the method applied in bringing the respective industrial outputs to a common denominator.

[14] It should be borne in mind that the Narodowy Bank Polski parities were derived on the basis of Polish consumption patterns, which *per se* gives greater value to the zloty *vis-à-vis* the korona and DM (E). Our own very rough calculations (details will be given in the study to be published separately) suggested that in 1957 Czechoslovak and Polish workers' earnings amounted to 0·81 and 0·71 respectively, with East German earnings = 1·0.

suggest that a collectivist centrally-planned economy, too, is not immune from strains if it is deprived of a minimum labour reserve to cushion frictions arising from miscalculations, the occupational and locational readjustments which inevitably require time, and other corrective processes. The fact that both economies—for, economic reasons, quite apart from political considerations—have had to tap such dubious 'reservoirs' as students, &c., at peak periods in agriculture, or (more continuously) prisoners' and soldiers' labour in mining, construction, and public works, is in itself a proof of the risks and disadvantages of relying on a hand-to-mouth supply of labour.[15] One of the first acts of the Polish post-October 1956 régime was gradually to dispense with this obnoxious method of supplementing regular labour resources, on both moral and economic grounds.[16]

How far did the mechanism operating in the two countries aggravate the difficulties arising from the lack of the cushioning labour reserves? The question is not easy to answer. With time, labour compulsion—never, in fact, as drastic as in the USSR whence it had been borrowed—tended gradually to weaken. Coercion has been wearing out, and has been yielding decreasing returns; political factors have also favoured its curtailment. Concurrently the allocation of labour has been decentralized and made to rely upon market forces.

A dilemma is involved. It springs from the contradictions between the working of the general allocational machinery and that of the labour supply. There is some inconsistency in a system which rests to a very high degree on direct 'physical' allocation, and at the same time relies on the push and pull of the market in marshalling the prime factor of production, a factor which, in addition, is one of the scarcest resources of both countries. (The push and pull is influenced chiefly by more or less orthodox instruments of economic policies, wielded in market economies).

Authoritative students have expressed their scepticism,[17] therefore, as to the ability of the market forces—in these circumstances—to channel the supply of manpower to the most needy

---

[15] By 1957 Czechoslovakia had to rely for more than half of her increment in non-agricultural employment on the recruitment of workers' wives and old-age and disability pensioners (*Hosp. Nov.*, 15 Sept. 1957).

[16] By the late 1950's Czechoslovakia, too, reduced her reliance on this method.

[17] Kalecki, in *Nowe Drogi*, nos. 11–12, 1956, p. 43. For an illuminating discussion of a *de facto* labour market see Nove, *Soviet Economy*, pp. 231ff.

sectors of the economy, in accordance with demand (as determined by the planners' social priorities).

The case of Czechoslovakia may serve as a good illustration. The inability of the mechanism to pattern manpower as required, especially skilled manpower, appears to be in that country a greater handicap to planned growth than the overall deficit of labour: mining apart (for various reasons it forms a category by itself) shortages of skilled staff have affected most acutely the key industrial branches (especially the iron-and-steel industry), rather than the less important. Significantly, the difficulty in shifting skilled personnel from the Czech to the Slovak regions has impeded the build-up of metallurgy and chemicals, that is, of branches assigned a strategic role in the industrialization of Czechoslovakia.

In a profoundly differing economic and demographic milieu, developments in the Polish labour market have given rise to still more doubts as to the validity of some basic concepts on which manpower policy has been built up.

As has been pointed out here, Polish post-war employment policies consciously promoted the absorption of labour into industry at a pace which would outstrip the current, actual needs. This was considered advisable both from the social and the economic angle. While remedying the social evils of open unemployment, it would, so it was believed, help the training and technological adaptation of 'green' labour. Thus it would help to create an outsize human framework for rapidly expanding industries. This policy which—it can well be argued—had justification in the immediate post-war years, lost most of it as time passed.

The actual effect of Polish policy has been the creation of artificial overemployment. Though this was deliberate at the outset, it tended with time to deceive the planners themselves. Worse still, as policy makers were bound to discover, beyond a certain point the overemployment thus created, far from paving the way to higher efficiency levels, had a retrogressive effect. It has tended to disorganize work, and to demoralize both management and workers. The swollen numbers have had a negative marginal productivity.[18]

How much of the surplus is actually redundant cannot be easily

[18] Iron and steel is an illuminating case in point, see below, pp. 197f.

measured or defined. But, to quote the analysis produced in the late 1950's by the Economic Commission of the Polish Council of Ministers:[19] 'It is estimated that the number of unnecessarily employed, compared with actual production possibilities, amounts, in industry alone, to no less than 0·5 million persons.' To see the figure in correct proportions one should bear in mind that it makes up half the total addition to the Polish industrial labour force throughout the whole period of expansion under the first development plan.[20] Excessive expansion of industrial unemployment has remained a serious problem of the Polish economy still in the 1960's.

REAPPRAISAL OF BASIC ATTITUDES

Such experience has caused a good deal of heart-searching, which in the post-1956 political climate has been outstandingly frank, and has entailed a rethinking of a doctrine professed in the previous period.

This has largely been determined by the famous critique by Marx and Engels of the Malthusian teaching. In this approach contradictions between economic growth and the growth of population are seen as inherent properties of the capitalist system. A 'reserve army' belongs, in such an analysis, to the mode of operation of capitalism. It is in fact the essential characteristic of the mechanism of the capitalist labour market that this 'army' is perpetually reinforced by workers pushed out of production. Parallel to this runs the process of the proletarianization of the peasantry, and—at a certain stage of development—chronic, disguised underemployment in peasant farming. On this line of reasoning, once the social revolution had removed the root cause of the proletarian 'reserve army', that is, once harmony had been restored between the productive forces and conditions of production, obstacles to full employment of available human resources disappear. It becomes then only a matter of intelligent planning to keep employment at the maximum possible level. In other words—almost by definition—in a collectivist, centrally-planned

---

[19] *Przeglad biezacej sytuacji gospodarczej kraju i zadania stojace przed polityka gospodarcza* (Warsaw, 1957), p. 24.

[20] Excessive employment was calculated at between 5 and 30 per cent, depending on the enterprise. This was roughly verified by an industrial survey which had shown that effective use of working time in industry ranged between 70 and 90 per cent (M. Kabaj, in *Nowe Drogi*, Nov. 1960).

economy, supply and demand adjust themselves to one another. Specific conditions in the Soviet Union seemed to strengthen the claim of this argument to universality.

On *a priori* grounds it can indeed be argued that, owing to this lack of consistency, the two centrally-planned economies have even less opportunity of shaping the flow of labour than market economies in otherwise similar conditions, particularly as regards population.

The experience of Poland has, first of all, called into question certain theoretical fundamentals of employment policy. Criticism since 1956 has widely admitted that the doctrinal framework supplied by the classics of Marxism is in crass discord with the observable reality. Kautsky has now received credit for rejecting the view of those Marxists who insisted that the change in the property system alone would automatically solve the problem of relative overpopulation, relative, that is, to the available capital.

However much the Malthusian theory, in its cruder form and wider claims, is open to valid criticism, it has forced itself on the minds of Polish analysts as a tool for a very broad interpretation of Polish developments—if only in its stress on the nexus between the demographic position and trends and the supply of the 'means of subsistence'.[21] In one (admittedly very special) sense, one could, in fact, say that the Malthusian spectre, which has been driven out from mature economies but still haunts so many underdeveloped areas, has become visible on the Polish horizon. This could not and did not fail to affect Polish population policies.

Moreover against Polish realities the meaning of the policy of full employment, which was previously understood to be a corollary of socialism, has now become severely circumscribed. It is widely realized that what happened in Poland actually amounted to a shift of disguised unemployment from agriculture to industry.

Once the doctrine of a necessary harmony between demographic and economic growths in a collectivist society had gone overboard, structural unemployment in such a society was acknowledged as a theoretical possibility. Indeed, it had to be when the doctrine was confronted with Polish economic life. It has now been realized that the two kinds of structural unemployment—the open and the disguised—may become inescapable alternatives.

[21] Cf. a very interesting discussion by A. Jozefowicz, in *Z. Gosp.*, no. 46, 1957

As seen by Polish students, other things being equal, a capitalist economy would tend to develop open industrial unemployment. A socialist economy, on the other hand, would gravitate towards disguised unemployment.[22] It would do so, first, because a collectivist economy creates a wider scope for manœuvring resources and removes some institutional inhibitions which are characteristic of capitalism. Secondly, because the specific mechanism of the labour market under socialism 'does not adequately register the degree to which the labour force is put to use'.[23] Hence capitalism would tend to concentrate disguised unemployment, other things being equal, in agriculture rather than in industry, while socialism, *vice versa*, would shift it to industry. Politically, let us add to this argument, it is, for obvious reasons, more expedient in a socialist state that industrial unemployment should be disguised rather than open.

Clearer thinking has made it easier to grasp the essence of the Polish dilemma. This in itself helps at least to avoid some mistakes which in the past stemmed from self-deception. It is now realized —as is explicitly stated in an analysis by the Economic Commission of the Polish Cabinet—that 'the difficulties which prevail in the labour market are not transitory in nature; on the contrary they must be expected to be aggravated in the coming years'.[24] For lack of a better solution half-measures have been advocated and in part applied. These include the extension of the school age. They also aim at reducing, or at least stabilizing, the employment of women, though putting the clock back is admittedly a very difficult matter once social habits have been changed.

Although the crux of the Polish dilemma is a large agricultural labour surplus, the Economic Commission even recommends discontinuing too rapid transfers of manpower from farming to industry, in order not to increase disguised unemployment in the latter.

Some of the problems involved have been, or will be, discussed in other parts of this study. One or two remarks on the substitution of labour for capital may be not out of place in the present context, even at the risk of repetition. It may appear poor logic to substitute in an economy such as the Polish one the superabundant factor for one which is very scarce. But there are qualifications to this

---

22 Kabaj, in Z. *Gosp.*, no. 26, 1958.   23 Ibid. p. 2.
24 *Przeglad biezacej sytuacji gospodarczej*, p. 23.

argument: the main one has been noted earlier. It is that, whatever the relative scarcities of labour and capital, a build-up of modern, capital-intensive technology, even out of step with the general environment, is imperative for a sustained growth-momentum; and there is in Poland an acute and justified consciousness of the danger of re-imparting to the economy a paralysing 'underdevelopment equilibrium'.[25]

Except for certain industrial branches which suffer from labour shortages due to specific—technical or economic—causes, there is comparatively little scope in Polish industry for capital outlay of the purely labour-saving type. But apart from this type, capital-intensive technological advance—where most desirable *per se*—still defeats the policy aim of creating maximum employment opportunities. The kind of rise in labour productivity which is worth paying for by additional capital expenditure creates, in Poland, a difficult dilemma: Professor Kalecki,[26] for one, has called for a discriminating approach to the postulate of raising productivity through extra investment under Polish conditions. No panacea, however, is within the reach of the Polish policy makers. Trying to solve the problem of the deep-seated structural underemployment of the nation's manpower and simultaneously to modernize and expand industry is tantamount almost to squaring the circle, if the assumptions on which the planner must work are a very narrow stream of capital from outside, reasonable progress in living standards, and no recourse to emigration.[27]

The latter assumption deserves special attention. Considering the general economic and demographic conditions one would believe that the three countries, now constituting part of one political group aspiring to close economic integration, would form an ideal area for a redistribution of manpower. It should be remembered that migration of labour to Germany—including that

[25] We have used the concept which Professor Nurkse so illuminatingly analysed and adopted, in *Capital Formation in Underdeveloped Countries*, p. 10.

[26] In *Z. Gosp.*, no. 31, 1960.

[27] There has been some emigration from Poland in recent years, mainly of those who opted for German nationality. It has partly been offset by Polish repatriates from the Soviet Union.

Poland was traditionally a country of heavy emigration. Between 1871 and the outbreak of the Second World War the emigration of people of Polish stock from the then partitioned Poland was of the order of 3·5 million. Cf. J. Zubrzycki, in *Population Studies*, no. 3, 1953, pp. 248ff. The wave of immigration restrictions to which the overseas nations resorted after 1918 tended to weaken this safety valve of the Polish economy. However, over the last ten years before the Second World War, emigration from Poland (seasonal excepted) amounted to about 750,000.

part which now constitutes the GDR—has been a secular phenomenon.[28] In fact it counterbalanced the general westward
migratory trend within the Reich. However, much as conditions
would seem propitious for resuming a flow of Polish labour to
areas of an acute deficit, the striking fact is that Polish emigration
came to a standstill. The inhibition of inter-country migrations of
labour within the area under survey may be accounted for
chiefly by psychological and political factors. Whatever the causes,
the failure of co-operation in levelling out the great disparities
in the labour-market position is one of the most conspicuous
deficiencies in the integration of the economies of the area.

[28] 'Seasonal' emigration to Germany amounted to 430,000 over the years 1927–38.
In 1938 about 63,000 'seasonal' emigrants to Germany were recorded.

CHAPTER III

The Growth of
Industrial Production

THE OFFICIAL INDEX FIGURES

WE shall now turn to the quantitative assessment of post-war industrial expansion in the area under survey.[1] Official index figures of growth in the three countries are shown in the following table.

Industrial Expansion Claimed, 1937–62

(1937 = 100)

	1948	1950	1953	1955	1960	1961	1962
Czechoslovakia	107	143	210	243	404	428	470
East Germany[1]		111	117	210	324	343	360[2]
Poland	148	231		487	758	830	900

[1] 1936 = 100.   [2] Estimate.

This table tells a story of remarkable successes. Over a quarter of a century which included one of the most ravaging wars in history, two industrially well developed and mature nations of central Europe—Czechoslovakia and East Germany—contrived to multiply their industrial output, the first five times and the second three and a half times. Poland's performance since the Second World War would appear to be even more spectacular: over the same period her production is shown to have risen ninefold. It will be even more impressive when compared with the period after the First World War: by 1938 Poland just regained the level of her

[1] This section summarizes a study by the present writer, to be published separately, which revises and extends up to the end of the 1950's a preliminary inquiry.

industrial production of a quarter of a century earlier. Czecho-slovakia's production in 1937 surpassed that of 1913 by one-third.

This impressive performance is, in fact, claimed for less than a decade and a half, namely from the time when post-war rehabili-tation was completed. In East Germany the period is shorter than elsewhere since there was a significant lag in the start of her reconstruction. The claim has sometimes been linked up with the thesis that some specific properties of the socio-economic model promote such progress.

It is true that on closer examination the official figures will themselves refute the additional claim sometimes made that the growth promoted by the model is continuously smooth and self-accelerating.

Yearly Industrial Growth Rates Claimed
(*percentages*)

	1949	1950	1951–5	1956–9	1956	1957
Czechoslovakia	19	16	11·2	10·0	9·5	10·2
East Germany	25	26	13·6	9·0	6·3	7·6
Poland	23	31	19·1	9·3	9·1	9·6

	1958	1959	1960	1961	1962	1963
Czechoslovakia	10·9	10·2	10·7	8·9	6·1	− 2
East Germany	11·3	12·3	8·2	6·2	6·1	4
Poland	9·8	9·9	12·0	10·5	8·3	3

Note: The industrial-growth estimate for 1963 has been based on data available for the first half of that year.

These figures indicate that the spurt at the turn of the 1940's was followed by a marked slowing down, roughly about the critical year 1953. After 1955, however, the rate of growth regained momentum and settled down, towards the end of the decade, at a level of about 10 per cent a year—a high rate, indeed, by any standard. A slowing-down of growth has, however, been discernible throughout the area since the beginning of the 1960's.

For purposes of comparison we may, perhaps, mention that in periods free from major economic depressions industry throughout the world has grown, on an average, by about 5 per cent a year.

Over the last four decades, the periods of the great cataclysms included, this rate was something like 4 per cent. Between 1937 and the mid-1950's Western Europe as a whole increased her output by about three-quarters. Her secular trend of industrial expansion may be set for the present century at about $3\frac{1}{2}$ per cent a year.[2] All in all it took Western Europe over half a century to quadruple her industrial production, and she doubled it over the quarter century which covered both the Great Depression and the Second World War.

When the claims of the three Central European countries are set against these other rates of growth the question may arise how far the former can be considered 'true'. Several factors tend to exaggerate the official indices of industrial performance. Some of these—for instance the absorption into industry of many handi-craftsmen and small-scale workshops—are connected with the post-war transformation of the economic and social system. No really satisfactory method exists for gauging the impact of factors of this kind on the indices. An even more important factor for Poland was the westward shift of the economy due to post-war territorial changes. As regards Czechoslovakia, on the other hand, we have not needed to make any allowance for the cession of the Sub-Carpathian Ukraine to the USSR, as the effect of this would be negligible.

SOVIET METHODS OF GROWTH MEASUREMENT

Other, more general difficulties arise in connexion with the measurement of industrial growth in any country, and more particularly in countries which subscribe to Soviet statistical concepts and methods. There is, of course, as Professor Hodgman puts it, 'no completely rational or intellectually satisfying'[3] solution of the problem of aggregating unlike physical units. Resorting to value—the only possible method—begs as many questions as it answers. Again, only very limited comparisons can be made between industrial production aggregates, particularly those derived from countries with different environments, models, and socio-economic philosophies, to say nothing of statistical conventions. No convention can claim for itself the virtue of providing a picture which is 'true' in some absolute sense, but a comparison

---

[2] Paretti and Bloch, in *BNLQR*, ix (1956), 186ff.
[3] D. R. Hodgman, *Soviet Industrial Production, 1928–51* (Cambridge, Mass., 1954).

of results obtained on the basis of varying conventions may distort the picture. It is the reckless conveying of unwarranted impressions distorted in this way, rather than the choice of one convention in preference to another, that is objectionable.

It is probably only due in part to doctrinal loyalty[4] that Soviet practice in the measurement of industrial growth has clung to what one might term the 'gross-gross' output concept.[5] (We have doubled the adjective 'gross' to avoid confusion with the Western usage of 'gross' merely to denote that no allowance has been made for wear and tear of fixed capital.)

The characteristic feature of the gross-gross method is the duplication of some components in the calculus: at each stage of manufacture the value of inputs obtained from other enterprises is included in the statistical product value. This contrasts with the widely accepted Western methodology based on 'value added' as the gauge of industrial performance: it eliminates the intra-firm flows and records the end-products; its rationale rests on the proposition that it is the value brought into being in the productive process which matters from the point of view of growth; in the last instance this convention rests on the tenet that the value added represents the newly created quantum of consumer satisfaction.

In the late 1940's—to quote the then Polish Vice-Premier in charge of economic matters, H. Minc—'the bourgeois methods of calculus' were discarded, and the statistical practices of the three countries were assimilated to Soviet concepts and techniques. A recomputation of the 1947 industrial output was published in Poland in 1949. It seems safe to believe that, at least until 1948, the Czechoslovak index was still computed on a method approaching the value-added basis; presumably this was true of East Germany for as late as 1950.

The adoption of the gross-gross rather than the value-added method influences the performance index in two ways. One of these relates to changes in the material-content—in 'material-intensity'—of industrial production, and Professors Gerschenkron and Erlich define,[6] with good reason, the process of industrialization as one of a change in the ratio of highly fabricated to 'low-

---

[4] An excellent discussion on the subject and a comprehensive bibliography can be found in G. Warren Nutter, *The Growth of Industrial Production in the Soviet Union* (Princeton, N.J., 1962).

[5] See above, p. 10.

[6] A. Gerschenkron and A. Erlich, *A Dollar Index of Soviet Machinery Output, 1927/28 to 1937* (N.Y., 1951). See also F. Seton, in *Bull. Oxf. Univ. Inst. Stat.*, Feb. 1958.

fabricated' commodities, to the advantage of the former: in other words industrialization is taken to mean a rising value-added in manufacturing in relation to the materials consumed during the process. By this token one would have expected the 'net' to outpace the 'gross', especially in a relatively undeveloped country such as Poland, at least over the first development period. There are good reasons, however, for believing that a countervailing influence stemming from the organizational structure has been at work.

Under the gross-gross method, other things being equal, when the number of recorded stages of production is increased the index is bound to move up; the reverse happens when they decrease. (Changes in the type—and value—of raw material would have a broadly analogous effect on the index.) To give the simplest example, results would depend on whether textile production was integrated in one enterprise throughout the period under investigation, or split at some stage into separate units for spinning, weaving, and finishing.

Similarly, duplication of intra-enterprise flows in metallurgy would depend on the degree of organizational integration of ore-mining, coking, and the making and finishing of pig-iron and steel. Under a more or less stable industrial pattern the impact of this kind of 'grossness' on the index would be on the whole 'neutral'. But structural shifts may provide opportunities for swelling the indices. To put the point in broad terms: moves towards specialization would tend to inflate the index, and moves towards self-sufficiency to deflate it. Similarly, decentralization may tend to impart an upward bias and centralization may work in the opposite direction. (From this angle the institutional reforms of the late 1950's would probably have in themselves a rather inflationary effect on the index.) Since—at least over long periods—incentive systems connected rewards with performance as measured by gross-gross output, firm managements naturally tended to swell the index artificially by appropriate manipulations of inputs (e.g. the use of materials 'bought' outside entrepreneurial units tends to improve the statistical performance; so, in some circumstances, does the re-processing of faulty goods).

The adverse impact of the gross-gross output method on the discipline of industrial planning and control incurred increasing criticism.[7] This critique has been accompanied by similar strictures

[7] See above, p. 10.

in the statistical literature of the three countries. A paper in the Polish statistical research journal concluded an inquest on the decade of Soviet-patterned practice in Poland with these words: 'Our signal achievement in the past period was undoubtedly the enormous increase in industrial production, yet no one is able to say what exactly this increase was; certainly the index numbers of gross output cannot tell us anything about it.'[8] East German writing and practice has endeavoured to evolve a methodology for eliminating the distorting effects of changes in the vertical structure of industry, and the consequent changes in inter-enterprise flows of products.[9] A suggestion to adopt the value-added method was made as early as 1956 by Professor B. Korda of the Prague Economic Institute at a conference on productivity measurement held in Prague at the end of that year. Similar suggestions also appeared about this time in the Soviet Union.[10]

Turning to the pricing problem, to state the obvious, some 'weights' must be adopted as an expression of value relations between commodities, and thus between producing industrial branches; and relative positions of commodities in any economy are liable to change over time: and the faster the qualitative and quantitative transformation of the economy, the more vulnerable an index must be on this count. By its very nature in a progressive economy, that is, in one where costs per unit are falling, a forward-oriented index (i.e. one based on prices taken from the past) of the

Laspèyres type: $\dfrac{p_0 q_n}{p_0 q_0}$ where p and q stand for prices and quantities; o and n for the base and the nth year, which is the type adopted in Eastern and Central Europe, gives an inflated picture

as against the backward-oriented Paasche type: $\dfrac{p_n q_n}{p_n q_0}$.

A dynamic process of industrialization as intensive as that experienced in the Soviet Union after 1928 would by its very nature rob the index of some of its significance. The manner in which Soviet statistical practice tried to patch up the initial

---

[8] J. Zagorski, in *Przeglad Stat.*, iv (1957), nos. 3–4, p. 208.

[9] Cf. *i.a.* E. Schmidt, in *Stat. Prax.*, no. 12, 1956, p. 193; Arnold and others, *Ökonomik der sozialistischen Industrie in der Deutschen Demokratischen Republik* (Berlin, 1956), pp. 122ff.; Behrens, *Arbeitsproduktivität, Lohnentwicklung und Rentabilität* (Berlin, 1956), p. 31.

[10] See *i.a.* A. I. Petrov and N. P. Lubimov, in *Plan. Khoz.*, no. 1, 1957, pp. 45ff. For a more recent criticism, see V. V. Novozhilov in V. S. Nemchinov ed., *Primenenie matematiki v ekonomicheskikh issledovaniyakh* (Moscow, 1959).

weights undermined the significance of the index still more: this consisted in bringing new products into output valuation at the cost price of the pioneering period which as a rule is a high-cost period; these initial high-cost prices were later corrected only very inadequately, if at all. A vast Soviet literature pointed out the distorting effects of pricing method.[11] While these methods were under fire in the USSR, they were nevertheless copied in the countries of her sphere of influence. The three Central European countries in particular originally based their gross-gross output indices on pre-war or wartime prices; and here too additions from current cost structures at the time of the first appearance of a commodity seem to have exercised an inflationary influence due both to the general upward trend of cost and prices and to the usually higher cost of 'pilot' production.[12]

The East German practice of pricing in the measurement of industrial performance has had some distorting features peculiar to itself. It relied until 1955 on what was termed 'measurement values'—*Messwerte*—the original base of which had been pegged to 1944 prices. These were manipulated rather arbitrarily, and adjusted by borrowing from current prices prevailing between that year and 1950. From 1956 onwards industrial gross output has been valued at 'constant' (f.o.b.) prices of the preceding year in most cases that is, at the actual ex-factory price. As against the East German index, both the Polish and the Czechoslovak series have been built up on prices actually prevailing at one stage or another. In both countries original post-war series were based on 1937 prices with some adjustments. In particular, the Polish one borrowed prices from 1937, excise deducted. From 1956 onwards 'comparable', that is, average-cost prices actually prevailing in 1954 or in planning for 1955 were substituted for the pre-war prices. Similarly the 1949–55 industrial performance was valued in Czechoslovakia at prices prevailing at the beginning of 1953, and for the subsequent period mid-1954 prices were adopted.[13]

[11] Criticism of the 1926–7 price base was aired as early as the mid-1930's. It gained strength with time. Cf. A. I. Rotshtein, *Problemy promyshlennoi statistiki SSSR*, vols. i (Leningrad, 1936), and iii (Moscow, 1947), *passim*.

[12] Gregory Grossman, *Soviet Statistics of Physical Output of Industrial Commodities* (Princeton, N.J., 1960), p. 129, notes, for a Soviet-type industrial economy, a general 'tendency towards devaluation of the specified unit of measure' as a result of pressure to fulfil the plan cast in physical units or value terms directly derived from them.

[13] Technically indices are constructed as base-weighted arithmetical averages. Series are built up of 'indicators' of quantities for relevant commodities; these are combined into index numbers at July 1954 prices.

In all these countries, prices as applied in gross-gross industrial output series are taken net of turnover tax.

In addition to industrial series proper each of the countries has produced more recently indices intended to reflect industry's contribution to national products, and intra-industrial (i.e. branch) contributions. Such series, expressed in current ex-factory sale prices, turnover tax included, have been published since the beginning of the 1950's in East Germany, and since the second half of the decade in Poland. At the end of the 1950's an index series of 'national income produced in industry' based on 1948, methodologically close to Western value-added, was published in Czechoslovakia (computed on 1955 prices).[14]

As can be seen, around the mid-1950's remote constant-price and arbitrarily patched-up structures were abandoned in index construction in all the three countries. Moreover, successive reforms carried out in the late 1950's made current prices more rational if not as an expression of scarcities, at least within their own terms, i.e. as an expression of production costs reducible in the last instance to the cost of labour.[15] At the same time a greater degree of stability in output patterns—a corollary of the slowing down of the rhythm of industrial growth—has improved the inter-temporal comparability of the current-price valuation. There remains, however, the question of a link-up with index series of the more distant past. Polish statistics alone have refrained, since the second half of the 1950's, from linking up heterogeneous series (though such 'patched up' series are sometimes officially referred to in Poland to substantiate claims to post-war industrial achievements); a recomputation of past indices into more or less homogeneous series does not seem to be contemplated as yet.[16]

[14] Net material product forming the basis of such 'net' series is defined, throughout the area, as gross value of commodities and 'material' services minus cost of commodities and services consumed and minus charge for depreciation. It is the deduction of the latter that constitutes the principal difference between this magnitude and value-added as usually defined in Western practice.

[15] See p. 15.

[16] Since 1957 the Central Statistical Office of Poland has begun work on an index of industrial production of the type

$$I = \frac{\Sigma^i q^w}{\Sigma w}$$

where $^i q$ stands for individual branch indices computed by the use of selected 'representatives', or, alternatively, symptoms such as employment, consumption of raw material or sale figures; w stands for weights. The index is to be close to the value-added method. Cf. J. Iszkowski, R. Kulczycki, M. Ostrowski and L. Zienkowski, in *Wiad. Stat.*, no. 1, 1957.

This method has been employed in the construction of the Polish perspective plan

THE METHOD OF MEASUREMENT EMPLOYED IN THIS STUDY

For some time past various attempts have been made in the West to recompute Soviet-type indices into series congenial to our mode of statistical vision. Some students have relied on the empirically established broad correlations between general industrial progress and a few 'physical-term' phenomena, such as the use of certain 'growth' materials—especially steel, energy (particularly in the form of electricity), and freight-hauls.[17] There are also ambitious attempts to recalculate Soviet indices by readjusting Soviet prices or applying foreign-price structures (to mention such pioneering works as those by Professors Gerschenkron, Grossman, Clark, and Jasny). Professor Hodgman's method—in which value-added weights for each industry branch are taken to be represented by rewards to labour—has also much to recommend it.[18] Each method has its advantages, but can hardly produce any 'ideal' portrait of growth, particularly where comparison with progress measured elsewhere in a different way is intended. On the other hand the fundamental issue which arises is whether prices derived from a Soviet-type economy can be used for a meaningful measurement of the growth process. Or one may wonder, as Hodgman does, whether it is consistent to divorce a given economy's system of values from its own specific pattern of consumption.[19]

---

extending into the mid-1970's (see above, p. 46). The growth dynamic reflected in this index appeared to be lower than that of the gross-gross index for the same set of branches and products.

Furthermore the Polish Central Statistical Office has carried out various checks of its gross-gross output index (this is referred to as the 'enterprise method'), by the use of a new series based on 215 product 'representatives'. The critique of the method has pointed to some of its obvious flaws, such as insensitiveness to changes in product-mix and quality and (where employment is taken as the relevant 'symptom') in productivity. A series based on a still wider range of 'representatives'—870 industrial products—has shown only marginal disagreement with that obtained by the traditional 'enterprise method'. In the latter the index stood in 1958 (1955 = 100) at 131 as against 127-8 in the '870 representatives' series. Cf. J. Iszkowski, in *Gosp. Plan.*, no. 10, 1960, pp. 12ff.

Information on pricing and branch weighting in the new index available to us at the time of writing has not permitted an adequate analysis of results.

[17] Cf. e.g. Seton, in *Bull. Oxf. Univ. Inst. Stat.*, Feb. 1958, pp. 1ff.; *Sov. Stud.*, Oct. 1960.

[18] Hodgman, p. 51. The results obtained for the USSR by different methods display, over a considerable span of time, significantly moderate discrepancies, oscillating for 1940 around half the official gross output index (1928 = 100).

[19] Hodgman, p. 19. Much light has been shed on the vexed problem of the rationality of weights derived from price-structures of a Soviet-type economy, in a polemic initiated by P. Wiles' analysis (*Sov. Stud.*, vii/2; viii/2) of the approach of Professors

Ours is an admittedly eclectic and rough method. While apologies are offered for its lack of subtlety, it may be pointed out that our choice of method has been partly dictated by the availability of statistical 'raw material'. At any rate, no more is sought than a very broad indication of what has happened. The actual procedures of building up our index-series are described in greater detail in our separate study.

Of all our series probably the least satisfactory, in at least one sense, is that for Czechoslovakia. Its weighting has been borrowed by us from the early post-war official Czechoslovak calculations which—this should be pointed out—somewhat improved on the pre-war method. It relies on a rather patchy combination of elements, i.e. of a given industry's 1937 share in sale values and labour force, and in motive power as recorded in the last pre-war Czechoslovak census (1930). The weighting of our East German index is basically derived from 1936 output values as computed by the Reichsamt für wehrwirtschaftliche Planung: these were converted by us from gross to net by means of the respective average all-Reich ratios derived from the same source. Finally our basic Polish index rests on the Polish post-war (1947) net valuation of industrial output in 1937 prices, excise excluded.

For each branch a dominant commodity has been selected as its 'representative'. 'Physical-term' indices of growth (in tons, kwh, metres) have then been applied on this basis to industrial value weights. The underlying assumption is that physical-term data are faithfully recorded by the official statistics of the countries concerned. There is every evidence to support the trust in these statistics on this count.

As in other similar attempts, engineering (as officially classified in the area: machine-building and metal-working, including the production of means of transport and precision instruments) has proved to be the problem industry. Its vigorous expansion makes it of paramount importance for the shape of the curve of overall

---

Hodgman and A. Bergson. The discussion revolves primarily around the question whether 'consumer's sovereignty' is a *conditio sine qua non* of rationality, or—and in what sense—the latter is reconcilable with the Master Planner's scale of preferences. The reader's attention is drawn to contributions made to this important debate by Joan Robinson, D. G. Hodgman, D. Granick, J. M. Montias, M. Dobb, F. Holzman, and K. W. Rothschild (*Sov. Stud.*, vii/3; viii/1 and 4; ix/1). There is a masterly discussion of the theoretical rationale of the appraisal of growth from the alternative angles of 'production potential' and 'welfare' in Bergson, *The Real National Income of Soviet Russia since 1928* (Cambridge, Mass., 1961), pp. 25ff.

industrial growth. Engineering is perhaps the worst offender in the official gross-gross output computations, owing both to the effect of duplications and to the artificial pricing of new products. The strong distorting effect of these factors on assessing performance in metal processing has been stressed in various contexts in the countries concerned. In particular East German literature has emphasized the distorting effect of inter-enterprise flows of materials.[20] To accept the gross-gross production series one would have to accept as a fact that, during the quarter of a century, engineering expanded nearly eightfold in Czechoslovakia, more than fivefold in East Germany and twenty-seven times in Poland.

Metal-working Industry, 1937–62

$(1937 = 1)$

| | Metal-working | | Consumption of steel |
	Gross output	Manpower	
Czechoslovakia	7·8	2·4	4·0
East Germany	5·3	1·8	2·5
Poland	27·0	5·9	6·6

No doubt the post-war expansion of this branch in Poland is most remarkable, but even when this is granted, the claimed increase does not seem empirically feasible. In 1937 production of British and West German engineering was about seventeen and twenty-one times respectively larger than the Polish. (The Industry and Materials Committee of the UN Economic Commission for Europe estimated the gross production of Polish, British, and West German engineering for 1937 or 1938 (in 1948 prices) at $235 million, $4,205 million, and $5,150 million respectively.[21] The implication of the Polish post-war gross-gross production index would be then that by now the output of Poland's engineering is

[20] Inter-industrial 'co-operation', in the official terminology, growing much faster than the output of machinery. Between 1953 and 1955 the gross output of machines rose about 20% and the index of inter-enterprise 'co-operation' by about 50%. In the precision and optical instruments branch the respective rates are 35 and 85%. Cf. Schmidt, in *Stat. Prax.*, no. 12, 1956, p. 193.

[21] *A General Survey of European Engineering Industry* (Geneva, 1951), p. 6. According to the same source Czechoslovak engineering production amounted in 1937 to $369 million. To accept the gross output indices, Polish output would now be two-thirds as large again as Czechoslovak.

more than half again as large as was Britain's at the outbreak of the last war—or nearly half again as large as that of Western Germany—which is a patently gross exaggeration.

When rejecting the official gross-gross output indices as the 'true' measure of performance one is still at a loss as to what to substitute for it. Here, unlike the non-engineering branches, the heterogeneity of the products-mix prohibits the choice of any 'representative' commodity in outputs.[22]

Broadly speaking, throughout the area, especially in the highly industrialized heart of the region, engineering has been affected by two chronic bottlenecks; labour and materials. To assume that something approaching value-added may be measured by the intake of manpower is hardly reasonable, since this would be tantamount to an assumption of more or less static productivity of labour. There are far better reasons for relying on metal input as a dependable symptom.

An analysis of historical data for Europe seems to justify the general inference that value-added indices of metal-working oscillate around those of metal consumption. In most cases the former tend to outstrip the latter, but it is far from a general rule; for our particular case we took into account the high 'metal intensity' of the post-war growth of engineering in the area.[23] A shift in this direction has been in particular a feature of East Germany's metal-working industries, although she is a traditional home of some branches—such as that of precision instruments—characterized by a very high degree of fabrication as against the weight of materials. We therefore accepted metal availability as a ceiling for metal-working output throughout the area, and as at least the first approximation to the measure of its progress. We have also, however, tried other approaches. One of these consists of taking the gross-gross production figure as the point of departure and 'tempering' its exaggeration by an allowance for the two bottleneck factors, that is, labour and material input. The obtained median has been used here for an alternative indicator of the performance of engineering, and thereby industry as a whole, with a strong warning as to its crudeness and arbitrariness.

With regard to Poland some attempt has been made to relate

---

[22] On problems faced in the recomputation of the engineering component in the Soviet-type index see A. Tarn and R. W. Campbell, in *Amer. Econ. R.*, Sept. 1962.
[23] See below, pp. 204f.

her overall post-war industrial growth quantitatively to the post-1939 territorial changes.

The two alternatives for engineering apart, our series are essentially those produced in our original publication, extended to cover the quarter of a century up to 1962. Corrections have been made where new statistical data appeared in the meantime.

New series have been computed by us as a check for both East Germany and Poland. The East German series differed from the old one mainly in that the range of branch 'representatives' has been widened. The same is also true of our new Polish series, but in that case the revision has been more drastic: the weighting had been based on actual 1938 'sale' values of output in the individual branches, converted by us to net. These series suggest a quite substantial scaling down of the Polish post-war industrial performance; for East Germany they did not yield results any different from the original one.

ESTIMATES OF INDUSTRIAL GROWTH SINCE 1937

Some of our principal findings are as follows:

1. Whether measured by the official indices, or by our own, Czechoslovak and Polish industries reached and surpassed their pre-war output levels as early as 1947 and 1948 respectively. On our own calculation the Polish pre-war output was regained in the present territory in about 1949. As appraised by the official method East German pre-war (1936) output was regained and passed by 1950—according to our method a year or two later. East Germany regained her former peak (1944) level only around the middle of the 1950's. The years mentioned here thus form the watershed in post-war rehabilitation: post-war industrial expansion can also, therefore, be conveniently viewed from these dates as alternative bases.

2. Over the quarter of a century after 1937 the output of Czechoslovak industry grew, according to the official gross-gross output index, nearly five times. On our method of calculation it increased about three times.

3. Whereas official statistics show East German industrial production to have been, by 1962, three and a half times that of before the war (1936), according to our index it roughly doubled; this implies an increase of about three-fifths over the 1944 peak level.

Industrial Growth, 1937–62: Comparison of Official Claims with Our Findings

(*per cent of 1937 levels*)

	Official index 1962	Our indices	
		I	II
Czechoslovakia	470	289	301
East Germany	360	213	231
Poland (*a*)	900	390	470
(*b*)	.	255	316

Note: Official index for East Germany as % of 1936 level. Index for Poland: (*a*) compares with pre-war levels within pre-war boundaries, and (*b*) within the post-war boundaries. Sets I and II of index numbers have been obtained by alternative methods of assessing the contribution of engineering. (See above, p. 118.)

Production data used as a basis of the index series for East Germany do not include the uranium-mining Soviet–German Joint Stock Company Wismut, and enterprises managed by the Ministry of the Interior.

4. The widest discrepancy emerged, not unexpectedly, in the measure of Polish industrial development. On our evidence the officially claimed rate of a ninefold growth over the quarter of a century has been reduced by about one-half; our alternative series suggest that, by 1962, Polish industrial output was three, four, or nearly five times the pre-war figure. Our calculations suggest that, in 1937, production in the present territory of Poland was half as large again as that in the pre-war territory. This does not however, invalidate the official contention that the industrial contribution of the territories in the West to the national total is now about one-quarter. The general inference is that by 1962, within the present boundaries, Polish industrial production was roughly between two and a half and three times the pre-war figure (or 70 per cent above it on our alternative count).

5. Our findings for East German industrial growth are in broad agreement with those arrived at by different paths, for the period

ending in the mid-1950's, by other students, especially by Dr Stolper, Dr Abeken, and 'Germanicus',[24] as far as they went. Official East German net-output figures have systematically lagged behind gross-output index numbers. As has been noted here, at the end of the 1950's Czechoslovak authorities produced their own net-output index series (the industry's contribution to material national income produced); it stood at 285 for 1961 (1948 = 100), suggesting that, over the period which followed upon post-war reconstruction up to the beginning of the present decade, industrial output increased two and a half times, rather than four times, as would appear from the official gross-gross output series.[25] Hence accepting the UN tentative estimate that, at the end of the reconstruction period (in 1948), the net value of industrial production was 3 per cent higher than before the war[26] (in 1937), the Czechoslovak net index number for 1961 would stand at 276 (1937 = 100), suggesting only a minor disparity with ours.

Polish official series show that industrial output as measured by its contribution to net material national product (Marxian definition) grew over the second half of the 1950's (1956–60) by less than one-half (48 per cent) rather than by three-fifths (59·6 per cent), as would appear from the gross-gross production index.[27] If this series is 'chained up' with one similarly constructed for the first half of the last decade,[28] the index number for 1960 would be 263 (1950 = 100). It would thus indicate, for the period 1950–60 a two and a half times increase in production rather than the three and a half times yielded by the gross-gross output calculation. The United Nations estimate just referred to suggests that by

---

[24] See references in my original study. It was only when the present study was completed that I acquainted myself with the final version of Stolper's detailed inquiry brought forward up to 1958. His broad conclusion, based on Western methodology and East German 1936 prices, suggests that, between 1936 and 1958, the output of East German industry—as measured by gross national product—increased by nearly one-half: by the same token it would have doubled over 1950–8 (see W. G. Stolper, *The Structure of the East German Economy* (Cambridge, Mass., 1960)).

[25] *Stat. roc., 1961*, p. 38. I have read a lengthy discussion of my series in J. M. Michal's *Central Planning in Czechoslovakia*, Dr Michal believes (p. 33) that it 'may somewhat have underestimated Czechoslovakia's industrial growth'.

[26] ECE, *Survey, 1949*. Estimate in 1938 prices. Obtained in two steps: (a) the prewar output arrived at by direct computation, and (b) the post-war figures calculated by applying appropriate index-numbers to the pre-war output value (converted into dollars).

[27] See W. Rogozinski, in *Gosp. Plan.*, no. 4, 1962, p. 4.

[28] A. Broner and R. Kulczycki, in *Wiad. Stat.*, Mar.–Apr. 1958. Growth over 1955–6 taken to be 6 per cent, see *Dochod Narodowy Polski, 1956* (Warsaw, 1958).

the end of the Polish reconstruction period (in 1949), the net value of industrial production was two-thirds as high again as it was before the war (in 1939).[29] Estimating then that, on this method, it was in 1950 about double its pre-war level, Polish net industrial output would be, by 1960, nearer five times the pre-war level in pre-war territory than seven and a half times, as shown by the gross-gross output series.

Last but not least, the result of a Polish comparison of the growth of heavy industry in the 1950's[30] may throw light on the impact of methodology in pricing on the measurement of performance. Heavy industry is defined as comprising the branches of fuels, metals, chemicals, building materials, and heavy engineering (production of machines and means of transport); twenty commodities were selected as their 'representatives' and weighted with 1956 Western European or specifically British domestic-market prices. The yardstick of growth is here total output during the eight years 1950–7 as related to a total of the 1949–51 triennium.

Output of Heavy Industries, 1950–7[1]

(total output in 1949–51 = 1)

		Computed indices	
Czechoslovakia		World	12
(a) official index	13	United Kingdom	9
(b) computed index	11	France	10
East Germany		Italy	12
(a) official index	.	Western Germany	12
(b) computed index	11		
Poland			
(a) official index	15		
(b) computed index	10		

[1] Figures rounded.

Source: Rychlewski, in *Gosp. Plan.*, nos. 1–2, 1959.

Note that on this showing, too, the Polish official gross-gross output claim is half again as high as the computed performance

[29] ECE, *Survey, 1949*, p. 3.
[30] Rychlewski, in *Gosp. Plan.*, nos. 1–2, 1959, pp. 64ff. 'Official indices' referred to by this source are gross-gross production indices; 'computed indices' are those obtained by the author.

figure; and the disparity is far lower in the case of Czechoslovakia. All these estimates may thus be taken as being at least indicative of the order of magnitude of the upward bias built into the gross-gross calculation. It is significant that, independently of Western studies in this field, an eminent Soviet authority has recently estimated that, between the start of the Soviet industrialization era and the mid-1950's, net production of Soviet industry increased thirteen fold, as against the twenty-one fold increase claimed officially on the basis of gross-gross production figures.[31]

As a corollary of the expansion, since the last war industrial structures of all three countries experienced a substantial transformation. One would presume *a priori* that the Polish change has been by far the deepest, but a precise and significant appraisal of the metamorphosis comes up against difficulties similar to those encountered in the treatment of industrial growth from other angles: structural shifts look different, depending on classifications and methods of aggregation, on relative prices, on the valuation principles (gross or net) adopted, and so on.

The impact of various ways of value-weighting may be well illustrated by the Polish case. The table below gives the shares of leading branches in gross-gross industrial output around 1960, obtained by the use of three different sets of prices.

Percentage Gross-Gross Industrial Output

	1959 current prices	*1960*	
		1956 prices	*Post-reform* current prices
Fuels	12·1	5·5	9·5
Ferrous metallurgy	4·1	7·1	8·6
Engineering products	24·3	22·2	19·7
Chemicals	7·4	9·0	9·0
Textiles	12·8	12·4	9·8

Source: Gosp. Plan., no. 3, 1961 and no. 1, 1962.

A glance at this table will tell us how, as a result of a price reform, manufacturing—both heavy and light—has been demoted. Clearly, before the price reform, the relative expansion of

[31] Strumilin, *Ocherki sotsialisticheskoy ekonomiki SSSR.*

the high-fabrication branches was exaggerated by keeping at an artificially low level the evaluation of raw and intermediate materials. Different pictures of structural change will also be obtained when criteria other than output are adopted, such as employment or wage bills. See our discussion of changes in man-power, on pp. 89f.

Ambiguities affect in particular references in official sources to changed ratios of the two broad branch groups, that is, of pro-ducer (or capital) and consumer goods industries, or alternatively of heavy and light industries. The heavy load of capital accumula-tion, i.e. of profits so defined plus indirect taxation, almost ex-clusively concentrated hitherto on consumer goods (when outputs were valued at current prices) had a particularly distorting effect. This may help to account, for instance, for the fact that during the crucial decade of post-war industrial development the shift in Polish proportions was only marginal: between 1949 and 1958 the share of consumer goods in the industrial total dropped from 53 to 49 per cent; the drop was somewhat more marked in Czecho-slovakia—from 50 to 44 per cent.

The table opposite juxtaposes some characteristics of the output structure of the three countries' industries of a quarter of a century ago with those which emerge from our weighting for the early 1960's and those of the official statistics for the latter period.

Our variant 1 yields a structure which fits in perfectly with that obtained from official statistics for East Germany in the early 1960's; it is also quite close for Poland. In both cases engineering has an identical position in the variant 1 and official computations; in both cases its share, as suggested by variant 2, is extravagantly high. (Note, on the other hand, that in the case of Czechoslovakia it is variant 2 that is nearer to the official one.) With all the emphasis, therefore, on the relativity of conclusions—relativity which verges on arbitrariness—one could perhaps venture this summary. The East German structure has undergone the comparatively smallest change, at least in respect of the domina-ting branch—engineering. It is safe to say that, in East Germany's case, the change is in the commodity composition of its output—in a shift towards 'heavier' products—rather than in the role of engineering within the industrial structure of the country. A corollary of the process is the rise in the role of chemicals and the decline in textiles, whose share appears to be cut by about one-third compared with pre-war. The same is broadly true of Poland and Czechoslovakia: in the latter, on our count, the proportion of textiles in total industrial output has been halved. Over the

	Engineering	Chemicals	Textiles
		(rounded percentages)	
Czechoslovakia			
Late 1930's	20	7	23
Early 1960's			
from official statistics	34	6	11
from our:			
variant 1	27	8	11
variant 2	32	8	11
East Germany			
Late 1930's	31	10	14
Early 1960's			
from official statistics	35	14	9
from our:			
variant 1	35	14	9
variant 2	42	13	8
Poland			
Late 1930's	10	9	15
Early 1960's			
from official statistics	21	8	9
from our:			
variant 1	21	12	10
variant 2	35	10	8

Note: Late 1930's = 1936 for East Germany, and 1937 for the two other countries. Early 1960's refer to 1961 as given by *Stat. roc., 1962*; *Stat. Jb., 1960/1961*; and *Maly rocz. stat., 1962*. All based on gross-gross output valuations.[32]

twenty-five years the share of engineering increased by something like one-half, and in Poland it was doubled. If this should be the standard, Czechoslovakia as well as East Germany would by now

[32] The share of engineering (machine construction and metal working) in net production on the accepted definition has been calculated by the Polish Central Statistical Office, for 1958, at 19·1 per cent, and that of textiles at 16·3 per cent. The disparity in share figures between gross and net calculation is particularly large for chemicals; the percentage in the latter calculation is 4 per cent. See *Dochod Narodowy Polski, 1957, 1958* (Warsaw, 1960).

rank with the industrial leaders of Western Europe, Britain and Western Germany. Here again one must make a strong reservation: international comparisons of industrial structures are probably even more treacherous than inter-temporal ones. In the particular case of engineering, differences in product-mix—especially in the proportion of capital goods, durable consumer goods, and last but not least, armaments—are no less relevant than mere percentage figures which refer the total to a national overall volume of industrial outputs.[33]

Our originally published study embraced a dollar valuation of industrial outputs reaching out into the mid-1950's, with an inter-country comparison built up on this basis. Because of the uncertainty involved these estimates were discontinued in the revised version of our inquiry. For what the results originally obtained are worth—and their value is very limited indeed—they would suggest broadly this: about the mid-1950's, on the total production basis, Poland became an industrial equal of Czechoslovakia, while East Germany's superiority declined. Considering that, since the second half of the decade, the industries of the three countries have developed more or less in step, this may be taken to be broadly true also for the early 1960's. In our showing, before the last war Poland's *per capita* industrial production was merely one-third of that of Czechoslovakia and one-seventh of that of East Germany; by the mid-1950's East Germany's *per capita* production was about one-third as large again as that of Czechoslovakia, and about double that of Poland.

What is certain, then, is that a process of levelling out industrial positions has taken place in the region. Consequently Poland has substantially risen in her industrial status. The same conclusion has been reached in the estimate carried out by the Hungarian Academy of Sciences: the main difference in the findings is that here East Germany falls behind Czechoslovakia on a *per capita* basis. A valid Polish comment has questioned this, however, and

[33] Heinz Emmerich, in *Ww.*, no. 3, 1939, p. 353, claims international comparability for the following percentage shares of metal working in the industrial total (rounded):

	East Germany	Western Germany	Czechoslovakia	UK	USA
1950	14	23	17	40	31
1958	31	32	25	43	32

No definition of terms is given.

has suggested that on this count the two countries are—we would say, 'are at least'—by now approximately equal.[34]

Member Countries of CMEA: Comparison of Industrial Status, 1961

	Czecho-slovakia	East Germany	Poland	USSR	Rumania	Hun-gary	Bul-garia	Albania
Total industrial output								
CMEA = 100	7·3	8·0	8·3	69·5	3·4	2·3	1·1	0·1
Poland = 100	88	97	100	840	41	28	14	1·3
Per capita industrial output								
CMEA = 100	167	147	88	101	59	72	45	21
Poland = 100	191	168	100	116	67	83	52	24

It may also be inferred from these estimates that the three countries of the region alone represent about one-quarter of the combined industrial potential of the CMEA partners, and nearly eight-tenths of the CMEA potential without the USSR. Another important inference is that between them the three countries of Central Europe command an industrial potential equal to one-third of that of the Soviet Union herself.[35] Soviet *per capita* output would equal about two-thirds of the Czechoslovak–East German average.

While any international comparisons of this kind must be treated with great caution, those of the CMEA as against Western countries are particularly precarious. We may, however, refer here to a recent conscientious effort to establish Poland's place *vis-à-vis* industrial countries of Western Europe.[36] The result of the inquiry is summarized in the table on page 128.

It would appear that by 1960, as far as total industrial production goes, Poland's level would correspond to one-third of the British, one-quarter of the West German, rather less than one-half of the French, and three-fifths of the Italian. (Since Czechoslovakia's and East Germany's total potentials are broadly of the same order as Poland's, the same is roughly true of each of these two countries

[34] *Materialy po ekonomicheskim voprosam sesii Vengerskoy Akademii Nauk v 1960 g.*, as quoted by A. Karpinski and B. Zielinska, in *Gosp. Plan.*, no. 6, 1962. Comment by the same authors.

[35] See also below, p. 320.

[36] A. Karpinski and M. Rakowski, in *Gosp. Plan.*, nos. 8–9, 1961.

as well.) On a *per capita* basis, on this showing, Poland would be in
the same class as Italy. The estimate is based on outputs of electric
power, fuels, crude steel, sulphuric acid, cement, cotton and

Poland's Industrial Output Compared with Four Western European
Countries

	Total		Per capita	
	1937	*1960*	*1937*	*1960*
UK	13	33	18	57
France	24	45	29	69
Western Germany	13	25	16	47
Italy	43	61	54	102

woollen yarn, and chemical fibres. As the authors of the study
rightly note, their findings tend to overstate the place of the less
developed countries, since—with higher technology and a more
refined output pattern—industrially advanced nations obtain
higher values of final products from the same material inputs.
Our computation for the mid-1950's (as mentioned, discontinued)
suggested that the total industrial output of Czechoslovakia and
of Poland represented about half the Italian and one-third of the
French level. The relative 'truth' may lie to-day somewhere
between. We would like to re-emphasize the need for a relativistic
approach in these matters.

CHAPTER IV

Energy

INDUSTRIAL growth is an energy-consuming process. Its history can, indeed, be written in terms of energy consumption. Only recently, however, have Europeans, in the West and the East alike, become increasingly aware of this fact of economic life.

RESOURCES OF PRIMARY ENERGY

Among the nations of Europe Poland is outstandingly well endowed in primary energy. Only Britain and Western Germany take precedence of her in total energy-wealth; and only the latter in energy *per capita*.[1] Czechoslovakia is less, and East Germany far less, fortunate. Measured per head, Czechoslovak resources are something like one-sixth, and East German about one-tenth, of the Polish figure. Poland possesses no less than four-fifths of the total wealth of the whole area. Since this is based almost entirely on hard coal, it is small wonder that the Poles look upon hard coal as the mainstay of their economic life. The tables on pp. 130–1 specify in greater detail each country's reserves of the various kinds of primary energy. A glance will show that the bulk of it consists of solid fuels.

Hard Coal

The hard-coal wealth of the area is primarily concentrated in Silesia—or, to be more exact, in the two Silesian basins. The Upper Silesian is by far the larger, in fact it is the largest continuous coalfield of Continental Europe, covering about 5,800 square kilometres.[2] The Lower Silesian basin—in the neighbourhood

[1] See table on p. 130.

[2] This is the figure broadly accepted by most Polish sources, e.g. F. Barcinski, *Bogactwa kopalne Polski* (Lodz, 1947), and by older German sources, e.g. C. Gaebler, *Das oberschlesische Steinkohlenbecken* (Katowice, 1909). Some later German authorities give a much larger area. P. H. Seraphim, *Industrie–Kombinat Oberschlesien—das Ruhr-gebiet des Ostens* (Cologne–Braunsfeld, 1953), puts it at 8,500 sq. km., 1,300 of which belong to Czechoslovakia.

These figures refer to the 'Great Upper Silesian' basin which includes the Dabrova, Cracow, and Ostrava–Karvina basins as well as that of Upper Silesia proper.

of Walbrzych—covers only about one-seventh of this area. The industrial exploitation of Silesian coalfields goes back as far as the mid-eighteenth century. It has had a chequered history over the following two centuries, marked by successive shifts in political sovereignties and the resulting changes in economic environment and policies. Its core owes the impetus of its initial development to the paternalist Frederician policies which aimed

Total and Per Capita Reserves of Energy

I. Estimate by UN, Department of Economic and Social Affairs, 1956

	Coal					Energy	
	Hard	Brown	Oil	Natural gas	Water power	Total	Per capita
	(In 10^9 electricity equivalent)					10^3 kwh	
America	11,299,672	1,272,290	72,094	66,710	905	13,771,765	39,597
Africa	613,712	633	243	.	1,531	2,145,636	10,159
Asia	3,169,488	21,938	131,892	849	1,228	4,552,167	3,171
Oceania	135,152	104,850	155	.	47	287,372	20,976
USSR	9,920,000	527,732	16,284	10,261	464	11,045,677	53,358
Europe	4,675,040	431,791	2,070	3,482	574	5,711,019	14,231
of which:							
Czecho-slovakia	48,000	31,250	12	0·3	7	86,262	7,013
E. Germany	1,800	122,500	.	.	2	126,300	6,902
Poland	1,088,000	24,325	32	.	6	1,118,357	42,202
Austria	176	5,843	354	.	40	46,373	6,721
Belgium–Luxbrg.	47,904	.	.	.	1	48,904	5,374
Denmark	.	125	.	.	.	125	28
France	96,000	1,050	60	64	60	158,674	3,699
Germany (FR)	1,792,000	157,500	593	.	16	1,966,093	38,400
Netherlands	32,000	20	173	.	—	32,193	3,066
Norway	64,000	.	.	.	105	169,000	
Sweden	800	1,600	.	.	80	104,720	
Switzerland	.	.	.	.	30	30,000	6,122
UK	1,368,000	1,200	6	.	9	1,379,022	27,093
Greece	.	5,000	.	.	4	9,000	1,154
Italy	5,696	1,072	8	742	52	59,518	1,237
Spain	64,000	3,750	.	.	32	99,750	3,500

Note: The following coefficients have been used: 1 ton of hard coal=8,000 kwh; 1 ton of brown coal=2,500 kwh; 1 ton of petroleum=12,500 kwh; 1 cu. m. natural gas=10·6 kwh. In most cases estimated water-power resources in kwh are based on capacity at Q^{95} or low water, assuming an annual utilization of 8,000 hours.

Source: *Peaceful Uses of Atomic Energy.* Vol. i, *The World's Requirements for Energy* (N.Y., 1956), pp. 99ff.

at the creation of an industrial armament base in Silesia for the rising military power of Prussia. The latter part of the eighteenth century and the early years of the nineteenth witnessed a vigorous

Total and Per Capita Reserves of Energy
II. Estimate by ECE (1958)

Type of Energy	Unit	Millions of units	Units per head of population[1]	Reserves as multiples of production in 1953	Electric power equivalent Total calorific value (10^9 kwh)	Per head (10^3 kwh)
Czechoslovakia						
Hard coal	t.	6,000	450	296	79,250	
Brown coal	t.	12,500	950	364		
Petroleum	t.	1	0·1	9·5[2]	12	
Natural gas	cu. m.	3,000	229	18·7	32	
Hydro power	kwh/ year	12,000	920	16·0[3]	12,000	
					91,294	6,975
East Germany						
Hard coal	t.	162	9	61	77,400	
Brown coal	t.	30,455	1,710	176		
Hydro power	kwh/ year	2,000	112	13[3]	2,000	
					79,400	4,453
Poland						
Hard coal	t.	135,000[4]	4,950	1,520	1,169,750	
Brown coal	t.	33,000	1,100	5,350		
Peat	t.	5,900	215			
Petroleum	t.	2·7	0·1	14·6[5]	32	
Hydro power	kwh/ year	13,500	490	5·0[3]	13,000	
					1,182,782	43,131

[1] Based on 1955 population.
[2] Based on 1955 output.   [3] Proportion harnessed in 1955.
[4] To a depth of 2,000 metres. Reserves at a depth of 1,000 metres, i.e. the more accessible deposits, are estimated at about 75,900 mill. tons.
[5] Based on 1956 production.
Source: ECE, *Possibilities of Electric Power Exchanges between the Countries of Central and South-Eastern Europe* (Geneva, 1958), Annex.

expansion in the parts of Silesia belonging to Prussia and to the Russian Empire. This was stimulated in the German Reich by favourable marketing arrangements arrived at with Silesia's Westphalian competitors and in the Russian Empire by the high tariff walls which secured a virtual monopoly of feeding the rapidly developing industries of the Polish 'Congress Kingdom' (the part of Poland allotted to Russia at the Congress of Vienna).

Over the three decades preceding the First World War the output of Silesian coal trebled and reached about 60 million tons, about 85 per cent of which came from mines within the German frontiers. As a result of the war Poland emerged as the principal partner in Silesian coal production, followed by Germany and Czechoslovakia—some three-fifths of the pre-1914 output area now belonged to her. New boundaries drawn across the existing production units and traditional markets entailed serious difficulties, which were very soon aggravated by the Great Depression. Success in exporting, above all to Scandinavia, particularly after the British coal strike of 1926, brought some relief.

During the short interlude of the Second World War the whole of the Silesian coal-producing area was, for the first time, united under a single political control. Post-war territorial arrangements preserved much of the unity of the Silesian basins, now exclusively in Polish and Czechoslovak hands. Czechoslovakia owns rather less than one-sixth of the Great Upper Silesian coalfield and nearly one-third of that of Lower Silesia. Partnership in the control of the sources of energy forming the basis of their economies thus seemed to predestine the two nations for economic integration.

Upper Silesia forms the core of Poland's hard-coal mining: it accounts for about 90 per cent of her known resources, and for a still greater share of her output. About the same proportion of the Czechoslovak deposits is situated in the Ostrava–Karvina basin, where four-fifths of the country's hard coal is mined; there are minor basins in the regions of Kladno and Plzen.

The meaning of estimates of mineral wealth depends on definitions. They may refer to proven, probable, and possible, to measured, or to inferred, reserves. In any case the economic value of the riches of the sub-soil varies according to their depth, depending on the changing technological conditions and—consequently —costs. This must be borne in mind when reference is made to various, very often conflicting, assessments.

Polish official sources appear to accept an estimate of about 85,000 million tons at a depth not exceeding 1,000 metres (135,000 million tons down to double that depth).[3] This, under

---

[3] *Rocz. pol. i gosp., 1959*, p. 446.

the surface mentioned above, would imply a formidable average of some 27 million tons per square kilometre—a concentration of coal believed to be the heaviest in the world. The leading German authority, Professor Friedensburg,[4] gives an estimate of about 150,000 million tons for the same depth. Professor Bohdanowicz[5] arrived at about 112,000 million tons to a depth of about 1,800 metres and 74,000 million down to 1,200 metres. V. H. Winston,[6] who provides an excellent résumé of estimates at various depths— which can be considered realistic under prevailing technological conditions—arrived at a probable total of about 100,000 million tons down to 1,370 metres. In another study[7] the same author accepts estimates of 112,000 million tons for Poland and 13,000 million for Czechoslovakia.[8]

Average Depth and Thickness of Producing Coal Seams in Selected European Countries

(*metres*)

	Depth	*Thickness*
Poland	325	3·50
United Kingdom	360	1·20
Western Germany	700	1·50
France	420	1·20
Belgium	800	0·80

Source: ECE, *Survey, 1951*, p. 162.

[4] F. Friedensburg, *Die Bergwirtschaft der Erde* (Stuttgart, 1942).
[5] K. Bohdanowicz, in Z. *Gosp.*, no. 21, 1946, p. 839. According to this source Polish reserves, to a depth of 1,800 metres, are distributed as follows (000 mill. tons).

	Upper Silesia	*Lower Silesia*
Proven	15·5	0·8
Probable	91·7	2·2
Possible	1·6	.
Total	108·8	3·0

[6] *In Amer. Slavic and E. Eur. R.*, xv/1, pp. 140ff.
[7] 'Mineral Resources', in N. J. G. Pounds and N. Spulber eds., *Resources and Planning in Eastern Europe* (Bloomington, Ind.; 1957), p. 80.
[8] K. König, *Der Steinkohlbergbau in Oberschlesien von 1945–1955* (Marburg, 1958), pp. 1–5, quotes German estimates for resources, down to 1,000 metres, of 74,600 mill. tons inside the present frontiers of Poland and 4,700–6,100 mill. tons in Czechoslovakia.

On the whole, Upper (but not Lower) Silesian hard-coal deposits are relatively close to the surface and are among the thickest in Europe.

Two-fifths and four-fifths respectively of the coal mined at the end of the 1950's was derived from seams up to 300 and 500 metres deep, and about half from thicker ones; nearly eight-ninths was obtained from seams with an angle of up to 25° only.[9] All this combines to form comparatively advantageous conditions for sinking and exploiting a pit, also, in particular, for mechanization, ventilation, vertical haulage, and general maintenance—a factor worth keeping in mind when the competitiveness of Polish coal *vis-à-vis* other coals, and fuels other than coal, comes up for discussion.

The quality of Silesian coal is high. Ash content in raw coal is very low, e.g. coal in the saddle-group seams (from which about half the Polish coal comes) contains about 3 per cent of ash. The heating value in Polish coals amounts to 7,250–8,600 kcal/kg:[10] the Czechoslovak average is stated to be 5,090 kcal/kg[11] Both types of coal are noted for their hardness; this and other qualities make them suitable for long-distance transport.

One special property of coal is of prime importance for industry. Coke carbon is still the sole chemical agent for the reduction of iron-ore in blast-furnaces. Suitability for coking is, therefore, a characteristic by which coal wealth can be judged as a basis of metallurgy. (This depends on various factors, among others on geological conditions.) About three-fifths of Czechoslovakia's output is cokable, and about two-fifths yields coke of a very high quality. Virtually the whole of Czechoslovak coking-coal output comes from the Ostrava–Karvina region. The proportion is much smaller in Poland—less than one-fifth only, and the quality of the coke is, on the whole, lower. But about two-fifths of the reserves in her smaller, Lower Silesian, basin is of good coking quality. Working conditions, however, are far more difficult than in Upper Silesia.

While, thanks to her Moravian reserves, Czechoslovakia is in a

[9] *Gosp. Plan.*, no. 11, 1959, p. 36.

[10] Data on quality of Polish coal mainly from Professor B. Krupinski, in *Polish Foreign Trade*, no. 3, p. 6.

[11] M. Rataj, in *Plan. Hosp.*, no. 5, 1957, p. 31, gives the overall average of coal mined in Czechoslovakia at 4,099 kcal/kg, the heat value of hard coal and brown coal being 5,090 and 3,492 kcal/kg respectively. The basis of classification has not been given.

more favourable position as regards both the overall ratio of her cokable coal and its quality, Poland is more fortunate in the size of her reserve.[12]

East Germany is endowed with only very meagre hard-coal wealth. This was indeed the chief weakness with which the Soviet zone was born as a separate economic body. Deposits are located mainly in the regions of Zwickau, Oelsnitz, and Freital.[13] There are minor deposits in the Poltz area and in the more recently opened-up fields of Doberlugk-Kirchhain. The three main coal-producing regions have reserves estimated—down to a depth of 2,000 metres—at about 110 million tons, a mere fraction per cent, of those of West Germany.

Brown Coal

The deficiency in hard coal in some countries has long since focused attention on brown coal as an important subsidiary source of energy in Central Europe—it has rightly been called the specifically mid-European type of coal. To quote Professor Friedensburg:[14]

The industrialization of what used to be Central Germany, promoted plan-wise out of defence considerations and constituting one of the most remarkable phenomena in German economic developments in recent decades, was based essentially on brown coal—spread over a large surface.

The East German brown-coal industry experienced a tremendous upsurge in the First World War, and was expanded thereafter.

East German total reserves in brown coal are estimated at about 25,000 million tons—a figure which may be only moderately increased by intensive geological surveys now in progress. It is located mainly in the Leipzig region (20 per cent), in Upper and Lower Lusatia (60 per cent), in the Mitteldeutsche Revier, centred around Halle, Bitterfeld, Merseburg, Zeitz (20 per cent), and in the small Oder basin cut roughly into halves by the post-1945 Polish–German frontier. The centre of gravity is shifting towards the Lusatian coalfields, which yield high-quality raw material for briquettes and coke, the more so as their deposits

---

[12] See below, p. 181.
[13] Germany (FR) Bundesministerium für gesamtdeutsche Fragen, *Kohlenindustrie in der sowjetischen Zone* (Bonn, 1951), gives the reserves of the Zwickau, Oelsnitz, Freital areas at 60·7 mill. tons, down to a depth of 1,200 metres.
[14] Friedensburg, *Bergwirtschaft der Erde, passim.*

occur in larger concentrations, which form mines containing 200–500 million tons or even more. Surface mining is virtually the only technique feasible on economic grounds: 98 per cent of the brown coal produced in East Germany is obtained from open-cast mines.

Czechoslovakia is the only one among the three countries whose solid fuel wealth is more or less evenly divided between hard and brown coal: the ratio being about 3 : 2 in terms of calorific content.[15] About four-fifths of her deposits of brown coal are found in north-west Bohemia, which represents 70 per cent of the industry in terms of output. Of some importance is the Slovak brown coalfield of Handlova (about one-sixth of her reserves); intensive exploration is in progress in small newly opened-up basins. Slightly more than one-quarter of her brown coal is derived from open-cast mines, but the proportion is rapidly declining; it was still nearly two-fifths around the mid-1950's.

Poland also has substantial resources of brown coal. Probable and possible reserves have, in fact, been estimated as high as 33,000 or even 38,000 million tons, which would place Poland third in Europe, after the German Federal Republic and East Germany but ahead of Czechoslovakia.[16] Her proved resources, on the other hand, are comparatively small. At any rate the abundance of hard coal has resulted—until very recently—in neglect of inferior fuels. The two principal fields, for which development projects are in hand, are situated in the Turoszow area, on the German frontier, and round Konin in Central Poland.

Brown coal varies in quality as between the three countries and the various fields. Different sources take the calorific value of Czech, East German, and Polish brown coal to correspond to a ratio of between 1·7–2, 4–4·5, and about 3 tons as equivalent to one ton of hard coal.[17] Classifications, however, vary greatly in drawing a border line between hard and brown coal (which makes, incidentally, for a high degree of uncertainty in statistics).

Brown coal is an increasingly versatile fuel. It lends itself to gasification—both for fuel purposes and for chemical synthesis.

[15] Rataj, in *Plan. Hosp.*, no. 5, 1957, p. 325. According to this source, solid fuels make up 99·79% of total reserves: of this, hard coal, brown coal, and lignites represent 57·86, 38·08, and 3·85% respectively.
See also J. H. Wszelaki, *Fuel and Power in Captive Middle Europe* (N.Y., 1952), p. 18.
[16] A. Strzeminski, in *Gosp. Plan.*, no. 1, 1958, p. 32; *Rocz. pol. gosp.*, *1959*, p. 446.
[17] ECE, *The Electric Power Situation in Europe in 1956* (1958), p. 19: ECE, *Survey*, *1948*, p. 236; *1951*, p. 227.

Because of its high weight-to-heat-value ratio it is most suitable as a fuel basis for power stations sited near coalfields. Generally speaking, because it is on the whole located eccentrically *vis-à-vis* the main industrial areas of both Poland and Czechoslovakia, it creates in both these countries a considerable transport problem: this is true also—if not to the same extent—of East Germany.

Oil

The area under survey is very poor in natural oil. In the last century Poland was one of the pioneering countries in the European oil industry. Already before the last war, however, her resources were dwindling. Over the quarter of a century after 1913 Polish output of crude oil was halved, falling to about half a million tons before the outbreak of the Second World War. With consumption at a very low level, even this comparatively smaller quantity was more than sufficient to meet Poland's requirements. The annexation of Poland's eastern territories by the Soviet Union after the Second World War deprived her of the most productive parts of her oil basin in the Drohobycz–Boryslaw area. Exploitation of oil resources is largely confined to the traditional sub-Carpathian oil regions, but successful prospecting for oil and gas is reported from the northern lowlands as well as the Carpathian foothills. Technical aid is provided under the CMEA arrangements. Recently new deposits of oil and high-grade gas suitable for industrial use have been discovered in the Mielec, Jaroslaw, Lubaczow areas (not taken into account in our table of resources); they have not yet been fully assessed, but are believed considerably to increase the proved reserves.

Czechoslovakia turns to the exploitation of her small resources of oil and natural gas mainly in the area forming the eastern extension of the Austrian fields. It is claimed that during the second half of the 1950's her proved reserves of oil were increased fivefold and those of natural gas doubled. East German resources are negligible.

Water Power

Hydraulic resources form a relatively small part of the three countries' total energy resources. East Germany, with the smallest potential, claims the highest degree of exploitation, roughly corresponding to the average for the whole of Europe. Poland, with the lowest degree of harnessed resources, has her largest potential concentrated on the Vistula.

It is only in Czechoslovakia, owing to more favourable topographical and geological conditions, that hydro-electricity plays even a modest role in power economy. About two-thirds of her exploitable resources are located in Slovakia, chiefly on the Vah, and are being harnessed as part of the programmes for the industrialization of eastern Slovakia. About one-third of the Bohemian potential is formed by the Vltava basin. Practical feasibility of exploitation is limited by the lack of workable sites, as well as by growing water requirements for human consumption and industrial and agricultural uses. As in Western Europe, in spite of technological advances, the capital outlay on hydro plants per unit of output is rising steeply. The formidable political and technical, as well as financial, problem of the utilization of the Danube waters by the riparian countries forms a category by itself.

Nuclear Fuel

Both Czechoslovakia and East Germany have relatively substantial reserves of nuclear fuel. Indeed Czechoslovakia can rightly be called the cradle of the atomic-fuel mining industry. Its history goes back to the eighteenth century, when uranium was identified in the Bohemian silver mines at Jachymov. (Maria Curie-Sklodowska's famous research was carried out on the uranium from that area.) The deposits originally mined are believed to be heavily depleted, but extraction has been extended in post-war years to the lead and zinc-mining regions of Pribram, and, more recently, along the Brdy ranges in the Vimpark–Kasparske Hory region, in the Summava Mountains, and in the Riesengebirge.

The intensive working of the original mines must have considerably reduced East German resources too, but here also the mining area has been widened owing to wartime and post-war prospecting. The centre of gravity of the East German industry still remains within the wider Riesengebirge area around Johanngeorgenstadt and the regions of Schneeberg, Aue, Oberschlemma and between Dresden and Freiberg.[18]

[18] During the negotiations of January 1957 in Moscow President Zapotocky of Czechoslovakia claimed that his country was one of the leaders in the world's uranium-ore mining. A similar claim has also been made for East Germany. Neither has been substantiated with any degree of precision.

Poland is also known to mine uranium in the Riesengebirge on a small scale, mainly in the Klodzko region; her resources have been considered to be unimportant, but it was stated recently 'that more good deposits of ore have been discovered'.[19]

To wind up this brief outline of primary sources of energy in the area under review, one remark may not be out of place. As has already been hinted at, even within their terms (and these are by their very nature narrowly circumscribed even in such industrially developed an area as is Central Europe), geological data provide a very relative picture of workable potential. Hence, in particular, calculations of the lifetime of reserves can be read only with the utmost caution. Changes in technologies tend radically to affect the picture—sometimes in a revolutionary way. So do the inter-acting changes in relative cost position, and economic feasibilities in general. Polish coal—the core of the area's energy potential—is a signal case in point. From the figures of the table on p. 131 for what they are worth, its resources would seem to be sufficient for a millennium and a half—in practical terms, inexhaustible. We shall see later how these appearances must be qualified.[20]

PRODUCTION OF PRIMARY ENERGY, 1937–62

During the last war, when the Czechoslovak and Polish hard-coal basins came under a unified control, the all-time peak of 116 million tons of hard coal mined was achieved (in 1943). On the other hand maintenance and safety were neglected, quality of output was lowered, productivity declined—though it was made up by additions to manpower, the substantial part of which consisted of forced labour. Despite dislocations, the progress made in the initial post-war rehabilitation of mining was indeed spectacular. Fuel was the key element in reconstruction. Poland entered into special commitments *vis-à-vis* the USSR. Ready markets were waiting for Polish exports in fuel-starved Europe. Moreover the first attempt at a Polish–Czechoslovak *rapprochement* in the economic sphere was greatly dependent on Poland's ability quickly to make up Czechoslovakia's own fuel deficits.

Within a few years, by 1948, both countries reached and sur-passed their pre-war levels of output. Thereafter the pace slowed

---

[19] Statement by the Government's Plenipotentiary for the Peaceful Utilization of Nuclear Energy, *Trybuna Ludu*, 14 Aug. 1958.
[20] See below, pp. 168f.

down. It was only in 1955 that the all-time peak could be regained. Expansion was more rapid in the old Polish lands than in the new Western territories: the latter lagged behind, owing both to the higher degree of exhaustion of deposits and a lack of sites for new mines.

Output of Hard and Brown Coal, 1937–60

| | 1937 | 1943 | 1945 | 1950 | 1960 | 1962 | Plans | | | |
							1965	1970	1975	1980
Hard Coal										
Czechoslovakia	16·7	24·2	11·5	18·5	26·5	27	36	..	38	..
East Germany	3·5	..	..	2·8	..	2·7	..	..	..	..
Poland—pre-										
war terr.	36·2	..								
post-war										
terr.	67·5	91·4	24·8	78·0	104	110	112–113	125	135	
Brown Coal										
Czechoslovakia	17·5	27·6	15·4	26·4	56	69	73	80	100	140
East Germany	101·0[1]	..	..	137·0	226	247	278	350	..	400–500
Poland	0·02	..	..	4·8	9	11	27	..	60	110

[1] 1936.

By the early 1960's Poland mined three times more coal than before the war within her pre-war frontiers. This implies a production half again as high in the present territory. The Czechoslovak increase in hard-coal output is of the same order.

This Polish and Czechoslovak rate of expansion in coal-mining corresponds broadly to that for the world as a whole. But it testifies to a considerable success when set against progress in Western Europe. Since the later 1950's the impetus has been lost in Central Europe, while Western European coal mining has suffered a set-back.

Thanks partly to her territorial acquisitions and partly to the rapid initial post-war pace of expansion, Poland has risen in rank as a coal producer. Her share in the world's output of hard coal has been doubled. Output per head of her reduced population has more than trebled. Indeed on a *per capita* basis she occupies the second place in the world, preceded only by Britain. On total output basis she ranks sixth in the world, that is, after the United States, the USSR, Britain, Western Germany, and China.

Cut off from the Ruhr hard coal, East Germany made an all-out effort to expand production of her local substitute. At the threshold of the 1960's her output was more than twice the pre-war quantity. On lower absolute levels Czechoslovakia's record was relatively still more spectacular, with more than trebled production and an increased share in world output.

Only since the end of the 1950's is more attention being paid in Poland to the development of brown coal and its production gradually expanded (see below, p. 169).

The output of oil has been more or less stabilized on its modest levels, but the end of the 1950's saw in Poland and Czechoslovakia a relatively considerable development in the production of natural gas.

Crude-Oil Production, 1937–62

(000 tons)

	1937	*1949*	*1950*	*1960*	*1962 (est.)*
Czechoslovakia	n.a.	n.a.	122	137	140
Poland					
pre-war terr.	501	.	.	.	.
post-war terr.	170	152	n.a.	n.a.	200

Gas is the competitive fuel *par excellence*; there is hardly any sphere of use where it could not technologically compete with other fuels. New discoveries and technological developments have drawn attention in both East and West to natural gas as a valuable source of energy. The main drawbacks in its industrial exploitation are the comparatively high fixed cost and its dependence on distributing networks. The size of the indigenous resources in the area is rather uncertain. Czechoslovak reserves have been estimated at about 3,000 million cubic metres, and Polish—at between 7,000 and 15,000 million cubic metres: the newly discovered gas field in the Lubaczow–Jaroslaw–Sedziszow area is known to have favourable geological conditions for development.

Before the last war Poland was producing about one-third of the whole of Europe's supply of natural gas at the then prevailing low levels. Though the loss of the greater part of her oilfields to the USSR caused a fall in gas output, a vigorous drive has made up for the early post-war decline. Stimulated by the rising demand for energy, and by pressure on other sources of supply, the share of gas in the area's energy economy is growing.

Production of Gas, 1960
(*ooo mill. cu. m.*)

	Natural	*Coke*	*Gas-works*	*Total*
Czechoslovakia	1·80 (est.)	3·57	.	6·2 (est.)
East Germany	.			
Poland	0·60	4·40	0·80	5·80

Source: UN, *World Energy Supplies* (N.Y., 1962), vii, 104–5. A cubic metre of natural gas = 2·22 cu. m. of manufactured gas. Blast-furnace gas not included (output in 1958 = 2,010 million cu. m.).

Throughout the area greater effort is being put into the collection and utilization of manufactured as well as of natural gas. Growing metallurgy provides an expanding supply of gas from blast-furnaces and coke ovens in addition to that obtained in the conventional gas-works, where the main raw material is coal. Expansion of oil-refining provides a source of tail gases. In all the three countries more attention is now paid, as has already been noted, to the gasification of lower-grade coals. In East Germany, until recently, the proportion of brown and hard coal used in the production of gas corresponded to about 2 : 3; it is expected soon to be reversed. In Czechoslovakia projects are in hand to gasify coal directly at less valuable coal seams.

The campaign for fuller utilization of gas resources is supported by an expansion of the distribution network. Long-distance gas pipelines have been built, or are under construction, throughout the region.

Data on the progress of uranium-mining are so scarce that only a brief mention of this can be made here to complete our summary of primary-energy production. All it is safe to say is that, in both Czechoslovakia and East Germany, the mining and concentrating of uranium ore form major industrial branches.[21] It is believed

[21] According to Dr Shimkin, the last known output data for the Czechoslovak mines refer to the inter-war and war periods: output reached a maximum of 32 tons of U_3O_8 in 1936 and dropped during the German occupation.

East Germany's recorded inter-war maximum was 400–450 tons of concentrate (with a uranium-oxide content of 2%).

Dr Shimkin estimates that production of U_3O_8 in the USSR and Central and

that employment in the East German industry amounted at its peak to 350,000, but that it was subsequently reduced in step with improvement in the originally very primitive techniques, and that, by the end of the 1950's, most of the sorting and loading and all the haulage had been mechanized and electrified. Considerable advances are also known to have been achieved in the technology of this industry in Czechoslovakia.

Little can be said with any degree of certainty about the prospects of the industry. Professor Friedensburg[22] estimated, around the mid-1950's, that production of East German uranium amounted to 3–4 per cent of the world total, but he expected a rapid decline as mining expanded in the United States, Canada, South Africa, and other countries.

CONSUMPTION OF PRIMARY ENERGY

Along with the steep rise of totals of energy produced and consumed in the region one or two characteristics stand out in the picture provided by the last section. First—in contrast to Western Europe—there has been a considerable degree of stability in the Central European consumption pattern: the displacement of coal by other fuels[23] has been far less marked here than in the West. Between 1950 and the early 1960's the share of coal in Western European consumption has dropped from three-quarters to about one-half. For the three countries it is still 80–90 per cent, the shift away from coal being comparatively the strongest in Czechoslovakia.

The second and interrelated feature is the continuing far greater reliance of Central Europe on indigenous energy. Already at the end of the 1950's Western Europe depended on outside sources for about one-third of the quantity consumed, while the three Central

---

Eastern Europe rose from about 10 tons in 1945 to about 150 by 1950. As against this, E. Kohl estimated the output of Czechoslovakia alone for 1950 as 400 tons and that of East Germany, in the Schneeberg district, at over 150 tons for 1948. Cf. D. Shimkin, *Minerals a Key to Soviet Power* (Cambridge, Mass., 1953), p. 147 and *passim*; E. Kohl, *Die metallischen Rohstoffe* (Stuttgart, 1954), p. 141; and V. H. Winston, 'Mineral Resources', in Pounds and Spulber, pp. 61ff.

An estimate in the *Financial Times* (13 May 1957) put the Soviet Bloc's output of uranium in 1957 at about 6,000 tons, about 800 tons of this being produced outside the USSR, half of it in Czechoslovakia and East Germany. According to the same source the Soviet Angara and Ukhta deposits alone may be producing 2,000 tons a year by 1960.

[22] F. Friedensburg, in *Der Volkswirt*, no. 47, 1956.   [23] See below, p. 154.

European nations were still having some overall surplus of output over use. But this is almost continuously—even if only gradually—falling. Moreover, the overall surplus conceals a growing specific deficit in liquid fuels. As the use of the latter rises and Polish exportable surpluses of coal decline, the area's energy economy finds itself in a rather precarious overall balance which, around the mid-1960's, may be expected to turn into an overall deficit, if only a marginal one.

Some—at least *prima facie*—striking facts will appear from an international comparison between the three countries' consumption of primary energy—both actual and planned for the middle of this decade.

Consumption of Primary Energy Per Capita
(*tons hard-coal equivalent*)

	1960	1965 (plan)		1960
Czechoslovakia	5·0	6·0	France	3·0
East Germany	5·0	.	Germany (FR)	4·0
Poland	3·1	3·6	Italy	1·6
			Netherlands	3·0
			Norway	2·38
Belgium–Luxembourg	2·8	.	Sweden	2·97
United Kingdom	4·74	.	Switzerland	1·67

Source: UN, *The Coal Situation in Europe in 1960/61* (Geneva, 1961).

Both Czechoslovakia and East Germany appear to have, on this count, a consumption level considerably higher than that of Western Germany, and quite close to that of Britain. Poland's *per capita* quantity is not far from the West German; it is higher than that of France, and roughly three times that of Italy. The three countries' area as a whole outstrips Western Europe by a considerable margin. Their *per capita* consumption would, therefore, seem to be well beyond that justified by their place as industrial economies.[24] However, comparisons such as this call for

[24] The exceptionally high consumption of energy in Poland has been brought out by J. Jedruszek's attempt to correlate it to national income (cf. *Ekon.*, no. 4, 1960, p. 813). According to this source the following quantities of primary energy were consumed in 1955 per $1,000 of national income (tons hard-coal equivalent): Poland

a number of very serious qualifications. Conversion of consumed quantities into conventional units (in this case into hard-coal 'equivalent' with conventional calorie content) conceals discrepancies in effective use, calorie for calorie. They arise from differences in the composition of quantities used, by sources of energy and by the final form in which they are used in a given country. The factors combined influence the overall efficiency of energy applied in a given economy; and in the particular case of the three Central European countries they tend to result in very high rates of consumption.

In the light of the data on *per capita* consumption summarized here, it may be of some interest to relate the area's levels of primary-energy consumption to the pace of its economic growth; and to compare developments in the three countries. Here again the experience of the three countries would fail to coincide with the usually observed relationship between changes in energy requirements and in national products: such observations seem to suggest that—as a rule—Gross National Product outstrips energy consumption. But here again the interrelation between the two is a rather complex phenomenon: it is influenced by such factors as the type of industrialization, the product composition, the relative importance of energy-intensive processes,[25] and efficiency in energy utilization. It is arguable that, on several counts, the conditions which prevailed in the countries under survey favoured rather a high rate of increase in the consumption of fuels.

The special circumstances of countries in process of rapid industrialization should also be borne in mind, particularly in the case of Poland, a country on the way towards gaining momentum in industrial growth. Under these conditions the use of energy may, in fact, tend to increase faster than national product, because of the rapid widening of the spheres of intensive energy consumption.[26]

A further element to be borne in mind is that gains in fuel efficiency may tend to follow—as often as not only with a considerable lag—the industrial development of a country. This is

9·35; France 2·75; UK 3·79; Germany (FR) 5·37; Belgium 3·87; Netherlands 3·67; Italy 2·36; Spain 3·38.

[25] E. S. Mason, and others, 'Energy Requirements and Economic Growth', in *Peaceful Uses of Atomic Energy*, i, 54.

[26] Ibid. p. 56.

particularly true where primary energy is comparatively abundant, as again is the case in Poland.[27]

Gross National Product, Industrial Output, Consumption of Energy and Electricity, 1956

(1937 = 100)

	Consumption of		Gross National Product		Industrial output	
	Energy	Electricity	Official index	Computed index	Official index	Computed index
Czechoslovakia	177	404	184	161	266	184
East Germany	148	223	...	141	224	136
Poland						
pre-war terr.		542	240?	156	535	251
post-war terr.	292			128		170
OEEC	139	307	144		182	
EEC	139	300	...		202	

Sources: Gross National Product, see pp. 000–00. Index number basis 1937, 1936, and 1938 for Czechoslovakia, East Germany, and Poland respectively. Industrial output, see above pp. 000–00. For Western countries see OEEC, *Industrial Statistics, 1900–1957* (Paris, 1958), pp. 8, 19, 22, 52.

Faulty allocational mechanism and, in a centrally planned system, a lack of rationally formulated energy policy may not be without blame for the abnormal use of energy. Only very recently have the three countires become alive to this need, and tried to develop an integrated approach to problems of energy economy.

The historical line of development in energy consumption points not only to its growth but also to a continuous structural change. A clear trend is discernible in the area as well as in most countries of Europe—a rising proportion of the processed at the expense of the primary forms of energy in both Poland and Czechoslovakia. By the late 1950's about two-thirds of their hard coal was consumed in processed form.

[27] Poland's average fuel efficiency, i.e. the proportion of gross energy-output ultimately utilized, is about 20%. This is slightly below the world average. The rate is about 34% in Belgium, 58% in Switzerland, 13% in Japan, and 6% in India. Cf. Professor Meiro (*Ż. Warszawy*, 24 Apr. 1957), and in *Peaceful Uses of Atomic Energy*, 'Contribution of Nuclear Energy to Future World Power Needs'.

It has been estimated that, over the century which followed 1860, the efficiency of the world's energy system roughly doubled (F. C. Putnam, *Energy in the Future* (N.Y., 1954)).

ELECTRICITY, PATENT FUELS, AND OIL

One line of development is the 'upgrading' of coal—by conversion into coke, gas, and patent fuels. Another—with a particularly strong nexus with economic growth—is the conversion of primary forms of energy into thermal electricity. Electricity helps to overcome the locational and other rigidities of an economy. It has a close link with technological progress. On the one hand it thrives on its spread. On the other it gives a forceful spur to advanced techniques. Higher technologies tend to raise the quantities of electric power consumed, but, as technology is perfected, it tends to reduce energy-inputs per unit of output. It is the countries with the higher ratios of electricity in total energy consumption which at the same time show the highest fuel efficiency.

Electricity is the industrial form of energy *par excellence*. More than two-thirds of the energy consumed in Western Europe in this form goes to industry. The proportion is three-fifths for East Germany, three-quarters for Czechoslovakia, and somewhere between the two for Poland.

Before the last war, even by German high standards, what is now the GDR was an area of very high power consumption, higher than that of the present Federal Republic. Between the outbreak of the war and the beginning of the 1960's East Germany's output—roughly corresponding to her use—increased two and a half times. Output rose nearly fivefold in Czechoslovakia and six and a half times in Poland (but only three and a half times within the latter's present frontiers). Both countries, in contrast to East Germany, improved their position in the world table. But East Germany—along with Britain and Western Germany—still occupies one of the leading places in this.

In contrast to total energy consumption, that of electricity has been rising in most of the expanding economies considerably faster than industrial output, a trend which in part merely reflects the substitution of this for other forms of energy. Between 1900 and 1937, and over the two following decades, the consumption of electric power in Western Europe increased tenfold and three times respectively, while industrial output rose approximately three and a half times and by four-fifths.[28] The behaviour of

[28] OEEC, *Industrial Statistics, 1900–57*; and *The Electricity Supply Industry in Europe, 1957–1975* (Paris, 1958), p. 35.

LIPP

electric-energy consumption since the war in the three countries under survey appears to have conformed to a broadly treated empirical rule of outpacing industrial progress, at least if the latter were realistically measured. The distance between the two was

Gross Output of Electric Energy, 1937–62

$(10^9 \ kwh)$

	1937	1950	1960	1962	1965 plans	1975	1980
Czechoslovakia	4·1	9·3	24·5	29	37·7	100	170
East Germany	14·0	19·5	40·3	45	63·0	.	.
Poland							
pre-war terr.	3·6						
post-war terr.	.	9·4	29·3	35	43·5–46·0	120	.

Gross Output of Electric Energy, 1938 and 1960

	Total output $(10^9 \ kwh)$			Output per head (kwh)	
	1938	1960	1960 (1937 = 100)	1958	1965 plan
Czechoslovakia	4·1	21·9	594	1·46	2·66
East Germany	14·0	40·3	288	2·00	3·50
Poland					
pre-war terr.	4·0	.	737	.	.
post-war terr.	6·7	26·4	358	0·83	1·36–1·41
World			495		
Britain	25·7	136·3	.	1·96	
Germany (FR)	32·4	118·9	367	1·84	
France	20·7	74·0	357	1·38	
Belgium	5·3	15·1	.	1·38	
Italy	15·5	54·3	349	0·90	
Netherlands	3·7	17·4	444	1·24	
Norway	9·9	31·0	312	7·69	

Source: Rocz. stat., 1959.

rather narrower than in the West; and the latter part of the 1950's saw a still closer parallel between them. This was in fact a phenomenon observable throughout the Soviet Bloc, the USSR included.[29] In East Germany and Czechoslovakia, production tended, at some stages, to outrun the support of electric energy. The supply of electric power has formed a continual brake on industrial expansion. A closer analysis of the bottleneck would turn to a large extent on the pattern of industrial uses of power.

A phenomenon generally recorded is that, as time goes by, more and more power is needed in industry, whether in relation to the value of goods produced or to the labour used up in their production. (A definite connexion exists between rising consumption of electric power and productivity per man.) On the other hand industrial use of electricity depends inevitably to a great extent on the structure of industry. In all industrial countries it is the producer-goods—and especially the capital-goods—sector of industry which takes the bulk of electricity. In Czechoslovakia and East Germany the proportion is exceptionally high—between three-quarters and four-fifths—higher, in fact, than in most nations of comparable industrial status. The spread of power consumption differentials is very wide—very often within the same industrial branch. For instance, in East Germany to produce a ton of 'Buna' synthetic rubber something like 40,000 kwh of electric energy are required; a ton of aluminium takes half this quantity; a ton of nitrogen 11,000 kwh, a ton of electro-steel 2,500, and at the other end of the scale a ton of pig-iron and of open-hearth steel take no more than 20 and 12·14 kwh.

As much as 68 mwh of electric energy are consumed in East German chemical industries per man, less than 3 mwh are needed in engineering, and less than 2 mwh per man in light industries. On a per-output value basis the discrepancies between the two industrial groups, even if not so pronounced, are still very substantial. Developed mining, basic-metal, and above all chemical, industries weigh particularly heavily on the energy intensity of a given industrial structure. A comparison between Czechoslovakia and East Germany also reveals national disparities for the same broad classes of industries, depending no doubt to a significant extent on specific patterns of both outputs and inputs.

[29] O. Bogomolov, in *Vopr. Ekon.*, no. 1, 1960, p. 19.

Consumption of Electric Power Per Man and Output Value in Various Industries

	Consumption per worker		East German consumption (000 DM of gross industrial value)
	East Germany (10^3 kwh)	Czechoslovakia (10^3 kwh)	
Basic industries	37·8	9·7	1·19
electric power	35·0		1·44
mining	25·5	20·8	1·53
chemicals	65·7	28·3	1·27
basic metals	31·4	20·7–67·7	0·56
Metal processing	2·7	3·9	0·11
Light industries	1·9		0·11
textiles	3·9	3·7	0·18
clothing	0·4	0·4	0·02

Sources: Stat. Jb., 1957, p. 316; Stat. roc., 1959, p. 163. East German data for 1957; Czechoslovak data for 1959. The former only refer to workers employed directly on production. Of the figures for basic metals the first refers to ferrous and the second to non-ferrous metallurgy.

These discrepancies explain some characteristics of the industrial consumption of electric power in the area. In the following table Poland stands out as the country with a comparatively low rate of overall industrial consumption per worker. (Part of the explanation may also lie in the general overemployment in Polish industries.) Moreover both Poland and Czechoslovakia show a very high share of mining and basic metals in the total power industrially used.

East and Western Germany appear to share the European record for consumption per man employed, and the exceptionally high proportion of chemicals—far above that of either Czechoslovakia or Poland—is a striking and important feature of their energy economy.

For a period in the 1950's there was a tendency to repattern the industries with a view to alleviating this pressure. Towards the end of the decade, however, the re-emphasized role of liquid-fuel processing and chemicals brought back the dilemma in all its sharpness.

Of the three countries it was East Germany which had the most highly developed system of electricity generation before the war. Based on very efficient power stations, concentrated in the last

Consumption of Electric Power by Main Industrial Sectors and Per Employee, 1960

	Percentage of total industrial consumption				Industrial consumption per employee (mwh)
	Mining	Basic metals	Manufacture of metal products	Chemicals & their products	
East Germany	17	8	8	46	9·5
Czechoslovakia	16	25	15	21	6·8
Poland	19	23	9	21	7·3
France	12	30	9	19	9·6
Italy	3	23	12	26	7·5
Britain	11	19	19	22	6·1
Western Germany	9	23	12	30	9·6

Sources: This table is based mainly on UN sources. However, according to the Czechoslovak report on the fulfilment of the second Five Year Plan, annual consumption per man increased from 8,100 kwh in 1955 to 10,700 kwh in 1960. These discrepancies may be due to differences in definition.

pre-war years in the neighbourhood of brown-coal mines, East German generating potential was in fact leaving a comfortable surplus over requirements. War damage and post-war Soviet dismantling deprived the country of approximately 2,600 MW in its most valuable plant: what remained represented a nominal capacity of 4,200 MW, with an average age of plant as high as thirty-five years: its effective capacity was only around 2,800 MW.[30] At the other end of the scale as far as electricity generation went, Poland was the most retarded in the area. With a population double that of East Germany she owned, in 1938, a capacity of only about 1,700 MW, by far the greater part of which was located within the territory that she was to retain after the war. The territories annexed by the USSR consumed only about one-seventeenth of Polish electric energy. The new Western territories,

[30] *Wirtschaftsdienst* (Dtsch. Inst. Wirtsch.–Forsch.), July 1955. Among the larger units the Trattendorf station lost nine-tenths, Leuna three-fifths, Finkelherd four-fifths, and Zschornewitz two-thirds of their respective capacities.

well equipped before the war and possessing about 1,500 MW, made an extremely substantial addition to the Polish potential. They were, however, affected by both war damage and Soviet dismantling. Stations with about 200 MW were completely destroyed and about 500 MW was partly damaged. Czechoslovakia emerged from the war with her modest capacity, 1,850 MW, almost intact.

It was from these levels that the modernization and expansion of generating plants was embarked on.

Altogether the thermal and hydro expansion added about 3,500 MW in Czechoslovakia and about the same in Poland (present territory), but it was only by the mid-1950's that East Germany regained the capacity of twenty years earlier.

The bulk of the additions to capacity in absolute terms was concentrated in thermal plant. But hydro capacities were expanded more or less *pari passu* except in Poland, where the share of water power in total power produced tended to fall over the 1950's. The same was true of Czechoslovakia for a time, but towards the end of the decade the lag was made up by capacities matured in an expanded programme. By the end of the 1950's the only country of the three where the share of hydro power in total output (about one-tenth) was of any relative importance was Czechoslovakia, where it was about one-third of the figure for Europe as a whole.

Most of the thermal plants in both East Germany and Czechoslovakia are fired with low-quality fuel: high-grade coal makes up only about one-third of the fuel used in the production of power in Czechoslovakia and a negligible proportion (rather less than 5 per cent) in East Germany, which holds the European record in this respect. In contrast, plants designed to use low-grade fuel have so far been making only a marginal contribution (about one-twentieth) to the capacity installed in Poland.

Progress has also been made in expanding and integrating the power-transfer networks. Poland has a 220 kv grid linking large energy-consuming industrial centres, i.e. the capital and the Lodz region, with Silesia. Similarly a 220 kv transmission line links the western and central industrial districts, while another one of the same voltage serves as a link with coalfields in Czechoslovakia. The goal is to add several thousand kilometres of transmission lines to the Polish network of 110 kv and over.

Czechoslovakia is in process of expanding her 220 kv distribution system, and building a VHF thoroughfare which would link the north-west Bohemian power-generating basis with Moravia and power-deficient Slovakia, and support the latter's industrialization—two-fifths of Slovak requirements will be met from such transfers. Additions of a comparable order are projected for the East German network: a 380 kv network will connect the principal East German consumption centres—Berlin, Halle, Leipzig, Karlmarxstadt—with the new Lusatian power-generation system.

PROCESSED COAL AND SYNTHETIC LIQUID FUEL

The progress made in some spheres of solid-fuel processing, especially in coking, will be discussed in other contexts.[31] A few words will be said here, however, on some of them.

Briquetting is of considerable relevance with regard to coals of low calorific value—low as related to weight—a factor of obvious importance for economic use at greater distances from the source. East Germany has traditionally been briquetting a substantial proportion—between one-third and two-fifths—of her brown-coal output. In Western Germany the proportion is still higher, amounting to about half the total. The output of briquettes has grown in step with the mining of brown coal; in contrast, only one per cent of Czechoslovak brown coal is being processed in this way. In fact, both in Czechoslovakia and Poland, more briquettes are being made of hard than of brown coal. In the production of 'synthetic' liquid fuels Germany has a long-established tradition. Before the last war she was the leading producer of 'synthetic' oil in Europe, and most of her plants were situated within the present frontiers of the GDR. The industry went through a period of vigorous expansion between 1939 and 1945, when it had to supplement the Reich's inadequate oil supplies. Production is at present concentrated in several hydrogenation plants at Leuna, Bohlen, Troglitz, and Lutzkendorf, the Fischer-Tropsch plant at Schwarzheide, and several smaller plants. All these were built before and during the Second World War and they have been in many cases reconstructed and modernized. Their capacity is estimated at about 2·7 million tons, including some 1·8 million tons of motor fuels. The output leaves, in fact, some surplus, chiefly exported to West Germany.

[31] See below, pp. 181f.

After the collapse of the Reich a few German-built plants were inherited by both Poland and Czechoslovakia. The most important plant in Polish territory, near Szczecin, with about 600,000 tons capacity, was dismantled and removed to the Soviet Union. At present only a small plant, at Dwory, is in operation (on the Fischer-Tropsch method) as a part of the chemical *Kombinat* 'Oswiecim'. It is considered by some experts to be uneconomic.

THE SHIFT TO LIQUID FUEL

To return to the question of the displacement of solid by liquid fuel: in the area under discussion this has been the delayed reflection of a trend which has gained momentum throughout the world over the last few decades and especially since the Second World War. Whereas at the end of the nineteenth century coal supplied about 95 per cent of the world's consumption of primary energy, the proportion was almost halved fifty years later. A higher heat-release coefficient, greater facility in regulating combustion, and other considerations of technology and costs have given a calorie derived from oil a strong competitive advantage over one derived from coal.

Attempts by the three countries—poorly endowed as they are with oil resources of their own—to expand their imports of crude oil and, *pari passu*, their refining potential have been handicapped both by difficulty in securing supplies within the existing foreign-trade framework and by the lack of sufficient plant. The refining capacity of each country has so far been small. Czechoslovakia's has, however, been roughly equal to that of the other two combined. Between 1938 and 1958 her processing of oil rose more than sixfold, and Poland's only by three-fifths.

Oil and Oil Products: Imports and Consumption, 1958

(*mill. tons*)

| | Crude Oil | | Refined Oil Fuels | | | | | |
| | | | | | Consumption | | | |
	Output	Imports	Output	Imports (net)	Total	Gaso-lines	Kero-sene	Fuel oils
Czechoslovakia	0·10	1·45	1·45	0·11	1·56	0·47	0·25	0·84
East Germany	.	1·10	1·03	−0·52	0·51	.	.	.
Poland	0·19	0·68	0·62	1·12	1·58	0·24	0·58	0·92

Source: UN, *World Energy Supplies 1955–58* (N.Y., 1960), pp. 86–87, 93.

Each of the three countries has embarked upon at least one vast project expected to come to fruition sometime in the 1960's. The new Czechoslovak refinery at Bratislava, another key component in the Slovak industrialization programme, is to reach a processing capacity of about 5·3 million tons of crude by the mid-1960's: by that time it will be solely responsible for approximately two-fifths of all domestic output of oil products. Further expansion now planned may increase the processing of crude by one-third in the second half of the 1960's.

The Polish plant of Plock is expected to refine about 2 million tons a year of crude around the middle of the decade and three times as much before the end of it. To meet requirements in the mid-1970's some 2½ million tons of petrol, 4½ million of diesel oil, and about the same quantity of fuel oil would have to be provided.[32] Hence the proposal to start before the end of this decade the construction of a second large refinery in the south of the country.

All the three large refineries in the neighbouring countries are connected with the programme of expansion in chemicals.[33] They rely largely on Soviet deliveries of plant and technology, and on Soviet supplies of crude. They will be served by an integrated transportation system—a crude-oil pipeline network 'Friendship' connecting them with the Volga oilfields, which rank amongst the most productive in the USSR.[34] The prime cost of freight via this pipeline—no doubt more economical than any other form of transport—is estimated to approximate per ton/kilometre to one-fifth and one-quarter respectively of the present cost of conveying Soviet oil by sea tanker or railway. The network, 4,000 kilometres long, with a system of pumping stations, planned to achieve sometime in the present decade the carrying capacity of 16–18 million tons a year, is a major venture in international co-operation. It starts at Kuibyshev and forks out on the Byelorussian frontier: its northern ramification is devised to deliver oil to Poland, and via Poland to East Germany, and the southern one to Czechoslovakia and Hungary. In Czechoslovakia it provides

[32] To match the estimated demand very-long-range programmes envisage refinery capacities of the order of 8·5 million tons by 1975. Each of the three plants envisaged is to have twice the potential of all Polish refineries existing in 1960.

[33] See below, p. 256f.

[34] Siting oil-refineries inland agrees with a new tendency also noticeable in the West: most of the new large Western inland refineries receive their crude oil by trunk pipelines from the coast.

crude directly to the Bratislava plant and to the refineries in the
western regions. Investment and operating costs will be shared
internationally. Poland, for instance, will obtain a ten-year credit
from East Germany, partly in kind (pipes) to cover the cost of the
sector of pipeline between Plock and Schwedt, and part of that
of the sector between Plock and the Soviet frontier. She will also
receive royalties on tonnage of oil conveyed.

A possible further extension towards the port of Szczecin would
make the trunk line usable southwards for oil supplied by tanker,
besides the main westwards and northwards direction, and thus
secure a greater flexibility to the supply system.

THE SOVIET BLOC AND THE ECONOMIC STRATEGY OF ENERGY

The long-range strategy of the three countries as regards
energy is closely bound up with the progress of collaboration, not
only among themselves but throughout the Soviet Bloc. For many
years after the war the pattern of collaboration was very simple:
Poland supplied most of the Bloc-partners' deficits in solid fuel and
Rumania most of those in liquid.[35]

The hub of the whole system, the USSR, despite her enormous
potential wealth, had for some years after the war serious difficulty
in satisfying her own dynamically growing requirements. For a
long time she was even a net importer of energy from the three
countries, compensating for substantial deliveries of Polish coal
with far smaller quantities of oil products, partly supplied not
from her own territory but, on her account, from Rumania and
Austria. During the late 1950's, however, the USSR gradually
began to take less Polish coal and coke. She also assumed (jointly
with Poland) responsibility for meeting East Germany's coal
deficits. In the 1960's she is increasing deliveries to East Germany;
and though she still buys some Polish coal and coke, she is at the
same time pledged to supply Poland with coking coal. Above all,
she has stepped in as chief supplier (with Rumania) of liquid (and
potentially also of gaseous) hydrocarbons.

In promoting, within her sphere of influence, the current trend
towards the consumption of liquid fuel, the Soviet Union has been
motivated by her appreciation of its economic advantages for the
Bloc. Her new policy has been made possible by her signal

[35] See below, pp. 300f.

progress in oil prospecting and production, and by the trebling of her oil output during the 1950's. Much of this she is obviously determined to market outside the Bloc—oil and its products are now her main earner of hard currency—but the rest may be sufficient to alter fuel consumption within it as radically, if not as rapidly, as in the Soviet Union herself or in Western industrial nations. The amount of Soviet oil earmarked for the three countries in the mid-1960's may be about 15 million tons of crude a year. The USSR has also undertaken to supply Poland with refinery products till the new Polish refining capacity provides a sufficient replacement. The clearest indication of the change in her role is, perhaps, her undertaking to supply East Germany, over the first half of the 1960's, with substantial quantities of oil (for expanding road transport, mechanizing agriculture, for the chemical industry, and even for power generation), as well as with 40 million tons of hard coal.

The new arrangements were made under the aegis of the Council for Mutual Economic Aid (CMEA), which has emerged as the centre of the surprisingly late and surprisingly timid effort towards some coordination of its members' energy economies. Only very slowly could the Council make headway in harmonizing the individual, national programmes of production and consumption. It has given its support to the dissemination of advanced technologies: it has tried to assist economically justified substitution of fuels by recommending some intra-Bloc exchanges, and the elimination of some particularly wasteful uses—of which the conversion of brown coal into liquid fuels in East Germany is but one instance. The CMEA has also sponsored some transfrontier exchanges of power; it has been agreed, for instance, to link the three countries by a 220 kv transmission line. Somewhere around the mid-1960's a power grid of 220 kv is scheduled to link the supply systems of the three countries, Hungary, and the Ukraine. As Western European experience has shown, linking up national grids offers substantial benefits due to differences in peak demands, but it is rather an expensive form of transport of energy.

Further, the CMEA provided at least the nominal frame for some limited co-operation between countries on specific energy products. A long time will no doubt pass before the CMEA-fathered ideas for Danube hydro power bear fruit. One of the two Czechoslovak–Hungarian Danube stations planned as a first step is expected to be in operation with a 130 MW capacity by the mid-1960's. Also under CMEA auspices, Poland's neighbours have committed some financial means in development of her coal resources—Czechoslovakia in a new Polish hard-coal mine, and East Germany in the Polish brown-coal basin.[36]

In the field of nuclear energy, in contrast to the conventional sources of fuel, co-operation inside the Bloc has from the first been close, though in a very special form safe-guarding the controlling position of the Soviet Union. The special régime for this form of energy is already dictated by its military importance. The countries of the area placed important contributions of nuclear fuel at the disposal of the USSR,[37] which in turn became the sponsor of nuclear-power development throughout her sphere of influence and provided the countries which had the greatest stake in this field with experimental equipment and technical knowledge. The Bloc's scientific and technical research has been pooled at the joint nuclear institute at Dubna in the USSR; and the latter country has undertaken to supply equipment for the industrial capacities planned by the three countries.

East Germany's immediate programme, up to the mid-1960's, assumes that to secure the desired pace of industrial growth no less than 6,500 MW will have to be added to her power-generating capacity. At least three very large stations are expected to be completed in the first half of the 1960's. Gas production is to be expanded even more rapidly than that of electric power.

Practically every new East German power and gas plant is based on low-grade fuels. The proportion of brown and hard coal in gas production—roughly two to three—is to be reversed. The central investment in the field of energy, and indeed of the whole economy, is the vast Schwarze Pumpe *Kombinat* absorbing about half the capital resources earmarked for energy, and as much as one-fifth of the country's total capital outlay. When at full strength—with a 'crew' of 16,000—it is to provide some 35 million tons of raw coal; and its processing plant is to yield some 6 million tons of briquettes, $2\frac{1}{2}$ million tons of coke, and nearly 3,500 million cubic metres of gas. It is to fuel its own 550 MW plant.

East German planners assume that the extremely high post-war increase in electricity consumption will subside after 1960 to

[36] See above, p. 141.   [37] See below, p. 169.

about 7–8 per cent per annum, a rate corresponding to the 'doubling in ten years' empirical rule of thumb adopted in several Western industrial countries. So far, however, demand has outstripped the programme, owing to the priorities accorded to several highly energy-intensive branches of industry. Even the increase of demand assumed by the planners would require 250 million tons of brown coal solely for fuelling power stations by the mid-1960's. Quite apart from the lifetime limits of brown-coal wealth, the mining and haulage of the tonnages involved would place an intolerable burden on the economy; the chronic delays in the progress of the Schwarze Pumpe project have underlined the difficulties.

On such considerations the East German 'perspective' plans assume a ceiling on brown-coal output: various versions put it at a level of between 350 million tons expected to be reached in 1970, and 450–500 million in the 1980's. More cautious versions foresee that, already in the 1960's, the output of coal-fired stations would meet no more than about half the increment in electricity consistent with the programmed growth of the economy.

Thanks to her more varied resources, Czechoslovakia has a greater range of choices and a wider margin of manœuvre than East Germany. To begin with she is the area's chief hydro producer,[38] and her long-term investment programme envisages the raising, sometime in the 1960's, of the proportion of hydro resources tapped, from about one-sixth to between one-half and three-fifths. Most of her energy, however, will still have to come from solid fuel.[39]

Her dwindling hard-coal resources are to cater primarily for metallurgical and chemical uses. Hence the emphasis on expanding the Ostrava–Karvina basin, which produces coking coal. This basin, however, has been continuously under considerable strain and has always been lagging behind the plans. It is at any rate believed that output will have to be stabilized at the mid-1960's target figure. This would, incidentally, relieve pressure on the labour market—an important consideration as regards Czechoslovakia's overall economic policy.

Like East Germany, though not to the same extent, Czechoslovakia will have to rely mainly on brown coal. The North Bohemian basin alone will have to provide the 19 million tons of

[38] See above, p. 152.   [39] See below, p. 170n.

conventional fuel needed for the 2,000 MW of new thermal capacity.[40] Brown-coal output is expected to reach nearly 75 million tons by the mid-1960's, but no more than 90 million by 1975. As the volume of low-calorie coal output grows, more of it is expected to be briquetted or subjected to underground gasification.

NUCLEAR ENERGY

The perspective programmes drawn up in the 1950's for a more distant future thus envisaged in both countries a substantial gap in the supply of energy from conventional sources, and assumed a shift to nuclear energy. In both countries they anticipated for 1970 a probable nuclear-plant capacity of the order of up to 3,000 MW, rapidly gaining momentum during the following decade—a trebled capacity by 1975 in Czechoslovakia and a fourfold rise around 1980 in East Germany.[41]

How far is this vision of the atomic age realistic? Any prognostication about the relative cost position of nuclear, as against conventional, power generation is affected by many elements of uncertainty, especially with regard to improvement in techniques, and relative scarcities of fuels. It may be assumed that over a foreseeable future the price of uranium ore and concentrate will continue to fall, and—at least in Western industrial countries—that the price curve of nuclear electricity will be falling over a long period before reaching a level of stability.

The essential point, however, to bear in mind is that in the overall cost of atomic power, capital items form the major part: in British calculations of the beginning of the 1960's depreciation and interest on fuel make up two-thirds, and fuel replacement and operating expenses only the remaining third, of the net cost-total (net, that is, of credit for plutonium produced); the range of these proportions is not likely to change materially in this century.

[40] Assuming 0·38 kg of conventional coal (7,000 kcal/kg) per 1 kwh with 32·4% fuel efficiency. At 7,000 operational hours a year the 2,000 MW correspond to 14,000 mill. kwh requiring 18·5 mill. tons of coal of 2,000 kcal/kg content.

[41] Cf. Professor Rammler's calculations in *Die Wirtschaft*, 29 Mar. 1957 and in *Neues Deutschland*, 4 Nov. 1958. See also *Einheit*, no. 12, 1956, pp. 1180ff.; F. Selbmann, in *Einheit*, no. 17, 1956; H. Hessel, in *Wirtschaft*, no. 3, 1957, and R. Jeczmionka, in *Wirtschaft*, no. 27, 1957. The latter source gives the estimated capacity of nuclear stations as between 2,000 and 3,000 MW. A. Schevchik, 'Prospects of Power Development in Czechoslovakia and The Part to be Played by Nuclear Energy for Peaceful Purposes', in *Peaceful Uses of Atomic Energy*, p. 141. See also F. Homola, in *Plan. Hosp.*, no. 9, 1955, and M. Kral, in *Pol. Ekon.*, no. 4, 1956, p. 276.

The most recent Euratom calculations assume that investment costs in nuclear plant, including the necessary stocks of fuel, will still average in the 1970's two-and-a-half times the outlay on conventional thermal stations.[42] Technical advance and competition from nuclear energy have already stimulated reduction of the latter, and will probably reduce it further.

Two more points should be taken into account. First, the building of nuclear plant means, to a certain extent, a shift in capital expense rather than an addition to it. A traditional thermal station entails investment in coal-mining and all ancillary facilities (or, for a coal-deficit country, an outlay of foreign currency on imported fuel), and also the capital cost of the distribution network, whereas nuclear power can be generated near the consuming centres. The second point, of special importance for Czechoslovakia, is that the average unit cost of capacity is much higher in a thermal than in a hydro station. More than double, in fact, in Western European practice, and this is more or less true for all three countries. The choice on economic grounds is therefore narrowed down where the alternative to nuclear power is hydro rather than conventional thermal sources of energy.[43]

Even with this qualification, and considering that capital charge is the dominating cost element, there is the prima facie inference that in Central Europe nuclear-power generation is at a greater disadvantage—*vis-à-vis* conventional—than in Western Europe. Because the relative cost calculation is still in flux, Western nuclear-energy programmes have undergone radical revisions over the last few years. Much of the enthusiasm for it which prevailed around the middle of the last decade was damped down by the beginning of the 1960's, when the glut of conventional energy[44] called for a substantial down-scaling of the cost of the latter in comparative calculations for nuclear energy. In the latest long-range British programme nuclear power is assumed to cost

[42] Cf. L. Armand, and others, *A Target for Euratom, Report to the Governments of France, German Federal Republic, Italy, Luxembourg, and the Netherlands*, 1957.

[43] Ibid. pp. 116ff., and OEEC, *Electricity Supply Industry*. Investment costs per 1 kwh for Czechoslovakia are given by J. Holubec, in *Nova Mysl.*, no. 8, 1957, pp. 717ff. in crowns as follows: Czechoslovakia, 3,500; USA, 2,250; UK, 1,950; and Western Germany, 1,350. This was obtained from a conversion rate of 300 kcs = 100 DM and it is rather difficult to judge how far the rate of exchange is realistic. According to E. Ziolkowski, in *Gosp. Plan.*, no. 8, 1956, the cost of installing kw capacity in Poland is about one-third above that in USA and Western Germany. The conversion on which this estimate rests may be no less arbitrary than that of Holubec for Czechoslovakia.

[44] See below, pp. 167f.

between 0·65*d*. and 0·7*d*. a unit compared with a halfpenny a
unit derived from an up-to-date thermal power station operated
on the coalfields:[45] nuclear electricity would thus appear to be
between one-third and two-fifths more expensive than conventional. The Kershaw 1962 report pointed out the uncertainties
of prognostication, but at the same time it stressed that no nuclear
power station in operation is competitive with the latest and most
efficient conventional power stations, and that there was no reason
to believe that those under construction would be competitive.[46]
It is safe to assume that the gap will be still wider in Central
Europe: atomic energy there would work out in the foreseeable
future perhaps 50 per cent more expensive than thermal.

The scarcity of capital in Central Europe was bound to lead to
a sobering reappraisal of the view, still fashionable a few years ago
among Czechoslovak and East German planners, that a nuclear
solution of their energy problem lay just round the corner.
Technological as well as financial difficulties have presumably
been encountered, while the USSR's new readiness to supply oil
must on the other hand have relieved their sense of urgency.

Early tentative calculations saw a major break-through in the
1960's for nuclear-power generation in Czechoslovakia and East
Germany. Programmes must subsequently have been delayed
and, as it seems, curtailed. Both countries are contenting themselves for the time being with one small station each, which are
intended to provide know-how and experience: nuclear-power
development will mark time till technological progress makes some
choices clearer.

POLAND AND THE FUTURE OF COAL

An obvious point of departure for the Polish long-range programme is hard coal, which up to now has supplied almost all its
requirements of energy and a substantial—even if declining—
proportion of foreign currency. (Much of what is said in this
section will also hold good for Czechoslovak hard-coal mining.)

Poland's problem is, of course, one of coal winning rather than
of coal wealth: it is the problem of securing an adequate flow of

---

[45] The cost of electricity in Western European nuclear stations has been calculated
as about half as high again as that in the new big coal–oil plants. Cf. Armand and
others, *Target for Euratom*, pp. 33ff. Cf. Great Britain. Ministry of Power, *The Nuclear
Power Programme*. Cmnd. 1083, 1960.

[46] Council of Europe, *European Energy Problems* (Strasbourg, 1962).

labour and capital to the mines. In spite of her favourable labour-market position, she has had difficulties since the war in manning her mines.

As in the coal-producing countries of the West, it is the supply of underground workers that has been the greatest headache in Central Europe. In Poland as well as in Czechoslovakia, coal-mining has been the industry with the highest labour turnover and wastage. To secure the numbers required both countries resorted at various periods to coercion, as well as to persuasion; but, since 1956, prison labour, and subsequently military labour (the coal corps) have been removed from Polish mines. At a later date Czechoslovakia, too, dispensed with military labour. Extraordinary measures, while in operation, inevitably affected the workers' morale and partly defeated their own purpose. It may be presumed that they were at least one of the factors which helped to lower overall productivity. The history of the post-war OMS—a rather synthetic index influenced as it is by the geological conditions of the pits, the state of equipment, and the organization of work, as well as by the men's morale—is, nevertheless, instructive. Over the quarter of a century which preceded the Second World War efficiency in mining—measured by this yardstick—recorded a spectacular leap, by one-half in Czechoslovakia, by nearly three-quarters in Poland. This, in fact, brought the Polish miner—admittedly working in geologically favourable conditions—to the very top of the efficiency table, far ahead of his fellows in the leading Western European coal-producing nations. From a post-war trough the productivity curve resumed its upward run. By the end of the post-war reconstruction period it stood more or less again where it was in the late 1920's. This is broadly true of the Czechoslovak miner. The goal explicitly postulated in the first Polish development plan, i.e. restoring the OMS to its pre-war level, has, however, never materialized. The period of that plan was, in fact, one of a steep decline. Improved labour conditions in general, and in the mines in particular, have resulted in somewhat better per-man yields since the mid-1950's. Nevertheless progress is slow and the Polish overall per-man output is not much higher than it was thirty years ago (about one-quarter above its level in 1914). It should in fairness be noted that Polish experience (like Czechoslovak) resembled that of the principal European coal producers: the general tendency appeared to be one of a levelling out of efficiency; countries with the pre-war highest OMS have recorded a decline, and the reverse trend is noticeable in the low-productivity areas. As a result the Polish miner now shares the leading place in the table of overall and underground OMS with the British, French, and West German miner.

Overall Output Per Man/Shift in Hard-Coal Mining, 1913–62
(*kg per worker*)

	1913	1929	1937	1943	1945	1949	1955	1962
Poland	1,090	1,270	1,738	1,210	840	1,328	1,163	1,487
Czecho-slovakia	970	1,009	1,404	.	.	1,086	.	.

Note: Czechoslovak statistics since 1950 only show yearly output per man. This was 347 tons in 1953 and 387 in 1960.

UN, *Coal Situation in Europe 1959/60* (Geneva, 1961) gives the output per man/shift for Czechoslovakia, in 1959, as 1,869 kg. If this magnitude is comparable enough it would place the Czechoslovak miner at the top of the European list.

As in the West, so in Poland—though not to the same extent—productivity in coal, and in mining generally, lags behind that in manufacturing. The solution of the human problem depends at least to some degree on capital outlay, to ease physical effort, to make the mines safer, and to provide transport and housing.

Heavy investment is, in fact, required to prevent an actual decline in extraction, let alone to promote expansion. Undoubtedly a good deal of effort has been put into the modernization and general technical improvement of Polish mines—in mechanized coal winning, power loading, haulage, and winding, as well as in sorting and washing plant (the importance of which increases as, with deeper mining, the quality of extracted coal deteriorates).[47] Part of the new equipment brought into mining

[47] By the end of the 1950's Polish mines roughly approached the British level of mechanization in cutting and underground haulage, but not in loading. For the three categories of work the Polish proportion was, in 1959, about 30, 90, and 23% respectively. About three-quarters of Polish underground work is electrified. About one-quarter of hard-coal output in the Czechoslovak Ostrava–Karvina area is obtained by the use of combines.

comes from domestic production, but something like half the machinery needed for new pits and about one-fifth of that for those under expansion has to be bought abroad.

By West European standards, adding one ton in capacity will cost about $35. Polish sources estimate the cost at 600–700 and 1,000 zloty for fuel and coking coals respectively, equivalent to $20–23 and $33. The vicissitudes of the Polish cost and price structures make it difficult to judge how far such calculations are realistic. But it may be presumed that, owing to the favourable geological conditions, the outlay for comparable capacities is lower in Polish coal mines than in most Western European countries. Five new mines, with a total capacity of 3·5 million tons a year, were put into commission over the six years of the first development period. Under all headings, i.e. including the maintenance of extracting capacity, well over $500 million was spent in mining.[48] It is probable that only three-fifths of what was required to sustain the working potential of the collieries was invested. The next development programme (1956–60) was almost twice as exacting as the previous one—it entailed the expenditure of some $800 million:[49] a quarter of the total industrial investment of the country. The (1961–5) programme involves roughly half as much again in capital expenditure. Thus expansion of coal-mining capacity—competing for capital with other urgent needs—puts a very heavy burden on national economy.

Finance is only one aspect of the growth problem of the industry. Hard-coal mining is an industry where investment takes a long time to mature. It takes about eight to ten years to sink a hard-coal mine in Western Europe; full output is reached within twelve to fifteen years. In Poland, for various reasons, the period can even be as long as eighteen years. It must also be borne in mind that

[48] This is the amount referred to as the equivalent of 24,000 mill. zloty mentioned by Professor Krupinski in his address to the Coal Committee, ECE, in March 1957 (*Neue Zürcher Zeitung*, 5 Apr. 1957). The amount spent over 1950–5 was given as 18,000 mill. zloty. However, the terms of reference are not certain. At any rate the currency conversion rates are, no doubt, arbitrary.

A. Strzeminski and Z. Twardowski quote the amount spent on mining over the six years 1950–5 as about 13,000 mill. zloty in 1956 prices. In the same terms the amount proposed to be spent over 1956–60 would be nearly 20,000 mill. zloty.

[49] A recent source, UN, *Coal Situation in Europe, 1959/60*, p. 63, would suggest that 'global investment' in the Polish coal industry rose between 1948 and 1960 from $26 mill. to $170 mill. The total spent over the period would amount to $1,230 mill. From the same source the annual investment per ton of output can be deduced as follows for the second half of the 1950's: (dollars per ton) Poland, $1.44; France, $2.70; Western Germany, $1.42; UK, $1.09.

construction of new mines draws away some qualified mining manpower from current production at the coal face, and thus affects output.

The Polish energy problem is also closely linked with the future of coal in world markets.[50] Immediately after the Second World War, against the background of the then existing political situation and the acute coal shortage, Poland was the advocate of Europe becoming self-sufficient in coal.[51] Her endeavours both to secure larger outlets in Western Europe and to interest Western Europe in the expansion of her output met with a good deal of understanding. The Western attitude was inevitably affected by the political split in Europe, but, after October 1956, Poland resumed her advocacy of a European approach to the development of her fuel wealth.

Meanwhile rising domestic consumption cut down Poland's export surpluses and her coal trade regained much of its traditional Western orientation.[52] In recent years she has reduced her sales to the Soviet Bloc rather than those to Western Europe, which have shown comparative stability. With reservations as to the relevance of internal cost for exports in world markets, it may be noted that Polish coal costs less than that of most Western European producers, because of geological differences, and a lower level of real wages. (Labour accounts for between one-half and three-fifths of the total cost per unit.)

Cost of Coal Mining, Late 1950's

($ per ton)

	Britain	Belgium	France	Poland
Total cost:	11·40	18·68	15·79	9·27
labour	7·25	8·75	8·19	4·31
materials	2·72	.	3·30	2·43
wear & tear	0·50	1·19	0·97	0·47

Source: T. Muszkiet, in *Gosp. Plan.*, no. 4, 1960. Polish cost converted into dollars at the rate of $1 = 24 zl.

---

[50] On Polish coal exports, see also below, pp. 291f.
[51] D. Wightman, *Economic Cooperation in Europe* (London, 1956).
[52] F. Rose, in *Mysl. Gosp.*, no. 3, 1958.

But although these disparities[53] tend to favour Poland very strongly, her position in Western European markets has been weakened by the new American competition. Polish coal prices in Western Europe since the Second World War have varied in response to changes in American 'landed price'. (They have reflected the fluctuations of its freight component.)

Apart from American competition, a more general factor has been added in recent years to the sense of precariousness of the Polish position in Western markets. Over most of the 1950's experts tended to assume that Europe—once exporter of energy—was heading towards an era of substantial and rapidly growing deficits, difficult to meet. It was generally believed that considerable quantities of coal would make one of the components of required imports. A forecast for 1975 anticipated, allowing for expected supplies of nuclear electricity and oil deliveries from other continents, that Western Europe would need imports of hard coal amounting to about 50 million tons a year.[54]

However, towards the end of the 1950's, Western European coal-mining was suddenly confronted with symptoms of a secular crisis. Indeed, the Western world has to readjust itself to an abundance of energy in all its main forms: prognoses of a continuous shortage of oil which had wide currency in post-Suez conditions have been also drastically disproved—it is now taken for certain that the oil-winning and refining potential is able to meet without undue strain the foreseeable rise in demand. Under

[53] A more recent UN source arrived at very similar magnitudes of total costs of production per ton: Belgium, \$18·5; Western Germany, \$13·8; France, \$14·8; United Kingdom, \$11·6; Poland, \$9·4. The percentage distribution of various cost items would be as follows:

	Belgium	Western Germany	France	Poland	United Kingdom
Manpower	54	54	62	45	63
Materials	31	35	24	27	22
Overheads & other costs	10	5	5	22	8
Depreciation	5	6	9	6	5

The same source draws attention to lack of full uniformity in the computation basis. In particular in Polish coal-mining the 'manpower' item does not cover certain costs of the transportation of miners (UN, *Coal Situation in Europe, 1959/60*, p. 58). But this does not affect the general conclusion about Polish labour costs being relatively the lowest. Moreover, at least in Upper Silesia, the cost of labour per ton is continually falling: between 1957 and 1959 it dropped from 94·5 to 91·1 zl./t. (ibid. p. 62).

[54] Two forecasts by the Coal Committee and the Commission for Energy of the OEEC are in broad agreement.

such conditions Western Europe's own coal is, and is likely to continue to be, increasingly uneconomical in competition with either oil or coal imported from the lower-cost regions of the world. This created a serious social and economic issue of a contracting industry in several Western European countries and, as noted by the 1962 Kershaw report, the greater the volume of permitted cheap coal imports—that is, imports from the United States and Poland—the more rapid the fall of demand for indigenous Western European coal. (According to this report, owing to the change in oil-coal price ratios, commercially exploitable reserves of coal in Western Europe diminished since the last war by as much as 85 per cent.) The remedial policies of the Western European countries have inevitably affected the chances of Polish coal exports: and although the principles of long-range energy policy of the Common Market envisage free entry for foreign coal after the transitional period, they stipulate the imposition of an overall Community quota for coal coming from the Soviet Bloc.

This blow to her hopes of Western markets could not fail to influence Poland's long-range coal programme. Rather unexpectedly this broadly resembles the Czechoslovak and East German programmes, even though the three countries' fuel reserves differ so much in size and composition. Hard-coal expansion is to go ahead, but only at a decelerating pace. An analysis of prospects up to the mid-1970's revealed that 'physical' and financial bottlenecks made it unrealistic to plan for more than a one-third increase of output. This would, indeed, be higher than the ECSC's proposal for an average yearly increase of about $1\frac{1}{2}$ per cent up to 1970. Poland's optimum output target has been set at about 135 million tons for 1975, and only a little over 100 million (the output previously scheduled for 1955) for 1965.

As in Czechoslovakia, the accent in hard-coal expansion is on coking coal. That means, in Polish conditions, concentrating expansion predominantly on the Rybnik district and the western and southern parts of the Upper Silesian basin, where it is more difficult and more costly (the cost per ton is about double the Polish average), with a comparative neglect of the rest of the coalfields.

With the coal glut reducing her chances of exports to the West, Poland, to meet her own needs in steam-raising fuel, turned to her indigenous substitute. It has been stressed before that Polish long-term plans rely on a possible maximum expansion in inferior fuels. The gain is double: in the time needed for developing mines and in the outlay of capital. It is estimated that brown coal in Poland needs between three and four times less capital than hard coal, ton for ton, and that the aggregate costs of mining may be between 25 and 50 per cent below the costs for hard coal per calorie. Most of the brown coal can be mined open-cast, which provides more scope for mechanization, hence output per man is 50 to 100 per cent above the Polish average, per calorie equivalent. These considerations prompted a substantial development programme in the two basins of Turoszow and Konin, which is expected to raise Polish output, with East German technical and financial support, from near nil in the beginning of the 1950's to just under 30 million tons in the mid-1960's and to double that quantity a decade later, eventually providing a fuel basis for up to 2,200 MW of power-generating capacity, and to reach a target of well over 100 million tons by 1980. Only marginal additions to power production—envisaged to advance more or less at the pace of the proposed growth in industrial output—will come from hydro sources. By the mid 1960's power stations fed with brown coal—Turoszow and Konin—are expected to represent nearly one-third of the country's power supply and two-fifths at the end of the decade. Sometime in the 1970's brown coal will catch up with hard coal, to occupy an equal status in Polish fuel economy.

For a time in the 1950's official Polish policy assumed a relatively considerable commitment in atomic energy. The argument behind this was that it is a stimulant and promoter of technological progress, as well as its fruit, and that since it opens a new era of industrial revolution, for a country to stand aside while the great adventure is in progress is perilous. Before the turn of the 1960's, however, it was evident that if countries richer in capital and pressed by their general shortage of energy—such as Czechoslovakia and East Germany—are wary of engaging themselves in the nuclear field, Poland should certainly keep out of it, at least within the planners' time horizon.

It is still, however, reasonable to foresee that—even if later rather than sooner—nuclear power will play a leading part among the sources of energy which are displacing hard coal and reducing its economic role to that of a raw material for the metallurgical and chemical industries. Poland, in spite of her inexhaustible resources of hard coal, is already caught up in this process. Hence her dilemma: being, paradoxically, forced to husband her wealth, will she have time to lay it out to full advantage? Will not she be forestalled by technological progress? Of the three European nations richest in hard coal, Britain and Germany founded their economic greatness upon it; Poland alone has not done so. Her dilemma, then, consists in how not to miss the revolution of yesterday rather than that of tomorrow.[55]

[55] The head of the Polish State Planning Commission, Stefan Jedrychowski, remarked in a recent article: 'There are often discussions about coal losing importance as fuel and about it being squeezed out by liquid fuels. Such a process is taking place in the capitalist world, but, in our part of the world, coal will continue to be the foundation of the energy balance for a long time to come' (*Nowe Drogi*, Feb. 1961); he added that Poland's two regular customers (Czechoslovakia and East Germany) may be expected to increase their buying of coal from her. Contrasting, in this context, the capitalist and non-capitalist worlds was presumably intended to convey the insensitivity of the latter in respect of the relative cost position of rival fuels.

CHAPTER V

Metal

T HE consumption of iron and steel (together with that of energy) has at the present time acquired the status of the most significant symbol and the accepted gauge of economic well-being and power. This need not necessarily imply that a growing iron-and-steel industry is an essential condition of the economic growth of a country—the example of a few rather atypical countries, in particular Switzerland, might be cited here. Nevertheless on empirical grounds it is not difficult to prove that in most cases a sufficient domestic supply of metal has been a corollary of economic development. Economic history can presumably be written in terms of tons of steel produced as well as of coal. This is as true of the late-comers to industrialization as it is of the oldest industrial nations.

THE IRON-AND-STEEL INDUSTRY BEFORE 1945

The view that economic greatness was inseparable from home-produced steel hardly needed external prompting in Central Europe. It evolved, as it were, almost automatically in one of the most powerful coal centres of the Continent. One may quote Keynes's famous saying on the German Empire 'built more truly on coal and iron rather than on blood and iron'.[1]

Naturally there was no room for 'steel patriotism' in the past in East Germany, that artificial product of the political arrangements that followed the Second World War. Within the highly integrated economy of the Reich, ferrous metallurgy was centred predominantly in the west, especially in the Ruhr coal basin (East Germany's share of coke-making was only about $\frac{1}{2}$ per cent and of steel-making only about 6 per cent); but the eastern region developed some specialized steel-making and finishing sectors, fed largely with pig-iron coming from the west, which in turn catered for the needs of the rest of the Reich. (East Germany contributed

[1] J. M. Keynes, *The Economic Consequences of the Peace* (London, 1920), p. 75.

about one-sixteenth to the Reich's output of steel.) The region's
pockets of metallurgy were patterned to accord with the regional
demand/supply conditions: the engineering of Berlin and Saxony
was a substantial provider of scrap, feeding local rolling-mills, and
at the same time was their customer. The relationship between
Berlin's electro-engineering and the Henningsdorf quality steel-
making was a case in point.

East Germany's Output and Intra-German Trade in Iron and Steel, 1936
(mill. tons)

	Pig-iron	Steel	
		Crude & semi-finished	Finished (foundry products)
Output	0·2	1·2	1·4
Net imports	0·3	0·1	1·0

Source: ECE, *Bulletin*, i/3, p. 34. Net imports of
finished products are a balance of 0·8 mill.
tons exported to western areas and 1·7 mill.
tons imported, of which 1·5 mill. tons came
from the west.

In contrast to this, the kernel of the iron-and-steel industries of
Poland and Czechoslovakia developed organically in a very close
geographical and organizational connexion with coal-mining.
This occurred within the framework of the states to which Poland
and Czechoslovakia succeeded on achieving political independence in 1919.

The first Silesian blast-furnace was built in the 1720's. Very
soon after this the Prussian conquest, which gave the province the
role of the principal arsenal of the Hohenzollern state, opened to
its iron-making an era of feverish growth. Later, when smelting
switched to coke in the nineteenth century, plants were mainly
concentrated within the triangle Gliwice–Bytom–Myslowice.
Similarly the southern Silesian coking-coal region—at that time
under Austrian sovereignty—became the home of the iron
smelting of Moravia.

Towards the end of the eighteenth century Upper Silesia alone among the areas of Continental Europe which to-day are the centres of heavy industry, appeared to give evidence of its promise for the future.[2] The following century saw a gradual ascendancy of the Ruhr over its Silesian rival, thanks to better supplies and access to raw material and to a more favourable marketing position than that of Silesia, situated as the province was on the far periphery of Germany. For a time Silesian iron-making sought outlets for its pig-iron across the border, in what was then the Congress Kingdom of Poland, and tried to obtain a firmer foothold there by establishing its steel-making subsidiaries.[3] A reversal of Russian tariff policies put an end, however, to this line of expansion. The industry languished in the shadow of the Ruhr giant;[4] at the end of the First World War its share dropped to about one-twentieth.

Protectionist policies favoured the development of ferrous metallurgy in the Russian-ruled Kingdom of Poland; this catered successfully both for local needs and for those of the wider markets of the Empire—it accounted for about one-tenth of Russia's total output—though it met with a gradually stiffening competition from other Russian provinces, and particularly from the growing metallurgy of the Ukraine.

The re-drawing of frontiers which followed the First World War brought most of the Upper Silesian metallurgy into the framework of one economy, together with that of the former Congress Kingdom. But, in both Poland and Czechoslovakia, the iron-and-steel industries—once enjoying the tariff protection and markets of the three Empires—were now to pass through the inevitable strains of readjustment and reintegration. This was soon to be superimposed on the painful business-cycle vicissitudes of the inter-war world. Serious marketing difficulties appeared. Both countries had relatively considerable surpluses of finished and semi-finished steel products over their domestic requirements, although consumption per head was uncomfortably low in Poland, especially in her eastern regions. They had to struggle hard for foreign outlets. This was bound to push them sooner or later into the arms of international cartels—the dominant feature of the

2 Professor Pounds, in N. J. Pounds and W. Parker, *Coal and Steel of Western Europe* (London, 1957), p. 50.
3 Ibid. p. 236.
4 W. Geisler, *Oberschlesien Atlas* (Berlin, 1938), p. 10.

inter-war landscape of the industry throughout the world.[5] Czechoslovakia joined the International Steel Cartel as early as 1927, Poland only followed suit eight years later, after having for a time exploited her position as a small but vigorous outsider. In both countries the industry was for most of the period ruled by strong domestic cartel-type organizations, shaping outputs or sales, or both. Their effectiveness was enhanced by government co-operation and control and, especially in Czechoslovakia, by a high degree of concentration. Three principal Czechoslovak concerns controlled about nine-tenths of the country's production of pig-iron and steel. Full advantage was taken of the relative prosperity achieved through cartellization, both external and internal, for technological advancement.

While in Czechoslovakia concentration combined with modernizing investment was vigorously pursued, the outbreak of the Second World War saw the Polish industry overburdened with a very high proportion of small, obsolete, and consequently inefficient high-cost units. It has been rightly noted that all the pre-war pig-iron-making capacity of the Sosnowiec–Dabrowa–Zawiercie–Siemianowice region could be profitably replaced by one single modern blast-furnace.[6] Efforts to remedy this malaise were undertaken in the late 1930's, when one small but modern steel plant was also constructed. But they came too late to bear fruit.

While Czechoslovakia roughly doubled her steel output over the quarter of a century after 1913, and increased by about one-half that of pig-iron, the Polish levels of 1913 could never be regained in the inter-war years. They were to be surpassed only under the drive of the German war administration—at the expense of insufficient maintenance. Territorial arrangements after the Second World War gave Poland control over the whole iron-and-steel industry of the now reunited Upper and Lower Silesia. But the capacity of the Polish industry—theoretically raised by about one-third—was severely crippled by direct war damage as well as by Soviet dismantling in the newly acquired territories. War losses amounted to about one-quarter in the old Polish lands and between two-fifths and one-half in the rest of the country.

[5] See 'The Influence of Iron and Steel Cartels' in *Europe—Nine Panel Studies by Experts from Central and Eastern Europe* (N.Y., 1954), annex II, and E. Hexner, *International Cartels* (Chapel Hill, 1945).
[6] 'Influence of Iron and Steel Cartels', p. 127.

When the new chapter of the industry's history opened, in 1945, production was disastrously low: about one-quarter of the pre-war level in Poland; about two-fifths in Czechoslovakia, where it suffered less war destruction.

Crude Steel and Pig-Iron Production: Inter-War Period
(*mill. tons*)

	1913	*1928*	*1936*	*1937*	*1938*	*1939*
Pig-iron:						
Czechoslovakia	1·1	1·6	1·1	1·7	1·6	1·5
Poland						
pre-war terr.	1·1	0·7	0·6	0·8	1·0	1·3
post-war terr.	·	·	·	1·3	·	·
Crude steel:						
Czechoslovakia	1·2	2·0	1·6	2·3	1·8	2·4
Poland						
pre-war terr.	1·7	1·4	1·1	1·5	1·5	1·9
post-war terr.	·	·	·	2·0	·	·

Note: Data for post-1937 years are not entirely comparable until 1944, since over that period the Olza area output was included with that of Poland and subsequently with that of Czechoslovakia.

Almost from the start the rehabilitation of the iron-and-steel industry was linked in both Poland and Czechoslovakia with ambitious programmes of general economic development. The steel industry in Germany was subjected, at least in theory, to a special inter-allied régime; the revival of East German metallurgy was to wait until the collapse of this régime in fact as well as on paper. In the meantime some four-fifths of the Soviet Zone's capacity was dismantled, and equipment was carried away to the USSR.

Development programmes, patterned on the Soviet example, axiomatically accepted the thesis that ferrous metallurgy was to be the heart of the expanded and reshaped industrial structure of all three countries. Steel industry being seen as the growth industry *par excellence*, the planners did not pause too long to consider whether, and to what extent, a national metallurgy was an economic proposition. The problems of a supporting materials-base were hardly discussed in the economic writings of the countries at the time. It is to these problems that we shall turn before the industry's expansion is analysed.

Metallurgy obviously depends on a steady flow of bulk material. To get one ton of finished steel, between 2 and 4 tons of ore (depending on metallic content), between $1\frac{1}{2}$ and 2 tons of fuel, and something like 1 ton of refractories, alloying, and other materials have to be brought together. Between them they amount to several times the tonnage of the end product. Some of the materials, though needed in quantity, can be disregarded, being commonly available. Fuel and ferrous metal, on the other hand, are the crux of the raw-material supply problem. The locational 'marriage' has normally a decisive influence on the structure as well as the size and the site of the industry. A few of the world's metallurgical centres have an accessible wealth of both the principal steel-making materials very near each other. The area under survey is not so fortunate.

Iron Ore and Scrap

On the whole it is becoming more important to have easy access to iron ore than to coal, because of the great economies which have been made over the years in the use of the latter in smelting. This trend works definitely against the area under survey. In all three countries iron ore deposits are meagre in area, and their metallic value is low and declining. Czechoslovakia is the best endowed country, and East Germany the worst, containing no more than 7–8 per cent of Germany's known resources.

The reserves of the industry's basic raw material amount to the equivalent of about fifteen years' requirements in metal, at the current rate of consumption.

Intensive efforts have been made throughout the area in the search for new indigenous reserves. Soviet geologists who took the lead in prospecting soon after the war encouraged the Polish authorities in the belief that, before the end of the first development plan, up to 40 per cent of the high target output of pig-iron would be covered from additional domestic sources. Such hopes failed to materialize. Much of the newly discovered beds hardly justified exploitation.

The traditional regions of Kielce in southern Poland and of Czestochowa on the verge of the Silesian basin—providing mainly lean siderite—have remained the centre of Polish mining. Czechoslovakia can claim about two-thirds of the three countries' resources. Her richest deposits form the Bohemian basin stretching

Main Iron-Ore Reserves

Orefields	Probable reserves (mill. tons)	Average iron content (%)	Iron contained in reserves (mill. tons)
Czechoslovakia			
Nusice–Zdice	334	35	117
Kosice	30	34	10
Olomuc	10	40	4
East Germany			
Thuringia	80	35	28
Poland			
Kielce–Radom	60	28	17
Czestochowa	87	30	26

Source: All data from ECE, Steel Division, *European Steel Trends* (Geneva, 1949), p. 115. Polish sources mention reserves as large as 500 mill. tons gross without further details of their location and Fe content.

out from the Plzen region beyond Prague. The Slovak basin extends from Banska Bystrica eastwards: only something like one-third of its deposits are considered economically usable—their main concentration is in the Kosice area. A third small basin with ores of high Fe content (up to about 60 per cent) stretches from the Olomuc area towards the Polish frontier. East Germany is the poorest in all resources among the countries of the region. Ores of the region are lean and have a high phosphorous content. The average Fe content of ores mined at the beginning of the 1960's was around 33 per cent in Czechoslovakia and Poland, and somewhat less in East Germany. The iron content of the East German reserves discovered since the war at Badeleben-Sommerschenburg is still lower (20–30 per cent Fe). Virtually all supply of ore has to be won by underground mining. None of the countries has any adequate resources of ferro-alloys.

Output of Iron Ore, 1937–62
(mill. tons)

	1937	1950	1959	1962	1965 (plan)
Czechoslovakia	1·65	1·95	2·87	3·5	4·50
East Germany	.	0·33	1·46	1·6[2]	
Poland	0·71[1]	1·46	2·01	2·6	
World	102	130	205		

[1] Pre-war territory: amounts in territories acquired after the last war are negligible.
[2] Estimated.

For several reasons the area is at a disadvantage, as compared with Western Europe, with regard to the other of the two metallic raw materials in steel-making. Supplies of scrap depend partly on the size of the metallurgical industry itself, since its 'circulating' scrap—their largest single component—is derived from steel manufacturing and finishing. Partly, also, they depend on the size of metal-working. Between them these provide the area's steel-making industry with about half the scrap it consumes. (Some rather small proportion of scrap consumed goes into metallurgical processes other than steel-making, in particular into iron found-dries.) The rest of the domestic supply is obtained from the scrapping of equipment and other durable steel-containing products. The Czechoslovak steel industry, the one best provided with domestic sources of salvage scrap, is backed by a total of about 100 million tons of steel put into the economy in the past. East Germany—otherwise similarly situated—had her reserves severely depleted by Soviet post-war takings. Poland's reserves in capital scrap are relatively the smallest, and so are her current supplies from engineering. All three countries may feel the strain around the middle of the 1960's, owing to the wartime shrinking of steel input into equipment, which would otherwise mature by that time for scrapping.

In so far as readily available, scrap is the ideal provider of metal. It is a good saver of capital, which otherwise has to be put into ore-mines, blast-furnaces, and coking facilities. The reduction of coke consumption alone makes it a preferable alternative to iron ore. The supply of ferrous metal has an obvious and direct bearing on the patterning of the iron-and-steel industry. A good deal of criticism was voiced, especially in Poland in the earlier post-war years, of the inter-war preferential expansion of steel-making capacities as against those in pig-iron, a policy which relied on rising imports of scrap. This 'disproportion' was attributed to the interest of monopolies in conflict with that of the country.

The pig-iron/steel ratio was actually falling in both Czechoslovakia and Poland. It was, indeed, lower in Poland than in most of the countries with a developed metallurgy at the time. (The exceptionally low rate in East Germany must be viewed from a different angle since steel-making had the West German hinterland.) But the policy was not indefensible under the prevailing supply conditions.

An interesting circular trend has been recorded. Throughout the world the earlier disparity between pig-iron and steel output was narrowed down after the 1870's. By 1914 the output of the two was more or less at par. Since then steel has tended to outpace pig-iron.[7]

The pig-iron/steel ratio in Western Europe has been in decline ever since the last war. In contrast, it has been rising systematically in Poland, and—far more steeply—in East Germany. Within a decade or so pig-iron consumption in East German open-hearth furnaces rose from about one-quarter to one-half of a ton per ton of product; the trend was reversed when imports of scrap were resorted to at the end of the 1950's. The same is true of Czechoslovakia since the beginning of the 1950's. By the early 1960's—under rather different metal-supply conditions—the Polish and Czechoslovak ratios—about 70 per cent—were near that of Western Europe.

Owing to the rapid expansion of iron and steel making on the one hand and the narrow limits of home supplies, an increasing part of requirements in metalliferous material has to be met from outside.

A tentative balance sheet of the metal supply of the three countries which we have compiled here would reveal this picture

[7] W. Isard, in *J. Pol. Econ.*, Apr. 1949, p. 120.

for the end of the 1950's. Scrap is making a considerable contribution, between one-half and three-fifths of overall requirements (quite a substantial proportion goes to iron-foundries).[8]

Balance of Ferrous-Metal Supply. End of the 1950's

	CSR	E. Ger.	Pol.	Area total
Consumption (mill. t.)				
Scrap	3·7	1·9	4·2	9·8
Iron ore (Fe content)	2·8	1·4	3·1	7·3
Total	6·5	3·3	7·3	17·1
Domestic supplies (mill. t.)				
Scrap	3·7	1·9	4·2	9·8
Iron ore (Fe content)	1·0	0·5	0·7	2·2
Total	4·7	2·4	4·9	12·0
Domestic supplies as % of total consumption	72	60	67	70
Home-raised ore as % of:				
total ore consumed	35	36	23	30
total metal consumed	15	12	10	13

Sources: ECE, *The European Steel Market in 1959* (Geneva, 1960), pp. 95, 112; *Stat. Jb.*, *1958* (East German data for 1957 partly estimated). Fe content of home-raised and imported ore estimated throughout at one-third and one-half respectively.

The area is importing about 5 million tons of ferrous metal. Domestic production corresponds to 30 per cent of the total ore supply: the proportion is lower in Poland,[9] but higher (approximately one-third) in Czechoslovakia. All in all, about two-thirds of the ferrous metal required in the two countries must be bought abroad. The surprisingly low figure for East German imports—rather under two-fifths for one and rather under three-

[8] In the late 1950's, 600,000 tons a year in Czechoslovakia and 800,000 in Poland.
[9] An analysis by K. Andrysik, in *Gosp. Plan.*, no. 12, 1958, gives 16% as the ratio of home-produced metal to pig-iron output, which agrees with our calculations. But he gives a ratio of primary metal to steel (68%) higher than ours.

fifths for total metal supply[10]—is only achieved through the more intensive exploitation of the relatively smallest resources: East Germany's is, in fact, the most precarious position. (It will be borne in mind that, besides ore, East Germany imports a quantity of pig-iron amounting to about one-fifth of her consumption.)

Metallurgical Fuel

The position of the area as a whole is more satisfactory in respect of metallurgical fuel than of metal. The state of its resources in coking coals has been previously mentioned, when it was also pointed out that both Czechoslovakia and Poland—but not East Germany—own vast resources. Still better is the area endowed with fuel needed in the steel industry outside the blast-furnace. In terms of overall quantities of coke produced, Poland has moved to the first place thanks to her mines in the new coking-coal-bearing regions; especially in Lower Silesia. Precisely half her coking coal is mined in the newly acquired western territories.

Output of Hard-Coal Coke
(mill. tons)

	1937	1950	1962 (est.)	1965 (plan)
Czechoslovakia (metallurgical)	3·5	5·4	8·6	11·6
East Germany			6·8	
(metallurgical)	.	.	3·3	
Poland pre-war terr.:	2·3			
present terr. Total	6·0	5·8	12·6	15·0
(metallurgical)	.	.	7·6	

However, Poland experiences a relative tightness in the supply of metallurgical coke, which makes up only a little more than half the total produced. The cause is the unsatisfactory quality, and indeed the deterioration, of coal in the charge of ovens, as an increasing proportion of coal mined is being coked. On the other

[10] Professor Friedensburg puts the proportion of foreign imported ores still lower. (F. Friedensburg, *Das Erzproblem der deutschen Eisenindustrie* [Dtsch. Inst. Wirtsch.-Forsch., Neue Folge, no. 39] (Berlin, 1957)).

hand, as extraction in Polish coalfields goes deeper, a greater proportion of cokable coal is found. Progress in bringing into operation new capacities in the coking coalfields has been too slow compared with the rise of requirements.[11] A contributing factor is the state of the coking industry. Since the war a considerable number of new batteries of coke-ovens have been commissioned within the framework of ferrous metallurgy. Yet it has still a considerable proportion of obsolete equipment: well over one-quarter of the coke produced comes from plant more than a quarter of a century old, compared with one-tenth for Western Germany. Per man productivity in Polish coking is more or less what it was before the last war, though it has been doubled since the post-war rehabilitation of industry began. It is still conspicuously below that of leading Western coke producers.

This helps us to understand why, by the beginning of the 1960's, Poland saw herself forced to import nearly one million tons of high-grade coke and coking fines, while her coke exports were more than twice as high. By the mid-1960's her coke imports may have to be increased to meet the requirements of the new modern furnaces: only by the mid-1970's are requirements expected to be met from domestic ovens.

A substantial part of Polish coke exports goes to East Germany, who is also the chief foreign customer of the Czechoslovak (and the Soviet) coke-manufacturing industry: by the early 1960's Czechoslovakia was selling abroad about $1\frac{1}{2}$ million tons, while East Germany was buying almost double that quantity. Co-ordination of the coking industry has become one of the fields of activity of CMEA. Exchange of coking coal against energy coal is being promoted within the framework of Czechoslovak–Polish co-operation. The precariousness of overall coke supplies has prompted the countries of the area to endeavour—in line with efforts throughout Europe—to make more rational use of available resources.

It was East Germany that must have been primarily in the minds of the authors of the 1962 CMEA declaration on the international division of labour when they pronounced the principle that only members of the CMEA adequately endowed with technological fuel and/or metal should develop their own full-cycle metallurgy. Certainly East Germany does not meet this

[11] See above, p. 168.

precondition. Her high dependence on imports has encouraged research into the production of pig-iron on fuel of lesser mechanical strength. This has made possible high-temperature coking of

Polish Long-Range Estimates of Coke Requirements
(mill. tons)

	1960	*1975*
Blast-furnaces	4·9	11·6
Other industrial uses	4·2	6·6
Heating	1·9	3·3
Export	1·7	2·0
Total	12·6	23·6
metallurgical coke	7·4	14·7

Source: Antoni Pienkowski, in *Gosp. Plan.*, no. 7, 1960, p. 18; small items unaccounted for.

brown coal, with working temperatures of 1,000–1,100°C, while until recently only semi-coking at 500–600°C was practicable.[12] An industrial supply of coke, the 'HTK' (*Braunkohlen Hochtemperatur Koks*) from the coking plant at Lauchhammer in Lower Lusatia, is based on local deposits with a high content of ash and sulphur. The HTK obtained in the new processes is used in small low-shaft furnaces: after an experimental stage at the Maxhütte, production of pig-iron on this fuel has been concentrated in the western steelworks, Kalbe, devised with the aim of utilizing the poor ores of the Badeleben and Harz districts.[13] (The cost of raw material is low.) The quality of HTK metallurgical coke has, however, been falling almost continuously since it was brought from the experimental stage into actual production. It is claimed that during the ten years of the Kalbe works' existence its costs have been cut by a third, while the output per furnace increased by two-thirds. On the other hand no more than between one- and two-thirds of the HTK supplied is reported to be fit for feeding to furnaces. Low and irregular quality of HTK is known to raise smelting costs substantially.[14]

[12] Cf. G. Bruckner, *The Use of Brown Coal High Temperature Coke in Low-Shaft Blast Furnaces*, in UN, *Advances in Steel Technology* (Geneva, 1956), i, pp. 103ff.
[13] See above, p. 177. [14] *Die Wirtschaft*, 11 Feb. 1959.

The tightness of the raw-material situation has stimulated energetic efforts in the area—in accord with the world trend—towards the raising, by various technological paths, of the yields per unit of inputs. The latter are very closely interrelated, but, broadly speaking, it is the reduction of the use-rates of coke which is the central goal in these endeavours. Both Polish and Czechoslovak rates are around a ton per ton of pig-iron—the Polish rate is still more or less what it used to be a quarter of a century ago and the Czechoslovak even higher.[15]

Specific Coke Consumption, 1960
(kg per ton of pig-iron products)

Czechoslovakia	960
East Germany	1,300
Poland	968
Belgium	891
France	1,006
Italy	752
United Kingdom	838
Western Germany	826

Note: The area's consumption for 1960; remaining countries 1959. Polish consumption was reported to have fallen still further in 1961 to 934 kg.

As for East Germany, with 1·3 tons per ton of pig-iron, corresponding to the Polish pre-1913 rate, she probably holds the invidious record for the highest specific consumption in Europe. In the Kalbe works the rate is even as high as 2 tons. This factor supports doubts as to the economic soundness of her iron-making industry.

At the present Polish–Czechoslovak levels of specific coke consumption, investment in these two countries in coal-mining and coking accounts for as much as two-fifths of total capital outlay on pig-iron production.

[15] In 1937 specific consumption of coke per ton of pig-iron was approximately 892 kg in Czechoslovakia and 1,070 in Poland.

The Beneficiation of Ores

As elsewhere the problem of coke consumption can be, and is being, attacked from various sides. One approach is the improvement of pig-iron-making machinery: as newer and more efficient furnaces are installed the rate of coke consumption should decline. Another is the beneficiation of ores. This gains importance as leaner ore is used in blast-furnaces. Enrichment also widens the range of usable ore and thus helps to raise the utilization of domestic resources. Various other processes are being more and more extensively applied in the area to increase the productivity of smelted material.

The tradition of ore preparation is old in Czechoslovakia (the first sintering plant was built during the last war at Kralovy Dvor), and it has had new impetus since the 1950's. Between the mid-1950's and the end of the decade the proportion of sinter in the total ore charge rose from about one-third to more than one-half, which is also now the proportion of sinter in the blast-furnace burden prevailing in Poland. The long-range aim—for about 1975—in Czechoslovakia as well as in Poland is to achieve a 100 per cent sintering of the burdens, preferably using self-fluxing sinter. The goal is interconnected with that of cutting down Czechoslovak specific coal consumption by the mid-1970's to about 815 kilograms per ton of pig-iron.[16]

The spectacular progress in preparation has, however, a complex effect on the cost structure of pig-iron making. Capital expenditure on enrichment and agglomeration facilities is very high: on Czechoslovak calculation they add about one-third to that of mining; preparation, even if carried out at the mines, would add about three-fifths to the cost of raw ore; in certain cases the cost is doubled. On the other hand sintering helps saving on both investment and operation costs at various stages of iron production from coking-coal mining up to blast-furnace operation. The net effect is not easy to establish—especially where pricing is as deficient as it is in the area under survey. Still more difficult is the appraisal of eventual gains where the alternatives are the use of beneficiated domestic ores or imports: claims of greatly improved competitive position made for the former in Czechoslovakia are not easy to check.

[16] S. Kasik, in *Plan. Hosp.*, no. 9, 1960, pp. 652ff.

EXPANSION OF THE IRON-AND-STEEL INDUSTRY

It is against the raw-material background outlined here that the vast expansion of the iron-and-steel industry should be set.

Development Programmes

East German expansion has centred on the two new *Kombinats*: the Niederschaftofenwerk at Kalbe on the Saale in the west, and the Eisenhüttenkombinat Ost at Eisenhüttenstadt (formerly Stalinstadt) on the Spree/Oder canal near Fürstenberg in the east. By the late 1950's the first had ten low-shaft furnaces. The other— built on the Polish frontier, and devised to be fed with Polish and Soviet coke and Soviet ore—became at the beginning of the 1960's the largest metallurgical centre of the country, equipped with six medium-size blast-furnaces producing well over a million tons of pig-iron a year, twice the original goal. It is to obtain a steel works based on the oxygen-conversion process. The only completely new post-war works in operation in Czechoslovak metallurgy is the NHKG—Nova Hut Klement Gottwald of Kuncice—at Moravska Ostrava; by the beginning of the 1960's it had 9 coke-batteries, 7 blast-furnaces, of which one is the largest in the country (ranking third in Europe), 4 open-hearth furnaces, and a rolling-mill. It produces about half a million tons of pig-iron; and an output of $1\frac{1}{2}$ million tons secures it one of the two leading places in Czecho-slovak steel-making. By the mid-1960's its steel output will be doubled. Its opposite number in Poland is the Nowa Huta Lenin Works. Poland's second new important metallurgical project— the Huta Warszawa in Warsaw—is intended to cater in particular for the needs of the automobile and aircraft industries and the shipyards.

On parallel lines a number of old hot and cold metallurgical works have been enlarged in all three countries. Under this heading comes the second-largest Czechoslovak metallurgical unit the Great October Revolution Works (TZVRSR), formerly Molotov Works, of Trinec, where a foundry has been operating since the 1840's. TZVRSR works partly on local poor ores. It now has six blast-furnaces with a total output of $1\frac{1}{2}$ million tons a year, which makes it the greatest pig-iron producer in the country; and four Siemens-Martin furnaces, producing about 2 million tons of crude steel. Its rolling-mill is probably the largest and most up to date in Central Europe, but its expansion is handicapped by the proximity of the Polish frontier.

A few more Czechoslovak plants have been expanded on a lesser scale. The Klement Gottwald Works (VZKG) of Vitkovice, started in the 1820's, has a coking battery, four blast-furnaces, Siemens-Martin furnaces, and a rolling works, with a crude-steel capacity of 1 million tons, which is still under construction. So is the former Skoda (now Lenin) Works of Plzen (200,000 tons crude-steel a year production), and the United Steel Works at Kladno in Bohemia (850,000 tons), established through the amalgamation of the Konev (Prague) and the Poldi Works.

Among the older Polish works, two—the Kosciuszko (started in 1802) and the Bierut at Czestochowa—were selected for the most thorough modernization and expansion (some planning error seriously affected the development programme for the latter). They received two additional blast-furnaces each; and between them they can claim a substantial addition to productive capacities from rather less than 300,000 to nearly 700,000 tons of pig-iron, and from 570,000 to 680,000 tons of crude steel. Some reconstruction has been carried out in smaller works—in both iron and steel departments of the Bobrek, Zawiercie, and Nowotko works, and in the steel-manufacturing works of the Batory, Baildon, and Florian concerns.

In East Germany an important reconstruction and development project was the Thuringian steel works Maxhütte at Unterwellenborn, built in the 1870's, dismantled and carried away to the USSR immediately after the war, and subsequently restored to new life when equipped with four new open-hearth furnaces and steel-making and rolling departments. Another large works almost entirely rebuilt is the Stahl und Walzwerk Brandenburg (eleven open-hearth furnaces with an output of 1·1 million tons of crude steel, and a rolling-mill). The quality-steel Riesa Works should also be mentioned here. Since the war a few mills of non-ferrous metallurgy have been converted to steel-rolling: by the early 1960's the country possessed a dozen steel works, half of which had finishing mills only.

The Nowa Huta (Lenin) Works may be considered to be representative in regard to siting, size, equipment, and structural pattern of the new 'giants'. Its main feature is a high degree of integration, which has, let us remark, in the Soviet-type metallurgical plant a rather wider meaning than in the West.

Built on the River Vistula in close proximity to the ancient capital of Poland, Cracow, it covers an area of about 10 square kilometres. It contains a system of coke-oven batteries with a capacity of 300,000 tons of coke; agglomeration and other ore-dressing facilities; four blast-furnaces with a capacity averaging 1,200 cubic metres, and a maximum of 1,386 cubic metres. The feature of the plant's pig-iron making is a full preparation of ore. It has also ten fixed open-hearth furnaces of 370 tons each; its finishing department includes a blooming mill with a capacity of over $3\frac{1}{2}$ million tons, a continuous hot wide-strip mill, a cold-strip mill, a tube-welding mill and a galvanizing plant. The way in which target capacities of the works have been successively raised reflects the problems with which technological advance and the economies of scale confront the planner. When the original blue-print was completed in the 1940's it anticipated a final output of about $3\frac{1}{2}$ million tons of crude steel a year, which is likely to be attained sometime in the mid-1960's. Its more recent variant (embodying the installation of several oxygen converters) fore-shadows a yearly production of about 6 million tons by the early 1970's. Technological advance in the world has silenced the strong criticism of such exacting targets, still voiced in the later 1950's; and still bolder revisions envisage a capacity of between 9 and 10 million tons of crude steel at some undefined date.

The Siting of Plants

One or two remarks may be made here in retrospect on these development programmes. First, the early post-war period saw a drive to the 'green-field sites'. Quite a few economic considerations militate against them: old units often provide a wider scope for internal economies; they call for less capital outlay on 'infra-structure'. But they may hamper expansion; new sites may give greater scope for coordinated, systematic, balanced growth and advanced technology.

As often as not choices have been slanted by considerations of general social as well as economic growth. The line of Polish economic strategy has been to promote industrialization outside the congested Silesian basin. Social and political motives added to the weight of economic arguments for the creation of the metallurgical centre around Cracow (Nowa Huta), thus to form the skeleton of a new industrial structure and 'radiate' socially by the formation of a proletarian core in the underdeveloped south. Similar factors influenced the original abortive Huko project of Slovakia.[17]

On the whole raw-material-deficient countries have been tending in recent decades to site their metallurgy at the sea-coast, possibly near to deep-water ports. Such, in particular, has been the impact on siting of the growing deficit in ores in Western Europe. In contrast, with very few exceptions—such as the small steel works of Szczecin—all the new metallurgical projects of the three countries are located inland, since they are all oriented towards the Soviet source of ore supply. This is true of the Czechoslovak NHKG as much as of the Nowa Huta and the Eisen-hüttenkombinat Ost of East Germany. The location of the latter was also motivated by its nearness to Poland who originally took over the responsibility for providing it with coke. However, it is a fact that inland location is traditional to Polish metallurgy: Polish as well as Czechoslovak steel-making has been concentrated in, or in the proximity of, coal basins. Such location of Polish metallurgy was in the past based on the coal-ore exchange between Poland and Scandinavia, especially with Sweden; it was served by the Silesia–Gdynia coal artery built in the inter-war period. No such shuttle service is behind the present Soviet-oriented locational policy.

In the case of Czechoslovakia the ore is transported to Ostrava via transhipment stations on the Soviet frontier, or from the Danube port of Komarno in Slovakia whence it is directed to the agglomeration plants.

There is little hope of alleviating the haulage handicap within a foreseeable future. The programmes of integrating the area's river systems with the inland-water network of the Soviet Union have been shelved because of the enormous cost involved. Rivers on which some of the 'giants' have been located, e.g. the Vistula in the case of Nowa Huta, or the Oder canal in that of the Eisen-hüttenkombinat Ost, are thought of as a supply of water (an important raw material, consumed in enormous quantities, which is sometimes overlooked) rather than as lines of communication.

There can be hardly any doubt in principle that metallurgy dependent on a very-long-distance overland haul of ores is at a

[17] See below, pp. 207ff.

disadvantage as compared with its competitors located close to the seaboard, let alone those operating near ore-mines.[18]

The Lure of Bigness

The size of an integrated operational enterprise is clearly dependent on that of its equipment. The modernizers of the industry in the area have been determined from the post-war start to provide the new and reconstructed plant with large-capacity equipment units. For a combination of technological as well as economic reasons, the size of furnaces has been increasing spectacularly throughout the industrialized world; indeed some units of the area which held records for size when they were planned have been rapidly outdistanced by the world trend by the time they materialized: blast-furnaces with a useful capacity of well over 2,000 cubic metres, and open-hearth furnaces with up to 500–600 tons, have been and are being installed in some other countries and are dwarfing the record-holders of the area.

Metallurgy, being essentially a mass-production industry, leaves plenty of scope for economies of scale. This is true of finishing as well as of lower stages. A continuous rolling-mill, to be an economic proposition, must be fed with a corresponding flow of material. Sectional-product and heavy-plate mills can be economical at smaller sizes but they need the support of very large primary rolling-mills, heavy slabbings and blooming mills such as those installed in the Polish Nowa Huta and Czestochowa, and the Czechoslovak Kuncice works. This is the kind of consideration which the architect of modern metallurgy had to bear in mind when balancing the capacities in Poland and Czechoslovakia. Not long ago the optimal capacity of steel plants was believed to be about 1 million tons of crude steel a year. The case of Nowa Huta shows how quickly target-capacity figures become obsolete.

No doubt there is a point beyond which the benefits of large-scale working become uncertain. To disentangle the numerous causes contributing to the appearance and to the location of this point on the productivity curve is hardly possible. As was noted by the Anglo-American productivity team, contemporary technology calls for far-reaching integration and for taking fullest advantage of the benefits from large production units and plants,

[18] See also, however, below, pp. 216f.

but every factor other than technical tends to put a ceiling on size: in particular the human factor and the absorptive power of the market for final outputs. Countries younger in industrial experience, which are very often attracted by the lure of bigness, are particularly inclined to forget the formidable administrative and organizational difficulties with which very large units confront those in charge of them.[19] Some at least of the disappointments and disillusions which were voiced in Poland—when public discussion became more frank after October 1956—may be attributable to these elements. It seems, however, that as the teething period passes such disappointments will be on the wane.

Specialization and the International Exchange of Products

Preserving a balance in the development of national metallurgies has proved an extremely difficult task to planners. True the imbalance was partly a result of a conscious policy which at least until the end of the 1950's was emphasizing the expansion of smelting capacity as the base of the industry. The development of its higher stages was deliberately postponed. Quite apart from this, however, the patterning of the product-mix of the final stages has confronted the planner, in the absence of a market mechanism, with a serious dilemma both in the national and in the international plane. The logical direction of policy for a small or medium-size country is to specialize as far as possible, and at the same time to secure as intensive as possible an international exchange of final products. (For industrially more advanced nations the parallel direction is to exchange products of finer finish against those of lesser refinement.) Let us recall that of the three countries, Czechoslovakia and Poland have traditionally been net exporters of rolled steel products. Since the last war, however, net exports have tended to decline.

It is not surprising that finished steel has become chronologically the first domain in which the CMEA tried its hand at harmonizing the industrial structures of its member-economies. Within a few years of its inception, i.e. as early as the beginning of the 1950's, it made its first attempts to standardize the manufacturing of some products and to allocate production. As a result of these efforts the overall ratio of exported finished steel to the total produced

---

[19] Cf. Anglo-American Council of Productivity, *Productivity Team Report, Iron and Steel* (London, 1952), p. 87.

was doubled for the CMEA region between 1950 and 1960, but it is still rather less than 5 per cent of output.

Technological Development

It was on the subject of technological levels of iron and steel capacities which came into existence since the war that Polish disappointments and criticisms were most vocal after 1956.

By now Czechoslovakia's own engineering is able to equip most of her new plant, but in Poland the core of the equipment of the leading units came, and part still comes, from the Soviet Union. Plants have been erected throughout the area on designs and technical documentation from the Soviet GIPROMEZ and under the supervision of Soviet experts. The personnel has been trained by Soviet technicians and generally the Soviet 'know-how' has been imparted. In fact, some of the leading new units in the area are replicas of some of those built in the post-war years in the USSR herself. They thus correspond in technology to some of the most up-to-date plants operating in the Soviet Union. One should accept the judgement of highly qualified expert witnesses, such as that of the British steel missions to the USSR, to the effect that, in broad terms, the standards of Soviet equipment and technology in coke, pig-iron, and steel-making are high, though not necessarily so in steel rolling.[20] (On the whole the Soviet Union, as it appears, has followed, and made good use of, borrowed Western experience.)[21]

However, a too indiscriminate copying in the past of Soviet examples with regard to size, design, layout, equipment, &c., and exclusive reliance on Soviet technology have not been an unmixed blessing. First, too little consideration has been given to tailoring national metallurgies to the material supply position, the capital/labour conditions, and in general to the given economic environment. A point which cropped up in the criticism appears to have been accepted by the Soviet authorities responsible for the Polish projects: in the earlier years the principal ruling in Soviet exports of plant-cum-techniques had been that projects should only

[20] H. W. A. Waring, 'Russia in the World of Steel', *Steel*, Apr. 1957. See also Iron and Steel Institute, *The Russian Iron and Steel Industry* (London, 1956).
[21] T. P. Colclough, in *Steel*, Apr. 1957. Mills G. Clark, *The Economics of Soviet Steel* (London, 1957), p. 272, points out that Soviet progress in techniques in recent years has been exclusively due to adoption, modification, and innovations of Western progress.

incorporate technologies tested in the Soviet Union.[22] It is this rule, combined with the very long gestation period of plant—the first phases of constructing the model Soviet-sponsored metallurgical plants, Nowa Huta and Nova Hut, lasted a full decade—that accounted for lags behind the more advanced technologies. In some sectors at least, especially steel rolling, the cutting off of the metallurgy of the area from the West might have had some adverse affect. Towards the end of the 1950's the Soviet Union agreed to revise the principles mentioned and to embody in the new projects, where advisable, British, American, and West German advanced techniques, even if untried in the USSR. Moreover, Poland at least, who by that time took over the responsibility for the equipment and general development of some of her metallurgical projects (in particular the Czestochowa Steel Works), tended to establish more direct contact with Western technological thought and practice.[23]

Installations now in hand or contemplated generally incorporate some advanced or even pioneering techniques. A few, particularly those concerning the raw-material stages, were mentioned in a previous section of this chapter.

Of other technological advances the one likely to gain ground in the area is the application of tonnage oxygen. Experiments are being conducted in Czechoslovak and Polish blast-furnaces. In Poland the cost of oxygen is believed to put a rather low ceiling on the economic feasibility of the process: but it is contended that mixture with natural gases in the experiments gave a two-fifths increment in output as well as a one-third cut in specific coke consumption. Development of this process has made it applicable to high-phosphorus iron; it is now in use in the manufacturing of special steels, alloy steels included, as well as of plain carbon steel, to which it was originally confined. These techniques are, *inter alia*, to contribute to the high target capacity of the East Slovak steel plant. The use of tonnage oxygen has also been the basis of the upward revision of the ultimate steel-making capacity of Nowa Huta.[24]

---

[22] Statement by the technical director of the Nowa Huta Works in *Trybuna Ludu*, 13 May 1957.

[23] Poland, *inter alia*, placed in the United States an order for a complete tin-plate plant to be attached to the new Nowa Huta cold rolling-mill. The plant, financed from American credit, is expected to operate in the early 1960's.

[24] B. Matuschka, 'Observations on the Technical Development of the New Oxygen Steelmaking Process (LD Process) in Austria and Other Countries', in UN, *Advances in Steel Technology*, p. 159.

The countries of the area, and especially East Germany (the Dehlens Works), are experimenting with continuous casting of steel slabs and billets (which permits of direct proceeding from molten steel to semi-finished sections). Rolling and finishing—an increasingly capitalized section of industry and one with the longest periods of capacity-gestation—has been left far behind in the queue for development projects. As late as the end of the 1950's roughly three-fifths of rolling plant was over thirty years old in Poland and over forty years old in Czechoslovakia.[25] But the turn of the decade witnessed some acceleration in the replacement of obsolete installations: by 1960 their share in output fell in Poland to about 45 per cent; it is expected to come down by the middle of this decade—when new projects on hand mature—to about one-quarter.

Productivity and Comparative Costs

The subject of productivity of the growing metallurgy of the area has been touched upon at various connecting points in preceding sections of this chapter. This will be supplemented now by a few 'synthetic' indicators which have gained considerable currency in its practice and literature.

First, productivity as related to equipment. This is commonly measured in the area by the two specific indices developed by Soviet practice, the yardsticks being respectively the volume of blast-furnace required to produce a ton of pig-iron, and the steel output per hearth area—in both cases calculated per day. (It will be noted at once that better performance is expressed in the fall of the former index and the rise of the latter.)

Gauged by the first yardstick, the efficiency of furnaces in the three countries—which has been rising and levelling out throughout the area ever since the early 1950's—is by now broadly on a par with that of the United States (a rate of about one cu. m/t/24 hours can be derived for that country for the end of the 1950's).

---

[25] Only about one-sixth of the plant was less than twenty-one years old in Czechoslovakia in 1956; plant erected half a century ago or earlier made up nearly one-fifth of the total. (Cf. J. Gracer, in *Plan. Hosp.*, no. 8, 1957, p. 50.) The age of Polish mills has been given for 1957 as follows: 51–60 years old 30%; 31–50 28%; 21–30 5%; 20 years and less 9% (Gwiazdzinski, in *Gosp. Plan.*, no. 3, 1958; see also S. Kawinski, ibid. no. 3, 1960; ECE, *Long-term Trends and Problems of the European Steel Industry* (Geneva, 1959), p. 11).

Efficiency of Plant in Metallurgy

	Blast-furnace volume required per day to produce a ton of pig-iron ($m^3/t/24$ hours)			Steel output per day per hearth area of open-hearth furnace ($t/m^2/24$ hours)		
	1948 or 1950	*1958 or 1959*	*1961 (plan)*	*1948 or 1950*	*1958 or 1959*	*1960*
Czechoslovakia	1·24	1·09	1·01	4·0	5·81	
East Germany	.		1·23	.	5·09	5·39
Poland	1·82	1·15	1·06[1]	3·14	5·30	5·95
USSR	0·98	0·77		5·36	7·56	

[1] 0·92 in 1965.

The series compiled here clearly picture the drive to make the utmost use of capital stock, though very often at the expense of maintenance, and consequently of the continuity of production. At any rate these series can be used only with the greatest circumspection in international comparisons for countries with different kinds and sizes of plant, different materials used, and varying methods and techniques—all of which bear unavoidably on efficiency as measured by these yardsticks. Professor Campbell rightly sounds a note of warning:

Soviet economists are very fond of making such comparisons of capital productivity and concluding that they prove the greater efficiency of their economic system and the chaotic wastefulness of capitalism. The conclusion is as dubious as the reverse one that we sometimes make on the basis of labour productivity comparisons. The high rate of utilization of capital equipment makes sense for the Soviet Union, but not for the United States. The relative abundance and cheapness of capital in this country [i.e. the USA] makes it rational for a firm to provide itself generously with capacity.[26]

The second gauge relates the industry's efficiency to its manpower. It is only too well known how precarious international comparisons of productivity are for virtually any industry, even for one with highly homogeneous outputs. The more so is it in metallurgy. Output per man depends, in addition to what one could consider as the men's efficiency 'as such', on various factors.

[26] R. W. Campbell, *Problems of United States–Soviet Economic Comparisons*, a paper submitted to the Joint Economic Committee of Congress (Washington, 1959).

These are, *inter alia*, the distribution of labour as between departments; the structure of industry; its organization; equipment operated, its size and age and technological conditions in general; quality of materials used in consecutive metallurgical process; output pattern. To insulate fully the influence of each of these elements on per man productivity is a virtual impossibility.

Labour Productivity in Iron-and-Steel Industry
(*tons per worker/year*)

	East Germany	Poland	Czecho-slovakia	Western Germany	Britain	France
Blast-furnace shops	228 (1957)	1,266 (1960)	951 (1960)	1,497 (1957)	1,130 (1956)	1,211 (1954)
Steel-making departments	308 (1957)	673 (1960)	689 (1960)	933 (1957)	936 (1955)	728 (1954)
Overall output of crude steel per worker in industry	.	52	70	.	126	111

Sources: Stat. roc., 1959; ECE, *Long-term Trends of European Steel*; Gwiazdzinski, in *Gosp. Plan.*, no. 12, 1958; ECSC, *Mémento statistique, 1958*; *Rocz. pol. i gosp., 1959*, p. 453.
  German data throughout from Dtsch. Inst. Wirtsch.–Forsch., *Wber.*, xxix/30, 27 July 1962, p. 132. Figures in brackets denote years. Data in the last line computed for 1957–8. Some data have been rather arbitrarily reconciled.
  It could be derived from additional data in *Wber.* that after 1957 East–West German disparity in the productivity of blast-furnace shops tended to widen. By 1960 the East German figure apparently equalled no more than 13·5% of the West German.

But with due caution some inference—if only a very broad one—seems to be sufficiently warranted. It is that the worker in the metallurgy of the area—especially the steel maker—is distinctly less efficient than his opposite number in advanced countries of the West, and that this discrepancy is particularly wide in the case of Poland.

In both Poland and Czechoslovakia, however, the productivity of metallurgical labour is continually improving. Over the short period of three years ending in 1958, output per worker in Czechoslovak blast-furnace shops rose from under 800 to well over 900 tons per annum (though it remained more or less stationary in open-hearth shops). Taking a longer perspective, output per worker in Polish blast-furnace shops increased nearly four times between the outbreak of the First World War (about 250 tons of pig-iron per worker in 1913) and the beginning of the 1960's. In both countries labour productivity may be expected to increase further with the rising efficiency of technological processes, and the commissioning of more effective installations. Czechoslovak planning authorities expect, for instance, productivity per man in the blast-furnace department of the East Slovak Steel Works to be three times the national average in the late 1950's, with equipment efficiency reaching simultaneously 0·6 cu. m/t/24 hours, which almost doubles the present national averages. For reasons touched upon here in several contexts, East Germany's record is one of exceptionally low productivity. This will be well brought out in an intra-German comparison. An analysis by the Deutsches Institut für Wirtschaftsforschung[27] would suggest that East German productivity per man in steel making and finishing is about one-third of West German: in pig-iron departments the proportion is even as low as one-seventh.

A Polish case study by a prominent student of the subject (J. Gwiazdzinski) is of considerable general interest. He has tried, first, to eliminate the impact of poorer materials in the late 1950's, since the Fe-content in the Polish blast-furnaces averaged 35 per cent as against 45–55 per cent in Britain and Western Germany: on this count some 10–15 per cent of productivity differentials could be accounted for. Around the mid-1950's the Polish average output per blast-furnace, when reduced to comparable terms, was 8 and 30 per cent lower than the British and West German respectively, and 21 per cent above the French; the British and West German open-hearth departments had an average of 35 and 25 per cent above the Polish. But the discrepancies in output per person employed were far wider: in West German, French, and British blast- and open-hearth furnaces respectively, it was 2·5, 1·8, 1·5, and 2·6, 1·8, and 2·4 times higher. Significant are the

[27] See table on p. 196.

findings for the most modern of Polish plants. The blast-furnace shops of Nowa Huta have—as one would expect—a very good productivity record by Polish standards: their output per worker is five times that of the oldest works and double the national average (1957). But although they have been devised by Soviet experts and provided with the most modern Soviet equipment their productivity is about one-third below the Soviet overall national average, to say nothing of the most up-to-date Soviet plants. The conclusion is that the primary cause of Polish low productivity is overemployment.[28] It is highly characteristic that overstaffing of iron-and-steel plants is highest precisely in works located in the areas where disguised rural unemployment is at its worst. We have thus touched upon the basic structural problem of the Polish economy.

While we are prepared to subscribe to these findings we cannot do so without some reservations, for there is still the case of Czechoslovakia—the country with diametrically different labour-supply conditions—to be accounted for. (The Polish case fits in well with Campbell's arguments.)[29] As has been remarked, Czechoslovak productivity—though satisfactory by Polish standards, especially in crude steel—is less so by those of advanced industries in the West. Whether any common organizational factors contribute to the international comparative disadvantage of the two countries may be a moot point.

We may now say something about the general cost-position in the industry. Here again we are, however, on ground which—particularly when international comparisons are intended—must be trodden only with the utmost caution.

The striking, if not really surprising, fact which emerges from a compilation of the British and Polish cost structures is the far lower share of the labour component at every stage of the Polish industry: combined for the two stages investigated—i.e. pig-iron and crude steel—the ratio is one of $1 : 4 \cdot 7$. While part of this disparity is most probably due to some differences in cost classification, it is obviously very wide and is certain to be so at later stages. British cost calculation would suggest that the cumulated labour cost of processes, from pig-iron making up to and including steel finishing, makes up almost one-quarter of the total cost;[30]

---

[28] Gwiazdzinski, in *Gosp. Plan.*, no. 1, 1960.   [29] See above, p. 195.
[30] Anglo-American Council of Productivity, *Iron and Steel*, p. 12.

in Poland it would appear to represent only about 6 per cent. Assuming then a considerable addition of (not too expensive) foreign ores, our 'guesstimate' would be that both Czechoslovakia

Cost-Structure of British and Polish Iron and Steel Making
(*percentages: rounded figures*)

	Britain	*Poland*
Iron		
Materials except fuel	40	52
Fuel	41	28
Labour	6	1·5
Balance	13	19·5
	100	100
Crude steel		
Materials except fuel	70	70
Fuel	9	7
Labour	8	1·5
Balance	13	21·5
	100	100

Source: British data relate approximately to 1950, see Anglo-American Council of Productivity. Polish data for first half of 1959, derived from Gwiazdzinski, in *Gosp. Plan.*, no. 7, 1960.

and Poland successfully balance out lower outputs per man in practically every phase of steel manufacturing by lower real wages (compared with Western metallurgies). On the other hand one would think that the cumulative effect of deficiency in materials, the structure of industry, and low per-man output rule out East Germany as an efficient producer, even when allowance is made for relative wage levels.[31]

Output and Steel Consumption since 1937

In a previous section of this chapter pre-war developments in

[31] A careful comparison carried out by the Dtsch. Inst. Wirtsch.–Forsch. (*Wber.*, xxix/30, p. 132) would suggest that real earnings of East German metallurgical workers are about 15 per cent below those of Western Germany. Related to per-man outputs this would still leave Western Germany with a per-ton labour cost less than half that in East Germany.

the area's pig-iron and steel industry were briefly described.[32] We can now take up the story where we left off. The table below summarizes the performance of the quarter of a century that followed. In overall quantitative terms this is no doubt a success story. The area as a whole increased fourfold its output of pig-iron; it more than trebled its production of crude steel. Poland's relative advance is particularly remarkable. On the eve of the

Pig-Iron and Steel Output, 1937–62
(*mill. tons*)

	1937	Pre-1945 peak	1945	1950	1962	1965 (plan)	1975
Czechoslovakia							
Pig-iron	1·65	1·7	0·6	1·99	5·2	7·65	
Crude steel	2·3	2·5	1·0	3·12	7·6	10·5	17–19
Finished steel	1·6			2·2	5·2 (5·8)[1]	7·3 (8·2)[1]	13·6
East Germany							
Pig-iron	0·2		0·21	0·34	2·1	2·15	
Crude steel	1·2	1·7?	0·3	1·00	3·4	4·63	
Finished steel	0·90			0·78	2·5	3·50	
Poland[2]							
Pig-iron	1·30	1·25	0·22	1·53	5·3	7·0	
Crude steel	2·00	2·40	0·50	2·35	7·7	9·0–9·1	13·0
Finished steel				1·85	5·2[3]	6·05	

[1] Incl. tubes. [3] Excl. tubes.
[2] Pre-war territory (1937): pig-iron 0·79, crude steel 1·47, finished steel 1·1.

Note: The coverage is not always certain, especially for pre-1950 data. Tube output is not systematically separated from rolled-steel tonnage. Polish and Czechoslovakia finished-steel figures include tubes from 1945 onwards. In 1959 tube output included in the recorded finished-material amounted to 0·55, 0·33, and 0·33 mill. tons for Czechoslovakia, East Germany, and Poland respectively.

First World War she ranked as a steel maker considerably higher than Czechoslovakia. On the eve of the Second, Czechoslovakia was producing half as much steel again as Poland. By the late 1950's they drew even.

Turning to a wider stage we shall find that the area's share in world output of both pig-iron and crude steel has risen (from 2·5 to 3·3 and from 3·7 to 4·5 per cent respectively). In other words the area has increased its output faster than the world as a whole. We shall also note that in the steel and iron race Poland's pace has been quite phenomenal among the countries of Europe, among

[32] See above, p. 175.

countries, that is, which started from at least the same level. More-over, because of the shrinking of her population, the rise in steel status is still more distinct if the per-inhabitant yardstick is applied. (The picture of her success is, however, considerably changed if it is drawn for the constant, i.e. the post-war, territory.) Czechoslovakia's record (trebling her steel output over the quarter of a century after 1937) is appreciable, though not unmatched by other European countries. Italy, for instance, before the war her peer in steel, outstripped her by the mid-1950's. East Germany's

Apparent Consumption of Steel Per Capita, 1913, 1936–8, 1960
(kilograms)

	1913	*1936–8*	*1960*
Czechoslovakia	94	95	496
East Germany	.	149	194
Poland	31	30	225
France (Saar)	131	132	306
Western Germany	180	264	525
Greece	18	24	.
Italy	38	52	187
Netherlands	166	136	278
Norway	110	136	275
Portugal	27	23	.
Spain	27	15	.
Switzerland	93	104	293
Sweden	112	218	545
United Kingdom	170	227	425

progress is relatively of the same order, and she makes an impressive showing in pig-iron, the output of which rose tenfold. It may be noteworthy that her share in the overall total rose for the quarter of a century from about $6\frac{1}{2}$ to about $8\frac{1}{2}$ per cent. But our discussion has brought out the artificiality of this achievement.

Having outlined the progress of industry which supported a considerable increase in the use of ferrous metal in the area, we may now try to trace some quantitative links between its consumption and industrial growth.

In both Poland and Czechoslovakia—but not in East Germany —steel consumption is undoubtedly above that which would be warranted by their status as industrial countries. Czechoslovakia

consumes nearly five times more steel *per capita* than before the last
war, and more than any of the most advanced nations of Western
Europe. Poland, consuming by now nearly eight times as much
steel as she did before the last war, beats Italy by a long distance.

Between the end of the 1930's and the 1950's total consumption
of steel in the area more than trebled. Parallel to this the shares
of the countries in the area's total markedly changed. Poland, once
at the bottom of the table, moved up to the top: East Germany,
which before the last war used as much steel as the two other
countries combined, now consumes less than either of them.

	Steel consumption	Industrial output	
		Official index	Computed index
	1959 (1937 = 100)		
Czechoslovakia	320	327	232
East Germany	196	300	179
Poland			
pre-war terr. (1937)	527	692	300
OEEC	167	194	
EEC	162	200	
France	210	178	
Italy	308	224	
Greece	283	233	
Netherlands	210	242	
Belgium	116	166	
Austria	295	248	
Sweden	216	201	
Britain	166	170	
Western Germany	208	258	

Sources: Steel consumption and industrial output of the countries
of the area: our own series. For the rest of the countries tabulated: OEEC, *Industrial Statistics, 1900–1957,* pp. 11, 89. Index
numbers for 1959 (1937 = 100): Western Germany for 1957
(1950 = 100).

Indeed steel consumption in Poland and Czechoslovakia grew
spectacularly fast when related to industrial growth, if the latter
is measured by our 'computed' index series. The disparity of

the phenomena would be less pronounced if official industrial gross-gross output indices were taken as the basis of comparison instead. While this would not agree with the post-war experience of Western Europe as a whole, it does agree with that of several of the Western European countries, including Italy.

It is, of course, safe to say in a very general way that steel consumption moves in sympathy with such symptoms of economic development as Gross National Product, industrial output (total or per head), and capital formation. But attempts to express correlation in some synthetic formula—particularly of a linear type—of universal validity have proved very hazardous.

A recent analysis[33] broadly suggested that, in the early stages of economic development, large increases in *per capita* steel consumption correspond to only small increases in the 'growth symptoms' mentioned; it is only as the growth process continues that the average percentage rise in *per capita* steel consumption connected with an increase in these 'variables' tends to fall. The elasticity declines fairly rapidly in relation to *per capita* national product, somewhat more slowly in relation to capital formation, and slowest of all in relation to industrial production. Finally, at very high stages of economic development, the decline in the coefficient relating steel consumption to industrial production may be somewhat quicker than in that relating it to investment. The coefficient of steel use against GNP declines, *inter alia*, because of the growing share of services (consuming little steel) and a parallel drop in the rate of capital formation.

Developments in the area do not conform at all closely to this broad pattern. The period under review covers a very strong leap towards the industrialization of Poland, when special priority was given to metal-using industries and building. (Even before the war Poland was a freak case as regards the extraordinarily high lead of steel consumption over industrial growth: completely out of relation with the observable European pattern.) This may account for an exceptionally metal-intensive growth of the Polish economy. Even in the two highly developed countries, however, heavy-metal input per unit of output value has also been increasing at a remarkable rate.

Several factors have contributed to what might be considered an abnormal use of steel in relation to overall industrial progress.

[33] ECE, *Long-term Trends of European Steel*, p. 122.

Not only did metal-working industries form the 'leading-link' in industrial expansion, but many of their products were highly 'metal-absorptive'. This was due partly to the product-mix chosen, partly, as has generally been admitted, to various technological deficiencies and operational shortcomings, to inelastic and irregular supplies of material which hindered economical

Steel Consumption Related to Gross National Product, *1955*

	Steel consumption (*mill. tons*)	Gross National Product (*$000 mill.*)	Steel consumption (*kg per $1 GNP*)
Czechoslovakia	4·1	7·6	54
East Germany	3·1	14·3	22
Poland	4·3	11·2	38
Belgium	2·7	9·9 (10·9)	28 (25)
France	10·4	41·7 (48·9)	25 (21)
Netherlands	2·5	9·6 (11·5)	26 (22)
Western Germany	21·4	49·0 (58·0)	44 (35)
Italy	5·7	22·1 (30·7)	26 (19)

Sources and Notes:
Steel consumption for Western European countries, from ECE, *European Steel Market, 1957*, p. 7. Dollar GNP from M. Gilbert and others, *Comparative National Products and Price Levels*, p. 23. We have been faced with the difficult choice between the two sets of GNP figures, one at the American and another at the European relative price weights. The second set has been adopted here in the main but bracketed figures in the table show that the results of a recalculation based on mean values of the two sets of countries would appear higher, and, correspondingly, European steel consumption per $ of GNP lower.

substitution, and so on. The combined and cumulative effect of these factors is that substantially more steel is consumed per unit of output value in Polish than in British, West German, or French engineering. According to a Polish expert estimate, at the end of the 1950's four-fifths again as much finished steel was used per dollar of engineering output in Poland as in Britain, and three-quarters as much again as in Western Germany.[34]

[34] Gwiazdzinski, in *Gosp. Plan.*, no. 10, 1960, p. 5.

Dr Kurowski's extremely interesting inquiry has led him to a generalized conclusion that because of what he terms a 'technical-quantity backwardness' of their metallurgies, socialist countries reach quantitatively the same levels of overall outputs and consumption, with higher volumes of steel produced and consumed than do capitalist countries. Indeed he suggests an empirical elaboration of a reduction coefficient which would allow for this signal phenomenon where comparisons of levels of overall development between socialist and capitalist economies are based on production and consumption of steel.[35]

This would bear out our own estimates (to be published separately) that more steel is used in the area per dollar of Gross National Product than in most of the leading countries of the West.

PLANNING FOR THE FUTURE

It is the exceptionally high steel intensity of industrial growth in the past that was seen by the planners at the turn of the 1950's as providing reserves for the future, in the sense that these would allow for the expansion of processing industries with a less than proportionate development of their metallurgical base. Metal working, in the broadest sense,[36] throughout the area is planned to grow fast—at a rate well over the overall industrial averages—and to occupy a leading role in the growth of exports. The objective is believed to be attainable, in different countries to a different degree, by a reduction of the metal content—in the first place the ferrous-metal content—per unit of output value in engineering, which would permit the cutting down of 'indirect exports' of metal. Such programmes assume that the metal weight of products can be brought down nearer to the standards prevailing in industrially advanced Western countries. They also assume a simultaneous repatterning of output: East Germany in particular intends to resume emphasis on certain less metal-absorbing sectors of engineering, e.g. electrical engineering and her traditional preferential sector of precision instruments.[37]

---

[35] S. Kurowski, in *Ekon.*, no. 2, 1962, p. 315.

[36] In Poland and Czechoslovakia it absorbs between two-fifths and a half of domestic steel consumption. In the late 1950's (1959) machinery industry in the narrower sense accounted for 26%, manufacture of transport equipment for another 7%, and that of metal products for 12%.

[37] A good deal of East Germany's economic difficulties since partition is attributable to deliberate patterning of both the metal-supplying and metal-using industries. On the one hand most of the metallurgical investment has been concentrated,

It is also hoped that rising efficiency in the finishing stages will allow a greater yield of rolled and finished products to be obtained from the same tonnage of crude steel.

The East German metallurgical programme for the 1960's is mainly based on further development of the *Ostkombinat*, which, after almost a decade's delay, is now to receive up-to-date steel-making and rolling departments, expected to operate by 1965. Its crude-steel capacity is ultimately to represent half the East German total, and its finishing department to turn out about five times the present East German tonnage. Emphasis is placed in these blueprints on high-grade steels the production of which is to rise two and a half times—the deficit in these steels will also be partly met through a thorough modernization of the Edelstahl-werk Freital special-steel works. The Riesa and the Finow works are to receive additional tube and pipe manufacturing facilities as a major contribution—along with that of the *Ostkombinat* to the programme of increasing the national output two and a half times. The construction-steel department will be enlarged in the Wilhelm Florin Henningsdorf Works.

The Polish programmes concentrate primarily on two large existing units while at the same time the old Silesian works are to be modernized.[38] As has been said already Nowa Huta holds the key place. In older works—Pokoj, Dzierzynski, Bobrek—old blast-furnaces are to be replaced by new ones of larger capacity.

since the war, on the lower stages of the iron-and-steel industry rather than on its finishing department.

At the same time emphasis in metal using has shifted towards heavy engineering. A quarter of a century ago the metal-intensive sectors of steel construction, ball-bearings, rolling-stock, ships, and equipment for metallurgy were making up only about one-twentieth of total turnover. It is precisely these sectors that have been forcefully expanded since the end of the war, while the share of such traditional products as textile and office machinery, and sawing, printing, paper-processing machines has been drastically cut. The role of optical and precision instruments, which made the East German metal industry world famous, has relatively also declined.

The tendency originated in German war economy but was strongly intensified after the war under the impact of Soviet reparations policies. In a more general way the post-war restructuring of metal-using industries, as well as their expansion, was carried out with a view to satisfying the requirements of equipment of the countries of the Sino-Soviet Bloc. However, these countries have not secured to East Germany a smooth supply of steel. In the 1960's the supply of steel is still one of the worst bottlenecks of the East German economy.

[38] The tendency is to continue in the very long run. Polish programmes assume that the entire 1980 output of crude and finished steel would come from the existing *kombinats*, with the possible exception of a new works producing extra-hard steels (Jedrychowski, in *Nowe Drogi*, Feb. 1961).

In steel-making about two-fifths of the open-hearth furnaces are to be shifted to automatic operation. Oxygen plant is to be installed in several works: around the mid-1960's oxygen-converter steel is expected to contribute about one-tenth to the Polish total. Higher stages of industry are to receive preferential treatment. The new and old modernized mills—in particular the electrified Kosciuszko Works—are to enable the industry to finish all the crude steel the country produces. The new Warszawa special-steel works is expected to cover the persisting deficit in high-grade steel: its yield of electric steel is to reach about 600,000 tons with correspondingly higher output in rolling-mills. (The country's total output before the war amounted to about 85,000 tons.) Thus it is hoped that sometime in the 1960's the proportion of special steels will reach that prevailing in industrially advanced countries. The tendencies described here are to continue until 1980: the long-run programme for the industry is based on the development of the existing plant.

The Czechoslovak expansion programme is similarly patterned. In Bohemia the main expansion effort goes to the Nova Hut Kuncice works, the production potential of which is being increased in all departments: it is planned to have in operation about the mid-1960's 3 coke-oven batteries, 2 more blast-furnaces, another steel works with 5 Siemens-Martin furnaces, and also 4 rolling stands. The capacity of Nova Hut is intended to approach 4 million tons of crude steel. New finishing capacities are also being installed in other plants. A large investment project is that of the tube and pipe making works of Chomutov. The notable point is that the industry of this developed economy has continued to be reoriented towards production of bulk steel. But it is likely that the new pressures for a more rational intra-Bloc division of labour will add urgency to a shift of emphasis to special steel. The United Steel Works, which specializes in high-grade steels, is planned to become one of Europe's leading enterprises in this field in the 1970's.

The largest project embarked upon is that of the East Slovak Hutny Kombinat—the Huko works of Kosice near the relatively richest deposits of the Slovak iron-ore basin. It is meant to be both a vital contribution to the metallurgical potential of the country and the heart of the general plan for the further industrialization of Slovakia. Initiated in the early post-war years the project was abandoned at the beginning of the 1950's, when it was discovered that the works would have no reasonably secure source of either fuel or metal. The project was revived towards the end of the decade on the assumption that a substantial proportion of ores and perhaps even of coking coal will be imported from the Soviet Union. Indirect, general benefits to the Slovak economy are apparently believed to outweigh the direct, high cost of the haulage of materials over very long distances. The Huko works is intended eventually to become the largest integrated enterprise of Czechoslovakia's ferrous metallurgy. Sometime in the 1960's when its main departments, including the oxygen-converter department and rolling-mills, come into operation, Kosice is planned to supply about 4 million tons of ingot and about $2\frac{1}{2}$ million tons of rolled steel: it is to be equipped with the first continuous hot wide-strip mill in the country. The project is broadly patterned on the Polish Nowa Huta, and as in the case of the latter, its target capacities have been revised upwards several times to take into account technological advance. As plans stand now, about 7 million tons of crude steel a year would be turned out about 1970, and eventually between 9 and 10 million tons by the middle of the next decade.

East Germany has at last accepted the implication of her structural dependence on foreign steel. By the mid-1960's her mills are expected to provide only between two-fifths and two-thirds of the rolled steel consumed in her economy.

East German Iron and Steel Imports, 1950–65
(mill. tons)

	1950	1961	1965 (plan)
Pig-iron	.	0·71	1·44
Rolled steel	0·34	1·54	2·27

In reverting to tradition from the past, the intention is to expand in the first place the higher-quality component of steel-making.

At the other extreme, Czechoslovakia feels more at liberty than her two neighbours to impart a simultaneously fast pace to all stages of her metallurgy. A noteworthy facet of her programme is the doubling of the output of pig-iron, in contrast to East Germany

where this is to increase only by a mere fifth. Indeed Czechoslovakia is the only one of the countries in the area where pig-iron
is to outstrip steel—which reflects differences in the position with
regard to both raw material (metallurgical coke) and the balance
of payments.

The decisive factor in the Polish slow-down is the realization
that a growth rate in steel above say 6½ per cent a year would
imply a more than proportionate demand for pig-iron, calling for
a corresponding expansion of blast-furnace capacity and higher
ore and coke imports. This would mean putting more of Poland's
scanty capital into the raw-material base of the industry thereby
further delaying the expansion of the finishing stages. It would also
increase the burden of raw-material supplies on the foreign payments balance, without sufficient chance of compensation by
expanded exports of engineering products.[39] The Polish plan for

Polish Ferrous-Metallurgy: Balance of Trade, 1959–65
($ million)

	1959	*1965 (plan)*
Imports	175	270
Raw materials	112	215
Exports	157	170

Source: Gwiazdzinski, in *Z. Gosp.*, no. 3, 1960. The
same source notes that in 1960 the average
price per ton of imported products was
higher by one-quarter than that of exported
products of metallurgy.

[39] It is the expansion of 'indirect' exports, i.e. of exports of metal in the shape of
machines, other equipment, and metal products, rather than of direct exports, which
secures substantial currency gains. An inkling of the difference may be obtained from
an interesting Polish estimate by A. Adamczyk, in *Gosp. Plan.*, nos. 8–9, 1960, p. 7:

Polish Direct and Indirect Foreign Trade in Steel, 1958

	Trade			Price of steel per ton (zl.)		Price of steel in indirect trade (price in direct trade = 1)
		Indirect				
	Overall (mill. tons)	mill. tons	% of overall	in direct trade	in indirect trade	
Imports	1·21	0·43	36	464	2,730	5·8
Exports	0·80	0·29	37	502	5,230	10·4

1961–5 has been criticized on precisely the latter ground. It has been suggested that the remedy lies in cutting down pig-iron targets and relying more on scrap which would also reduce investment costs per ton of end product.

Neither of the two factors mentioned is felt to be similarly compelling in the case of Czechoslovakia: if the plans of the two countries are implemented she will regain from Poland by 1965 the first place as steel producer of the area.

A further deceleration in steel also characterizes the Polish long-distance programme. The 1975 plan is of quite considerable interest both for its substance and methodology. It is the only known exercise in programming of this kind so far revealed in any detail for any of the centrally-planned economies. It has arrived at an optimum target of $12–13\frac{1}{2}$ million tons of crude steel for 1975, implying a defeat for the school of thought which advocated a sustained quick-march. Had the advice of the latter been heeded, the target would have been fixed at the extravagant level of 31 million tons—roughly the present output of Britain and France combined. It was calculated by its protagonists at a rate of 11 per cent. i.e. that recorded during the first post-war development period: the rate of 8 per cent per annum recorded in the second half of the 1950's, when projected to 1975, would yield a 20-million ton target.

The decelerating Polish rate would thus come down to that obtaining in several Western European countries. It would be appreciably below the tempo which prevailed in leading steel-making countries at the earlier stages of their industrial development in the nineteenth century. The deceleration itself would agree with the fairly general, empirically established fact that the rate of growth of steel consumption decreases as its absolute level rises.[40]

The 1975 target has been obtained from a detailed estimate of demand, a method considered more reliable—especially in conditions of a rather reduced predictability—than the alternative of an extrapolation from trends and of correlating consumption to other growth phenomena. Nevertheless the Polish programme figure is quite close to the trend value estimated by the ECE Steel Commission. That estimate started from a free-hand extrapolation of steel consumption in the past half-century and allows for

[40] See above, p. 203.

probable developments in indirect steel exports, and the likelihood of specialization in industries with high steel-input coefficients: values arrived at were checked against implications in the overall economic developments. Two lines, one for slowly developing and one for rapidly developing countries, were plotted on the same principle to describe the relationship between the average annual increase of *per capita* steel consumption and the consumption level of 1951; they cover the period from the late 1950's to the target year around the mid-1970's.[41] Both Poland and Czechoslovakia are well above even the upper line, and East Germany is below it.

Steel Consumption and Production, 1972–5
ECE estimate—Trend values

	Consumption		Production			Surplus or deficit (mill.tons)
	Mill. tons	Kg/per cap.	Mill. tons	Av. rate of increase p.a.	Kg/per cap.	
Czechoslovakia	10·7	649	13·0	6·4	789	2·3
East Germany	7·3	405	5·0	2·8	277	2·3
Poland	11·5	390	13·0	6·2	441	1·5

Source: ECE, ibid. p. 141.

On these estimates Poland and Czechoslovakia as steel producers would move more or less in step, and around the third quarter of this century the area as a whole would be turning out rather more than 30 million tons a year (crude-steel equivalent of finished steel). Consumption would be of the same order: a Czechoslovak surplus and an East German deficit would cancel one another out, so that Poland's modest surplus of about 1½ million tons would be at the same time that of the area as a whole. East Germany would have to import approximately one ton of steel in every three she utilized.

On such assumptions the gap between Polish production and consumption levels and those prevailing in Western European highly industrialized countries would become still narrower: in

[41] ECE, *Long-Term Trends and Problems of the European Steel Industry*, p. 129.

consumption standards Poland would almost draw level with East Germany, while Czechoslovakia would consolidate—on a *per capita* basis—her place among Europe's highest steel consumers in a class with Britain, Sweden, and Western Germany.

Steel Production and Consumption: Trend Values, 1972–5
(kg per capita)

Country	Produc-tion	Consump-tion	Country	Produc-tion	Consump-tion
Czechoslovakia	789	649	Italy	326	320
East Germany	277	405	Netherlands	363	524
Poland	441	390	Sweden	688	625
France	621	545	UK	668	611
Germany (FR)	671	653			

Source: ECE, *Long-Term Trends of European Steel,* pp. 130, 141.

It must be observed, however, that even this perspective does not seem to agree with the vision of the Czechoslovak long-range plans. Its details have not been disclosed but the statement of policies to be pursued until 1970 makes it clear that metallurgy is to remain 'in the forefront of industrial development'. The scanty information available points to a 1975 output target as high as 17–19 million tons of crude steel implying a *per capita* quantity of 1,100–1,250 kilograms (about 13½ million tons of rolled products). The planners seem to expect a very high rate of saving of steel in home consumption: within the coming fifteen years input of steel in the metal-working industry (which absorbs about 70 per cent of Czechoslovak steel production), is hoped to be cut—*pro rata* of gross output value—by about 45 per cent. Greater thrift in metal uses combined with a very high 1975 output target would help to meet domestic consumption, and at the same time to boost direct as well as indirect imports. The forecast for 1975 appears to assume a division of labour within the orbit which would give Czechoslovakia—along with the USSR and Poland—a much more important role as supplier to its steel-deficient countries than do the ECE forecasts.[42]

[42] See especially Z. Pucek, in *Plan. Hosp.*, no. 4, 1960, p. 256; and also Gracer, ibid. no. 6, 1959, p. 420.

It is also known that Poland has submitted to the Council for Mutual Economic Aid a tentative programme for the 1980's which signifies a break with the cautious plan for the future of the industry which we have mentioned. According to this new variant, Polish steel production would keep pace with that of Czechoslovakia, so that by 1980 a goal of 24 million tons would be reached.[43] The striking point about this alternative is that it assumes expanded supplies of Soviet pig-iron as well as of ore. The future will show whether the Soviet Union is prepared to underwrite Polish and Czechoslovak assumptions.

ACHIEVEMENTS AND PROSPECTS OF CENTRAL EUROPEAN METALLURGY

In their expansive effort all three countries, though to a varying degree, experienced many setbacks and disillusions. It has been mentioned that several major projects were found to be misplanned at one stage or another: the shelving of the steel plant for a decade in the Stalin Works in East Germany is only one of the cases in point: no less striking is that of the Bierut (Czestochowa) Works in Poland: a small, old plant singled out in the early post-war years for development into one of the leading metallurgical centres, as a part of the policy of rapidly raising the pig-iron-making potential: only when two blast-furnaces were already installed was it discovered that the underlying requirement analysis was basically erroneous: expansion was halted and the capital sunk remained semi-idle for years.

Gross miscalculations with regard to the supply of fuel and metal for the Czechoslovak Huko project formed one of the counts in the indictment against those accused of sabotage in the notorious political Slansky trial (1952). Indeed one could say that almost every programme went wrong with regard to either size or pace or effects: at one stage or another severe imbalances appeared. Capacities, both in volume and in composition, lagged behind resolutions. Nevertheless, as has already been pointed out, the fifteen years after the Second World War did witness remarkable progress. The three countries were, in fact, being carried on the tidal wave which was sweeping Europe and the whole world. (Never, for instance, has the mature British steel industry moved faster.)

[43] P. Jaroszewicz, in *Nowe Drogi*, no. 11, 1962.

However, at least in the one country of the area where public opinion has been given more chance to voice its doubts, the wisdom of the expansion policy has come to be very seriously questioned on several counts, which because of their general importance deserve at least a brief discussion.

First, it has been argued that heavy investment in steel plant is now more risky than it used to be: that though the first half of the twentieth century has seen some significant technological advances, the second seems to be opening up new vistas of fundamental, truly dramatic changes in technology. There may be something in this, but how much only the future will tell. In an industry in which it takes long years for the costly equipment to be planned, constructed, and run in, the risk of being badly outpaced by progress is admittedly particularly heavy. But can nations which are bent on dynamic growth afford to wait? A risk of the kind with which we are dealing here has always been the lot of the late-comer, and may be viewed as the price he has to pay for getting other people's costly experience cheaply. He can hardly escape from it in this particular case without affecting his chances.

The next point of criticism has been that the enormous effort concentrated on steel corresponded to a conservative 'uniform schema of Stalinist accelerated industrialization',[44] which with its priorities for iron (inherited from the nineteenth century) and for steel was already hopelessly out of date when transplanted to the area. There is something in the argument that the contemporary hierarchy of growth materials has deprived steel of its paramountcy, especially where an exaggeratedly one-sided developmental strategy is concerned. But the case of steel versus other materials cannot easily be stated in clear-cut terms, at least not for a foreseeable future. In contemporary economies chemicals do, in fact, tend to outstrip the growth of the industrial body in general and of steel in particular: over the twenty years after 1938 Western European industrial and steel output less than doubled, while that of chemicals trebled. Moreover the countries under survey have a not inconsiderable natural wealth to form a sound foundation for a chemical industry: certainly no less ample (and in some sectors definitely more so) than that supporting indigenous steel.[45] Polish calculations, at least, for what they are worth (the

[44] J. Kurowski, in *Z. Gosp.*, no. 2, 1956.   [45] See below, pp. 240f.

vagaries of price and cost structure justify a question-mark here) would suggest that chemicals do not yield lower returns on capital: nor do chemicals appear to compare unfavourably with steel as a foreign-exchange earner. On either count, however, the assessment would depend on the respective structures of metallurgy and chemical industry, since capital-output ratios and foreign-currency-earning abilities vary as from one product to another. On the other hand, for a capital-deficient nation, modern chemicals—promising as they may be—are anything but an easy field of industrial expansion. They have no doubt the lure of great adventure: but because of their dynamic force they carry correspondingly great risks of rapid obsolescence.[46]

At any rate one cannot too hastily assume a losing battle between steel and its competitors. For one thing, experience seems to suggest that the newer materials tend to create new needs to which both they and steel tend to adjust themselves. In some spheres of consumption competition may in part result in a repatterning of the uses and production of steel rather than its elimination: this is particularly the case in building, where substitution of reinforced and pre-stressed concrete for steel is compensated by a widening application of some steel products. No doubt plastics and light metals are making, and will make, inroads into various uses which have hitherto been a steel monopoly. In the view of ECE, however, 'it seems unlikely that during the next fifteen years aluminium and plastics will make a marked impact on steel consumption as a whole.[47] This forecast is based on the hypothetical calculation that even if the pace of expansion of the two were to equal that of steel of a century ago, their combined output would amount to a margin only—rather less than one-tenth—of a validly estimated volume of needs met by steel. In a word, steel is still, and in the foreseeable future will be, inextricably interwoven with the process of economic growth. It is still the most expressive, closest companion of investment. Steel is still the scaffolding and the bone structure of a growing economic body, and it is almost certain to remain such within the time-horizon of the present-day economic planner.

As we have seen, if the economies under survey are to sustain their growth impetus, a flow of steel supplies of, say, 30 million tons a year has to be assured for 1975. True, this does not imply

[46] See below, p. 236.   [47] ECE, *Long-Term Trends of European Steel*, p. 138.

per se the necessity for national self-sufficiency in steel. But the alternative, that is to say, an adequate flow of steel from outside, seems to be hardly a practical proposition where magnitudes of the order mentioned are involved; at least hardly practical from the angle of the foreign-payments position.

However, when this has been said the more general question of the viability of the domestic steel industries remains still to be answered.[48] Thus we are again thrown back to where we started. First—to the twin problem of resources and location.

Long-range projection on the supply-and-demand position in steel-making materials must proceed, among other things, from some assumption as to alternative metal inputs. It is reasonable to expect that the area will continue to rely on its own supplies in the main, as far as scrap is concerned. With self-sufficiency in scrap the tonnages of metal imported to secure the programmes' steel outputs would still be enormous.

Can a healthy industry be built up and grow with an ever increasing reliance on foreign metal? As we have pointed out, towards the end of the 1950's the area was dependent on foreign trade for about three-quarters of the ore charged into its blast-furnaces. This proportion is bound to go on rising. It may go up to perhaps 90 per cent by the mid-1970's if the expectations for steel-making materialize, and home resources are used sparingly. But then the difference between Western and Central European countries, when a very long view is taken, is only a matter of degree. At the turn of this decade, for instance, Britain may depend on foreign ores up to 70 per cent (in Fe content). Continental Western Europe will have to shift the pig-iron/steel balance so as to step up the ratio of pig-iron. This, and growing steel production, may force the six industrial leaders of the Continent (ECSC) to import, by the early 1970's, something like two-thirds of the ores required, that is, double the ratio of the mid-1950's. Moreover they are passing through a drastic change in the geography of ore supplies, about two-thirds of which, not long ago, used to come traditionally from Lorraine and Scandinavia.

---

[48] The Chairman of the Polish State Planning Commission, Jedrychowski, in *Nowe Drogi*, Feb. 1961, blamed the climate created by doubts as to the purposefulness of developing metallurgy as an element contributing to underfulfilments of its targets. (In 1960 6·7 mill. tons of crude steel were produced as against the planned 7 mill. tons.)

Western, no less than Central, Europe has to look farther afield for ore. Around the mid-1960's the ECSC countries are likely to import about one-third of Fe consumed from outside Europe. Western Europe is already importing ores from the other hemisphere. The problems of securing distant sources of supply, of investment in transportation and beneficiation of ores, in reducing coke consumption and so on, are thus the common headache of Western as well as Central European metallurgy, though admittedly a greater tightness in the capital-supply position makes them more painful for the latter.

Foreign ore in Central Europe means to-day and in the foreseeable future, primarily the Soviet ore. The Soviet Union is responsible for about three-quarters of ore imported to the region in metallic content; (the share is lower in Czechoslovakia and East Germany—about two-thirds and a half respectively), and this implies a ratio of more than a half of all the ores smelted. Moreover the USSR is also virtually the only supplier of pig-iron. The proportion of Soviet supplied metal will inevitably continue to grow with the growth of capacities. Is the USSR able to provide all the metal needed to balance out the area's deficit? It has been suggested by an eminent student of Soviet metallurgy—Professor Clark[49]—that in spite of a fabulous stated ore wealth there were good reasons why the USSR should like to import at reasonable prices high-grade Western ores under the guise of supplies to Poland. However, a subsequent visit to the Soviet iron-and-steel industry impelled him to qualify this judgement in view of the notable achievements found there in the field of beneficiation of low-grade ores: indeed as a result he has revised his views on the general policy of location and development of both Soviet and Soviet orbit metallurgy.

The USSR's ore reserves are by far in excess of her needs over the foreseeable future. However the economic value of Soviet iron wealth is limited by its geographical location as well as by its grade and quality.

Intensive efforts have recently been made to open up new iron ore sources particularly in the Urals. But it is the Ukrainian Krivoi Rog ore-fields which still make the backbone of Soviet-European metallurgy. Although their powdery form and high

---

[49] M. G. Clark, *Economics of Soviet Steel*, p. 179 and '*Steel in the Soviet Union*' (American Iron and Steel Inst., 1959), edited by him.

silica content reduce their value, the quality of Krivoi Rog ores is otherwise satisfactory. (They have a low content of both phosphorus and sulphur.)

The comparatively shortest distance, plus a sufficiently high Fe content—averaging about 55 per cent in deep-mined ores—which reduces the cost of a long haulage, makes these the most economical support for Central European metallurgy among all Soviet ores. The Soviet Union's own metallurgy is gradually shifted to an increasing use of lower-grade open-cast Krivoi Rog ores which carry about 36 per cent Fe (being magnetic they are easily concentrated).

An alternative source to Krivoi Rog is the ore-fields of Kerch. They are believed to be three times larger than those of Krivoi Rog. But their Fe content is far lower than that of the rich ores of the latter and they are highly phosphorous.[50]

Since the initial programmes of iron/steel expansion in the area were conceived, there might have been at times some hesitation in the Soviet overall policy for the area's metallurgy. Central European countries seem to have been encouraged to obtain additional ores from non-Soviet sources, *inter alia* from overseas sources, both inside and outside the Sino-Soviet Bloc, including such distant countries as China, Brazil, and India; and these imports are expected to grow in absolute tonnage. But what is known about the arrangements for deliveries of ore in the 1960's would point to firm as well as extremely heavy Soviet commitments.

By the mid-1960's Soviet imports may amount to 25 million tons gross (including equivalent of pig-iron) and reach double that volume by the end of the decade. Since the USSR does experience some difficulties in living up to obligations incurred, it is probable that the allocational patterns for ore in her own metallurgy have been rearranged in such a way as to give the area some priority claim on the most efficient Krivoi Rog material.

A political factor which creeps into this problem calls perhaps for a brief digression. It is believed that an expansion of metallurgy so very heavily dependent on Soviet raw material has

[50] Cf. M. G. Clark, *Economics of Soviet Steel;* C. D. Harris, 'Industrial Resources', in A. Bergson ed., *Soviet Economic Growth* (N.Y., 1953), pp. 176ff.; D. Shimkin, *Minerals —Key to Soviet Power* (Cambridge, Mass., 1953), pp. 50ff., and Iron and Steel Institute, *Russian Iron and Steel Industry*, p. 8.

permanently placed in the hands of the Soviet Union a powerful
tool of effective political pressure and thus dangerously mortgaged
the political future of the area. It is in fact suggested by some
exponents of this view that the intention to provide such an instrument of pressure stood at the cradle of the expanded industry. It
seems, however, that the reverse causal connexion between the
danger of political pressure and the dependence on foreign raw
materials can be legitimately argued. It is not the dependence on
Soviet ores and other raw materials that creates political risks but,
vice versa, it is the political supremacy which enables the Soviet
Union to make the dependence on her supplies more onerous.
Shorn of direct means of political pressure, the Soviet position as a
supplier of key material for the area's industry, in particular as a
supplier of metal, could give rise to no more apprehension than say
that of Scandinavia. And, *per contra*, so long as the USSR wields
effective levers of direct political influence in the area, the
reliance on her raw materials—and especially on ores—neither
adds appreciatively to her political strength in the area, nor
makes much difference to the political status of the countries
concerned.

The realization of this—in addition to considerations of her own
iron ore supply position—has contributed to the encouragement
clearly given to Central European countries to look for ores to the
outside world.

While thus, we believe, the political risks of a heavy reliance on
Soviet ores are not as great as is so often suggested, the problem of
viability must still be analysed in economic terms. On this point
we have to refer the reader back to our discussion of relative
productivities and costs. We may summarize and restate our
belief that the iron-and-steel industries, as they grew and are growing, are fairly capable of economic existence. In the present
context the accent is, however, on the proviso that the metal
supply be not too burdensome. The first question—one would
ask then at this point—is how relatively expensive is Soviet metal
in the area? Comparability of ore pricing is not free from pitfalls
because of the differences in the terms of delivery as well as in the
form, grade, and quality of material available from different
sources. Czechoslovak sources define Soviet price as a median
between the cheapest and the dearest price charged by other
leading exporters. The relevant fact is that the Soviet ore price for

Bloc countries—quoted f.o.b. frontier of the customer—is, according to an independent inquiry,[51] somewhat below that obtained by the USSR in transactions with outsiders. (This contrasts with certain indications of an overall price discrimination.)[52] The USSR, when promoting the expansion of metallurgy in the area, appears to have taken upon herself the responsibility for providing ore at a reasonable price and for absorbing some part of the burden arising from the locational disadvantage.

At the beginning of the 1960's suggestions, framed as a well-founded critique of the lack of coordination in the CMEA area, were put forward for more far-reaching alleviations of this burden. A lower ceiling was proposed for domestic mining in the ore-deficient countries. It is being pointed out that there is little logic in using—say in Poland—home ores which entail, in comparable terms, a capital investment outlay and operational cost between three and a half and five times heavier than even the poorer Soviet European ores.[53] An essential corollary of the postulate is a scaling down of the Soviet price charged to socialist economies. Even those who doubt the realism of this approach suggest a rationalization of the area's metallurgies broadly on the following lines. First, to confine inter-orbit trade to high-grade ores, enriched and agglomerated if necessary by the producing nation. Here it will be noted that at least one country—less short of capital than others, i.e. Czechoslovakia—is contributing to the development of ore-enriching installations in the Krivoi Rog basin. A Czechoslovak credit for this purpose is to be repaid with ore supplies. Secondly, an increasing substitution of pig-iron for ore in the Soviet supply of metalliferous material to the CMEA

[51] Horst Mendershausen's analysis (*R. Econ. Stat.*, xlii/2, p. 154) suggests that the price the USSR charges the orbit countries for her ores is about 18 per cent below what she obtains in trade with other countries.

[52] See below, pp. 318f.

[53] In the USSR the average cost of mining and enriching—up to 55–60% Fe—the Kursk and the poorer Krivoi Rog ores amounts to 340–410 Rbs/ton: the similarly computed outlay on the Polish Czestochowa ore would amount to about 2,350 zl/ton Fe (for poorer ores up to 4,500 zl/ton Fe). At a purchasing-power parity based on relative wages levels, this was calculated to yield for Poland an investment cost between three and a half and five times higher per ton, which is also roughly true of operating cost per ton Fe. Cf. A. Markowski, and M. Rakowski, in *Gosp. Plan.*, no. 6, 1959, p. 10.

This does not necessarily mean that furnace efficiency is higher in every respect when Soviet, rather than at least some domestic, ores are used. Some comparison of the respective contents and efficiency indicators for the Ukrainian Krivoi Rog and the Polish Czestochowa ores, when used in a Polish blast-furnace of 500 sq. m., has been given by Adamczyk, in *Gosp. Plan.*, no. 11, 1956, p. 5.

members would both reduce the transport burden and save the heavy cost of investment in the raw-material stage of the industry.

One may detect a historical irony in the fact that Polish attitudes have thus gone full circle over the last decade and a half: what was seen as a sin of pre-war metallurgical development now appears a virtue. Whether and to what degree these lines of policy, which have in fact been increasingly discernible in relation to East Germany, would be conceded by the USSR in relation to the two other countries of the area, and how far this would enable them to narrow the cost differentials in steel-production, is a point on which one could not risk a forecast.[54]

NOTE ON NON-FERROUS METALS

In various industrial uses non-ferrous metals support, and in part compete with, steel consumption. This note will sketch in a few words the area's potential and progress in this field.

Zinc and Lead

The only abundantly available non-ferrous metal in which the area abounds is zinc, owing to Polish resources. These rank among the richest in Europe in metal content, and among the world's largest. Located mainly in the Bytom area—in close neighbourhood with hard coal—they formed in the past the basis

Lead and Zinc Reserves

(000 tons metal content)

	Poland	East Germany	Czechoslovakia
Zinc	3,900	203?	3
Lead	400	600?	20

Source: Winston, 'Mineral Resources', in Pounds and Spulber eds., *Resources and Planning in Eastern Europe*, cf. table on p. 222n.

of the flourishing Upper Silesian zinc industry. Smaller deposits are worked in the Olkusz district. The lead content in the ores, though between one-half and one-eighth that of zinc, helps to make Polish production of concentrates more economical. East

[54] See reference to Professor Kalecki's statement on p. 303.

Germany is richer in lead—with (according to some estimates) rather more than half a million tons of this metal in her subsoil.[55]

How economical Polish zinc production really is in any comparative sense is rather difficult to say. There is a *prima facie* high probability, that, as far as costs go, Poland—along with other, older, European producers—falls behind the new overseas suppliers of zinc and lead concentrates and perhaps also those of refined zinc and pig-lead. Metal content in Polish ores steadily declines: sulphurous ores are rapidly dwindling; enrichment of galmans is considerably more expensive since it entails substantial consumption of coke and coal amounting to about 30 and 9 per cent of the oven load respectively. In advanced industrial economies both zinc and lead suffer from the competition of more 'modern' rivals: lighter metals and plastics. Lead in particular is being displaced by other materials as the source of

[55] East German reserves in non-ferrous metals have been usefully summarized by an authoritative source as follows:

Metal	Location	Size of deposits (tons)	Metal content (per cent)
Copper	Mansfeld Sangerhaus	170,000 Cu .	1·1 –1·3 1·3 –1·6
Lead	Freiberg Brand Mansfeld (combined with copper)	} 15,000–50,000 Pb {	1·23 0·3 –0·5
Zinc	Freiberg Brand (combined with lead) Mansfeld	. .	1·0 –1·25
Tin	Altenberg Ehrenfriedersdorf Rodewisch Tannenbergsthal	} c. 5,000 Sn {	0·21–0·5
Nickel	Hohenstein–Ernstthal Callenberg Kuhschnappel	} 40,000,000 (gross) {	0·8 –1·0
Wolfram	Rodewisch	c. 2,000 WO₃	.
Antimony	Oberboehmsdorf	c. 1,000 Sb	5

Source: Dtsch. Inst. Wirtsch.–Forsch., *Wber.*, no. 6, 1958. Data based on surveys carried out in the early 1950's. Resources of copper and lead are believed to be considerably higher in the light of later findings, see *Wirtschaftszahlen aus der SBZ*, p. 40.

protective dyestuffs. As 'natural' sulphur becomes available[56] production of sulphurous concentrates loses some of its former importance because of the by-product, sulphuric acid.

Under prevailing conditions Poland strives to make the maximum use of her wealth. Whatever cost calculation would suggest on other grounds, zinc has a secure market at home as a foreign-currency saver, and no less secure outlets in the USSR, Czechoslovakia, and East Germany, and generally in the Bloc, which takes about 70 per cent of Polish exports, amounting to about 90,000 tons of metal a year.

Plans for the 1960's envisage substantially increased production, partly based on poorer galman ores and waste (about 6 and $5\frac{1}{2}$ per cent Zn respectively). The comparatively lower cost of fuel and labour appears to favour imports of concentrates, where distance from sources would not make transport unduly expensive, as for instance from Bulgaria. At 1959 prices production of a ton of zinc from foreign 50–60 per cent concentrates would give a hard-currency saving of 33 zl. per $. About two-fifths of Polish-produced zinc is at present based on such imports. Technologically the Polish zinc industry is rather retarded—certain processes have not changed for decades, though some advance has been made since the war in both smelters and refineries. Electrolytic processes now account for about two-fifths of the total output, as against one-sixth before the last war. Modernization of plants and techniques (partly based on British licence), as well as expansion of plant, is to contribute to higher outputs planned for the middle of the 1960's.

One of the major investment projects planned for the 1960's is the non-ferrous metallurgical *Kombinat* in Miasteczko Slaskie in Upper Silesia. It will be composed of zinc-oxide, zinc, and lead producing departments, supplemented by a department producing rare metals (cadmium and bismuth), and it will be combined with a sulphuric-acid plant. Some 70 per cent of the primary material it will handle is expected to be recovered from slag from non-ferrous works in the Katowice and Krakow voivodships.

Copper

Until recently East Germany, owning the Mansfeld basin—the largest in Europe with nearly 150 square kilometres of deposits—

[56] See below, pp. 241f.

was the only source of copper in the area. In the early 1950's Polish mines sunk in the Grodziec–Zlotoryja district of Lower Silesia yielded the first small quantities of material. Since then Polish production has increased and gradually approached East German output.

The area's potential position has dramatically improved since vast deposits—claimed to be equal to those of Northern Rhodesia and thus among the richest in the world—were discovered near Lubin–Sieroszowice in Lower Silesia. Alternative estimates place them after those of the USSR, Rhodesia, Chile, and the Congo. Surveying is not completed yet, but geological conditions are known to be very difficult and have caused some disappointments in the initially envisaged time-table of exploitation. As now planned, three mines—of which one is already under construction—would come into operation in the second half of this decade. The smelting and refining of the ores from the 'new copper basin' are to be initially concentrated in the Legnica plant which came into operation at the end of the 1950's. (It processes concentrates with a 15% Cu content from the 'old basin'). Later on a new one is likely to be constructed, presumably at Glogow.[57]

An acceleration of programmes may result from a provisional Polish–Czechoslovak co-operation agreement concluded in 1961. This envisages Czechoslovakia's participation in the setting-up of a Polish copper 'basin' broadly on the same principles as those ruling her active interest in Polish hard-coal and sulphur.[58] Czechoslovakia will provide Poland with some equipment and in return will receive copper and electrolytic copper as repayment of credits granted for the construction of plants.[59]

Aluminium

None of the three countries has sufficient resources of raw material to support aluminium production on any considerable scale. Czechoslovakia and Poland make use—within modest limits—of poor native materials. The economics of aluminium must also allow for the exceptionally heavy consumption of power in its production: about 18 Mwh (Polish standards) are required per ton for reduction of the metal. In spite of serious doubts as to economic viability, the cost calculus being what it is, it was

[57] Z. Karst, in *Gosp. Plan.*, no. 12, 1960.
[58] See above, p. 158 and below, p. 241.   [59] See below, p. 313n.

decided in the 1950's to build up large domestic productions, mainly on bauxites imported from Hungary. The East German industry, deprived by Soviet dismantling of a substantial part of its alumina and aluminium-manufacturing facilities, was revived and given new impetus, in the traditional centre of electro-metallurgy at Bitterfeld. New industries were created in the mid-1950's in both Czechoslovakia and Poland. Plant complete with 'know-how' was provided by the Soviet Union. Towards the end of the decade the three countries reached a combined output of about 90,000 tons, of which about two-fifths came from East Germany. At the end of the 1950's imports of bauxite amounted to 40,000 tons a year in Poland and 15,000 in East Germany. Discrepancies reflect differences in the availability of domestic raw materials.

Experience has encouraged further expansion of the production potential for the 1960's. Poland has the lead in relative tempi of development. Her aluminium plant near Cracow passed its originally planned capacity by about 50 per cent by the end of the 1950's. It is to be doubled again during the 1960's and another plant, expected to reach two-thirds of its ultimate target capacity in 1970, is being built on parallel lines near Konin—the shift in location of the industry reflects the growing role of brown coal as the source of Polish supply of energy. However, all three countries have still to import some quantities of this metal. Czechoslovakia committed herself to financing the construction of some aluminium plants in the USSR: her investment there is to be repaid with supplies of aluminium from the new works.

Other Non-Ferrous Metals

Indigenous tin is available in the area from the small residual Erzgebirge deposits owned by Czechoslovakia and East Germany. The Erzgebirge and Silesia also provide the area with small quantities of various rare metals. Czechoslovakia has a small reserve and a corresponding output of antimony. Poland produces some quantities of bismuth and cadmium (a metal of use in the technology of atomic energy and dyestuffs), and endeavours to recover germanium—important in production of electronic equipment—from her zinc-lead ores. Some silver is mined in East Germany and Poland, where it is combined with lead deposits. On the whole the area has been known to be poor in polymetallic ores.

But the surveying of the Polish 'new copper basin' seems to suggest that silver, cadmium, molybdenum, and wolfram will be found in its ore deposits.

In spite of its growth Polish production of light non-ferrous metals is still relatively very low. The Polish ratio of one ton of aluminium produced per one ton of steel corresponds to about one-third of the world average (1959). The same is broadly true of consumption: the Polish per head figure is about half that of the world as a whole.

Consumption figures *per capita* are considerably higher in the two other countries. But in both Czechoslovakia and East Germany less aluminium and copper are consumed *per capita* than in either Britain or Western Germany.

The low level of use of non-ferrous metals in East German engineering is brought out a survey—made *ad valorem* in comparable terms—for the two parts of Germany.

Consumption of Non-Ferrous Metals in Engineering
(kg per 000 DM of output)

	Western Germany	East Germany
Copper	8·03	2·83–2·89
Lead	3·3	3·77–4·08
Zinc	4·14	1·68–1·70
Tin	0·17	0·08
Nickel	0·21	0·18
Aluminium	4·81	3·39–3·77

Source: Cf. Dtsch. Inst. Wirtsch.–Forsch., *Wber.*, no. 37, 1958.

This is believed to impair the quality of some engineering products.

The area is dependent on substantial imports of non-ferrous metals. The Soviet Union is its main supplier. Imports from her include copper (though she herself is a heavy net importer of this) aluminium, cobalt, antimony, tin; the latter was partly bought by the USSR from China and re-exported to Central Europe. Imports of these materials entail a considerable burden on the balance of trade: only Poland's trade in non-ferrous metals is balanced out or shows at times some surpluses—thanks to her exports of zinc.

Some relief could be expected from a more rational substitution of material. To quote a Polish source:

A view prevails among experts well informed about our [i.e. Polish] raw-material balances, that elaboration and a subsequent consistent application of a rationally evolved programme defining substitution of non-deficit non-ferrous metals, or wrought iron, or perhaps plastics for deficient metals (e.g. aluminium for copper and lead) is an urgent and important task.

CHAPTER VI

Chemicals

VERY few developments in contemporary industrial history have matched in importance the progress in chemicals, even if these lack an appeal to popular imagination comparable to that of steel, so often identified with economic power. Chemicals have been, in the past few decades, one of the most buoyant sectors of all advanced industrial economies. They are conditioned by, and they themselves condition, the overall technological progress. Their impact is indeed all-pervasive. They are feeding practically every industry, including agriculture. They are still in almost continuous flux, based on an interplay of science and technology which has few precedents in industrial history. They in turn spread change throughout the economic systems. The growth of this highly heterogeneous and extremely diversified industry—turning out thousands of products—defies attempts at adequate aggregative treatment. Only some selected aspects of it can be dealt with in this very brief survey.

THE CHEMICAL INDUSTRY IN THE THREE COUNTRIES

An indication of the relative position of the chemical industries before the last war may form perhaps a convenient point of departure. This is the picture, expressed in terms of shares of all-European chemical production, measured by contribution to national net products (in percentages): Czechoslovakia 3·8; East Germany 11·0; Poland (pre-war territory) 0·4, (post-war territory) 0·9.[1]

---

[1] Derived and re-computed from data in ECE, *Survey, 1948*, pp. 237, 243.

All-German share given by this source is 39·5%, the East German proportion of which has been taken by us to be 28%.

The addition to the chemical industry gained by Poland in the Western territories is not reflected in these figures, since they do not allow for war damage or dismantling. The figure for chemical production in the Western territories derived from the ECE data is equal to about 45% of that in pre-war Poland.

These percentages would suggest that East Germany alone was producing half as much again as Czechoslovakia and Poland combined. This may be taken as being broadly correct.

As Dr Haber points out in his excellent study[2] the Central European chemical industries arose, independently of each other, in the basin of the Rhine and along the banks of the upper and middle Elbe. In the outcome of this process before the last war Germany topped the list of European chemical producers. She was indeed one of the birthplaces and classic countries of the modern chemical industries of the world, and East Germany had more than a fair share in the patrimony of the whole Reich. Between the wars—by the mid-1930's—East German chemicals, developed mainly on brown coal and salt, accounted for approximately 30 per cent of the Reich's total, whether in terms of output values or manpower. The territorial centre of the industry was the present Land Sachsen Anhalt (at that time the Prussian province of Sachsen and the Land Anhalt), which alone was responsible for over half East German production. Powerful chemical concerns were built up in some domains in which East Germany gained primacy: its Leuna Werke became the largest European producer of 'synthetic' oil[3] and nitrogenous products. Broadly speaking Western Germany led in finer products, but even there her position was not undisputed. The East German concern Agfa of Wolfen, for instance, established for itself a near-monopoly in photographic articles. During the Second World War German chemicals moved eastwards,[4] as they did in the first war. New plants were located in what is now East Germany, which rapidly expanded capacities, particularly in branches not dependent on imports curtailed during the war. The industry suffered considerable war damage, followed by extensive dismantling: thus one of the leading units of the industry, the Leuna Werke, lost one-third of its capacity as a result of direct war destruction while another third was removed by the Soviet occupation authorities. In some cases the loss of capacity through dismantling amounted to one-half or more, which may, perhaps, be representative of the

---

[2] L. F. Haber, *The Chemical Industry in the Nineteenth Century* (London, OUP, 1958), pp. 43ff.
[3] See above, p. 153.
[4] Both world wars—and the preparations for them—gave a spur to the development of East German chemicals. The country's largest industrial *Kombinat*, Leuna Werke, was started in 1916.

industry.[5] It is only owing to the inclusion of a considerable part of the chemical plants into the SAG system that it survived to form the basis of the expansion in the 1950's.[6]

The pre-1945 all-German chemical production and markets formed an extremely complex interwoven whole; Western Germany relied on East Germany for a substantial part of her supply of sodas, technical nitrogen, and potash, while the latter was dependent on the west of the country for organic acids and finer derivatives. The East's dependence on the supply from the West of dyestuffs and pharmaceuticals was to have a notable effect on the economic relations of the two parts of the country in post-war years.

By the mid-1950's East Germany was able to claim for her chemical industry—the output of which regained its 1938 value volume—second place after the USSR in the Soviet Bloc. A good West German source concedes East Germany's claim to the sixth place in the world as a chemical producer; but at the same time, it points to a considerable decline in relative status: her percentage-share of world output appears to be a mere third of what it was before the war. This reservation will apply to her more recent claim to rank seventh in the world and, in fact, second on a per head basis.[7]

Over half the output comes from the country's 'big' six—Leuna, Buna, Bitterfeld electro-chemical *Kombinat*, Agfa Wolfen, Farbenfabrik Wolfen, and Piesteritz. A very important centre is being developed around Lauchhammer for the processing of by-products from the new coking plants, and the fully automatic 'Leuna II' is becoming one of the country's leading producers of phenol, caprolactam, ethylene, and polyethylene production.

The industry employs a quarter of a million people—9 per cent of the country's total industrial labour force. It is the branch with the highest share of overall industrial imports. It contributes about one-seventh to the total gross value of industrial production, on the official method of calculation, and about one-sixth of its total output goes into exports. It is indeed one of the mainstays

[5] Germany (FR), Bundesministerium für gesamtdeutsche Fragen, *Die chemische Industrie in der S.B.Z.* (Bonn, 1952.)

[6] Leuna Werke may exemplify the pace of reconstruction of the part of industry taken over by the system of *Sowjetische Aktiengesellschaften*, and working directly for the Soviet Union. By 1949 pre-war levels of output were regained, and by 1954—when the SAG was wound up—they had been doubled.

[7] *Die Wirtschaft*, 11 Apr. 1962.

of the East German balance of trade: about one-quarter of all earned foreign exchange is credited to chemicals. As East German input-output tables indicate, half of its production goes to industry and construction: besides the chemical industry itself its main customers are the motor, textile, and building industries.

Share in World Output of Chemicals (end of the 1930's and mid-1950's)

	$ *Thous. million* (*1954 prices*)		*Percentage share in world output*	
	1938	*1954*	*1938*	*1954*
East Germany	1·28	1·24	7·5	2·4
Poland	0·16	1·04?	0·9	2·0?
USA	5·12	22·00	29·9	43·0
Britain	1·47	3·80	8·6	7·4
Western Germany	2·00	2·94	13·4	5·7
France	0·96	2·00	5·6	3·9
Italy	0·70	1·20	4·1	2·3
Belgium	0·29	0·52	1·6	1·0
Netherlands	0·19	0·42	1·1	0·8
Switzerland	0·13	0·40	0·7	0·8
USSR	1·41	6·90	8·2	3·5

Source: A. Metzner, *Die chemische Industrie der Welt* (Düsseldorf, 1955), p. 16. Note inconsistency with the ECE calculations (p. 228), due it seems to different methods of valuation.

The chemical industry of pre-war Poland was mainly confined to heavy chemicals, substances of simple chemical structure produced in uncomplicated processes. The leading plants were those of Tomaszow Mazowiecki (rayon), Pabjanice (pharmaceuticals), and Moscice (nitrogenous fertilizers). Hence the country had to rely heavily on imports for various organic and fine chemicals. Although the share of the Western territories in the all-German chemical industry was only marginal, amounting as it did to about 2 per cent, they made a valuable contribution to the modest Polish chemical potential. The output of the branch in these territories equalled approximately half that of pre-war Poland. It was considerably increased during the war, since chemical factories serving the German war effort were transferred to, or established in, the area, especially works connected with coal processing, and mineral dyestuffs based on zinc. Several large units were built up, such as the Oberschlesische Hydrier-werke A.G. at Blachownia, employing about 11,000, the I.G. Farbenindustrie Heydebreck works at Kedzierzynia, employing about 30,000 (their production was closely interconnected), and the largest of the new plants, the Anorgana (now Rokita), at Brzeg Dolny. As in East Germany, much of this potential was reduced through war damage and dismantling. But what remained has helped to build up a vigorous industry during the expansion of the 1950's.

There are a few leading factories in Poland each representing between 2 and 4 per cent of her total chemical output. These are the Blachownia, the Rokita, and the Dwory-Oswiecim works of organic chemicals and the nitrogen works of Tarnow and of Kedzierzyn, each employing between 7,000 and 8,000; also the rubber works of Grudziadz, nitrogen plants at Chorzow, the man-made-fibre plants of Tomaszow Mazowiecki, Gorzow and Jelenia Gora, with a labour force of 3,500 to 5,500 each. The chemical *Kombinat* of Oswiecim, the nitrogen Kedzierzyn factory, the sulphuric-acid factory at Wizow, the soda factory of Janikow, and the cellulose-fibre plant of Jelenia Gora have been built or completely rebuilt since the war. About one-fifth of Polish capacity is believed to be technologically obsolete. Of the rest, about one-tenth embodies up-to-date equipment and know-how.

Although retarded, the Polish chemical industry had, already before the war, a comparatively high share of overall manpower and output value. By the early 1960's it employed nearly 180,000 —about 6 per cent of the industrial total—and accounted for roughly the same share of gross output at the official method of computation (including the chemical-raw-material and rubber industries).

Polish calculations, for what they are worth, suggest that Polish output of chemicals per head reached by 1960 the average level of Britain, West Germany, France and Italy put together. To accept the evidence of the calculations quoted above (p. 231) the Polish chemical industries around the middle of the last decade moved up quite close to the East German. It was in order to underline our doubts as to this valuation and the validity of the inference that we inserted a question mark in the table. The wide pre-war gulf between the two has certainly, however, decreased, at least quantitatively. There can be no doubt as to East Germany's qualitative lead.

Only 3 per cent of Polish output is exported; and exports are still confined mainly to the few traditional items—soda, carbide, electrodes, products of coal-tar distillation (some start has been made with dyestuffs and pharmaceuticals), and there is still an import surplus in the overall balance of trade in chemicals.[8]

Share of Chemicals in Exports—end of the 1950's
(*percentages*)

E. Germany	Poland	UK	W. Germany	France	Netherlands	Belgium	Norway	Italy
25	4	8	11	8	9	8	9	7

Whether the yardstick is output or labour-force, the Czechoslovak chemical industry is by far the smallest in the area. However its production would seem to be more diversified than that of the Polish industry—especially in inorganic chemicals. Around the end of the 1950's it employed about 60,000, some 5 per cent of the national total, and its share of gross output was also about 5 per cent.

The industry has spread throughout the country. A considerable part of it is centred in the century-old traditional area of Ostrava, where it is inter-linked with coal processing and metallurgy. A substantial proportion of chemical plant is out of date, but in addition to new construction, some of the old plants have been intensively modernized, such as the Zaluzi-near-Most (Stalin)

[8] Chemical exports equal only about a quarter of imports. In spite of the post-war development of the industry, the proportion has not changed materially. But before the last war finished or semi-finished products—pharmaceutical articles, dyestuffs, organic products—predominated in Polish imports: at present a high proportion is made up of raw materials. A substantial part of imports classified as chemicals now consists of oil products (30 per cent): imports of potash necessitated by the loss of potash mines account for 9 per cent, raw materials for other fertilizers, for another 4 per cent. Raw materials for the chemical industry proper account at present for about two-fifths of Polish chemical imports. Plans for 1965 envisage a 14 per cent share of chemicals in the Polish total of exports. Cf. S. Gieszczynski and M. Niesiolowski, in *Gosp. Plan.*, no. 11, 1960, pp. 1ff.

Chemical Industry: Share of Industrial Manpower and Output,
1958 or 1959

	Manpower		Share of industrial output (per cent)	
	(thousands)	per cent of industrial total	In gross production value	In value added
Czechoslovakia				
(a)	50	3·1	4·1	9·1
(b)	62	3·3	5·1	
East Germany				
(a)	264	9·7	13·8	
(b)	326	11·9	13·5	
Poland				
(a)	129	4·6	4·5	9·6
(b)	141	4·7	5·2	
Western Europe (OEEC countries)	·	·		10·3
Belgium	73	4·6		5·6
France	245	4·9		12·4
Western Germany	399	4·7		9·8
Italy	·	·		19·8
Netherlands	·	·		10·7
Austria	34	3·1		7·7
Denmark	12	3·3		8·3
Greece	·	·		17·0
Norway	21	4·6		13·7
Sweden	·	·		5·6
Switzerland	28	·		·
United Kingdom	466	4·5		8·5

Sources: For the three countries' manpower and shares in gross industrial production—*Stat. roc., 1959*; *Rocz. stat., 1959*; *Stat.
Jb., 1959*; *Plan. Hosp.*, nos. 6–7, 1958. Data on Western Europe
obtained or derived from OEEC, *Industrial Statistics, 1900–
1957*, pp. 4 and 6.

Data under (a) refer to chemical industries as classified in
official statistics. Data under (b) include for Poland the rubber
and soap industries; for Czechoslovakia the rubber industry,
and for East Germany, the cellulose and paper industry.

On the whole data under (a) seem to provide a better base
for comparison with Western Europe.

For Czechoslovakia manpower comprises manual workers only: for all the other countries it covers wage-earning and salaried staff.

works and the Chemical and Metallurgical Production *Kombinat* at Usti-on-Elbe.

The industry sells abroad about one-tenth of its production—a ratio just below the average for all industries.

Relative Position of Chemicals in the Industrial Body

The position of chemicals in the industrial bodies of the respective countries, its relative size, and its role against the European background, are hinted at in the preceding table. At the risk of repetition a note of warning will be sounded here, again for the sake of emphasis, as to the comparability of data. It is affected by the many difficulties encountered. Not the least of them are due to the differences in classification and in the drawing of branch and sector frontiers. More serious obstacles to comparability arise from the differences in methods of valuation which have been treated at length before.

The share of chemicals, in each of the three countries, in the industrial net product—about 10 per cent of the aggregate—closely approaches that prevailing in Western Europe. It is also safe to say that by any method of measurement it is on the upgrade in the area, as it is throughout industrial Europe: the average share of the chemical industry in the overall European industrial structure has, in fact, increased approximately threefold since 1900.[9] In this sense a high share of chemicals reflects the secular trend in reshaping industrial bodies. Too much should not, however, be read into comparisons on this count: it will, for instance, be noted that the highest place in the table is held by Italy, who, thanks to her large oil-refining branch and traditional interest in staple-fibre production, created a chemical industry well ahead of her overall level of industrialization. On the other hand the two leading chemical producers, Britain and Western Germany, who between them are responsible for half European production, show no more than an average proportion of chemicals in total product.

The key structural feature which stands out in the table on page 234 is the high—well above the average—labour productivity

[9] Paretti and Bloch, in *BNLQR*, no. 39, 1957, p. 214.

in this industrial branch. In Western Europe taken as a whole it employs only about one-twentieth of all industrial labour. But its contribution to value-added in industry is twice that proportion. This characteristic would be less pronounced if gross-output statistics were taken as a basis for the three countries. A relatively high proportion of fabrication costs in chemicals secures for them on the whole a higher share in net, rather than in gross production on which the official valuations are based in the area.

Polish calculations of cost structures suggest that this is a branch with exceptionally low marginal capital-to-output ratio. These findings may seem, however, somewhat suspect as to their basis and meaning for an industry characterized by a rapid rate of change, one with a high rate of obsolescence and requiring more and more complex, and consequently expensive, plant.

Marginal Capital/Output Ratio in Polish Chemical Industry: End of 1950's

Whole industry	1·7	Rubber	0·8
Inorganic chemicals	1·7	Dyestuffs, varnishes	0·3
Organic chemicals	0·8	Man-made fibres	1·6
Chemical raw materials	1·8	Synthetic fibres	1·4
Great synthesis	1·5	Plastic materials	0·4

Source: Compiled from T. B. Kozlowski, in *Gosp. Plan.*, no. 4, 1960, and other Polish sources.

They are, indeed, disproved by the experience of economies with more rational price and cost structures. In particular they go against the results of dependable British investigations.[10]

It is the manufacturing of inorganic chemicals and the mining of chemical raw materials which show the relatively highest investment to output ratios. These are as divergent as 6·5 for some of the mined materials as against 0·4 for plastics and 1·4 for synthetic fibres. Here again suspicion may arise as to how intermediate materials are supplied to the higher-stage-fabrication plan at artificially low prices. Even if allowance is made for such distortion it seems credible that it is the heavy-chemicals sector which calls for the relatively greatest investment.

[10] There is a well-reasoned discussion of this point in the excellent study by W. B. Reddaway, 'The Chemical Industry', in Duncan Burn ed., *The Structure of British Industry* (Cambridge, 1958).

As against the findings questioned, estimates of a falling trend in the ratio may seem more plausible. According to Polish official sources 2 zloty had to be invested under the first development plan to achieve an increase of output of one zloty; the investment required dropped to zl. 1·70 in the second half of the 1950's and is planned at zl. 1·30 for the present half decade.[11] We shall return to the implications of this.

Performance and Programmes

The late 1950's witnessed a growing consciousness that in chemicals the area was retarded as compared with the more important producers in Western Europe. The distance is particularly marked as regards the scope and type of products: the range of more refined items is smaller than that typical of the advanced industries. The predominance of basic sectors of heavy inorganic chemistry in Poland has already been pointed out. Czechoslovakia, and, still more, East Germany, are, it is true, closer to the Western pattern. Yet, in fact, even East Germany is lagging behind industrial Europe in certain up-to-date organic chemicals. In Poland the outputs—per head of the population— of representative inorganic products were, in the mid-1950's, between two and a half and five times smaller than in the leading Western countries: those of more complicated organic products were up to forty times lower. Production of some of the chemicals most characteristic of contemporary progress was either non-existent or in its infancy.

A few words on comparisons between the two Germanies. As against Western Germany there is a very strong East German lead in calcium carbide and fertilizers (due primarily to potash wealth). East Germany is also ahead of the Federal Republic in several other heavy chemicals such as chlorine, calcium and caustic soda, and primary ammonia, all of which form a solid basis for the developed chemical industry; she lags behind, however, in sulphuric acid. But, in the range of 'modern' chemicals, the lead indisputably belongs to Western Germany. In some aspects the pre-partition picture has tended to perpetuate itself; in fact some of its features have tended to accentuate themselves more strongly than hitherto.

[11] Statement by the Minister for Chemical Industry to the Central Committee of the Party, 23 Jan. 1960.

Statistically measured, chemicals have been, at least in Poland and Czechoslovakia, one of the main 'leading links' of industrial expansion in the post-war period, though overshadowed by engineering. Eastern Germany, which already at the start of the period possessed a developed chemical industry, does not conform to this pattern. Until the mid 1950's her chemicals were advancing only just in step with overall industrial output.

Programmes for the 1960's accord to chemicals a distinctly preferential rate of growth throughout the area. It is more than double the overall industrial average in Poland and nearly attains that ratio in Czechoslovakia. In the latter country the locational policy favours the concentration of new plants in Slovakia, such as the East Slovak Chemical *Kombinat* and the Losovice nitrogen-fertilizer factory. Chemicals together with iron and steel are to constitute the backbone of Slovakia's industrialization. In East Germany progress is planned to be half again as fast as in the industry as a whole.

The rethinking of the industrial strategy of the Soviet Bloc has resulted in East Germany being assigned the role of the principal country in chemicals—in certain aspects a pilot-producer even ahead of the Soviet Union. In this she has been assured of the USSR's support in terms of an adequate flow of some raw materials in which she is deficient—and, on a modest scale, the necessary finance.[12] It has been stressed by the Soviet leaders that the Germans, being pioneers in chemistry and having developed outstanding skills in some of its sectors, should be placed accordingly in the intra-Bloc division of labour.

The division of labour in chemicals is the concern of the special permanent committee of the CMEA, with headquarters in East Berlin, which deals with economic, technical, and scientific co-operation in this branch. Since 1958 it has adopted various resolutions aiming at greater specialization in a number of individual products, including fertilizers, synthetic materials, synthetic rubbers, and fibres. Co-operation is being extended to embrace research as well as the provision of the requisite projects, machines, and chemical equipment. Measures have been drawn

[12] See statement by N. S. Khrushchev on 9 July 1958. A pledge of a Soviet loan for the development of the East German plastics industry was reported in 1958. It is to be used specifically for the construction of a polyvinyl chloride plant. Repayment is to be carried out in rising yearly supply-quotas of that product, beginning with 20,000 tons in 1961.

up for securing and coordinating the raw-material basis. Co-ordination has been extended to cover whole important areas in the use of chemicals such as the use of plastics in building. In the early 1960's specialization under the CMEA schedules was claimed to cover more than four-fifths of the chemical production of member economies. The meaning of the claim is not easy to interpret.

As these words were being written Poland's very-long-range programme—the only one in the area—was revealed as a comprehensive whole aiming at consistency. With an expected increase of net output, over 1960–75, by four and a half times, chemicals are to continue as the most dynamic element in overall industrial growth. Their nearest followers, engineering and power generation, would grow only threefold. The plan proceeds from an expectation that, in accordance with the observed trend, the marginal capital (investment)-to-output ratio will go on declining in this and the next decade.[13]

Assuming that by the mid-1970's the ratio drops to about 1·0, total capital outlay over the fifteen years following 1960 would be

Polish Programme for Chemicals, 1956–75

	Output—total (000 tons)		Output per capita (kg)	
	1956	Anticipated 1975	1956	1975
Sulphuric acid H_2SO_4	481	2,210	17·5	59·0
Soda ash	214	1,040	7·2	27·8
Nitrog. fertilizers N_2	175	815	6·4	21·7
Phosphate fertilizers P_2O_5	123	650	4·5	17·3
Chlorine	19	215	0·7	5·7
Plastics	12	300	0·4	8·0
Synthetic fibres	0·8	75	0·03	2·0
'Natural' fibres	58	175	2·1	4·7
Rubber products	75	310	2·8	8·3
Synthetic rubber	—	150	–	4·0
Sulphur	14	750	0·5	20·0

Note: The CMEA discussed these problems at its Prague session in Dec. 1958.

Source: Pojda and Zajac, in *Gosp. Plan.*, no. 8, 1958, p. 30. *Per capita* outputs for 1975 given for anticipated population.

[13] Note that the ratio does not say anything *per se* as to the relative burden of investment in a given industry. Assuming equal ratios, an industry with higher-cost outputs entails heavier investment—in absolute terms—than one with lower-cost outputs.

of an estimated order of $3,000 million.[14] This gives an idea of the order of magnitude of the effort implied in the programmes.

All in all, investment patterns do display some shifts in favour of the advanced stages of manufacture.[15] But the major part of investment in chemicals has still to be directed to the production of heavy materials which feed non-chemical industries and agriculture as well as to the manufacture of the higher-stage chemicals. Costly development of the indigenous raw-material basis is a policy dictated partly by the determination to develop each country's own natural wealth and partly by balance-of-payments considerations; it inevitably reduces the capital resources which can be put into the more 'sophisticated' chemicals. Sectoral allocation of investment in the Polish long-term programme is so conceived as to bring about a *per capita* output of the most important chemical products by 1975 roughly equal to that in industrial Western European countries around 1955. But, seen against the formidable pace of advance in applied science and chemical technology, twenty years make an extremely long period of time. In no other area of industrial life is planning two decades ahead more of a crystal-gazing exercise than it is in chemicals. This makes chemicals highly representative of the dilemmas which face the capital-deficient nations as they try to catch up and keep abreast with the industrial leaders of the world.

RAW MATERIALS

The three countries as a whole may be considered moderately well provided by nature with the basic materials required by the industry. Limestone is abundant over vast areas. There is also plentiful salt, especially in East Germany (in the Stassfurt area), and, still more, in Poland (in Bochnia, Wieliczka, Ciechocinek,

[14] J. Pojda and M. Zajac, in *Gosp. Plan.*, no. 8, 1958, p. 32. The zloty amount is about 92,000 million. Conversion rate of $ = 30 investment zloty may be warranted.

[15] These are the percentage shares of major sectors of chemicals in the total investment outlay on the Polish chemical industry over 1950–60:

Year	Fertilizers & raw materials	Chemical synthesis	Inorganic chemicals	Staple fibres	Synthetic fibres	Plastics	Dyes, pharmaceuticals, &c.
1950–5	30·1	8·6	16·3	15·3	3·6	1·2	8·8
1956–60	24·5	19·2	12·7	7·7	3·4	5·6	9·4

Source: *Przemysl Chemiczny*, no. 3, 1958.

and other areas); the latter's reserves have been estimated at 150 million tons. Resources are sufficient for a larger-scale production of soda, chlorine, and so on. Centres of chemical industry have an adequate supply of water—at least as raw and cooling material, if not as a source of energy.

Sulphur

Of other essential substances, sulphur has been, until very recently, a deficit material. The area has had to build up its production of sulphuric acid primarily on indigenous pyrites, supplemented more recently by anhydrites, and on considerable pyrite imports. But the position underwent a radical change when, in the 1950's, vast resources of native sulphur had been found in the Tarnobrzeg and Piaseczno regions of Poland. These have not yet been adequately surveyed, but tentative estimates are as high as 95–110 million tons of pure sulphur in ores with about 20–25 per cent S content. On these estimates Poland would own nearly one-fifth of the globe's reserves, closely following Mexico, the country richest in sulphur.

	Resources (mill. tons)	S content in ore (%)	Yearly output around 1958 (000 tons)
Mexico	110	25	1,500
Poland	95	20	13
USA	90	25	5,600
USSR	70	10	40
Italy	30	8	245
Japan	15	40	195

The geological conditions of Polish deposits are difficult; their exploitation calls for vast investment on mines and processing installations and on the infrastructure—transport and housing in the new basin. In time Polish sulphur is expected to go a long way towards meeting the requirements of the Soviet Bloc as a whole— three-quarters of the exports planned for 1965 is expected to go to the CMEA area. Czechoslovakia has been financially engaged in its development.[16]

[16] See below, p. 313. It has been suggested that sulphur recovered from brown coal mined in the northern basin could meet a major part of Czechoslovakia's requirements in this chemical. See O. Mesaros, in *Plan. Hosp.*, no. 4, 1961, p. 316.

About 1960 the first mine, at Piaseczno, and the processing plant of Machow were in operation. By the beginning of this decade a yearly output of 132,000 tons was achieved. The material was delivered to consuming industries as sulphur and sulphur dioxide gained from the burning of waste ore. This quantity is expected to be trebled by the middle of the decade.

Phosphate Rock

None of the countries of the area has any adequate indigenous supply of phosphates. There are scattered resources of poor phosphorus-bearing materials in all the three countries, with a P_2O_5 content of up to 15 per cent after enrichment; small quantities of industrially usable material are recovered in steel making. All three countries draw their imports of phosphate rock mainly from the Soviet Union, whose own resources under exploitation are, however, insufficient to cover the deficits. Most probably no radical improvement in the phosphorus supply can be expected in any of the countries from prospecting in progress.

Potash

Among raw materials in which the area is exceptionally well provided by nature, potash salts deserve a special mention. Partition left with East Germany most of the German potash wealth of the Harz, Werra area, Hanover, and Mecklenburg regions. She is believed to own about one-third of the world's known total resources, which form the basis of expanded fertilizer production. About three-fifths of East German potash output is sold abroad, mainly to Soviet Bloc nations. Under a special CMEA arrangement Czechoslovakia is committed financially in East German potash production in return for a stipulated supply from this source. With about a million tons of K_2O shipped a year, she is in fact the leading exporter of potash in the world. On the other hand, hopes staked on Polish potash—found in the Klodawa region—have not been justified as yet. These resources have not yet been analysed as an economic proposition: one suggestion is that Klodawa ores should provide salts for general industrial use, while fertilizer salt would continue to be drawn from East Germany. Production of Klodawa potash—at an initial level of about 100,000 tons a year—is expected to start in the late 1960's.

Cellulose

In the not too distant past the area's timber was an abundant base for chemicals. Wartime destruction, territorial losses, and a rise in the consumption of timber have reduced availabilities. At any rate none of the countries is able to expand plantations of fast-growing, cellulose-yielding trees.[17] Poland alone exports some quantities of wood-pulp, but she is herself short of refined cellulosic raw material and imports some 80,000 tons a year—half the cellulose she needs in the chemical industry—most of it from Finland. In the other two countries home supplies also account for only a fraction of requirements, met mainly from Scandinavian sources and the USSR. Poland and Czechoslovakia have recently secured a source of low-cost cellulose from Rumanian reed plantations, in the development of which they co-operate financially and technically. With the view to saving her timber resources, East Germany is entering into similar arrangements with Bulgaria, where straw-cellulose production is being developed.

Coal

Coal—both brown and hard—gives the area's chemical industries both energy and ingredients for an extremely rich range of products (in some cases the two functions of coal appear in the same process). In addition to gas—town gas and coke-oven gas—carbonization of coal is providing the area with its important breakdown-products. Coke, with which we dealt as one of the pivots of the iron-and-steel industry, is—via calcium carbide—the source of acetylene. The latter, in addition to being an essential material in other branches—to name only engineering, where it is indispensable for welding, and construction—is one of the mainstays of the aliphatic synthesis industry. It is the source of hydrogen and carbon monoxide in the fabrication of synthetic ammonia, methanol, and urea. On this route, through the Fischer-Tropsch

[17] All the three countries have expanded their production of cellulose since the Second World War.

Output of cellulose, 1937–58

	1937	1958	1937	1958
	thous. tons		share in world output per cent	
Czechoslovakia	.	365	.	1·1
East Germany	205	325	0·7	0·7
Poland	93	236	0·2	0·5

RIPP

Production of Basic Chemicals
(ooo tons)

	1937 or 1938	1955	1959	1960	1961	1962[1]	1965
Sulphuric acid (SO₃)							
Czechoslovakia	165	383	513	553	600	643	560
East Germany	369	483	564	596	660		1,005
Poland	180	450	611	680	794	703	1,140
Chlorine (HCl)							
Czechoslovakia	.	69	65	74			110–20
East Germany	4	8		55	67		
Poland							
Caustic soda (NaOH, sodium hydroxide)							
Czechoslovakia	30	82	100	115	115		140
East Germany	124	257	304	327	306		.
Poland	22	101	158	174	186	200	255
(Na₂CO₃, soda ash)							
Czechoslovakia	.	94	100			70	140
East Germany	378	459	564	594	540		.
Poland	89	211	437	500	536	646	660
Calcium carbide (300 l.C₂H₂/Kg)							
Czechoslovakia	.	78	91	104			.
East Germany	.	793	888	922	950		1,180
Poland	64	211	280	321	360		.
Ammonia, synthetic (NH₃)							
Czechoslovakia	.	.	457				
East Germany	.	293	.	477			
Poland	33	167	325	346			
Phosphate fertilizers (P₂O₅)							
Czechoslovakia	61	98	135	146	167	181	.
East Germany	32	.	138	166	175	180	284
Poland	43	132	174	197	235	280	360
Nitrogenous fertilizers (N)							
Czechoslovakia	24	60	133	140	144	160	.
East Germany	229	.	329	334	335		386
Poland	43	154	258	271	282	300	480
Potash (K₂O)							
East Germany	953	.	1,528	1,666			2,128
Poland	108	.	.				.
Synthetic rubber							
Czechoslovakia	.	.	.		.		.
East Germany	.	72	84	87	88		105
Poland	.	.	5	20	31	35	50
Plastics							
Czechoslovakia	.	.	53	60	78	97	180–90
East Germany	.	.	93				311
Poland[2]	.	4	40		69		185
Synthetic fibres							
Czechoslovakia	.	.	1·5				21
East Germany	.	.	6·7				39
Poland	.	0·5	4·5		6·0	6	29
Organic dyestuffs							
Czechoslovakia	.	.	.				.
East Germany	.	8	8				.
Poland	2	7	10				.
Chemical fibres							
Czechoslovakia		49		62	69		
East Germany							
Poland	8	54			83	82	

[1] Polish production of polyvinyl chloride and polyester in 1962 has been estimated at 15,000 and 8,000 tons respectively.
[2] Partly estimated.

process—in wide use, especially in East Germany—coke is the source of different aliphatic intermediates.

Coal thus makes a signally intimate triangular interlink between the three leading sectors of the industrial system—energy generation, metals and chemicals. It indeed well deserves the name of the universal raw material *par excellence*.

BASIC PRODUCTS

No more is intended than a very fragmentary survey of developments in some key fields of the industry, because of its extremely wide ramifications and the lack of documentation. Large vital sectors—to name only dyestuffs and medicinal and pharmaceutical products—are left out of the account, which, therefore, should be considered as no more than an attempt at an illustrative case story.

Per Capita Output of Certain Chemicals, 1960

(kilograms)

	CSR	East Germany	Poland	France	Italy	UK	Western Germany
Sulphuric acid	41	42	23	44	42	52	59
Soda ash	8	56	18	19	10		20
Chlorine			0·3	7·3	3·7		11·8
Ammonia	3		2	7	4		12
Fertilizer:							
nitrogen (N)	10	19	9	13	13	8	20
phosphate (P₂O₅)		18	7	21	7	8	17
Plastics (materials)	5·1		2·3	6·6	5·1	10·9	17·7
Man-made fibres			2·4	2·7	3·3	5·2	4·2
synthetic			0·16	0·99	0·7	0·76	0·95

Sulphuric Acid

To begin with basic inorganic chemicals: we should perhaps first say something about developments in sulphuric acid, which—in spite of the astonishing advances in 'newer' substances—is still reigning supreme in chemicals. Most of it—in the area as a whole, well over one-half—is absorbed by the fertilizer industry, in the production of superphosphates and ammonium phosphates. But what remains forms an essential support in the area for the manufacture of dyestuffs, plastics, man-made fibres, and so on. Outside the chemical industry, other branches, such as textiles and metals, are also among its users. The technology of acid production is interdependent with the raw materials used. Since about the turn of the century the continuous 'contact' process has predominated, providing heavy concentrates of wide industrial application. But, as has been pointed out, until recently the position as far as sulphur-bearing material is concerned has been precarious. The area has relied on comparatively less efficient material—and this has been one of the handicaps of this sector—partly on by-products of, or waste sulphur recovered from, other industries. Thus, before the war, Polish acid-making was dependent for two-thirds of the sulphur content of its output on by-products of the zinc industry.

Since the last war pyrite-burning plants have been supplied throughout the area largely with imported material. In the 1950's the industry tended to shift to local calcium sulphates, gypsum, and anhydrites. It has been allied to the production of cement and thus has helped to satisfy the fast-growing demand from building trades: in the manufacture of acids from anhydrites the joint product—clinker—serves as the basis of cement production on approximately the same scale in tonnage. A comparatively more complicated form of anhydrite processing is, for instance, the technical basis of the new large Polish plant of Wizow, in Lower Silesia, working on locally found raw material; this is also true of the still newer plant at Busko Zdroj. Similarly in East Germany, the leading post-war plant, Agfa Wolfen—turning out 200,000 tons of acid and 170,000 tons of clinker cement—is processing indigenous anhydrites. So will another German factory of comparable capacity at Coswig on the Elbe, the first kilns of which went into operation in 1960. This is expected ultimately to become the largest plant of its kind in the world. (Until the Coswig plant helps to overcome the deficiency some smaller units under construction or completed—at the Freiburg zinc plant, at Salwedel, Premnitz, and Oranienburg—are expected to provide some relief.) Germany played an important role in the development of sulphuric-acid manufacturing. It is largely to her chemists and technologists that the discovery and industrial use of the process for the catalytical production of concentrated acid is due: she has pioneered in the application of the contact-acid process. However, the limitations of the raw-material basis and the insufficiency of manufacturing facilities are the cause of a really critical sulphuric-acid bottleneck in East Germany. (It has been noted that under-development in sulphuric acid has long been characteristic of East German chemicals.) The task of widening this bottleneck has become the more urgent as plans for the production and exports of 'new' materials involving appreciable additions to acid con-sumption have had to be implemented. Some observers have suggested that East Germany's vast build-up of acid-manufacturing capacities has been treated in the CMEA arrange-ments as her counterpart for the Soviet-stipulated supplies of oil, hard coal, and phosphate rock.

Czechoslovakia's acid output has been based chiefly on inferior indigenous pyrites, with an S content as low as 12 per cent (18 per cent is usually considered the lowest limit of econom-ical use). For various reasons expansion of Czechoslovak capacity has been accompanied by a significant rise in both capital and running costs per ton of output.

The raw-material prospects of the industry of the area as a whole have improved considerably since the Polish sulphur wealth was discovered.[18] (Technologically the natural-sulphur-using process is more efficient.) As the flow of supplies is widened from the new source, natural sulphur will be increasingly replacing sulphur-bearing material in Poland and Czechoslovakia, and to a lesser extent in East Germany. The Polish 'basin' is to include a sul-phuric-acid plant, with an ultimate output of about 400,000 tons, and a factory making phosphoric acid and phosphate fertilizers; about one-quarter of the country's estimated 1965 output of the latter is to be produced there. In the meantime Tarnobrzeg sulphur is to be used in a smaller plant at Torun with a capacity of 100,000 tons, forming part of a phosphate-fertilizer factory believed to be the most up to date of its kind in Central Europe which was opened about 1960.

Czechoslovakia's new installations at the Moravian chemical works, Postorna, have been devised to produce acid from pure sulphur obtained by her from the source jointly developed.

Around the middle of the 1960's about 50 per cent of the sul-phuric acid produced in Poland will be based on natural sulphur: the rest on other home-derived materials. (A sulphuric-acid plant is to be installed in the new Miasteczko *Kombinat* of non-ferrous metallurgy.)[19] The proportion of materials other than Polish

[18] See above, p. 241.   [19] See above, p. 223.

natural sulphur will be, in the foreseeable future, higher in Czechoslovakia, and East Germany does not seem to rely on Polish sulphur to any comparable degree: in the late 1960's about 70 per cent of her vastly expanded output of acid is still to come from anhydrite processing plant.

Alkalis

East Germany and Poland have a long history as alkali producers. German soda-manufacturing was started in what is now East Germany—at Schoenebeck on the Elbe, around 1800, and Polish development also goes far back into the last century. It has supported various trades both inside and outside the chemical branch—in the first place soap manufacturing, but also rayon, textiles, and paper and glass making.

Throughout the area the predominant technique in alkali production has been the Solvay process: it is thus largely emancipated from the link with sulphuric acid which is so strong in the Leblanc process. (Until they were nationalized in the 1940's, the principal Polish and Czech plants were actually controlled by the Solvay concern.) The Solvay process relies basically on brine (about $1\frac{1}{2}$ tons per ton of soda), limestone (roughly the same quantity), and coal—and coke (about half the tonnage of soda ash)—as its chief raw materials, and these are the location determining factors. Since the last war the—formerly Solvay-owned—Polish factories producing soda ash, caustic soda and crystal soda—those of Matwy and Borek Falecki, have been considerably expanded and modernized. Progress has been still more spectacular in East Germany, the chief soda producer in the area, where output rose tenfold. Substantial reconstruction and expansion is also being carried out in Czechoslovakia, whose only factory dates from the beginning of this century: a large investment is hoped to lower cost and reduce the soda deficit. At present this deficit is met by imports, mainly from East Germany and partly from Poland.

Chlorine

Recent Polish and East German additions to caustic-soda capacities rely chiefly on the electrolytic process based on brine, which supplies sodium hydroxide, chlorine, and hydrogen. It has technical advantages, though these are offset by a large consumption of power. In its application, in preference to the ammonia-soda alternative, requirements of chlorine are the determining factor. Siting of chlorine-making plant generally depends on the supply of electricity (by Polish standards some $5\frac{1}{2}$ mwh are consumed per ton). Unlike some other 'traditional' inorganic chemicals, chlorine has not suffered any decline in demand in recent years. Indeed, from being a less desirable companion of the soda-making trade, it is gaining an increasingly independent role in industrial life. Its wide application in the production of plastics, in addition to its more traditional uses, such as chlorinated solvents, has raised its importance in more recent years. Indeed the shortage of chlorine, together with that of phenol, has been the principal bottleneck in the expansion of the plastic-material sector in the area in general, and specifically in East Germany. However the largest single producer in the area is the East German Elektro-chemisches Kombinat Bitterfeld, a complex unit producing a vast range of inorganic as well as organic chemicals and believed to hold the all-European record for chlorine. Since the last century Bitterfeld has been one of the major centres of the German electrochemical industry. Its works had close connexions with the Allgemeine Elektrizitäts Gesell-schaft: they were originally designed to electrolyse potassium chloride to caustic potash, and subsequently turned to electrolysing brine to caustic soda and chlorine; and then to the production of bleaching powder. The links between electrochemistry and non-ferrous metallurgy are worth noting here. The Bitterfeld *Kombinat* is followed in rank by a new electrolytic plant of the Buna Works. Polish chlorine comes mainly from the Oswiecim and Rokita plants.

Calcium Carbide

Among the basic inorganic chemicals, calcium carbide deserves special mention. Though threatened with growing rivalry,[20] it stands every chance of retaining one of the dominant roles in the chemical industries of the area: demand for products of acetylene derivatives, far from declining under the impact of competition, is in the ascendant. Calcium carbide is likely to preserve this role in spite of the disadvantages of its production. In addition to

[20] See below, p. 258.

limestone and coke (650–720[21] kilograms per ton by the East German and Polish standards) it requires very great quantities of power: some $3\frac{1}{2}$ mwh (Polish average) are consumed in producing a ton of carbide in ovens at 2,500° Celsius. (The alternative of what has become the conventional electric furnace, i.e. one in which coke is being burnt in oxygen, has found, for various reasons, little application in the area.) This weighs very heavily on the energy requirements of carbide-based chemicals, e.g. 90 per cent of the power needed in the production of nitrogen is accounted for by calcium carbide alone.[22]

New carbide furnaces are under construction at the Chemische Werke Buna. When the new capacities are on stream, this works, 90 per cent of the processing operations of which are based on calcium carbide, and which now ranks as its largest single producer in Europe, is expected to become the largest unit in the world, with a yearly output of about 800,000 tons. The three other principal East German carbide producers are the Stickstoffwerk Piesteritz, Elektrochemik Hirschfelde, and Leuna.

East Germany's two neighbours are also intensively investing in this section of the industry. Besides the older Czechoslovak plants—the Sokolov and Lobkovice factories—the newly erected Novaky factory is to be appreciably enlarged. Czechoslovakia hopes by the mid-1960's to cover an increased domestic consumption and to be able to export a certain amount to other Bloc countries.

Nitrogen-Ammonia and Fertilizers

Some components of the area's fertilizer sector were mentioned when raw-material resources and basic chemicals were discussed. Only a few remarks will be added now. Nitrogen-ammonia is one of the pivots of the sector. The range of the industrial application of nitrogen and nitric acid is very wide and still expanding: it embraces such various uses as the fabrication of explosives, plastics, synthetic fibres, dyestuffs and pharmaceuticals, but the bulk of it is directed to fertilizer production. Technical nitrogen makes up a marginal fraction of total output.

Germany was one of the pioneers of the industry; and earlier in

[21] Polish pre-war coke consumption approximated to about 600 kg per ton of carbide. The post-war increase is a pointer to the technological deterioration of the processes.

[22] See below, p. 251.

this century its centres crystallized along the lines corresponding to the geography of resources. The first German factory of *Kalkstickstoff*—based on calcium carbide, on the Frank-Caro method—was put into operation in 1905 in what is now East Germany—at Westregeln, near Magdeburg. The needs of a siege economy—envisaged before, and embarked upon in 1914— acted as a powerful scientific and technological stimulus. The supply of ammonia, which early in this century was obtainable only from gas and coke-ovens works, had to satisfy the steeply rising demands from rival civilian and defence uses. The invention of the Haber-Bosch technique enabled the Badische Anilin und Sodafabrik to put into operation in the Ruhr area, as early as 1913, the first German large-scale plant for ammonia synthesis based on fixing atmosphere nitrogen. Very shortly thereafter, during the First World War the same concern commissioned a second plant, which owing to considerations of strategy as well as fuel supply was located at Leuna near Merseburg.[23] Leuna was thus destined to become one of the chief centres of the East German chemical industry. The monopoly of the Chilean nitrate fields was effectively broken. (Before the Haber-Bosch technique was applied half the nitrogenous material had to be imported.) Subsequently the cyanamide process has been perfected and technological altern- atives have been evolved.

At the outbreak of the last world war East Germany ranked among leading European producers in this domain. After the war, however, expansion was damped down and her share in the world's output fell, in contrast to the two other countries of the area, which pushed forcefully ahead.

Poland started her production of nitrogen from the air at the end of the 1920's. It was expanded subsequently in the inter-war period in the plants of Moscice (now Dzierzynski) near Tarnow, and of Chorzow. The period following the Second World War saw a further growth of this sector through the reconstruction of the old plant and new additions. Substantial capacities were added at the Tarnow factory: in the rebuilt Kedzierzyn *Kombinat* the manufacturing of ammonia is the basic department.

In the early 1950's a very considerable advance was recorded in securing a greater contribution to nitrate-fertilizer output from

---

[23] On these developments see, e.g. H. Schall, *Die chemische Industrie Deutschlands* (Nürnberg, 1959), pp. 57ff.

the 'coking-chemical' branch. A basic reconstruction of the old Chorzow factory—expected to result in the 1960's in a doubling of its output—has been undertaken chiefly with a view to using coke-oven gas resources as its prime material. The discovery of natural-gas resources in the south of Poland gave an impetus to plans for a radical shift in the raw-material basis in this industry; especially in the modern installations of the Tarnow plant, 'Tarnow II', based on the Italian Montecatini method. When it reaches its ultimate pro-grammed capacity sometime in the 1960's, about a thousand tons a day, the plant will be producing the equivalent of the total annual Polish production recorded at the start of the decade.

Another nitrogen-product factory in Pulawy,[24] based on natural gas, is expected to be commissioned in the later years of the present decade. The complete equipment for this plant is to be supplied to Poland by Czechoslovakia in connexion with the latter's interest in the development of the Polish 'copper basin'. The plant is scheduled to process some 800 million cubic metres of natural gas and to have an output of just under half a million tons of ammonia and half that quantity of acetylene. (At full capacity the new plants are hoped to save about 2 million tons of coke a year.) By the middle of the decade Poland is likely to take over from East Germany the lead in this industry.

The underdevelopment of Czechoslovakia's ammonia industry has been a good deal criticized. An interesting analogy has been noted: Czechoslovakia and Belgium have roughly the same out-puts of coal and coke, yet the latter produces nearly four times more nitrogen, mainly from coke-oven gas. Programmes for the 1960's strive to make up for the lag. The output of the principal Bohemian supplier is to be steeply raised in the Lovosice works and the Nitro Ostrava plant; by the mid-1960's the Zaluzi-near-Most plant is expected to turn out five times more ammonia than before its reconstruction (1957); the Duslo chemical works, under construction in the South Slovak lowlands, is expected to take over responsibility—in the early 1960's—for nearly one-third of the nitrogenous products turned out in Czechoslovakia.[25]

[24] Complete equipment for this plant is to be supplied to Poland by the Czecho-slovaks in connexion with the copper credit. (See above, p. 252.) The factory is planned eventually to reach a capacity of 1·35 tons of ammonia—or 700 tons of nitrogenous fertilizers—a day.

[25] Two further factories, the Chemko at Strazske and the Spolana works at Neratovice are to be opened. Czechoslovakia is also to supply a plant of 700,000 tons capacity to Poland in connexion with the copper deal.

A short digression may not be out of place here, to indicate a link-up of the chemical industry with other spheres of the economy. The interdependence of the fertilizer sector with agriculture and other domains of economic life is a good case in point, though it is far from being the most complex among those which face the choice-making central planner.

All three countries have set exacting goals for agriculture for the first half of the decade, and propose to reach them chiefly through intensification. Some data on the programmes are compiled in this table.

Fertilizer Usage and Farm Yields, 1958–65

Country	Commercial fertilizers applied (kg of nutrient per ha arable land)	Livestock (head per ha of farmland) Cattle	Pigs	Four main grains	Pota- toes	Sugar- beet
Poland						
1958–9	40	41	60	16	131	255
1965 plan	80	52	81	18	160	250
Czechoslovakia						
1958–9	100	60	72	18	.	299
1965 plan	160–200	.	.	27	.	325
East Germany						
1958–9	190	58	129	25	150	313
1965 plan	.	.	.	31	245	385
Western Germany	252	82	100	28	236	349
Denmark	138	103	174	37	223	390
France	91	53	23	21	172	340
Italy	48	57	67	81	178	300

Sources: J. Zaleski, in *Gosp. Plan.*, no. 8, 1959, p. 44; and L.S., ibid. no. 3, 1960, pp. 45–46; J. Marecki, ibid. no. 11, 1961.

The programmes envisage a steep stepping up of fertilizer usage. It is to be doubled in Poland; in Czechoslovakia the increase will be even steeper. Poland is among the lowest consumers of fertilizers in Europe, although in the past two decades their use has risen fivefold. Broadly she wants to be in 1965 where Czechoslovakia was in 1958; (see table above). The first unknown in the central decision-makers' calculation is the response of yields to fertilizing: recorded data show a wide variation in time and space:[26] some

[26] Incremental ratios computed for the post-war period, up to the mid-1950's for Poland, Italy, France, West Germany, and Belgium have been found to be about 10, 40, 28, 15, and 9 kg of wheat respectively, per 1 kg of nutrient.

more or less arbitrary assumptions have to be made. The Polish calculation appears to be this: the incremental ratio of yields to fertilizers in the recent past was 5·3 kg of grain per 1 kg of pure nutrient; this 'efficiency coefficient' is anticipated to rise by one-quarter, i.e. to 6·7 kg, through better techniques of husbandry, &c. On this basis, to reach the yield-targets about 2·53 million tons of pure nutrient will be needed; of this, given the planned livestock population, some 1·23 million tons of commercial fertilizers would have to be supplied from industry.[27]

Next, the resource-allocation for the postulated supply of fertilizers has to be checked against alternatives. Take nitrogen: what would be the impact on coal-mining and foreign trade? A ton of nitrogen would save, through higher yields, some 6 tons of imported grain, say $360; but, against this, the 5 tons of coal and coke needed to produce it, and withdrawn from potential exports, imply a loss of $60 in foreign exchange. The second check may be made on the basis of investment efficiency. Direct capital outlay in Polish agriculture, per 1 zloty of net output, is believed to be of the order of 1·70 'investment zloty'. On the other hand 1 zloty invested in the productive facilities required to get 1 ton of N (including a Lurgi plant to replace, for heating purposes, the coke-oven gas used up in the production of nitrogenous fertilizers, plus the required corresponding capacities in mining—and so on, all along the line) would yield a rate of 0·65 zl. This—if data are to be trusted—is well below that which is characteristic of direct investment in agriculture. In other words, the argument boils down to a contention that in a sense the coal-miner and the worker in a chemical factory are more efficient producers of grain than the farmer. Consequently it would be a sound policy for raising foodstuff outputs to shift as high a proportion as possible of resources on a national scale, from the farms 'directly' to the coal-mines, coke-ovens, and chemical plants.

Doubts as to how the Polish capital-to-output ratios mirror reality have been indicated in a previous context. Moreover the calculation reproduced here may sin by ignoring some technological limitations and operational optima.[28] But at least it reflects

---

[27] Zaleski, in *Gosp. Plan.*, no. 8, 1959, p. 44.

[28] The Polish 1975 programme envisages a rise of grain yields, i.e. up to 21q ha. The authors contend that a higher supply of commercialized fertilizers, though theoretically feasible, could not be absorbed by peasant agriculture, cf. Kalecki, in *Nowe Drogi*, no. 8, 1958, p. 31. Some grain deficit is assumed to persist.

the general way in which the central planner's mind has to work when he is making his strategic choices.

Organic Chemicals; Coal Derivatives

Germany is one of the cradles of the organic chemical industry built up on the technologies for separating and refining crude benzoles and tar. They are separated into a range of primary distillates and, as far as tar is concerned, pitch: crystallization, distillation, application of acid or alkali provide the vast number of intermediate derivatives used in chemical trades. Within the all-German economy East Germany developed less than a proportionate share of the fundamental benzole and coal-tar distilling industries. Its location appears to have been chiefly determined by hard-coal deposits and river systems; the important dyestuff and related sectors have been located mainly in the Rhine and Main areas. It will be remembered, for instance, that the brown-coal Bitterfeld basin attracted the Aktiengesellschaft für Anilinfabrikation, better known as Agfa, to Wolfen: but around the turn of the century its Wolfen plant withdrew from tar processing and concentrated on photographic articles, which made East Germany one of the leaders in this domain.

One of the factors to be borne in mind is that this sector of the industry has close ties with metallurgy as well as gas works: it draws its basic materials from the coking departments of iron and steel works. However, expanded in East Germany in the last two decades or so, it is far more advanced there than in the two other countries of the area. Both Czechoslovakia and Poland export lower-grade products of the carbon-chemical industry while importing the more refined ones. Czechoslovak critics point in particular to the underdevelopment of the manufacturing of dyestuffs and pharmaceuticals, in spite of the potentially rich starting basis. They point out that while their country is on a par with the United States in *per capita* output of hard-coal tar, she is far behind in its derivatives.[29]

Poland has the lowest proportion of processed coal to be found anywhere in the leading coal-mining countries; and the chemical characteristics of her coals give only a partial explanation of this disparity.

[29] J. Slamma and J. Hon, in *Nova Mysl.*, no. 8, 1959, p. 698.

Coking and Chemical Processing of Extracted Coal
(*per cent of total output*)

Western Germany	Britain	France	Poland
46·2	24·6	30·7	13·8

Source: Pienkowski, in *Gosp. Plan.*, no. 2, 1958, p. 25.

A large proportion of plant is out of date, and average efficiency of processes is very low. It has been calculated that by performance standards of the most modern plant—such as that of the coking department in the Nowa Huta Works—the country's yearly loss through inefficient processing amounted to 80,000 tons of tar, and 12,000 tons of benzole.[30]

As late as the end of the 1950's the bulk of coke-oven gas was wasted from the point of view of a possible usage in chemicals. Nor was the proportion high in Czechoslovakia—about 3 per cent in the late 1950's. Against this poor record virtually all coke-oven-produced gas is utilized in chemical processing in East Germany. It is fair, however, to note that in Poland the proportion of the total output of tar and benzole chemically utilized went up, between the late 1930's and the late 1950's, from 6 to 15 per cent; about one-third is believed to be the desirable minimum.

Petrochemicals

It was only towards the end of the last decade that the countries of the area—as indeed of the whole Soviet Bloc—became actively interested in the development of petroleum-chemical industries, although the manufacturing of a growing range of organic chemicals from petroleum has undoubtedly been one of the most remarkable developments on the industrial stage of the world. The 1950's saw a doubling of the output of petrochemicals in the industrialized West;[31] a further doubling is anticipated within the

[30] Ibid.
[31] By the end of the 1950's in the United Kingdom about 50% of all basic organics was made from oil. A spectacular increase took place in Western Germany: petroleum chemicals accounted in 1958 and 1959 for 29 and 40% respectively of total basic organic production, OEEC, *The Chemical Industry in Europe, 1959–60* (Paris, 1961), p. 21.

coming half-decade, a signal measure of dynamic growth. By the end of the 1950's about half of all basic organics in Britain was made from oil, and two-fifths in Western Germany.

Scarcity of indigenous oil and the uncertainty of supplies from outside have been but one of the causes of its underdevelopment in the area. The shift to a new raw-material basis in chemicals became pronounced in the area at the start of the decade, and was interrelated with the policy of widening the fuel basis. Pledged supplies of Soviet oil, and the construction of a trunk pipeline and vast new refining capacities, are considered just as much a part of the development of petrochemicals as of fuel supplies.[32] Substantial catalytic cracking capacities have been programmed. Petrochemical facilities are to be added in the early 1960's to the crude-oil refinery at Schwedt-on-Oder, and at the new lubricating-oil plant, Lützkendorf, where part of the Soviet-imported oil will be processed.

Similarly Czechoslovakia proposes to link up petrochemicals with the processing of oil in the existing and new plants—at Pardubice, Kolin, and Kralupy Slovnaft. Facilities to be installed in Kralupy Slovnaft and commissioned in the early 1960's will make it the chief producer of synthetic rubber and support the production of plastics. Poland too intends to build a petrochemical works, in conjunction with the new large refinery at Plock expected to provide around 1963 basic materials for synthetic rubber, plastics, synthetic fibres, detergents, &c. The double-purpose drive is to be in full swing before the end of the coming half decade.

Petroleum as the basis of chemicals has various indisputable technological and chemical advantages. The vast expansion of oil-refining capacities dictated primarily by fuel needs creates *per se* considerable opportunities in the chemical field. Petroleum processing also helps to stabilize chemical production and ensures a smoother supply of raw material. One of the features of the oil-processing industry is a negligible rate of wastage. It has made increasingly deep inroads into chemicals as a potential competitor with coal in organic and inorganic chemicals. In the organic-chemical sphere it has gained a particularly outstanding position in supporting the manufacture of various products such as plastics, synthetic rubbers and fibres, solvents, detergents, and

[32] See above, p. 157.

pesticides. It has obtained a foothold in inorganic industry, among other things as a source of hydrogen for the manufacture of ammonia.

Hence the advent of petrochemicals—which in a wider sense include chemical processes based on gas as well as oil—has confronted the planners with a tricky problem in patterning the chemical industry. The problem is comparatively easier where oil and gas each provide an exclusive path for some products. (Higher olefins are unobtainable from coal.) Once the decision is made to produce certain articles—this is particularly the case with certain 'synthetic' materials—there is no choice as to the basis. It is more complicated where patterning involves choices of alternative routes, via coal or petroleum, both being technologically open and commercially feasible. Under some conditions the steep rise of demand for organic intermediates from such expanding users as the plastics industry would, by itself, cause a turning, sooner or later, to petroleum as an additional source of material; but in a country such as Poland, very rich in coal and (potentially) in its chemical by-products, the choice on economic grounds is far from clear-cut.

The case of the two rival hydrocarbon base-materials—acetylene and ethylene—may serve as an illustration of some difficulties for the choice-maker. Ethylene has been extracted in the countries under review, on a modest scale, from coke-oven gas. A demand for a larger flow of this material leads to petroleum. A widely practised method—the cracking of low-octane liquid-petroleum fractions—provides this hydrocarbon, as well as other important chemical substances such as propylene, butene, and butadiene (also methane and hydrogen). Acetylene, on the other hand, can be economically obtained, and in the area it has till now almost entirely been obtained, via carbide although it can also be made from either liquid petroleum or natural gas. The different physical properties of ethylene and acetylene may make one or the other more suitable under particular conditions or for particular purposes. Ethylene has, for instance, the great advantage that it can safely be turned into (and stored as) liquid. But over a fairly wide range, through appropriate routing, the two hydrocarbons can well be interchangeable, say, in products of vinyl-chloride and thus of its polymer PVC. Thus the decision to adopt one of the two rather than the other, as well as the choice of the path of producing it, must rest on economic as well as technological considerations.

Gas versus Coke

The tapping of resources of natural gas in Czechoslovakia and Poland has given a new stimulus to a structural shift in the raw-material basis in the great synthesis. In Poland the chemical processing of gas would be centred on the Tarnow *Kombinat* situated as it is only about 20 kilometres from the new gas fields of Dabrowa Tarnowska.

The tendency in both Czechoslovakia and Poland is to cut down the use of coke as a prime chemical material (by Polish standards nearly 2 tons of coke are needed to produce a ton of synthetic ammonia), 'classical' coking being subordinated essentially to the needs of metallurgy.[33] The Polish—Tarnow—project largely eliminates coke from that plant as a technological raw material. In the raw-material input of the ammonia-nitrogen branch as a whole, its share is expected to be cut from 85 per cent in 1960 to about 50 per cent in 1965, and consumption of natural and coke-oven gases to increase sixfold.[34] At the level of the country's planned 1965 chemical production the gases would replace something like 600,000 tons of coke—a valuable saving considering the tightness in coke supplies.

The chemical industry is expected to receive between one-third and two-fifths of all natural gas consumed, which is a high proportion by the standards of countries with advanced chemical industries and abundant natural-gas supplies. The total supply of natural gas to the Polish economy is estimated for 1965 at around 1,000 million cubic metres, possible deficits being met by imports of up to one-third of this quantity from the Soviet Union. This would, however, require the solution of the technical problems of long-range transport. In addition, the chemical industry would use a sizeable proportion of coke-oven gases, and in time—following the planned rise in oil refining—refinery tail

[33] Before the last war Polish consumption averaged about 1,500 kg of coke per ton of ammonia, which is also roughly the present East German (Leuna), figure; in 1959 consumption amounted to 1959 kg, some efforts have been made since to lower this average. The high consumption rate is due to earmarking the best coke for metallurgy: cf. Pienkowski, in Z. *Warszawy*, 2 Feb. 1961.

[34] These and other data are derived from very valuable articles by Pojda and Zajac, in *Gosp. Plan.*, nos. 1–2, 1959 and 7, 1960.

gases are expected to be available for chemicals in Poland as in the
two other countries of the area.

In the re-routing programme for Polish chemicals ammonia is
given first priority in the re-distribution of available gases. Its
cost may be cut in this way by as much as two-fifths (about half this
rate where coke-oven rather than natural gas is applied). The rest
of the gas available for chemical industry is mostly being turned
to the production of acetylene (1,000 cu. m. of natural gas
replaces about 1.8 tons of coking coal in acetylene production, and
one and a half tons of other coal), to form a basis—cheaper by
one-quarter—for its various derivatives, especially in plastic
materials and synthetic fibres. The main saving of the branch
will come from cutting down the pace of expansion of calcium
carbide and thus of the great quantities of electric power it
requires.

Any attempt to evaluate the programmes for re-patterning the
bases of the chemical industries of the area will probably assume
that the share of petrochemicals is bound continuously to rise in
any case, as a corollary of expansion of the chemical industry as a
whole.

Synthetics

Against the background of the previous section, a few more
words will be said about the group of organic products on which
the attention of industrial policy-makers in all three countries has
centred in recent years. The ubiquitous applicability of synthetic
raw-material products of polycondensation and polymerization,
and their phenomenal versatility, account for the conquests they
make. There can be no doubt that they are in the forefront of the
contemporary revolution in chemicals.

Synthetic Rubber

Among 'growth' materials belonging to, or linked with,
chemicals, rubber has a special place for many reasons. Various
sectors of the economy depend on it. (The comparatively low
rates of consumption in the area, especially in Poland, have an
obvious connexion with the area's lag in automotive road transport.) In accordance with the world trend, synthetics have been
gradually displacing the 'natural' product in the area's consump-

tion—partly in response to changes in relative cost and foreign-payment conditions, and partly to progress (quantitative and qualitative) in synthetic production.

Around the beginning of the 1960's synthetics were making up about one-quarter of all the rubber used in Polish and Czechoslovak manufacturing (as compared with one-third in Britain, whose consumption of synthetic rubber is, however, comparatively low because of her connexions with the Malayan natural-rubber plantations). The proportion is to rise steeply in the 1960's, and it is already higher in East Germany.

East Germany is, in this domain too, one of the world's pilots. ✗ The plant at Schkopau on the Saale, between Merseburg and Halle, erected in 1939 was one of the first installations of its kind. This was the original industrial application by I. G. Farbenindustrie of their remarkable research achievements, inspired by the desire to make their country's war economy independent of imports, which had led to the Buna-synthesis (a name derived from the two materials used—butadiene, technically obtained from acetylene, and natron used as a catalyst). In the middle of the Second World War the Schkopau plant's output amounted to about 118,000 tons, but the industry lost about one-tenth of its capacities through bombing and an estimated half through subsequent dismantling by the Soviet authorities. What remained was operated in a SAG enterprise. After a drop to one-third of its peak level, output reached about 90,000 tons towards the end of the 1950's, rather more than half of which went into exports. The rebuilt Schkopau rubber works are believed to be somewhat obsolescent when judged by Western standards.

As against other leaders in the field, East Germany has been technologically rather conservative. The basic product at the Schkopau Works—accounting for about half its output in value terms—is at present a general-purpose synthetic, a styrene-butadiene copolymer with butadiene predominating; a proportion of the output consists of certain special-purpose rubbers. Some departure from the classical methods towards a 'synthetic-natural' rubber has apparently been made on an experimental basis. The 1960's are planned to be a period of fundamental re-routing of production from coal to petroleum.

German planners estimate that alternative investment and current cost ratios of the rubber obtained from 'cracking' gas and from carbide are as favourable to the former as 1 : 1·7–1·9 and 1 : 1·1–1·25 respectively.

To meet the special requirements not satisfied by the type of synthetic produced the country has to import a certain amount of natural rubber. But at the same time rather more than half of its output of synthetic rubber is set aside for exports. Czechoslovakia and Poland are among East Germany's leading customers.[35]

The construction of large-scale synthetic-rubber-manufacturing facilities is the central investment project planned for Czecho-slovak chemicals in the 1960's. The original plans, drafted almost a decade ago, rested on an exclusive carbide basis. Cost considera-tions and energy deficiencies caused several years' delay. Meanwhile the plans were revised and integrated with the petrochemical programme. Czechoslovak expansion is to receive a new impetus when the large Kaucuk plant at Kralupy for oil-based synthesis comes on stream sometime around 1963. At the first stage it is to be fed with base intermediates from the Zaluzi (Stalin) Works. When the Kaucuk plant is completed home production is expected gradually to reduce rubber imports and eventually to eliminate them towards the end of the 1960's, when it reaches full capacity.

Polish synthetic production started at the end of the 1950's in a plant belonging to the Oswiecim concern. It is equipped pre-dominantly with Soviet machinery and based on a Soviet licence. (Russian scientists arrived in their research at a butadiene-rubber almost simultaneously with I. G. Farbenindustrie. The seizure in 1945 of the Schkopau equipment and personnel helped technical development of the synthetic-rubber branch in the USSR.) The Polish factory, however, even when it was installed, was con-sidered to be behind the advanced standards. It was fitted in with Oswiecim's coal-carbonization system, but a programme for the late 1960's envisages a switch to a petrochemical 'route' with an ultimate output of 50,000 tons and a widened range of products, including special purpose rubbers, and perhaps even the

[35] The area's foreign trade in rubber at the end of the 1950's is reflected in the following table (000 tons 1959 or 1960):

	Czechoslovakia	East Germany	Poland
Natural rubber	14	−23	32
Synthetic rubber	12	−49	17

Minus denotes exportable surpluses.

'synthetic-natural' rubber. Around the mid-1960's domestic production is to cover half the country's use of rubber. Polish calculation suggests that, at full efficiency planned, the cost of a ton of Oswiecim butadiene alone would roughly correspond to a world-market price of styrene-butadiene rubber of the kind manufactured at Oswiecim. (The reliability of the frame of choice provided by such dollar calculations is rather uncertain.) A Polish commentator on the Oswiecim plant remarked incisively:

The problem of synthetic rubber lays bare certain weaknesses of our investment planning. The chemical orchestra lacks harmony. . . . Various things happened—there have been constructions built ahead [of feasibilities], there have been under-invested projects, or some [affected] by deficient co-operation or support in supplies. It is not only chemicals which suffer from this malaise.[36]

Plastics

Comparatively little headway was made in the area until very recently in the domain of synthetics, outside the special sphere of rubber. Even East Germany, who, considering her pioneering record since the 1920's in both fundamental research and technology, would seem predestined for an active role in this field confined herself to the production of a few materials, chiefly polystyrene and PVC. (She has been an exporter of both these articles for some time.) Production is based on the carbide-acetylene route, mainly at the Buna plant, and to a lesser extent in the Piesteritz nitrogen works. The other two countries imitated her on a smaller scale: Poland made a start in 1957 with an insignificant output of PVC at the Oswiecim works, her chief producer of acetylene.

It was only at the turn of the 1950's that the profound transformation in industrial materials which occurred elsewhere attracted practical attention. The self-accelerating technological progress in polymers can, indeed, be viewed as a revolution.[37] It has by now profoundly affected almost every branch of industry and a wide sphere of final consumption. The flexibility of the

[36] W. Dudzinski, in *Z. Gosp.*, no. 15, 1959, p. 6.
[37] Over the decade and a half following 1940 the world's output of plastic materials rose tenfold. Within this period world production of steel doubled, that of copper rose by 28%, of zinc by 60%, of lead by 12%; output of tin declined by 23%. World production of plastic materials is expected to rise fourfold or fivefold and reach 15 million tons a year by 1970.

properties of the new materials, great adaptability of shape and colour, ability to meet various requirements, great resistance to inclement climatic conditions—all this has helped the continuous widening of the scope of their uses.

To single out but a few fields of application of the new constructional materials, 'plastic engineering' has become an important component—or rather an extension—of the traditional machine and equipment producing industry. The ease with which the materials lend themselves to shaping by the various techniques give them a unique position in this industry. About one-half of all plastics produced in Poland is to be directed to engineering.

Another field of a mass application of plastics is the building trade. By now, in one way or another, these replace practically every conventional building material, including timber.

Where choices have become wider, decisions have to be determined by technological and economic calculation. To give a few examples: Polish sources accept Soviet data which suggest that (apart from lowering the weight and increasing the lifetime of products) a ton of new materials applied saves up to 3–5 tons of steel and reduces labour input up to 5–6 times. East German experience would suggest that the use of plastics in building reduces the cost of pipes by one-fifth and that of floors by between one-quarter and two-fifths.[38] Binding and packaging is yet another application: the efficiency of plastics, measured in relation to weight, is believed to be up to three times that of paper and so on. How far these data do reflect realistic cost relations may seem, however, to be uncertain. W. B. Reddaway remarks (p. 254): 'Plastics are not in general *cheap* materials . . . plastics are frequently used for the sake of the special properties which they give to the finished article rather than for the sake of cheapness.'

An important factor to be taken into account—though not to the same extent for all the three countries—is the relative 'energy intensity' of plastics. According to East German sources, technically equivalent outputs of plastic materials, steel, and aluminium involve power requirement at the ratio of 1 : 5 : 8, even

---

[38] When the substitutability of plastics for traditional material is discussed one should also bear in mind the 'complementarity effect' in the use of the former: to give one example, relevant for our case history: the use of plastics in construction calls forth an extra demand for reinforcing steel rods.

where plastics are produced on the very power-intensive carbide-acetylene rather than the oil-ethylene path. Here again our few examples may give an indication of the interplay of technological and economic considerations. In turn the latter may be, as often as not, a composite effect of factors which do not necessarily point in the same direction: higher investment but lower operating cost, or vice versa. And what is true for one country is not necessarily so for another. East German calculations suggest a 1 : 3 : 5 ratio for respective investment outlays in plastics, steel, and aluminium. But the relative position of steel would be more favourable in the Czechoslovak and Polish ratio.

Targets for the middle of the decade in both the production of plastics and their fabrication into finished articles have been set high enough to support consumption goals of 5 to 18 kilograms per head, with Poland at the bottom and East Germany at the top of this range, which would bring the usage nearer to standards prevailing in Western Europe.[39]

East Germany has made rapid progress, particularly in articles which by now form her traditional line in this field. The Buna Works have become Europe's largest single manufacturer of polyvinyl chloride; by the middle of this decade output is expected to reach 140,000 tons a year. Some East German processes—such as a catalytic low-pressure polymerization of ethylene evolved in the late 1950's—have developed successfully enough to become attractive to chemical industries in advanced Western countries.

Generally, emphasis is to be placed—in agreement with the trend noticeable in the West—on thermoplastic rather than on thermosetting materials. (Thermosetting plastics generally obtained by polycondensation, i.e. those which permanently retain the shape to which they have been hardened, include three major families of material: phenolic, aminoplastics, and polyester and alkyd resins. Dissoluble materials, thermoplastics—usually products of polymerization—which are at present in the forefront of advance, comprise the 'grand trilogy': polyvinyl chloride, polyethylene (or polythene), and polystyrene.) Outstanding among new thermoplastics is the group of polycarbonates.

As has been noted, expansion is related in these programmes to the expected general growth in petrochemicals—in agreement

[39] *The Economist*, 30 Dec. 1960.

with the general swing observable—in most of the plastic-producing countries. Time-tables as well as goals vary in the three countries. The most exacting is the East German programme: it rests chiefly on the expansion in the Leuna and Buna works. It is expected that about 1965 the new Leuna II Works will commission petrochemical cracking facilities to secure a wide flow of propylene and ethylene sufficient for the intended build-up in plastics.

Programmes in the two other countries are similarly framed. They appear to assume that when momentum is gained during the 1960's—in some cases during the 1970's—a wider flow of starting materials, based on liquid and gaseous feedstock,[40] would provide an abundant supply of intermediates in addition to those available on the coal-carbide route.

As has been mentioned, East Germany is already exporting a certain amount of the established products of the sector, chiefly PVC. If outputs and consumption keep to their long-range plans Poland hopes to join her as exporter, in the latter 1960's, of PVC and acrylics from the new Tarnow II plant, of polystyrene from Oswiecim, and probably of polyethylene from the petrochemical department of her great new oil refinery.

Man-made Fibres

What has been said so far of plastic materials is also largely true of completely synthetic fibres: the two sections of industry are very closely connected at their starting bases and through various intermediates; it is, in fact a feature of the progress in this field that they tend increasingly to overlap.

All three countries possess well-established branches of what by now have become the 'traditional' man-made fibres. Indeed, Czechoslovakia and East Germany rank—on a *per capita* basis—among the leading producers in the world. Poland's production and consumption of man-made fibres are comparatively low but her share of the total of fibres used—over one-third—is also one of the world's records. Rather more than one-quarter of the fibres handled in Polish textile factories is made up of man-made

[40] Propylene is perhaps one of the most telling examples of possibilities which the shift to the oil-basis opens to chemicals, since this is a by-product of any refinery that produces raw materials for petrol, diesel oil, and petrochemicals, and one which has very few other uses. Hence the industry can offer large quantities of this commodity at a low price. It is used in producing the plastic polypropylene, outstanding for some of its properties, such as exceptionally light weight.

material; viscose rayon forms the bulk of this, and there is a small proportion of protein fibres.

Although inventions and innovations in fibre-forming synthetic polymers had revolutionized and continue to revolutionize this branch, even in the most advanced countries, the purely synthetic fibre is not likely to squeeze out, in the foreseeable future, the old viscose type. In fact there are some signs of a come-back of the cellulosic fibre in certain specific uses, although this is damped down by the scarcity of cellulose. 'Natural' fibres—cotton, wool, silk—also display a remarkable tenacity in the face of competition from their rivals. But a deficit in the expensive raw material in 'traditional' textiles (both 'natural' and man-made) involves a heavy load on the foreign-trade balances, about $200 million a year in the case of Poland, and turns attention to full synthetics.[41]

Synthetics have in this field a long and interesting past in the area. As early as the beginning of the 1930's the 'artificial silk' factory of Wolfen experimented with the spinning of a poly-vinchlorid fibre evolved from a German patent dating back before the First World War: the Second World War disrupted these pioneering developments. Perlon fibre was industrially produced before 1945 by the I. G. Farbenindustrie in its factory at Gorzow from the intermediate caprolactam supplied by Leuna Werke, which is still its leading producer. The Gorzow plant was dismantled and shipped to the Soviet Union after the war and afterwards reconstructed by Poland.

Since the 1950's all the three countries have been developing their fully-synthetic branches, starting from polyamides. Progress up to the turn of that decade was, however, rather slow, except perhaps for a few articles such as perlon, which is the established German version of nylon, particularly adaptable for the manufacture of wool-like materials and blending with natural wool. East Germany has been able to sell her licence to some Western countries which may be perhaps an indication of the efficiency of this process.

The 1960's are seen as a period of a major break-through in the structure of fibre production. Within a rising total the proportion of viscose rayon is to remain more or less stable, while that of synthetic fibre is to go up steeply, at the expense of cotton, wool,

[41] A. Poraj, in *Z. Gosp.*, no. 40, 1960.

and jute. Considerable additions to capacities are patterned accordingly. In Poland terylene plants are being built in Silesia, at Blachowina and Torun (based on an ICI licence and imported British equipment), and the existing facilties at Jelenia Gora and Gorzow are being enlarged. Czechoslovakia is expanding and modernizing her man-made-fibre plants, Cerna-on-Luznice, Opatova, Plana, and others.

In East Germany a strong emphasis is being put on expanding both range and size of outputs in traditional (perlon-type) products, with a corresponding increase in the production of caprolactam. More recently attention has been paid to the development of acrylic fibres. Substantial quantities are expected to be supplied about 1965 by a new plant to be installed at the Premnitz rayon works, though the industry appears still to be struggling with some technical difficulties. Production of a polyester fibre, started at about the same time, is being centred on the Chemiefaserkombinat Guben in the Frankfurt-on-Oder area, where one of the largest projects envisaged in the 1960's for chemicals is devoted to this product, and where a pilot plant for filament is also to be commissioned.

As in plastics throughout the area, the technology of synthetic fibre is shifting from coal to oil, and efforts are being made towards a closer integration with the spinning and weaving sections of traditional textiles.

One additional point deserves mention when programmes of development in 'new' chemicals are discussed. Elsewhere progress in this field has been very closely interrelated with the designing and equipping of modern plant—a plant adequate for complex, continuous, large-scale process—controlled with a sufficient degree of precision, carried out under specific conditions (ultra-high or ultra-low temperatures, pressures, and so on) and complying with specific quality standards: this is a field giving far more than average scope for mechanization and automation. 'Modern' sectors in leading Western countries have been fortunate in possessing well-developed, technically up-to-date chemical engineering at their elbow. Indeed the spectacular progress made would be unthinkable without them.

It is not surprising that equipment, and—particularly in Poland—the supply of skills, proved to be a chronic bottleneck.[42]

[42] On the deficient supply of equipment see Dudzinski, in *Z. Gosp.*, no. 23, 1960.

Technologies have proved harder to master, and teething troubles to be more prolonged, than was anticipated.

Generally speaking it has been felt that technological developments in the sphere of synthetic materials had to be oriented towards the West to a greater degree than in other fields, because of the considerable technological retardation throughout the Bloc, the USSR included. Around the turn of the 1950's Poland entered into a contractual arrangement with Imperial Chemical Industries which made available to her the 'know-how' and a licence for the production of polyester fibre, under the name of Elana. A consortium of the three Central European countries and the main oil and natural-gas producer in the Bloc outside the USSR—Rumania—has turned to ICI for the purchase of its 'know-how' on polyethylene, the highly versatile material the penetration of which into various industrial and household uses has been truly spectacular. British firms are designing a plant for each of the four countries, as well as specialized equipment.

CONCLUSION

This chapter dealt with a single branch of industry, one making a comparatively modest contribution to national products, and did so in a fragmentary way only. Nevertheless it pointed to some questions of general relevance. These stem from the fact that chemicals form a singularly important integrating sector of a modern economy. Time and again have we met links and 'bridges', interdependence, complementarity and competition, whether of products, of resources required in their production, of production 'routes' or of technologies. We have seen these complexities enhanced by the fact that in many cases the interconnexions and repercussions cross the frontiers of the branch itself: to recall only those reaching out from chemicals into the spheres of fuels, metals and textiles, building materials, engineering, agriculture, or foreign trade.

The fast pace of progress adds yet another factor—time—to the numerous elements which complicate choices.

Where, and in so far as, competitive markets operate, solution of the tricky problems which arise would be provided automatically. Some illuminating investigations have shown the intricacy of strategic decisions even where monopolies or oligopolies prevail. (Over a wide area of the chemical industry, of course, imperfect competition still prevails either in market economies or where intervention of the public hand is strong.)[43] In centrally planned economies, where public intervention is on a global scale, strategic decisions become even more difficult. 'Weighing up' alternatives, difficult in general, becomes even more of a problem where unreliable value-yardsticks—faulty as opportunity indices—fail to give the planner guidance for his choices. In this sense chemicals will reflect his difficulties in the search for an optimum.

[43] Reddaway, *passim.*

CHAPTER VII

Foreign Economic Relations

SELDOM has a period of less than a quarter of a century witnessed such dramatic changes in foreign economic relations as those which have occurred since 1938 in Czechoslovakia, East Germany, and Poland. They occurred under the combined impact of a number of factors: a far-reaching transformation of socio-economic structures and of institutions; the severance of historically developed economic ties and the forging of new ones; the paramountcy of the political and economic *raison d'état* of the ideological grouping that engulfed the area; and the philosophy of foreign trade to which the nations of the area have subscribed since the war. First, however, a few words should, perhaps, be said on the historical background.

HISTORICAL BACKGROUND

Czechoslovakia

Before she was shifted into the new frame of the Soviet Bloc, Czechoslovakia was one of those industrially advanced European countries which lived by intensive world-wide trade and widely ramified connexions with the world capital market. Over most of the inter-war period she had a sizeable export surplus: her only trade deficit between 1925 and 1928 was in the trough years of the Great Depression. She had almost continuously a handsome surplus on her current foreign-payments account.[1] Considerable Czechoslovak investment in industrial and financial enterprises abroad, and still heavier foreign investment[2] in Czechoslovakia were outstanding features of her inter-war economic position.

Up to 1918 Czechoslovakia had secure and sizeable outlets for her industry in the agricultural *hinterland* of Austria-Hungary. For a few years, as it were by the force of inertia, the traditional

---

[1] Part of the surplus was being used to reduce the substantial foreign debt: Czechoslovakia had been saddled with a heavy debt at the threshold of independence.

[2] In 1935 900 mill. and 1,400 mill. kcs. respectively (League of Nations, *Balances des paiements* (Geneva, 1938), p. 213).

directions and pattern of her foreign trade survived the Habsburg Empire. But the frontiers drawn after the First World War and the policies of the successor states, which embarked on a more or less successful industrialization drive, were bound to remould them. A wave of protectionism spread throughout Czechoslovakia's old markets. In the early 1920's the old industrial nucleus of the former empire—Czechoslovakia and the Austrian Republic—between them still shared one-half of the imports of both Hungary and Jugoslavia. Before the outbreak of the Second World War this proportion had declined to less than one-fifth. The last ten years of peace saw an almost exact halving of Czechoslovakia's share in the total imports of the agricultural countries of south-eastern Europe: (Bulgaria, Greece, Hungary, Roumania, Turkey, and Yugoslavia). Meanwhile Germany's share doubled.[3] Indeed the period, and particularly its latter part, was one of almost continuous retreat in the face of a forceful economic onslaught by Germany, who by ingenious manipulations was able to tie up her exports with bulk purchases of local raw materials.

It is only fair to note, however, that Czechoslovakia made a determined attempt to fit her foreign trade into her new politico-economic position, and to adjust herself to the inevitable industrialization of the hitherto primarily agricultural economies of the Danubian basin. During the 1930's this was attempted partly within a political formation, the Little Entente. Czechoslovakia took an active part in the development of chemical industries in Yugoslavia and Roumania, of metallurgical industries in the latter, of steel industry in the former, besides expanding her previously established interests in the Danubian textile industries.[4] She also sought outlets for her industries beyond her traditional sphere.

Against this background it is small wonder that the collapse of Germany after the Second World War should have aroused hopes that the time had now come for Czechoslovakia—the economically most advanced country of the region—to fill up the vacuum, and to replace Germany as the principal provider of industrial goods, especially of products of heavy industry.[5]

---

[3] League of Nations, *Europe's Trade* (Geneva, 1941), pp. 46, 51.

[4] A. Basch, *The Danube Basin and the German Economic Sphere* (N.Y., 1943), p. 157.

[5] This was emphasized for instance by President Benes early in 1946. Cf. W. Diamond, *Czechoslovakia between East and West* (London, 1947), p. 137; and D. W. Douglas, *Transitional Economic Systems, the Polish–Czech Example* (London, 1953), p. 292.

Poland

The two inter-war decades were a continuously trying period in Poland's foreign economic relations. The industries of the Congress Kingdom lost their established Russian markets for metal products, textiles, and other manufactures.[6] The agricultural lands regained from Prussia lost their markets in East Germany. Silesian heavy industries had to fit themselves into the new economic frame.

For a while most of Poland's foreign trade still moved within the circumscribed region of her Western neighbours, Austria, Czechoslovakia, and, above all, Germany. Russian markets appeared to be irretrievably lost when cut off by the Revolution. The year 1924, when an economic war broke out with Germany, was a turning-point. Poland was, in fact, one of the few countries of the region which successfully resisted absorption into the German economic sphere. To retain economic independence she endeavoured to push her trade further afield. Over the ten years which preceded the Second World War Poland's exports to Britain doubled, measured as a percentage of her total exports, and Britain took over much of the position previously held by Germany. Over the same period Germany's share in Polish exports was cut by one-half.[7] Poland tried to expand her sales outside Europe so as to obtain the means of paying for the raw materials she lacked. By 1938 such exports made up more than one-third of the total.[8]

The Achilles heel of the Polish inter-war economy was foreign payments. Her balance of payments was almost entirely dependent on trade. Some of her traditional sources of foreign exchange— emigrants' remittances in the first place—tended to dry up in the restrictionist inter-war world. Hence the 'neo-mercantilism' of her policies. To quote a historian of the period:

The so-called active trade balance (excess of exports over imports) was a motto very popular with the public. Sometimes this was exaggerated into a 'foreign-trade-balance complex'. The enforcement of equilibrium in returns of imports and exports over short periods, not only for a given year, but even over single months, imposed a neo-mercantilistic imprint on the economic policy, impelling it to ever-increasing controls and restrictions.[9]

---

[6] See above, pp. 173f.
[8] Ibid.

[7] League of Nations, *Europe's Trade*, p. 52.
[9] Zweig, p. 98.

For various reasons, attributable partly to internal conditions and partly to foreign relations, Poland's access to foreign sources of capital between the wars was limited and shrinking. Records with regard to the Polish inter-war balance of payments are not sufficient to produce a fully documented picture. Over the last fifteen pre-war years surpluses of exports over imports were twice as large as deficits. This may suggest some net additions to foreign investment, since stocks of gold and foreign assets remained more or less unchanged over the period.[10] But the Great Depression started a rapid efflux of foreign capital which does not seem to have been checked until the outbreak of war. Poland inherited a substantial foreign engagement in both her extractive and manufacturing industries. In the larger concerns (limited companies) which controlled most of the large-scale plants the size of foreign investment nearly equalled that of Polish capital. Over the last few pre-war years this foreign investment declined in both absolute and relative terms,[11] partly because of a deliberate government policy of strengthening the Polish element in the control of national industry. Before readjustment after the First World War was completed it was violently disrupted by the outbreak of the Second. It had always been dominated by that perennial weakness of the Polish economy: anæmia in capital supply.

East Germany

One would hardly be justified in treating pre-1945 East Germany as an individual unit from the angle of foreign trade (she accounted for roughly one-quarter of the Reich's trade). The basic fact which stands out in her trade position is the intricate cobweb of commodity exchanges with other parts of Germany on which she relied. Between two-fifths and one-half of her total output was exported to other areas of Germany. Broadly the same proportion in consumption was met from inter-regional trade. The regional interdependence of Western Germany as measured by the same two yardsticks was less than half that of East Germany.

Being so much smaller, East Germany needed to rely more on the rest of the country. Specialization on arable farming made her

---

[10] Zweig, p. 100.
[11] The ratio of Polish to foreign capital in limited companies changed, between 1932 and 1937, from 1 : 1·1 to 1 : 1·4, League of Nations, *Balances des paiements*, p. 185.

dependent on exchanges of crops against animal products. The very high degree of industrial specialization was a still stronger contributory factor. Her principal industrial branch, metal processing, was dependent on raw and semi-finished materials

Commodities	Exports in relation to output (%)		Imports in relation to consumption (%)	
	To other German regions	To foreign countries	From other German regions	From foreign countries
Agricultural				
Western Germany	6	—	12	12
East Germany	31	3	19	11
Industrial				
Western Germany	22	18	21	12
East Germany	49	15	55	6
All				
Western Germany	18	13	18	12
East Germany	43	11	45	8

Source: ECE, *Bulletin*, i/3, p. 28.

supplied by the Rhineland and Ruhr. In the first years after the war it was widely believed that an ampler food basis secured to East Germany a healthier and a more independent economic structure than that of Western Germany. Subsequent developments were to disprove this and to demonstrate that the historically developed degree of East Germany's inter-regional dependence and particularly her dependence on industrial raw material supplied by regions from which she was now cut off were bound to have an adverse effect on her viability as a separate economic unit.

POST-WAR DEVELOPMENTS

By the end of the 1940's state foreign-trade monopolies on the Soviet pattern were established in both Czechoslovakia and Poland. Residual private foreign trade survived for some time in East Germany under strict state supervision. Pre-war instruments for directly and indirectly influencing foreign trade were either discarded or lost their economic relevance. Foreign trade was placed under the direct control of a central authority and sub-ordinated to the overall economic plan. It was only by the end of the 1950's that some tendencies appeared, especially in Poland, towards a marginal devolution of foreign-trade decisions to the enterprises concerned.

Something more will be said about the quantitative developments in foreign trade.

Share of World Trade, 1929–62

(*per cent*)

	1929	*1938*	*1950*	*1962 est.*
Czechoslovakia	1·7	1·4	1·13	1·4
East Germany	2·0	2·0	0·72	1·7
Poland	1·0	1·0	1·05	1·2

Source: Maly rocz. stat., 1939, p. 164; ECE, Survey, 1957, and Bulletin, xv/i.

Notwithstanding the post-war growth of her industrial body Poland's share in world trade has been comparatively static, as soon as it settled down around the pre-war percentage. This was 1 per cent or so in the inter-war prosperity year of 1928, the same in the last year of peace, and in the late 1950's. A falling trend in Czechoslovakia's share in world trade—noticeable already before the war—was not arrested until the early 1950's. Around that decade Czechoslovakia was restored to her 1938 position in world trade. But she has not regained that of the late 1920's.

Similar developments have been noticeable in the case of the other industrial country of the area. In 1938 East Germany's share in world trade was not much less than that of Czecho-slovakia and Poland combined. By 1950 it was only a mere third of what it had been then. This was largely accounted for by the high proportion of unrequited exports on reparations account. When the heavy burden ceased a marked recovery became noticeable, but even by the end of the 1950's East Germany's share in world trade was somewhat smaller than two decades earlier. In fact, this way of reckoning tends to underestimate the fall, since inter-regional trade saw a far steeper decline, and much of it had to be replaced by trade with other nations.

Gross National Product, Industrial Output, and Foreign Trade, 1937–56

	1956 (1937 = 100)			*1959 (1937 = 100)*		
		Gross National Product			*Industrial production*	
	Foreign trade volume	*Official index*	*Computed index*	*Foreign trade volume*	*Official index*	*Computed index*
Czechoslovakia	183	184	161	239	350	232
East Germany	144		141	217	300	179
Poland:						
pre-war terr.	192	240?	156	244	692	300 [254]
post-war terr.			128			203 [170]
OEEC	157	144				
World	170					

Sources: GNP, from calculations to be published separately. Index-number basis: Czechoslovakia, 1937, East Germany, 1936, Poland, 1938.
Industrial output, see pp. 106f.
For Western countries, see OEEC, *Industrial Statistics, 1900–57*, pp. 8, 19, 22, 52; and idem. *Statistics of National Product and Expenditure, 1938 and 1947–55*. Index numbers for GNP cover the years 1938–55.

Volume of Foreign Trade (in 1956 prices)

	1938	*1950*	*1953*	*1956*	*1959*	*1962*
Czechoslovakia:						
$ 000 mill.	1·42	1·72	2·23	2·58	3·39	4·44
1938 = 100	100	121	157	183	239	302
East Germany:						
$ 000 mill.	1·89	1·04	2·45	2·73	4·13	4·73
1938 = 100	100	55	130	144	217	250
Poland:						
$ 000 mill.	1·04	1·56	1·85	2·01	2·56	3·53
1938 = 100	100	150	168	192	245	311

Sources: $ values in current prices taken from League of Nations, *Europe's Trade*, p. 83; and ECE, *Survey, 1957*. Converted into 1956 dollars by the use of unit value indices for world trade in UN, *Stat. Yb., 1957*.
Pre-war East German share in all German trade taken to be about 22%: 20% share derived from ECE, *Bulletin*, iii/3, p. 28, plus 2% for the estimated share of East Berlin.
Index numbers for foreign trade of OEEC countries and world trade derived from UN, *Stat. Yb., 1957*. Base year in both cases 1938.

This must also be borne in mind when examining the correlation of foreign-trade volume with industrial output and Gross National Product—the volume of trade, that is, after the effects of price changes have broadly been eliminated (see table above). By the late 1950's, however, progress in foreign trade appears to have been more or less commensurate with the other two symptoms of economic development in East Germany and Czechoslovakia, but not quite so much so in Poland. (This is the case if the yardstick of our series rather than the official index, for both industrial output and Gross National Product, is used.) It may be of interest to note that the foreign-trade volume of the Eastern part of Germany increased less than that of the Western—the part far less dependent in the past on inter-regional exchanges. The increase in the foreign-trade aggregates implies, of course, a still greater one in *per capita* figures—for Poland and Czechoslovakia, but not for East Germany. Poland alone, however, has considerably surpassed her *per capita* trade-levels of the inter-war peak years.

Foreign Trade Per Capita, 1928–61

(comparable (1956) dollar prices)

	1928	1938	1950	1961
Czechoslovakia	248	99	137	297
East Germany	262	114	59	259
Poland	63	30	62	106

Gauged by the same yardstick, the two highly industrialized nations of the area were, by the early 1960's, still well behind the two leading industrial countries of Western Europe: Britain and Western Germany.

Foreign Trade Per Capita, Central and Western Europe, 1962

(dollars)

Czecho-slovakia	E. Germany	Poland	W. Germany	France	UK	Italy
300	259	118	482	331	456	216

The yardstick should of course be used with great circumspection—its relative relevance can only be appraised against the given economic background. But it seems safe to say that, in spite of the spurt achieved in the later years of the past decade, foreign commerce is still undersized. The disparity between the two Germanies on this count is a striking phenomenon.

Finally, it is tempting to assess the proportions of national product for the area and income passing through foreign transactions. Unfortunately the pricing and costing methods—and the divorce of internal and foreign-trade prices—make any attempt in this field extremely hazardous.

A quite interesting—and at least methodologically acceptable—Polish attempt to relate exports to adjusted GNP arrived at a strikingly low percentage; when set against Western European levels, it bears comparison only with that for Italy.

Exports as Percentage of Adjusted GNP, 1957

Poland	France	W. Germany	Italy	Netherlands	Norway	UK
10·1	17·5	24·1	13·0	45·2	33·0	24·5

Source: B. Wojciechowski, in *Gosp. Plan.*, no. 8, 1959, p. 23. Polish product and exports adjusted to something approximating factor costs: for the sake of comparability non-material services are deducted from Western GNP data. Other approximate computations suggest lower Polish percentages: e.g. J. Krynicki, *Problemy handlu zagranicznego Polski* (Warsaw, 1958), p. 214, arrived at about 8·5% for 1955, and T. Witt and J. Dorozynska, in *Handel Zagraniczny*, no. 8, 1951, at 7·5, 8, and 7 per cent for 1955, 1956, and 1957 respectively.[12]

The proportion—about one-tenth—agrees broadly with the writer's own very rough correlation of dollar estimates of national income and foreign trade; (broadly the same percentage—11 per cent—can be derived as a ratio of exports to final uses of national product from Polish input-output tables for 1959). It is referred to here with an underscored proviso that no more than a very broad approximation should be read into it.

[12] In his address to the Sejm, Professor Lange estimated that imports were expected to amount to 16·2 and 14·7% of distributed national income in 1961 and 1965 respectively; the percentage would be 14·6 and 15·7 of national income in exports. But the computational frame of these data is uncertain. See *Trybuna Ludu*, 11 Feb. 1961.

Exports as Percentage of Gross National Product, 1956

Czechoslovakia	East Germany	Poland
18	11	10

The high percentage arrived at for Czechoslovakia may, in particular, be open to doubt: indeed some official Czechoslovak statistics—whose terms of reference have regrettably not been disclosed—seem to imply a figure far lower than ours.[13]

We may refer with no less diffidence to certain estimates carried out in the area for assessing the share of industrial production absorbed by exports. A Polish calculation found that exports represent in that country about one-sixth of net output (at prime costs)—a proportion lower by far than that recorded in any Western European industrial nation.

Export as Percentage of Net Output at Prime Costs

	Poland	France	W.Germany	Italy	UK
Industry	16	27	29	14	31
of which					
Mining	34	23	38	25	26
Engineering, iron & steel, & metal working	19	29	39	15	41
Chemicals	17	29	41	25	30
Textiles & clothing	8	32	13	19	38

Source: B. Wojciechowski, in *Gosp. Plan.*, no. 8, 1959. Data refer basically to 1957.

Czechoslovak assessment yielded a lower proportion, 11 per cent, but this had been presumably obtained on a gross-output

---

[13] Dr J. M. Michal, *Central Planning in Czechoslovakia*, p. 96n. has arrived at 12–14% as the exports/national income ratio for 1957, but he rightly warns his reader of the uncertainties of the price basis.

For 1958 the foreign-trade-turnover/national-income ratio was stated by a Soviet source to be 'very close' to 28% for both Czechoslovakia and East Germany. See *Vn. Torg.*, no. 10, 1962, p. 30.

basis.[14] An East German estimate for a rather remote year of the early 1950's arrived at a somewhat higher percentage than the Czechoslovak (14·75 per cent; gross commodity output after elimination of intra-branch duplications).[15] East German official sources seem to share the view of most independent students that it is the underdevelopment of foreign trade which forms a serious brake on the economic progress of the country, more dependent as she is than any other of equal industrial rank on imports of such basic growth materials as rolled steel, non-ferrous metals, hard coal, and metallurgical coke. Only to a certain extent can the handicap be relieved by domestic inferior substitutes, in some cases at a high cost in terms of scarce factors of production, which recoils on the growth process.

Awareness of the handicap of underdevelopment in foreign trade has prompted the countries of the area to plan that it shall grow more or less *pari passu* with industry in the 1960's. Foreign trade is, however, by its very nature one of the most uncertain, the least 'plannable' sectors with which the national planner has to deal. It can indeed be argued that their high dependence on foreign trade is precisely what places the planning experiment of the industrial Central European nations—especially East Germany and Czechoslovakia—in a category apart. Here the experience of such a largely self-sufficient country as the Soviet Union has only a limited relevance.

There is some interrelation between the unreliability of foreign trade from the planning angle, the growth policies pursued, the confining of foreign commerce to basic growth commodities, and the keeping of trade—to a very high degree—within the group of planned economies. These constraining tendencies had a cumulative effect on both the size and the pattern of foreign trade. On the latter an ECE study very appositely remarked:

The result of concentrating trade on 'essentials' imported so far as possible from other countries of the area (which were committed to

---

[14] *Stat. roc., 1959*, p. 363; no terms of reference stated. The percentage-showing in individual branches in the same year (1958) was:

Metallurgy	Engineering	Chemicals	Rubber	Glass	Textiles	Paper
9·4	18·1	3	18·4	37–34	11·4	15

[15] Kohlmey, in *Ww.*, no. 1, 1958, p. 71, calculations for 1954.

very similar development programmes) was that for every country the possibilities of changing the level or composition of its trade to compensate unforeseen domestic scarcities were very limited.[16]

Commodity composition and geography of the countries' trade will be analysed presently. (Some aspects of foreign trade which have contributed to a lack of flexibility will be taken up in other contexts.)

THE NEW COMMODITY PATTERN

Any analysis of commodity pattern of trade, of its changes in time, and comparisons between countries (on the basis of the usual statistical information) can give no more than a very general reflection of reality. No more than this should be looked for in the tabulation on the following page. Two principal factors affect the picture. First, it reflects the combined effect of changes in price relations as well as in quantities: this concerns comparison over time. Secondly, (which concerns comparison both in time and in space) any break-down of imports and exports composed of a great variety of different goods into statistical categories is always more or less arbitrary. This warning should be borne in mind especially when comparisons are made between pre- and post-war positions. It is also only with these qualifications that a few broad remarks will be made here to point out some structural similarities and dissimilarities between the countries of the area, and to trace the overall directions of changes.

Structural demarcation lines within the area are reflected in the table with sufficient clarity. East Germany was before the war and she is to-day primarily an exporter of industrial finished products. Their aggregate proportion to total exports changed moderately over the last two decades, being of the order of approximately two-thirds of the total. But drastic changes have occurred within the broad category. Manufactured consumer goods have yielded their leading place to machinery and equipment. This is roughly also what happened in Czechoslovakia where the change has been in fact even more drastic. On the import side both countries rely heavily on foreign raw materials, forming rather more than one-half in Czechoslovakia and rather less than one-half in East Germany. In both countries primary products—food, fuel, and

<hr/>

[16] ECE, *Bulletin*, xi/1, p. 39.

raw materials—represent between them nearly three-quarters of the total.

Both sides of the Polish foreign-trade balance are in distinct

Foreign Trade: Commodity Composition

(*percentages*)

	Czechoslovakia		East Germany		Poland	
	1937	*1962*	*1936*	*1961*	*1937*	*1962*
Exports:						
Machinery & equipment	6	48	28	52	2	30
Raw materials & fuels	47	29	n.a.	30	43	39
of which:						
Fuels & energy	n.a.	n.a.	n.a.	n.a.	18	n.a.
Metals	n.a.	n.a.	n.a.	n.a.	7	n.a.
Chemicals	n.a.	n.a.	n.a.	n.a.	17	n.a.
Manufactured consumer goods	37	20	n.a.	14	n.a.	11
of which:						
Textiles, clothing & shoes	33	n.a.	20	n.a.	n.a.	n.a.
Food, &c.	10	5	n.a.	4	37	14
Imports:						
Machinery & equipment	10	25	n.a.	16	19	33
Raw materials & fuels	68	51	n.a.	44	n.a.	47
Manufactured consumer goods	6	3	n.a.	14	19	7
Food, &c.	16	19	n.a.	25	n.a.	14

though shrinking contrast with those of the two other countries. It is somewhat less marked when comparison is made with Czecho-slovakia rather than with East Germany. Poland too was and is heavily dependent on raw-material imports. Indeed the share of raw materials in her imports roughly equals that of East Germany. But the proportion of foodstuffs is considerably below that in the two more industrial countries, where it oscillates between one-fifth and one-quarter of all imports.

Not long ago disparities were wider in exports, but the 1950's brought Poland nearer to her neighbours' pattern. Before the war the overwhelming bulk of Polish exports consisted of foodstuffs and raw materials. Between them three principal items, food, fuel, and timber (in this order of importance), contributed almost four-fifths of the total. Their role has shrunk, yet at the beginning of the 1960's they made up two-fifths of Polish exports: conversely the formerly insignificant exports of manufactures achieved a sizeable proportion, with a steadily rising share of capital goods. This process continues: thus the structure of Polish external commerce at the threshold of the 1960's may be defined as one typical of an economy in rapid transition. Generally the shifts in structures of economies, as reflected in the composition of the trade of the area, can be looked upon as partly superimposed on trends noticeable in the world at large. Thus, first of all, a large increase in the relative role of machinery and transport equipment, and the corresponding decline in that of textiles and miscellaneous, mostly 'lighter' manufactures, is a phenomenon which the three countries share with all the industrial and semi-industrial areas of the world.

On the other hand the area under survey shows some interesting differences in the lines of development in foreign trade as against other areas of similar industrial structure. Thus imports of basic food produce have been declining in importance more or less consistently in Western Europe over the last thirty years or so. (Western Germany appears to be an exception, obviously attributable to the disruption of intra-regional exchanges.) The tendency is explainable by the rise in agricultural productivity and a continuous growth of the population's real incomes: basic foodstuffs are characterized by low income elasticity. A more detailed analysis which is to follow will show an opposite direction of development in the food trade of the three countries, including Poland.

Broadly speaking the pressure of import requirements of raw materials—the concomitant of industrial growth—on the balance of trade, is more or less common to all industrialized and semi-industrialized areas. But on the whole it makes itself felt more strongly in the three countries under discussion than in the West. There are several reasons for this. First, methods of appraising success in manufacturing and incentive rewards—to enterprise and its personnel—have been biased towards large volumes and heavy weights. Other than organizational causes have contributed to this result. Further, there is a long-range trend in the industrial world showing a gradual, relative decrease of the raw-material input per unit of output of processed goods, which is partly due to the spectacular rise in the production of synthetic substitutes:

between the outbreak of war and the mid-1950's the ratio of the 'natural' raw-material input to output fell from one-quarter to less than one-fifth. The area has been falling behind the leading countries of the West in some of the main fields of technology which have widened the scope of economical substitution (chemicals, metals). Yet another contributing factor is the specific nature of some outlets: requirements of new markets have, in many cases, entailed heavy-weight outputs.

Engineering Products

A few remarks will now be added to what has been said earlier on foreign trade in certain important groups of commodities.

Engineering has established itself since the war as the principal export industry throughout the area. Exports of capital goods have been influenced by pulls in two opposite directions—on the one hand by internal demand for investment goods, on the other by the demand in foreign markets and the need for foreign currency. A balance had to be struck sometime with the sacrifice of domestic needs, as was the case with Czechoslovak and East German exports of equipment for power stations. While Czechoslovakia was suffering from an acute insufficiency of power-generation plant she installed abroad during the post-1948 decade thermal and hydro capacities of over 3,100 MW.[17] This also applies for East German and Polish transport equipment. Armaments tended to mortgage a part of productive capacities which would otherwise have worked for export.

The truly spectacular rise of engineering to the role of the principal export industry throughout the area is clearly shown in the table on p. 283. Its share in East German exports—already high before the war—has been doubled: at the beginning of the 1960's it made up as much as one-half of the national total. In a sense the phenomenon has been still more striking in the two other countries. Czechoslovakia, whose engineering sales abroad represented, before the Second World War, a mere twentieth of total exports (she was a net importer of machinery and equipment), came—as far as this proportion goes—on a par with East Germany.[18] In pre-war Poland the contribution of engineering to

[17] *Hosp. Nov.*, nos. 51–52, 1959.
[18] In fact the disparity shown in our table is partly due to differences in classification. On the Czechoslovak classification the share of engineering in East German exports would be one of about 50%.

export was quite negligible: post-war years—especially the 1950's
—saw its rapid increase; by the end of the decade it passed the
one-quarter mark; it is expected to be close on two-fifths by
the middle of this decade. Broadly, the share of machinery and
transport equipment in East German and Czechoslovak exports
corresponds to that prevailing in the leading industrial countries
of the West, specifically Britain and Western Germany.

Engineering has also become, throughout the area, the export
industry *par excellence* from the angle of the proportion of its
products traded abroad. In terms of value about 30 per cent of
East German engineering output—which is almost exactly the
overall West European rate—is destined for exports. The Czechoslovak proportion—roughly one-fifth—is well over that of France.
The Polish proportion has been rapidly approaching this figure.
It was about one-sixth at the beginning of the decade, and is
planned to go up to one-fifth around 1965.[19] As one would

Exports of Engineering Products as Percentage of Output, 1960

Belgium	46	Czechoslovakia	18
France	16	Poland	16
Western Germany	45	East Germany	30
Italy	28	of which:	
Netherlands	40	heavy machinery	37
Sweden	33	transport machinery	35
United Kingdom	34	ships	50
Western Europe (OEEC)	33	precision & optical	
		instruments	45
		textile machinery	45

Sources: Western data from OEEC, *The Engineering Industries in Europe*
(Paris, 1961), p. 105. Data for the three countries of the area
from various official sources. The deficient international comparability should be borne in mind.

A key to some striking differences in estimates would be
provided by the Polish input–output tables for 1959: a 15%
ratio would represent the share of exports in the structure of
'final goods' produced by engineering, and the 7% ratio, the
share in the uses of its 'global production'.

---

[19] Note that a one-fifth proportion had already been achieved by the end of the
1950's according to some statistical data. This may underline the caution required
in using such calculations.

expect, the ratios are considerably higher for some ranges of products, such as ships and rolling-stock in Poland (about three-quarters of the total at the beginning of the 1950's, this is now about one-seventh). Similarly the East German ratio of exports in some sectors, such as shipyards (about 80 per cent), factories producing precision and optical instruments, heavy machinery, textile machinery, and a few others, is well over the average.

Although far behind the two principal European exporters of engineering products, Britain and Western Germany, each of whom sells to the tune of $4,000–4,500 million a year, East Germany and Czechoslovakia are comfortably placed among the major exporters of Europe. East Germany, following the big two and France, takes the fifth place in the world and a fourth place in Europe. Czechoslovakia is located in the medium class along with such important sellers as Sweden, Italy, the Netherlands, and Belgium–Luxembourg. Hers is the place in the world on a par with Japan. Poland rapidly moves up from the lower bracket of the table.

European Exports of Engineering Products, late 1950's

(*$ million*)

Czechoslovakia	692	9	USSR	798	6
East Germany	980	4	Italy	761	7
Poland	285	14	Sweden	707	8
			Netherlands	609	10
W. Germany	4,579	1	Benelux	518	11
United Kingdom	4,221	2			
France	1,368	3			
Switzerland	831	5			

Sources: The three countries' national statistics; for Western countries OEEC, *Engineering Industries* (1959), p. 63. Western European data may be overstated in comparison with those of the three countries owing to differences in classification, especially of consumer goods. Figures in frame denote the place in European export.

No doubt this is the branch which has every opportunity to remain in the foreseeable future the most dynamic single export branch of the area's economy. East Germany's expansion in this respect is especially noteworthy.[20]

Around the middle of the 1950's East Germany overtook Czechoslovakia by a considerable distance as the area's principal exporter. (Her previous statistical lag behind Czechoslovakia will appear larger, however, than the real one, if East German deliveries to the USSR under the reparation system—not recorded in trade statistics—are taken into account.) Between them, at the end of the decade, the three countries were fast approaching a level of $2,000 million worth of engineering products annually sold abroad. East Germany and Czechoslovakia could claim net exports of well over $1,000 million. Against this, notwithstanding the rapid growth of both her output and exports of machinery and equipment, Poland, along with the USSR, Bulgaria, and Rumania, still belongs to the net-importer group of countries of the Bloc.

Towards the end of the 1950's, however, Polish exportable surpluses of capital goods have tended to grow at a quicker pace, thanks partly to increasing capacities and partly to stabilization of domestic investment needs. The fall in foreign earnings from other exports called for a compensating intensified export drive in engineering products. At the same time this branch was able by the late 1950's to meet roughly four-fifths of the economy's requirements in equipment for new installations, replacements, and repairs. The 1960's are likely to see Polish self-sufficiency on balance in capital-goods trade.

The nature of engineering outputs, consisting as they do of many thousands of various finished goods, as often as not highly individualized, presents serious obstacles to any direct measurement of competitiveness. Official criticism has pointed time and again in each of the countries to what would seem to be resistance to technological advancement. A fairly recent Czechoslovak survey noted that 'leading officials underestimated the role of technical development and were satisfied with the production of obsolete items'; that 'progressive technical methods were so far applied only haphazardly'; and that, in particular, the engineering industry 'was not prepared to satisfy the demand for mechanization and automation equipment in national economy'. According to the

---

[20] On the restructuring of East German engineering after the Second World War see above, p. 206n.

same survey there are in Czechoslovakia some 178,000 machine-tools and forming machines—one machine for every 1·5 workers—but only some 21 per cent of the total are machines with a high degree of mechanization and automation, as against 40 per cent in the United States.[21]

One could quote scores of similar exhortations from the other two countries as well. They may be—and very probably are—intended as a spur to technological improvement. But one can detect a few factors which have tended since the war to reduce the competitive powers of this particular branch.

One is the continuous sellers' market, the security of outlets within the Soviet-Bloc group of countries which are virtually insulated from the impact of effective competition by advanced Western engineering industries. In fact, from the very start, the post-war geographic reorientation of outlets and the adaptation of a substantial part of outputs to the requirements of economies at an early stage of industrial development tended in themselves to divert the two leading producers away from their traditional lines of sophisticated products. Of necessity they had to concentrate on basic equipment for industries, transport, and agriculture. (Poland made these sectors from the beginning of her expansion in engineering, its chief domain.) In particular East German engineering had been traditionally oriented towards production of highly finished equipment—such as precision and optical instruments, printing and food-processing—for which material was imported from the Western regions of the Reich.[22] But to meet the preferential demand of the USSR during the war reparation period and after, and generally of customers in the Sino-Soviet trading area, she had to shift her output pattern towards metal-intensive products. (Note that, of her total exports of engineering, roughly half goes to the Soviet Union and another two-fifths to other countries of the 'Socialist Group'. The remaining tenth is sold in equal parts to capitalist and to underdeveloped countries.) In the event much of the 'know-how' acquired in the past had been inevitably wasted (though of course a good deal of new has been gained). Further, though absorptive on the whole, the new post-war markets have proved, at least in certain lines, too

---

[21] Report to the Central Committee of the Communist Party, by its Secretary, Oldrich Cernik (23 Sept. 1959). The report also noted that of 450 novelties exhibited in Brno in 1957, one-fifth had yet to be put into production.

[22] See above, p. 206.

narrow to permit of an efficiency-stimulating product-mix. A few more handicapping elements have been mentioned in other contexts, to recall only the chronic shortages of materials—one of the factors accounting for the heavy weight of machines and equipment in relation to capacity. A survey of Czechoslovak engineering carried out in the late 1950's noted that the difference in weight between Czechoslovak products and comparable products of leading countries is of the order of 20–30 per cent.[23] The same survey stressed that many machines and installations supplied by the Czechoslovak industry did not comply with the highest technical standards, and that its weakness lay particularly in the finish.

Some of the handicaps—perhaps the most obstinate ones—are common to all three countries to a degree that warrants the suspicion that they may stem from the actual operational conditions of the industry. Hence the eradication of certain of its ills and flaws is anything but easy; considerable effort has been undertaken, however, since the later 1950's, towards raising technological levels. A systematic large-scale retooling of the industry has been in progress in Czechoslovakia[24] and East Germany. Some repatterning of outputs has been carried out. This has been combined with endeavours to enforce a more rational division of labour within the Soviet Bloc. It is noteworthy, however, that still in the 1960's the 'parochialism'—to use the expressive term of official criticism—of this vital branch was a matter of great concern to Czechoslovak leadership. It was found that engineering in this small-sized economy was manufacturing four-fifths of the world's nomenclature for this industry, and this state of affairs affected the technological level: it was stated to inhibit automation, a factor of manifest significance under conditions of the structural labour shortage. At the same time a growing proportion of outputs has been moving towards markets where it has been exposed to keener Western competition with regard to quality and adaptability, as well as terms offered.

---

[23] See article by Cernik, in *Rude Pravo*, 4 July 1958. Some interesting data on the weight of comparable Czechoslovak, British, West German, and American machinery can be found in *Hosp. Nov.*, no. 13, 1958. See also statement by O. Simunek, chairman of the Czechoslovak State Planning Commission and Czechoslovak representative on the Permanent Executive Committee of the CMEA, on quality standards of engineering products (*Rude Pravo*, 17 July 1961).

[24] Report on the fulfilment of the Second Five Year Plan (*Rude Pravo*, 20 May 1961), and Simunek (*Rude Pravo*, 14 Sept. 1962).

It has been noticed here that since the war, East Germany for instance, has been outstripped by Western European, American, and Japanese competitors: in those branches precisely which once formed her traditional field of specialization and from which she was deflected in the post-war years. As she and other countries of the area have become growingly aware of the difficulties of meeting Western competition on some old-established ground, an additional stimulus has evolved for the (partly politically motivated and conditioned) export drive to underdeveloped countries outside the Bloc.[25]

The area's foreign trade in metals was discussed in an earlier context: so also was trade in energy.[26] It may not be out of place, however, to stress once again in the present context the quite exceptional role coal had in Poland's commerce and to note some changes which have occurred in more recent times.

Coal

It used rightly to be said that a 'coal monoculture' was the outstanding characteristic of Polish exports. In the first post-war decade coal (and coke) contributed between two-fifths and three-fifths towards Polish foreign-currency earnings (in trade). But since then the proportion has been halved. This is to a large extent the result of a double process: first, a sharp decline in relative price, and, secondly, increased 'indirect exports' of coal, i.e. of the growing quantities used in the production of exported goods, in particular of coke, metallurgical products, zinc, soda, nitrogen fertilizers. It may be fairly safely forecast that at least the second component of the process will continue. It is indeed expected that, sometime towards the end of the present decade, indirect exports of coal will overtake the direct ones.

A parallel phenomenon is a geographical shift of Polish coal exports. In the late 1940's and the early 1950's the socialist group of countries was taking 16–18 million tons a year (including coke). This gradually fell to about 7 million tons by the end of the 1950's.

The most significant phenomenon in these developments is the reduction in the quantities supplied to the USSR: from about 12 million tons in the early post-war years to about 3 million by

[25] About 90% of Polish engineering exports goes to the socialist Bloc.
[26] See above, pp. 191 f. and 186 f.

the end of the 1950's.[27] (In fact by that time the USSR had not only drastically curtailed her dependence on Polish coal and committed herself to providing some quantities to East Germany,

Polish Exports of Coal and Coke, 1924–65

(mill. tons)

	Exports of Coal				Exports of Coke
	Total	*To USSR & Central & Eastern Europe*	*To Western Europe*	*To overseas countries*	
1937	11·0	.	.	.	.
1953	24·2	17·3	6·8	0·1	1·8
1961	17·5	7·9	5·6	.	2·1
1965 (plan)	16·8	8·4	.	.	2·0

Note: Pre-war average of exports to Western Europe amounted to 11·3 million tons (1936–8), including 1·7 million tons exported from parts of Silesia which at that time belonged to the Reich.

Source: J. Dzierzynski and Edward Rose, in *Zachodnia Agencja Prasowa*, no. 38, p. 11.

---

[27] The quantities of concessionary deliveries of Polish coal to the Soviet Union were fixed by an agreement of August 1945. Poland was committed to supply 8 mill. tons in 1946, 13 mill. tons per annum in the following four years, and 12 mill. tons a year until the occupation of Germany ended. These quantities were halved by a subsequent agreement concluded in March 1947.

The arrangement was apparently made in lieu of a joint Polish/Soviet company for the exploitation of Polish mines in the new territories, originally proposed by the Soviet Union: Soviet contribution to this company was to be the claim to war reparations from the coal-bearing areas incorporated into Poland. Coal supplied under the arrangement was priced at the mere cost of transport to the Soviet frontier. Cf. S. Mikolajczyk, *The Pattern of Soviet Domination* (N.Y., 1948), pp. 157–8:, A. Zauberman, in *World Today*, no. 3, 1954, p. 134, and V. Winston, in *Amer. Slavic and E. Eur. R.*, xv/1, p. 55.

Deliveries under the arrangement ceased as from 1954. All in all some 65 mill. tons of coal were provided. Taking the average world-market price of $14–15, the USSR's gain amounted to $900–950 mill. By a November 1956 agreement Poland's outstanding debt to the USSR of $525 mill. was declared repaid by previous Polish coal deliveries below world-market prices.

Poland is pledged to deliver, over 1961–5, to the USSR on the average 4·8 mill. tons of coal and 0·6 mill. tons of coke a year; on the other hand the USSR is to supply a yearly average of 0·4 mill. tons of coking coal.

but appeared as Poland's competitor in Western markets in her quest for hard currency.) As has been pointed out before, Poland's policy is to stabilize hard-coal—and coke—exports until the mid-1960's at roughly the level of the late 1950's, and to direct a maximum proportion towards free-currency markets. The objective implies a continuous decline of coal as the foreign-exchange earner (even assuming a halt in the fall of its price in world markets).

The era of 'monoculture' is definitely over. It is difficult not to perceive in this a symptom of Poland's economic advancement, though the transition may be rather painful.

Nuclear Fuel

A sector of trade in energy commodities treated so far apart from the rest is that of nuclear fuel.

Immediately after the war the Soviet Union put her hand on the production of nuclear raw material throughout her sphere of influence. In East Germany she obtained virtual control as the occupying power, in Czechoslovakia her interests were established on a treaty basis which was revised after the 1948 political coup with a view to strengthening her position.[28] In Czechoslovakia the industry is organized in a national enterprise, the S. V. Jachymov; in East Germany in the last Soviet–East German joint company, the Deutsche Sowjetische Aktiengesellschaft Wismut. The latter took over in 1954 from the original, exclusively Soviet, organization which was formed in 1946 and operated under the system of the economic enclaves, the SAGs, until these were wound up.

Estimates of the Soviet Union's own, statistically undisclosed, output of uranium and barium bearing ores, and that of the three countries, show wide discrepancies. It is consequently hard to say what is the actual role of East German and Czechoslovak supplies in the Soviet overall nuclear-energy economy. There are reasons to believe that their role was considerable over the first post-war decade and a half or so. But it is also fairly safe to assume that owing to post-war prospecting, especially in Kazakhstan and Siberia, in addition to earlier discoveries in the Ukraine, the Caucasus, and the Urals, supplies of indigenous fissile material have greatly improved, and consequently the Soviet Union's

---

[28] J. Kasparek, in *Russian R.*, Apr. 1952, pp. 97ff. According to this source the 1945 agreement gave the USSR a monopoly of the purchase of all uranium ore mined and also of its products.

dependence on Czechoslovak–East German supplies has markedly diminished. It is not unreasonable to foresee that she may ultimately be ready to release adequate supplies to the countries of the area to meet the needs of their own energy economy. But she seems determined to preserve the monopoly of processing the countries' ores in her own territory.

Textile Raw Materials

On the import side, textile fibres may deserve at least a brief mention. They used to be called a 'hump' on the area's balance of trade. For a time after the war, the low-priority policy for consumer-goods industries tended to curtail the load. By the mid-1950's, however, a change of policy led to a rapid growth in Polish cotton-goods output. East Germany felt she must, in any case, expand her cotton industry because of her separation from the Western regions. Before the war she produced only about one-seventh of Germany's total output of cotton goods, but three-fifths of her woollens. The inter-regional textile trade had consisted, therefore, basically of the east–west exchange of woollen for cotton goods. Hence a considerable increase in East Germany's post-war imports of raw cotton. By the end of the 1950's these had doubled, as compared with pre-war, approaching those of Czechoslovakia, who regained her pre-war levels of consumption. The Soviet Union is the principal supplier of cotton to the area: in more recent years, however, Egypt has covered part of its requirements. Czechoslovakia has become the area's chief trader in Egyptian cotton. In the late 1950's about 30 per cent of her raw-cotton imports was derived from the UAR. Part of this she re-exports. But the fast expansion of Soviet cotton growing seems to outstrip that of processing capacity; the USSR in the long run is likely to become the exclusive supplier. She tends also to become a considerable source of raw wool, most of which comes at present from the sterling area.

Foodstuffs

Before the Second World War the two industrial nations of the area had quite a comfortable equilibrium in their overall food trade. This was turned after the war into a continuous and considerable deficit, particularly heavy in the case of East Germany. Poland, previously dependent only on imports of tropical foods and vegetable oils, had traditionally substantial surpluses in her food trade. These fell drastically and at times turned into deficits. Food imports have become a major foreign-payments problem throughout the area, to Poland as well as to East Germany and Czechoslovakia.

Substantial imports of grain—exceeding 6 million tons a year by the early 1960's—have become a regular feature. Before the war the occurrence and size of net grain exports depended on the year's harvests, but in the mid-1930's they were more or less constant and fairly substantial. East Germany had a lead with 1 million tons exported a year. By the end of the 1950's each of the three countries imported about 2 million tons, the two more industrialized countries buying both coarse and bread grain and Poland chiefly the latter. Most of the grain imported is coming from the Soviet Union. But since the second half of the 1950's, Poland has been able to obtain substantial quantities from the United States at favourable credit terms. The year's crop has remained a crucial factor for Poland's import capacity and thereby for the overall position of her economy.

Faced with the necessity of substantially supplementing the population's diet with foreign food, the two industrial countries are trying to contain or reduce imports of animal products; though they have to reconcile themselves to more generous imports of fodder in support of animal husbandry—a policy which has had, so far, only limited success.

In the 1930's Poland built up for herself an important foreign market in animal products, especially in bacon and tinned meat exported to Britain. (Her traditional livestock exports were already showing a gradual decline.) After the war, in the changed situation, while importing food grain she has tried to keep the home supply of fodder for the growing livestock population, (especially of pigs fed mainly on rye and potatoes) in step with the rising demand for meat and other animal products. At the same time she is striving to expand her foreign sale of products of intensive agriculture. Polish exports of animal products to the USSR, quite substantial in the 1940's, gradually petered out; Britain once again became Poland's principal, and indeed most valuable, outlet for meat products, which, along with coal, formed the basic support of the free-currency section of her balance of trade. Poland's exports of meat—partly compensated by imports—amount to about one-tenth of domestic output, though in nutritive equivalent, only to 30 per cent of imported grain. Yet with rising consumption her home market suffers from endemic supply crises.

As for the more industrialized countries of the area, it is more than dubious in the light of experience whether the East German policy objective of entirely eliminating foreign supplies of animal products within the foreseeable future stands a chance of materializing.

A note may be made here of the difference (broadly pointed out earlier) between trends in the industrialized part of the area and in Western Europe. In the mid-1930's Western Europe as a whole relied on imports for more than one-quarter of the grain it consumed. Twenty years later this ratio had fallen to about one-fifth; at the same time dependence on foreign meat and other animal products dropped to a marginal proportion. The opposite trend in the area can be accounted for by the relative stagnation of agriculture, coupled with changes in the pattern of consumption.

THE GEOGRAPHICAL DIRECTION OF TRADE AND THE SOCIALIST WORLD MARKET

No other single fact equals the new political attachments in intensity of impact on the foreign economic relations of the area. Only the surface of the momentous change is mirrored in statistical data.

We shall not describe in detail the chain of events which gave the commodity exchanges their new geographical mould. Nor does space allow of a detailed description of the new network which absorbed by the end of the 1950's between three-fifths (Poland) and three-quarters (the other two countries) of all trade as against one-tenth or so twenty years earlier.

The pattern which has evolved is a signal mixture of old and new. It virtually detached the three countries from many traditional markets in Western Europe and other parts of the world. On the other hand it gave back to Czechoslovakia much of her traditional trade with some of the former successor states of Austria-Hungary from which, as we have noted, she was being gradually cut off by the rising tide of economic nationalism between the wars. The new pattern violently disrupted East Germany's ties within the closely knit economic body of Germany.

On the other hand it redirected her trade towards Eastern Europe
—and the Balkans in particular—the target of the forceful German
thrust in the 1930's. It tended to renew the old trade links between

Share of the 'Socialist Group' in Foreign Trade

(percentage of total trade)

	1937	*1948*	*1954*	*1961*	*1965* (*plan*)
Czechoslovakia	11	31	75	72	75
East Germany	(17)[1]	75	75	73	75
Poland	7	40	70	60	66

[1] All-German trade.

the three neighbours, Germany and Czechoslovakia, Poland and
Germany which had been weakened in the 1930's but strengthened
again in the intervening era of German conquests. It brought
back—this time in magnified dimensions—the Soviet outlets for
East German industry, which played such an important part in
the German trade of the early 1930's. It established new contacts
between the economies of Poland and south-eastern Europe.
First of all it restored—in a profoundly different shape—Poland's
pre-1913 trade links with what used to form the Imperial Russian
markets. Connexions with China were, until the conflict, in a
sense the resumption of the pre-war drive towards far-away
overseas outlets. So was the expansion of trade—outside the Bloc—
with some other undeveloped countries of the Far East, as well as
the Middle East and Latin America, inspired though it was as
much by political as by economic motives.

The very logic of the Soviet Union's general strategy in her new
sphere of political and ideological paramountcy called for a
wedding of its countries into an economically harmonized group.
Creation of what has come to be termed the socialist world market
was indeed understood to be a historical necessity stemming from
the common political interests and philosophy. The process of
forging the system was neither entirely continuous nor smooth.
No sooner had the rudiments of normal economic life been
restored after the war in Poland and Czechoslovakia than both
began to gravitate towards their traditional trade networks.

Soviet predominance tended to recede particularly fast in Czechoslovakia, who had to turn to the West for certain goods not readily available at that time in the USSR. By 1947 the Soviet Union's share in both her exports and imports dropped to a mere 5 per cent. It is a moot point how far the Soviet Union could, on principle, tolerate the continuation of this trend, which was in any case reversed by the reflex of happenings on a wider international stage.

The turning-point is, by common consensus of Western students, Soviet opposition to (and the cutting off of Poland and Czechoslovakia from) Marshall Aid and the European economic cooperation to which it gave rise. The virtual collapse of any appearance of coordinated Allied rule in Germany removed the tenuous obstacles the USSR was encountering in the fitting of her Zone's economy into the new framework. Restrictive measures embarked upon by the United States in 1948, and subsequently extended to the whole of East–West trade by her allies, could not fail to add to the Soviet Union's sense of urgency in building up a homogenous trading group, and in strengthening its discipline. (It is not intended here to weigh up this effect of Allied policies against the West's gains, in terms of security, from retarding the pace of the Soviet armament drive.) Programmes of industrial expansion set afoot by that time tended, in any case, profoundly to affect the traditional demand/supply positions and the corresponding geographical pattern in each country's trade.

Looking back, it is the year 1953 which appears to mark the start of a new phase. A measure of relaxation in the international political climate and in the internal politics of the Bloc opened up possibilities for some readjustments in trade directions. Severe strains and stresses in the area's economy aggravated by its isolation from world markets prompted a shift towards more flexible outlets which would provide 'hard' currency and thus greater freedom of manœuvre in imports. Last but not least, as time passed, Western restrictions dictated by defence needs tended to wear themselves out.

The political isolation of East Germany's régime in the world outside the Bloc (lack of diplomatic relations and normal trade treaties), the greater degree to which the economies of the Soviet Union and East Germany became complementary (owing, though not exclusively, to developments under the régime of war reparations) all tended to make the latter's dependence on the Bloc's intra-trade especially strong. The Berlin crisis gave a new impulse to a further tightening of East Germany's economic ties with the USSR, as a correlative of the drive for severing the residual links with Western Germany.[29] The concept of a special East German–Soviet *Wirtschaftsgemeinschaft* was evolved in the early 1960's; it has been argued that, economic motives apart, 'political ideological' considerations require that a country of East Germany's type 'marches together in the first rank with the most progressive country of the socialist world, one with the highest developed science and techniques. . . .'[30]

At the other extreme, in Poland, the political events of the autumn of 1956 favoured the re-establishment of somewhat closer commercial and financial contacts with the Western world. Yet, on the other hand, such new tendencies have been counteracted by a discernible emphasis on tightening the political and economic cohesion of the Bloc. As time passed the new foreign-trade structures gained their own powers of self-perpetuation, if only because the interwoven production patterns matured and consolidated. Towards the end of the 1950's the Soviet-Bloc countries were dependent on mutual deliveries for about half their cotton, three-fifths of their rolled steel, between three-quarters and almost the whole of their fuels, iron ores, pig-iron, and fertilizers, and—a point of particular consequence—for about four-fifths of their equipment. In spite of the newly professed favour for a fuller development of East–West commerce, the share of intra-Bloc trade in the area's total has been stabilized.

Since the mid-1950's the worst features of this relationship have been relaxed. The Soviet 'get-rich-quick' policy characteristic of the early post-war years, gave way to one of greater consideration for the interest of the partners. Grossly discriminatory prices, well typified by the case of Polish coal deliveries, were discarded. The régime of reparations and of Soviet-owned and run enterprises— the SAGs—which had previously so severely crippled East German economy was wound up. While political motives, in intra-trade and generally in the Bloc's foreign trade, have presumably retained greater room in trade policies than is common in market economies, the weight of economic factors distinctly increased.

[29] See below, p. 308.   [30] R. Bauer, in *Ww.*, no. 2, 1962, p. 187.

A few more salient elements deserve to be stressed when the USSR's trade with the area is discussed.

The first is the vital position the area holds in the Soviet Union's

Share of the Soviet Union in Foreign Trade:
Czechoslovakia, East Germany, Poland

	1937	1945	1947	1953	1962
Czechoslovakia					
Exports	1	13	5	36	38
Imports	1	33	5	39	38
East Germany					
Exports	.	.	.	46	40
Imports	.	.	.	47	49
Poland					
Exports	1	93	28	38	35
Imports	1	91	25	27	31

own network of foreign trade. It accounts for nearly two-fifths of the Soviet Union's commodity exchanges with the world. East Germany alone accounts for half that share, the other half being divided more or less equally between Czechoslovakia and Poland. Trade with them absorbs as much as three-quarters of all Soviet merchandise exchanges with all the European members of the Bloc: indeed an appreciable part of the—relatively substantial—expansion of Soviet foreign trade after the Second World War is attributable to it. Since the end of the 1950's East Germany has occupied, even if intermittently, the first place among the Soviet Union's customers. China—whom she had displaced around 1960 as the Soviet Union's trade partner—was, for a time, East Germany's only serious rival for primacy in the Soviet table.

Before the last war, as industrialization progressed, the Soviet Union tended to maximum self-sufficiency. That trend was moderated after the war, partly as a consequence of the formation of the new trading system under her leadership. Thus, in that system the area—and more specifically East Germany and Czechoslovakia—has taken over the role which, in the 1920's, was held by the Reich and, in the late 1930's, by the United States and the United Kingdom, as the supplier of machinery and equipment.

(In 1928 Germany had a one-quarter share in both Soviet exports and imports: this dropped to about 4 and 8 per cent respectively before the outbreak of the war.) The USSR is still a heavy net importer of machinery and equipment. She imports twice as much as she exports: her yearly overall surplus of imports is about $750 million. But with the three countries' area the surplus approaches $1,000 million. Nearly three-fifths of the capital goods bought abroad by the Soviet Union come from the three countries, which top the list of her suppliers: East Germany alone being responsible for about three-tenths of the Soviet total.

True, Czechoslovakia's share is smaller, about one-fifth in the early 1960's. None the less she occupies an important place as the leading—or one of the leading—provider of some essential kinds of equipment. In the late 1950's she supplied the Soviet Union with more than one-third of all imported metal-working machine-tools and rolling-mill equipment: over one-half of power-plant and sugar-refinery machinery, two-fifths of the diesel engines, nine-tenths of the lorries, two-thirds of the river boats and almost three-quarters of the motor-cycles.

Even Poland—although her share in the Soviet total is the smallest (about 8 per cent)—sells twice as much machinery and equipment, in value terms, as she buys from the USSR. Three-quarters of Polish engineering exports to the USSR consist of rolling-stock and ships—Polish shipyards are a substantial provider for the Soviet merchant navy.[31] These products make up well over one-quarter of Polish total exports to the USSR. In the case of East Germany and Czechoslovakia the proportion is between one-half and three-fifths.

[31] There have been some discernible shifts in Soviet buying of engineering products. Broadly speaking, as time passes it moves away from standardized and 'bulk' machinery to more specialized equipment. This is especially true of metal-forming and metal-working equipment. Rather more than 40% of machine-tool imports—*ad valorem*—comes from East Germany, about one-third from Czechoslovakia, and about one-fifth from Poland. The area has been the leading supplier of transport equipment to the USSR. For a period the overwhelming proportion of exports of the expanded Polish and East German shipyards—as well as of the rolling-stock output of the area—went to the USSR. Some 1,750 locomotives and 20,000 trucks were delivered by Poland alone over the first post-war decade. Towards the end of the 1950's the USSR tended to reduce her buying of ships, but the buying of ships from Poland was maintained at a level of about $30 mill. The vast Soviet railway-electrification project found expression in the growing orders for electrical rolling-stock placed in the area.

Poland takes about one-tenth of Soviet exports of engineering products, half of which are in complete factory sets.

Turning to the other side of the trade position we shall note that, in the late 1940's, the Soviet Union was still heavily dependent on, and drew heavily from, the area's supplies of primary produce. But ten years later, by the late 1950's, the picture had radically changed. True, the area remained a substantial source of supply to the Soviet Union for some essential raw materials—such as uranium from East Germany and Czechoslovakia, potash salts from the latter, zinc from Poland—but, on the whole, net additions to the USSR's own supplies in vital raw materials fell to nil, or became marginal; conversely, traditional exports of some raw materials were substantially stepped up. The USSR now became a net supplier to the area of finished and semi-finished metals, as well as of ores, and of energy, in the shape of both solid and liquid fuels. The growing supply of oil was making her an

Commodity Composition of Soviet Trade with East Germany
and Czechoslovakia, 1960 or 1961

	Soviet imports from		Soviet exports to	
	East Germany[1]	Czecho-slovakia[2]	East Germany	Czecho-slovakia
Machinery & equipment	57	49	6	22
Raw materials	28	20	72	49
Food	–	4	22	27
Industrial consumer goods	15	27	1	1

[1] 1961.   [2] 1960.

Sources: A. Suk in *Plan. Hosp.*, no. 5, 1960, and other sources.

important provider of chemical materials; and her position as the chief supplier of foodstuffs was enhanced. (The two industrial countries of the area absorbed between them nearly half the USSR's total agricultural exports. The latter's food imports from the area—very heavy in her lean post-war years—become confined by the late 1950's to sugar bought from the Poles and Czechoslovaks.)

USSR's Share of Raw-Material Imports. End of 1950's and mid-1960's[1]

	Czechoslovakia			East Germany			Poland		
	1965	1958	1965	1965	1960	1965	1965	1960	1965[2]
	000 tons	% of total imports		000 tons	% of total imports		000 tons	% of total imports	
Coke				1,550		58			100
Crude oil	5,200	99		4,800	95	90	3,100	100	100
Iron ore	10,100	72			100		8,200	75	80
Pig-iron				1,435		100			
Rolled steel				1,560	80	75			
Copper		50		44		100	9	25	
Aluminium		98		85		95		34	100
Phosphates	118	61		320	95		360		
Rubber (synth.)	19	58		28				32	100
Sawn timber				1,545	90	80	250		100
Cellulose		71		122		45			
Cotton	60	53		152	80			60	
Wheat		97		100				50	
Butter		80					9		

[1] 1965 refers to 1965 trade agreement.   [2] From Soviet Bloc countries.

To sum up, except for Poland—trade with whom has a less clear-cut character—the USSR plays *vis-à-vis* the area the typical role of a raw-material hinterland rather than that of a supplier of industrial commodities—a role which strikes one as unusual for a politically paramount power.[32] Since the end of the 1950's Poland, too, has endeavoured to reshape the structure of her Soviet trade so as to bring it closer into accord with this overall pattern: that is, trying to substitute an increasingly large proportion of manufactures for the shrinking quantities of coal—once the mainstay of her exports to the Soviet Union. It is safe to forecast that this tendency will continue, and gather momentum.

[32] Roughly two-fifths of Czechoslovak and East German imports from the USSR, and rather more than one-quarter of Polish imports, consist of agricultural products, as can be seen from these data for a few years in the 1950's. In contrast these products form a negligible proportion in the area's exports to the USSR.

However, at an Academy of Sciences conference the participants of a Polish debate on the 'perspective' plan were warned by its author that 'if the Soviet Union does not propose to expand her production at a quicker pace [than the Polish one] . . . that means that she has no unlimited volume of raw materials at her disposal. Raw-material resources of the Soviet Union are enormous, but the output [presumably of raw materials] is also limited by technico-organizational factors.' See reference to Professor Kalecki's contribution, in *Ekon.*, no. 1, 1959, p. 136.

Trade between the Three Countries

As has been noted, the three countries—Czechoslovakia, East Germany, and Poland—form the core of the East European trade network, by virtue of the fact that between three-quarters and four-fifths of all trade conducted by the European members of the CMEA is done by this group of three. (Among the countries forming the 'world socialist system' there are those whose industrial economies are the most foreign-trade-oriented: Soviet estimates suggest that East Germany's and Czechoslovakia's shares in the 'system's' foreign trade are double[33] their shares in its total industrial output, and Poland's is about one-third higher.) But what is the trade of the countries of the area among themselves? An attempt at an answer may be usefully started from Czech–Polish economic relations.

Most of the inter-war period was marked by a political estrangement between the two neighbours.[34] Although their economies were in that period complementary to a higher degree than they are to-day, their mutual merchandise exchanges played a strikingly insignificant role in the respective trade bills. It was widely anticipated that political and territorial changes brought about by the Second World War would result in drawing the two countries much closer in the economic field. This belief inspired the early post-war agreements on economic co-operation. Although tentative and cautious they tended distinctly towards paving the way to organic ties in the future. They created a framework for coordinating agencies. Coordination of investment was contemplated. Partnership was envisaged in construction of some plants on Polish territory to be equipped with Czechoslovak machinery. Czechoslovakia was granted special rights in the use of the harbour of Szczecin and the Oder navigation. Very little of these arrangements materialized at the time. Czechoslovakia no doubt did play a major part—second only to the USSR—as the supplier of equipment for the rehabilitation and the initial expansion of Polish industries. Her share in Polish foreign trade, which in 1938 amounted to about $3\frac{1}{2}$ per cent, was three times as

[33] See *Vn. Torg.*, no. 19, 1962. This source mentions the following shares in industrial output computed for 1958 (per cent): Czechoslovakia 6, East Germany 7, Poland 6·5, USSR 60; and in foreign trade: Czechoslovakia 12, East Germany 14, Poland 9, USSR 35.

[34] For an excellent general background of Polish–Czechoslovak relations see Hugh Seton-Watson, *East European Revolution* (London, 1950), *passim*, especially p. 343.

large fifteen years later. But a decline set in at that point. By 1957 Czechoslovakia's share in Polish commodity trade was halved as compared with the 1953 peak. Similarly Poland was one of the few among Czechoslovakia's chief customers who showed a rapid fall in Czechoslovak trade.

At the turn of the decade, however, deliberate action was taken to restimulate Polish–Czechoslovak economic relations. Joint bodies have been formed and entrusted with the task of expanding scientific, technological, and economic co-operation in the domains of industrial production, raw-material supply, and foreign trade. Commodity exchanges have tended again to expand and at the same time to come nearer to the pattern usual between industrial countries; engineering products, almost nil in Polish supplies to Czechoslovakia a decade ago, by now make up about two-fifths. Predictions current in the West that the sharing of control of the Silesian basin—the Ruhr of the East—would *per se* cement the two economies into an *Ostkombinat*[35] have failed to materialize. However, various factors do work towards closer links. The proximity of the Silesia–Cracow and the Ostrava–Karvina industrial regions is only one of these; the other is Poland's emergence as an important source of two raw materials, sulphur and copper, and Czechoslovakia's ability to finance their development. Once again Poland's and Czechoslovakia's planners are inclined to see the countries as forming one 'complex'; and it remains to be seen how far new programmes (reaching out to 1980) for its integration into, as it were, a sub-unit within the Bloc will materialize.

It was East Germany's industrial revival—perhaps rather more than Poland's progress in industrialization—especially as a producer of capital goods, that at least for a time affected Polish–Czechoslovak economic relations. Towards the mid-1950's she took over a large part of the responsibility—second only to that of the USSR—for meeting Poland's needs in investment supplies. By early 1960's East Germany was responsible for nearly one-quarter of Polish imports of machines and other capital goods.

Over most of the post-war period Poland's trade with her two

[35] See e.g. P. H. Seraphim, *Industrie-Kombinat Oberschlesien das Ruhrgebiet des Ostens*. The failure of the *Ostkombinat* to materialize is discussed in an interesting passage by Johannes Polaczek, *Die Entwicklung der oberschlesischen Montanindustrie in den Jahren 1945–55* (Marburg, 1958), pp. 133ff.

highly industrial neighbours has been following a closely similar pattern. In each case between one-half and two-thirds of supplies from Poland's partners has consisted of machinery and equipment, supplemented by some essential raw and semi-processed materials, such as potassium salts and synthetic rubber, liquid fuels from East Germany. The overall shift in Poland's foreign-trade composition towards the end of the 1950's also found, however, some reflection in trade with her two neighbours. At the beginning of the 1950's nearly nine-tenths of Polish supplies, such as coal, coke, zinc, some basic chemicals, consisted of raw materials; Polish export of capital goods was non-existent; towards the end of the decade Poland was energetically trying to push her manufactures —especially machinery—into two neighbouring markets; by the beginning of the following decade investment goods were making up one-third of the total, the share of agricultural products markedly declined.

On the whole, within the similar pattern of trade, East Germany has shown for a time more flexibility and has found more scope for stimulating mutual exchanges. Consequently, as early as the beginning of the 1950's she displaced Czechoslovakia as Poland's second-largest customer. At the end of the 1950's the volume of East German trade with Poland was half again as large as that of the latter with Czechoslovakia. Still more spectacular has been Poland's fall in Czechoslovakia's list of traders. East Germany gained a comfortable second place in this list, while Poland moved down to the fourth and fifth place in her exports and imports respectively, preceded in exports by the Soviet Union, East Germany, and China, and in imports by the Soviet Union, East Germany, Hungary, and China, in that order.

The capture by East Germany of the vital place in both Czechoslovakia's and Poland's foreign trade—notwithstanding the differences in their economic structures—is a phenomenon which merits special emphasis. But again the early 1960's have witnessed a certain weakness of this process. Of the observable causes one appears to be the anæmia which has affected the East German economy and another a still more accentuated orientation of East German engineering towards the absorptive Soviet market. An inter-connected factor seems to be Poland's rising freight-bill for East German–Soviet transit through her territory; this would seem to have exercised a downward pressure on East German buying of

Polish goods; Polish imports from East Germany are nearly twice the value of East German imports from Poland.

Similarities and dissimilarities of structure may influence trade in various ways. (In the post-war period total trade among the world's leading industrial countries increased faster than did their exports of manufactures to the rest of the world.) It is well established that amongst market economies of similar size a large manufacturing production is usually accompanied by a large exchange of manufactures. Indeed, the same tendency seems to be brought out by the post-war gravitation towards each other of the two highly industrial economies of the area. In 1953 East Germany still held only the fifth place among Czechoslovakia's trade partners. By the end of the 1950's she became her second most important customer, preceded only by the USSR.

Admittedly, a substantial slice of mutual commerce is made up of raw and semi-processed materials. Under these headings Czechoslovakia and East Germany trade coking coal, kaolin, and some foodstuffs against potassium salts, brown-coal briquettes, sulphur, &c. But capital goods account in mutual exchanges for about three-fifths and one-third of East German and Czechoslovak supplies respectively: two-fifths of imported Czechoslovak machinery and equipment comes from East Germany; and this is twice the share these items constitute in total Czechoslovak imports.

As has been noted in another context, in the intra-area trade pre-war geographical patterns tended to restore themselves in a remarkable fashion. This is true, at least as far as the position of East Germany is concerned. On the other hand Czechoslovakia has tended to replace for East Germany, in some respects and on a very moderate scale, her pre-war intra-German exchanges.

Intra-German Trade

Although they have increased almost continuously in the 1950's German inter-regional exchanges corresponded by the end of the decade, at a purchasing power parity, to no more than one-sixth of their pre-war size (when they constituted roughly half of all East German external trade, that is, foreign plus inter-regional trade). At the beginning of the 1950's the proportion was a mere fifth and it dropped to about one-tenth in the early 1960's. None the less they do form a very substantial component—between two-fifths and three-fifths—of the whole of East Germany's trade outside the Sino-Soviet world. In some commodities—especially rolled steel—they are indeed of prime importance to the East German economy. Generally speaking, however, the composition of German inter-regional exchanges has undergone, since the war, no less appreciable changes than their size. Machines, together with other metal products, represent no more than between one-quarter and one-fifth of each side of the mutual balance of trade, the bulk of the merchandise trade being formed by essential primary goods and semi-manufactures. The exchanges suffered from various technical handicaps. The principle of a rigid balance over comparatively short periods was but one of them. Towards the end of the 1950's a growing East German deficit heavily obstructed trade between the two parts of Germany. The beginning of the 1960's saw an agreement to ease some of the technical rigidities. Soon thereafter restrictions imposed as a result of the Berlin crisis demonstrated once again the sensitivity of inter-regional exchanges to changes in political climate.

The aftermath of this crisis has been, since the beginning of the 1960's, a determined drive towards the ultimate elimination of East Germany's dependence on intra-German links. A concept of a closer East German–Soviet 'economic community' has been evolved (see p. 290). While the Soviet Union declared herself ready to replace any shortfalls in West German deliveries the East German leadership awoke to the fact that the cobweb of German economic ties is, in fact, still tighter than would appear from the quantitative measure of inter-zonal links and this is true in particular in respect of technological interdependence. Hence efforts to sever these links, especially through a shift towards Soviet technological standards.[36] This, however, entailed a considerable diversion of East German resources and caused new and serious frictions. Whatever the ultimate outcome of the process of such re-structuring, it has proved to be more protracted, dislocating, and costly than was expected by the leaders of East Germany.

East–West Trade and Western European Integration

Here a very brief digression on the area's East–West trade may be called for. Having reached its post-war trough around 1953 this

[36] See A. Lange, in *Ww.*, no. 7, 1961.

trade, and specifically trade with Western Europe, passed through a phase of moderate revival since the later years of the decade. This could be accounted for by political and economic factors operating on both sides, and gave rise to some optimism for the future. It has been borne out by a continual expansion in the 1960's, but certain new and more permanent obstacles have become visible.

Trade with Western Europe
(*percentage of total trade*)

	1937	*1950*	*1953*	*1962*
Czechoslovakia				
exports	58	31	14	16 (7)
imports	62	30	15	17 (8)
Poland				
exports	56	30	22	28 (10)
imports	72	38	27	23 (7)
East Germany				
exports	.	12	16	
imports	.	12	12	

Note: If intra-German trade were *included*, the East German series would read, for the respective years:

.	25	22	19
.	31	19	19

The bracketed figures in the right-hand column denote the share of the EEC countries.

By that time it became evident that Europe's trade was entering a phase of tighter regional concentration. While, on the one hand (as was noted before) security embargoes in East–West trade were on the wane, on the other Western regional preferences were evolving within the framework of the EEC and EFTA. In their first impact these preferences would appear to affect East Germany rather than Poland; manufactures make up about two-fifths of total East German sales to Western Europe, with a considerable proportion of engineering products. Two points, however, must be borne in mind. First, intra-German trade which, as we have said, accounts for about two-fifths of East Germany's European East–West trade is exempted from the EEC arrangements in respect of commerce with outsiders. Secondly, there is good reason to believe that it is precisely because of its comparatively large proportion of manufactures that Czechoslovak and East German East–West trade has shown a comparatively lesser expansive force than that of the rest of the Bloc, quite independently of Western European integration.

On the other hand Poland has some cause to feel that Western European integration is bound to impair her position in Western European markets. As has been pointed out, her coal exports were bound in any case to decline owing to the glut in Western markets. She is therefore all the more concerned about the future of her food exports. To her the decisive contingency is the access to the Common Market of Britain, who takes first place among her hard-currency markets. All in all, about one-quarter of Poland's total exports go to Western Europe and half of this consists of farm products. Clearly she cannot consider with equanimity any EEC régime of discrimination in this field. The fact that in their East–West trade the countries of the area, as indeed all Soviet Bloc countries, confine themselves to what are considered to be the most necessary imports (largely technologically advanced equipment for which there is no substitute in the Bloc markets) narrows their elbow room.

Underdeveloped Countries

The survey of the geographical patterns of foreign trade may be concluded by pointing to the increasing role of trade with non-European retarded economies—outside the socialist group. The subject was touched upon in the more specific context of machinery and equipment exports. The direction of exports in manufactures, especially in capital goods, to Africa, the Near, Middle, and Far East, and Latin America rather than to industrially advanced countries, has been increasing ever since the mid-1950's. Czechoslovakia was the original leader in the drive but East Germany is gradually catching up with her.[37] Towards the end

[37] Czechoslovak imports from underdeveloped countries consist almost exclusively of raw material and food. Equipment forms three-fifths of exports to these countries (*Cz. Foreign Trade*, Oct. 1963). This structure is almost typical of East German trade. In Polish exports equipment represents rather less than one-third of the total (*Z. Gosp.*, no. 23, 1962).

of the last decade the volume of the three countries' trade with the developing regions outside the socialist camp roughly approached that of the USSR herself, a telling measure of the contribution to the general strategy of the camp *vis-à-vis* these regions.

The drive has been favoured by the experience gained in catering—within the socialist camp—to the needs of nations at the early stages of industrial development, and the adaptation of outputs to such needs. Particularly valuable has been from this angle the experience in providing entire 'projects'—complete with blueprints, equipment, technological 'know-how', services of experts in the construction and running of the plant, and training facilities for local personnel. It is only right to note that the drive has been inspired—to say the least—by political as well as by commercial considerations; that some economic benefits to each side have been compensated for, to a certain extent, by disadvantages; and that, as time passed, its benefits tended to be affected by diminishing returns to both sides. It has also been favoured, among other things, by the readiness of the economically underdeveloped countries to enter into barter arrangements securing bulk sales of their primary produce, mineral and agricultural raw materials. This, in the eyes of the trading partners, has often compensated for the lower qualitative standards of some of the equipment received as against Western supplies.

Share of Underdeveloped Countries in the Area's Trade, 1962
(Percentage)

Czechoslovakia	East Germany	Poland
11	5 (est.)	8

The more onerous aspect of the trade drive into the underdeveloped countries is its finance. The ability of the exporters of engineering products to offer adequate credits is clearly of prime importance. In many cases the countries of the area have shown themselves willing to sell their goods at comparatively low prices, as well as at very generous credit terms.[38] Political motives—the

[38] OEEC, *Engineering Industries*, pp. 98, 121.

buying of goodwill of the non-committed nations (largely coterminal with those of the underdeveloped world)—have added to the high requirements of capital normally involved in exports made up to such a high degree of investment goods. Over the decade which followed 1953 the three countries committed between them well over $800 million in low-interest medium-term credits. Clearly the area can ill afford to compete with capital-abounding nations in trade involving heavy engagement of capital.

FOREIGN PAYMENT POSITION

Scarce as is statistical information on the foreign commodity trade of the area, it is abundant in comparison with that on the overall foreign payment position. Few data are published on 'invisibles'; very few are revealed on the state of foreign debts and claims; no information at all is disclosed as a rule on foreign-exchange and bullion holdings. Only very indirect and very incomplete indications may be gained from the behaviour of trade balances, and other symptoms, and from announcements on foreign credits. Pledges rather than use are normally revealed for the latter. It is safe, however, to assume that none of the three countries has had, at any time since the war, any appreciable stocks of gold or hard currencies. All the evidence there is seems to suggest that their trade has been conducted on a hand-to-mouth basis.

By the end of the 1950's all the three countries of the area had an adverse trade balance with the USSR. East Germany was able to dispense with visible export surpluses in this trade only towards the end of the last decade, when her last financial obligations *vis-à-vis* the USSR connected with her post-war status came to an end.

Poland has had considerable overall trade deficits over practically the whole of the post-war period, large deficits with the Bloc being accompanied normally by surpluses in the trade outside it. Towards the end of the last decade those surpluses, too, shrank and turned into deficits, but these could be met by proceeds from Western credits.[39] An appreciable proportion of Poland's intra-

---

[39] See below, p. 315. However, Poland's payment position *vis-à-vis* her Bloc partners seems to be adversely affected by their tendency to secure from her, as it were *via facti*, unscheduled credits. The Chairman of the State Planning Commission remarked that this position is at times 'too good' since 'our "avoirs" sometimes exceed the rational level'. Cf. *Nowe Drogi*, Feb. 1961.

Bloc deficits, of the order of about $100 million a year, is being offset as a rule by earnings from shipping and railway services, those from transit in the USSR's trade with East Germany making a particularly valuable contribution.

In contrast to Poland, Czechoslovakia's position has been the strongest in foreign trade and payments in the area. Her trade has shown almost consistent export surpluses overall as well as within the Bloc. She has apparently used these for granting modest loans—chiefly inside, but in part also outside the Bloc—to under-developed economies in support of the trade drive.[40] Practically every member of the Bloc has benefited from Czechoslovak credits at one time or another, the largest ones so far have been pledged to Poland as Czechoslovak participation in the development of Polish hard-coal, copper, and sulphur extraction.[41] Even East Germany has been among the recipients of Czechoslovak credits. (Czechoslovakia participated with the USSR in financial assist-ance for the expansion of East German potash mining.)[42]

On the face of it East Germany's position would appear similar to that of Czechoslovakia. This, however, is belied by persistent symptoms of an acute tightness. These have continued even after East Germany's obligations under the occupation régime towards the USSR came to an end. The strain became indeed critical as soon as more consideration for living standards entailed a more liberal import policy in the consumer-goods sector.

SOVIET FINANCIAL SUPPORT

Throughout the post-war period the Soviet Union has been standing by with financial support to countries exposed to strains.

[40] See above, p. 310.

[41] The largest transaction of this kind is that connected with the development of Polish copper. Altogether Czechoslovakia pledged credits to Poland to the amount of $200 million: of these $112 million for the copper project, $88 million for the sulphur project and the remainder for coal-mining. The 'copper credit' will be, in fact, used partly for the purchase of a nitrogen plant to be installed at Pulawy and partly for certain deliveries of metallurgical coke, cement, and other goods. In each of these three cases loans bear 2% interest. Poland can draw upon the credits pledged over periods of years. Up to between one-half and two-thirds of the credits is made available to Poland in the shape of Czechoslovak equipment. Repayment in copper (and copper products), coal, and sulphur is scheduled to start after the projects have been com-missioned, which is planned for 1961–6, 1964–70, and 1969–79 respectively. Poland is pledged to sell some quantities of sulphur, coal, and copper during periods of ten, twenty-five, and five years after the repayment of loans has been completed.

[42] The total loan granted amounted to about $60 million, half of which came from Czechoslovakia and half from the USSR. Repayment is arranged in potash deliveries to the credit-giving nations.

Financial assistance has been provided by her partly in commodity credits, partly in convertible foreign currency. Most of it had a connexion with investment projects in which she has been interested. Thus, Poland obtained, under different headings over the post-1946 decade, loans to the equivalent of about $1,000 million: more than half of this was made up of loans granted in support of the first development programme, especially in connexion with two projects: the Nowa Huta steel works and the Zeran car factory.

Between the mid-1950's and the early 1960's East Germany obtained credits from the USSR amounting to nearly $900 million, of which over one-third was in gold and convertible foreign exchange, to ease her position in hard-currency markets, and about the same proportion consisted of loans to finance her investments, most of which were earmarked for the chemical industry. Later in the 1960's the USSR pledged herself to assist East Germany financially in connexion with the policy of a further eastward reorientation of her economy.

It is only fair to emphasize that over a period of years the strains which the USSR was relieving in this way were, to a large and decisive extent, of her own making. Symptomatic of the new phase was the cancellation, agreed in November 1956, of all the outstanding Polish debts, amounting to about $525 million, as a compensation for the underpayment of Poland's coal deliveries to the USSR in the past at a nominal price. (See p. 292n.)

The cost of Soviet finance is very moderate: the rate of interest is in fact exceedingly low. But the overall terms are rather onerous: most of the loans are of a relatively short-term type: repayment of the longer-term credits has never been extended over more than ten years and as a rule begins within a year or two after deliveries for a given project have started. Above all, the size of loans has been inadequate to 'lubricate' the growth of assisted economies.

WESTERN AID TO POLAND

In the meantime, since the mid-1950's Poland—alone within the Soviet Bloc—has been so fortunate as to be able to turn for financial assistance to the West. She has secured various credits, the most important of which are from the United States. These have been granted on extremely advantageous terms: a proportion being repayable in 25–40 years. A substantial part of these aid credits has been spent on purchases of agricultural products, mainly grain, from United States surplus stocks. These are being repaid into a blocked Polish currency account in Poland. While there are arrangements for the reconversion of this account into dollars at some later date a predominant part of it is likely to turn out, in fact if not in name, to be a gift rather than credit.

The vast American credit has enabled Poland to run over a long period a substantial deficit in her East–West trade. To see the post-1956 American aid in the right perspective one may perhaps note that by the early 1960's it equalled in purchasing power between three and four times the American loan Poland secured in the late 1920's to form a basis for her financial system. Moreover a substantial proportion of the pre-war loan had to be sterilized in bullion; and one of the conditions of the loan was the appointment of an American economic adviser in Poland. The question whether a Poland politically tied to the Soviet Bloc can reasonably stake hopes on the continuation of American 'lubricating' of her economic growth on this impressive scale creates a fascinating dilemma for which we shall not try to suggest a solution here.

POLISH PAYMENTS DIFFICULTIES COMPARED WITH EAST GERMAN

As has been pointed out in this section, East German difficulties on this score are of a very specific character. They have been aggravated, moreover, by her exports being of a type which entails considerable credit-giving. To some extent these difficulties are, in fact, circular. Pressed by the deficiency of capital and driven by the need to secure means for the purchase of foreign raw materials and food, she has had to export over periods too much of her output of capital goods, considering the heavy needs at home for retooling her severely decapitalized economy. Insufficient replacement and addition in her capital stock tended in turn to recoil on her productive efficiency and thus on her competitiveness.

The Polish case is the more familiar one of a capital-deficient country, with a strong population pressure, which becomes out of breath in the course of an intensive industrial growth. It is a not uncommon phenomenon that growth processes 'bump' against the ceiling set by the feasible limits to imports which in turn are rigidly determined by export availabilities (both being in part influenced by the needs of a fast-growing population). We may conveniently recall in this context the illuminating findings of those engaged on drafting the Polish long-term 1960–75 economic vision. As Professor Kalecki has stated: 'In the course of work on the perspective plan it appeared time and again that the bottleneck in economic development was foreign-trade balance, that is, the difficulty of balancing the necessary increase in imports by a corresponding one in exports.'[43] It is tight foreign exchange as well as lack of capital—two aspects of essentially the same bottleneck—which have held back attempts to re-accelerate Poland's industrial expansion in the 1960's.[44]

THE SOVIET BLOC: TERMS OF TRADE AND PRICING POLICY

With some seven-tenths of the countries' foreign commodity exchanges moving within the boundaries of the Bloc, the terms of intra-Bloc trade have naturally had a signal influence on their economies.

For most of the period under review the subject was shrouded in secrecy, although at different times some hints, very often conflicting, have been dropped.[45] As early as 1951 Soviet authority maintained that the socialist countries' camp 'tended towards its own price basis and its own money scale of settlements, in conformity with its social structure' and has discarded world prices in its members' relations. No light was shed on what was the concrete bearing of the common socio-economic structure on pricing inside the orbit. A decade later the idea of the Bloc's own price structure gained new significance, and indeed urgency, in connexion with the efforts towards a more efficient integration. It was given a formal sanction by the 1962 conference of the Bloc's ruling parties and formulated in the 'Fundamental Principles of the International Socialist Division of Labour'. These rules call for perfecting the system of price formation of the world socialist market in such a way as to create conditions for a 'gradual change over to an independent basis'. The principles recommend keeping in mind

---

[43] *Nowe Drogi*, no. 8, 1958.

[44] It will be noted that growth models evolved in recent years by Polish students concerned with the application of mathematical techniques in planning operate with two ultimately scarce factors, capital and foreign exchange (see p. 316). In this they resemble, and perhaps draw inspiration from, Professor Chenery's model for developing economies. See his 'Application of Interindustry Analysis to Problems of Economic Development', in *The Structural Interdependence of the Economy*, Tibor Barna ed. (Milano–New York, 1956), p. 381.

[45] I. Zlobin, in *Vopr. Ekon.*, no. 7, 1951, pp. 89ff.

the requirements of expanding member economies and improving the intra-CMEA division of labour, but they do not seem to have moved beyond vague generalities.

So much for the objective for the future. Too little is known to permit a complete analysis of principles and actual pricing in operation within the Bloc.

The official Soviet textbook of political economy has this to say on the subject:

Commodity prices in the world market of socialist countries are stable. They are fixed by voluntary agreement concluded by partners who enjoy equal rights with mutual interests fully respected. This excludes any kind of discrimination or non-equivalence in commerce. There is no multiplicity of prices such as is the feature of foreign trade of capitalist countries.[46]

A more recent statement by a Soviet authoritative source[47] formulates the intra-Bloc pricing method as follows: (1) there is a 'planning principle' in the intra-Bloc commodity exchanges which 'precludes any elemental processes of price formation'; (2) trade in the world socialist market is based on 'equivalent exchange'; (3) prices are 'coordinated and fixed in a contractual manner'; and (4) they 'remain stable' over a long period. The notion of 'equivalence' has not been defined, nor has the manner in which it is secured. With these reservations it seems safe to say that at least a point of departure in intra-Bloc pricing is formed by world-market price relations at some stage; however, as these price relations are kept 'frozen', they tend in time to deviate from the price structure obtaining in world markets. Moreover it would appear that certain readjustments are obtained on a 'contractual' basis. Thus, in addition to deviation from world prices, those prevailing within the Bloc may differ as between pairs of its members. Analyses of trade statistics for the late 1950's suggest, for instance, that East Germany paid to the Soviet Union less than either Poland or Czechoslovakia for such materials as wheat, crude oil, iron ore, manganese ore, iron and steel. There is no evidence to show to what extent differentials of this kind reflect the strength of the economic (or political) bargaining positions of trade partners.

Broadly speaking, sometime before, or around, the middle of the

46 *Politicheskaya Ekonomiya* (Moscow, 1958), pp. 66off.
47 V. Sergeyev, in *Vopr. Ekon.*, no. 7, 1962, p. 144.

1950's the operation of prices grossly weighted in favour of the Soviet Union was terminated. In particular it is contended that uranium is being bought by the USSR from Czechoslovakia and East Germany at 'fair' world-market prices.[48] It is less certain, however, whether any price differentiation has been practised at a later date by the USSR *vis-à-vis* her partners within the Bloc, as compared with other sources of supply and outlets.

A continuing price discrimination—in a specific sense—during the later 1950's has been pointed out by an illuminating study[49] carried out by Dr Mendershausen on a wide sample basis for Soviet exports to, and (on a substantially narrower one) for Soviet imports from, the orbit. In so far as it goes, the analysis suggests that—taking Soviet business with European free markets as the yardstick—the orbit countries were more or less systematically underpaid, over a number of years, for what they sold to the USSR and were overpaying for what they bought from her.

The evidence provided by this and similar inquiries[50] is not entirely conclusive as to the overall *net* loss of the USSR's partners from business with her. Because of the nature of their exports to the Soviet Union, composed as these are to a high degree of manufactures varying in kind and quality, it is scarcely possible to derive from trade statistics a satisfactory set of comparative prices. (It is precisely because the three countries' imports from the USSR consist largely of homogeneous primary goods that a considerably more representative set of import prices could be compiled.)[51] It thus cannot be excluded as a feasible contingency that the three countries' losses on imports from the USSR were fully or partly compensated, or even over-compensated, by gains on their exports, especially on exports of equipment.

[48] Originally the price paid to Czechoslovakia only covered some costs plus a profit margin. At a later stage the respective clause of agreement was given the interpretation of including full mining and loading costs (cf. J. Kasparek, in *Russian R.*, Apr. 1952). In the case of the East German company it was asserted that the USSR pays for the concentrates delivered 'as for any other export commodity', which covers production costs and a 10% margin profit credited to the East German Government as the co-proprietor. That would correspond to the stipulations of the Soviet–East German agreement reported in March 1957. Cf. broadcast statements by Selbmann and Grotewohl of 11 Nov. 1956, and 6 Mar. 1957 respectively.

[49] *R. Econ. Stat.*, xlii/2 (May 1960) (linked with a previous study by the same author, ibid. xli/2 (May 1959)).

[50] See e.g. a paper presented to the Assembly of Captive Europe Nations in July 1960 by Jan Wszelaki (Soviet Price Discrimination in Export to East-Central Europe).

[51] A Czechoslovak official source insisted that prices adjusted according to established rules were giving Czechoslovakia—in her trade with the USSR—a gain of between 5 and 15% over those obtained in her trade with capitalist countries.

Moreover, as would appear from the Mendershausen inquiry, prices charged on something like one-third of the Soviet Union's exports to her Bloc are below those obtainable by her in trade with outsiders. Iron ore, as we have noted, is a case in point. Yet another factor which complicates the issue is the Soviet policy of undercutting prices of some commodities as a means to widening outlets: questions of cost and profit in the sense these terms carry in the West play a small role in the decision-making of Soviet-type foreign-trade organizations. Here an important case in point is oil. It seems to be the fact that Bloc partners pay for oil supplied by the Soviet Union far higher prices than those she charges outsiders; but at the same time Soviet prices charged to Bloc partners would appear to correspond roughly with those prevailing in world markets. The case of Soviet trade in oil with the two Germanies seems to provide support for this view.[52] It is with these qualifications that one may accept as an established fact that, *caeteris paribus*, if these countries were able to turn to free markets for the bulk of the primary materials they import they could save a considerable amount of foreign exchange. The *caeteris paribus* clause includes in particular the assumption that these countries would have ready markets for their own products where they could earn the sufficient quantities of free-market currencies.[53]

The question has been asked whether Central European countries have not turned into an economic liability to the USSR. It has been suggested that at least since the late 1950's, Poland has been a burden on the Soviet economy:[54] still more, and in a less qualified form, would this be the case in regard to East Germany. To have a clear meaning in this context the terms 'liability' and 'asset' would have to be more precisely defined. It may be validly argued that the area ceased to be the source of windfalls which it was for the Soviet Union in the first post-war decade. But the benefits derived from the area under his influence or control by

[52] See *Guardian*, 21 June 1962.
[53] Since I wrote these words I have acquainted myself with broadly similar views expressed by Franklyn D. Holzman, *R. Econ. Stat.*, May 1962. Professor Holzman interprets Soviet pricing as an effect of the Bloc as a 'customs union' rather than in terms of a 'raw bargaining power' as does Dr Mendershausen. The customs-union effect, as understood by Holzman, is that each member 'price-discriminates' against the other. It is the maintenance of the 'union' (and thereby making member nations refrain from trading with outsiders) rather than price discrimination which reflects the Soviet Union's superior power.
[54] See V. Winston, in *Problems of Communism*, no. 3, 1958, pp. 14ff.

the leader of a *Grossraumwirtschaft* can hardly be thought of merely in terms of direct and calculable gains and losses.

Even under the assumption of fair terms of trade and of a supply of Soviet finance to the area, it is of decisive importance for the USSR to possess within the area of her political supremacy a powerful and versatile base whose pattern of production could be geared to her requirements. The essential point is that access to supplies from such a base—especially the metal-processing base—cannot be denied to her by any politically motivated embargo, let alone impeded by foreign-exchange difficulties. The latter factor is of no small weight, considering the order of magnitudes involved.

A tentative balance sheet of benefits and disadvantages is still more difficult to draw from the point of view of the countries of the area, even under the premise of 'fair terms' of trade with the Soviet Union.

Russia's potentialities have always exercised a magnetic power of attraction on the industrialized nations of Central Europe, especially Germany. From this angle the new intimacy of East Germany's economic relationship with the Soviet Union would appear as a paradoxical fulfilment of an long-cherished aspiration, though in a hardly desirable political constellation.

In Czechoslovakia the advantages of close economic links were argued even prior to the February 1948 *coup d'état*.

People in the Western countries [so Dr. Ripka argued at that time] [55] often fail to understand why we are so interested that the USSR should purchase from us the largest possible quantity of our heavy industrial products. The answer is simply that our best possibilities for the sale of these goods appear to be in the USSR and in Central Europe, and not in the Western markets, owing to the high industrial capacities of those countries. The Soviet Union will be able to take many of our products whose selling price is mostly payment for man-hours of work that has gone into their fabrication, and whose export is thus peculiarly advantageous for us.

It may not be surprising to see the lure of the Soviet Union thus forcefully expressed at the time when memories of Czechoslovakia's frustrations in competitive markets during the hard years of the

[55] Address at the Session of the Trade and Craft Committee of the Constitutional National Assembly, reported in *Czechoslovak Economic Bulletin*, no. 57 of 1946, as quoted by Margaret Dewar, *Soviet Trade with Eastern Europe* (London, RIIA, 1951), p. 22.

inter-war era were still fresh. In fact the reasoning behind the words quoted is essentially the same which a decade later underlay the official emphasis on the benefits Czechoslovakia drew from an exchange of the fruits of her work against materials in the highly absorptive Soviet markets.[56] Moreover a desire for close economic co-operation in the region between the Black Sea and the Baltic has been traditionally very much alive in Czechoslovakia, though it would not, of course, be irrelevant for these aspirations that this materialized under Soviet tutelage.

When the subject is approached from Poland's standpoint one cannot overlook that the twenty inter-war years were only an interval in a century-and-a-half-old link with Russia's economy. There is the historical lesson of unquestionable benefits gained in the economic sphere by Poland from this attachment, between the Napoleonic Wars and the First World War. The issue has been almost continuously in the focus of Polish thinking, though in a changing economic and political set-up. At the turn of the last century it was taken up in a brilliantly written essay by Rosa Luxemburg[57] who forecast the vigorous growth of a capitalist economy in Russia and its organic merger with that of Poland, a merger seen as a historically inexorable and highly beneficial process. In a debate which continued over the following decade or two critics argued that, as Russia's industries grew, the interest of the Polish economy would be subordinated to them.[58] (Let us note parenthetically that no sooner did the ink dry on Rosa Luxemburg's words than demands for discriminatory policies against Polish industry became vocal in Russia.)

If Rosa Luxemburg's opponents were able to point to the dangers of Poland's industry being sacrificed to the interest of that of Russia, the risks involved in subordination to a foreign economic *raison d'état* are magnified potentially when this no longer operates in an interplay of market forces, but is enforced in a family of centrally planned economies, likely to be influenced by the leader country.

It is with this very serious qualification that one can properly assess the view—by no means confined to the politically biased—

[56] President Zapotocky's statement to the Prague College of Technology, 15 Feb. 1957.
[57] Rosa Luxemburg, *Die industrielle Entwicklung Polens* (Berlin, 1898).
[58] For an interesting outline of these polemics see the memoirs of one of their participants, A. Wierzbicki, *Wspomnienia i dokumenty* (Warsaw, 1957), pp. 161ff.

that ties with the Soviet Union carry for her orbit a promise of economic advance.[59]

Another important factor deserves consideration. If we may revert again to the historical analogy, the expansion of the Russian-oriented industries of the Congress Kingdom was supported by the flow of capital from the West, from France, Britain, and Germany. The Soviet Union has not been able so far to provide the sphere of her political influence with capital on an adequate scale. The effect of capital deficiency hampers the economic growth of the area and is likely to do so in a foreseeable future (with the possible exception of Czechoslovakia).[60] Whether, and in how distant a future, the Soviet Union might be able to assume the function of a supplier of capital in the required dimensions is open to speculation. The enormous needs of her own expansive economy, needs which must be expected to grow— absolutely and (as recent experience suggests) even in relation to national product—as the grandiose plans for opening up the vast regions in her North and East are implemented—are bound to reduce the availabilities of Soviet capital for Central Europe. These will be inevitably reduced still further to the extent to which the Soviet Union commits herself to the financial support of the underdeveloped countries, both inside and outside the 'Socialist' world. In a word, a tightening rather than an easing of the capital-supply position of the USSR and her orbit seems to be justifiably predictable. And it is well arguable that the Soviet Union's capital hunger and its consequences are among the elements which have left the strongest impact on the mutual relationship between her and the orbit from the day she gained political supremacy after the Second World War. (Hardly any elements exist for speculation on the prospect of a wide flow of Western capital to the countries of the Soviet sphere of political control. The sizeable financial aid which, as has been noted, Poland obtained from the West after 1956 would suggest that such a contingency cannot be entirely excluded, at least not under certain circumstances.)

To conclude these remarks it may be only right to note that our treatment of the links between the USSR and the countries of her

---

[59] Cf. J. Marczewski, *Planification et croissance économique des democraties populaires* (Paris, 1956), i, 93f.
[60] See above, p. 313.

orbit—of Central Europe in particular—isolates one of their aspects: in real life the impact of Soviet-type mechanism is also involved in these links. Above all it is indeed an extremely far-reaching abstraction from reality to ignore the powerful extra-economic factors which come into play.

THE SOVIET BLOC: THE MECHANISM OF INTEGRATION

Having closed the digression on the advantages and disadvantages of Soviet Bloc membership, we propose to add some remarks on the process of its integration and the interconnected subject of the mechanism by which it is being promoted.

This section should begin perhaps by once again reminding the reader that both the nature of the USSR's economy and her post-revolutionary history had hardly elicited any practical interest in problems of the rational coordination of a group of national economies. Only when the phase of 'building socialism in one country' came to its close did the subject become of more than academic relevance. Further, for reasons mentioned earlier, it was only in the 1950's that the Soviet leadership awoke to the need for rational patterning of the Bloc's member-economies. As time passed by the price to be paid in terms of efficiency for autarchically inclined national systems was growing, particularly so in the case of the small-size mature economies of Central Europe dependent on intensive commodity exchanges,[61] through whatever machinery this can conceivably be secured. A vague concept of division of labour has been only slowly gaining recognition. It took still longer to think out its implications: the process of evolving a consistent operational mechanism is still far from completed.[62]

It may also be noticed, if only in passing, that there is inherent conflict between the principle of an international division of labour and the postulate of the 'complex', that is, an all-round development, still so strongly stressed in the Soviet theory of economic growth, with a renewed accent on its universal validity. Demonstrably, however understood, international division of labour implies the antithesis of 'complexity' in the expansion of the

---

[61] The subordinated function in Soviet thinking transpires from the definition of the role of foreign trade 'under socialism' in the official Soviet textbook of economics. Foreign trade is defined as a 'supplementary' source for the expansion of output, taking advantage of achievements of world techniques and improvement in the supply of consumer goods (*Politicheskaya Ekonomiya*, 2nd ed., p. 540).

[62] The subject of this section has been discussed by the present writer in *Problems of Communism*, no. 4, July–Aug. 1959, pp. 23ff.

economy, the imparting to it of bias in favour of production patterns which secure efficiency.

Integration on the Level of Trade

Further, the mechanism by which international division of labour operates is, in practice—from our point of view—of no lesser importance than the principles of economic strategy subscribed to. The essential point is that, until comparatively recent times, the family of centrally planned and controlled economies has endeavoured to integrate its system essentially on the level of trade. Dr Myrdal has rightly stressed the paradox of confining the tools of integration to commerce in the part of the world where the states wield unprecedented and unlimited powers over all means of production.[63] It is true that already at an early stage a coordinating organization was formed to act as a mechanism for harmonizing the associated economies, but until well into the 1950's the Council for Mutual Economic Aid kept to the role of provider of a more or less nominal aegis over bilaterally made trade arrangements. (The CMEA, which was established in 1949 as a counterpoise to the OEEC and Western European consolidation under the Marshall Plan, started its active life years later.)

Quite apart from the impact of historical elements on his attitudes, the central planner and controller is inevitably (and understandably) disinclined—as has been pointed out in previous contexts—to rely for the materialization of his plan in essential sectors on sources of supply and outlets beyond the plan and his control. This is, in fact, one of the most potent among the various factors which tend to depress the planned economies' foreign trade generally. True, it is a contributory element to the preference for intra-Bloc exchanges as against trade with free-enterprise, market economies. Within the Bloc some measures could conceivably be taken (and have been taken) to mitigate the insecurity. The main instrument for this purpose is a trade agreement with a quantitatively fixed commitment. (Such a commitment is only exceptionally feasible in dealings with countries where the state holds no monopoly of foreign trade. Quantitative arrangements with these are, as a rule, of the nature of quotas for the general orientation of the partners rather than obligations.) Gradually,

---

[63] G. Myrdal, *An International Economy* (London, 1956), pp. 147ff.

the periods of such agreements have been extended so as to synchronize them with national plans. Yet even this—as has been found out—has failed to provide a satisfactory answer to the problems of the coordinated expansion of a centrally-planned trading group.

International trade can be an adequate coordinator of free-enterprise economies where a free, competitive market integrates them along the lines of a comparative advantage. (This should be read as no more than a general proposition; we by-pass such problems as the full use of productive resources.)[64] Indeed, in an extreme formulation, free trade is an efficient 'integrator' without any need of institutional integration. In centrally-planned economies whose patterns of production are consciously insulated against external pulls and pushes, there is incomparably less scope for achieving overall integration along the lines of maximum efficiency—whatever the notion of efficiency adopted may be—through the operation of trade alone. One of the impediments is the bilaterality of intra-Bloc commerce conducted within the frame of agreements which are concluded between pairs of its member countries and as a rule stipulate strictly balanced exchanges of goods.[65] Students of the problem inside the Bloc who have analysed the inclination to bilaterality stress that it 'compartmentizes' intra-Bloc exchanges, depresses their potential volume to some low common denominator, and reduces opportunities and freezes resources; in a word, causes quite considerable waste[66]—which is more than proportionate for economies highly dependent on foreign trade.

(Attempts to infuse a measure of multilaterality into intra-Bloc business have proved unworkable owing to technical difficulties. A partial solution was sought in a limited measure of intra-Bloc transferability of trade balances.[67] As one would only expect, this could give little practical relief: national economic plans would be

[64] See *i.a.* J. Tinbergen, *International Economic Integration* (Amsterdam, 1954), p. 107.

[65] Among members of the Bloc, bilateral clearing agreements are the rule: these are concluded as a part of commercial contracts. A marginal degree of elasticity is provided by 'swing' credits fixed as a percentage of trade turnover. It is only where a non-member community (notably Finland) enters as a partner that multilateral clearing facilities have been arranged.

[66] See *i.a.* S. Polaczek, in *Z. Gosp.*, no. 4, 1956; Cz. Niewadzi, ibid. no. 25, 1956; and V. Kaigl, in *Pol. Ekon.*, no. 4, 1956, pp. 238ff.; and G. Kohlmey, *Der demokratische Weltmarkt* (Berlin, 1956), p. 224.

[67] Principles of clearing accounts were elaborated by the CMEA foreign trade committee in Jan. 1962.

obviously thrown out of gear if substantial unscheduled demands
for commodities could be made by a third country in virtue of an
acquired balance which had been formed in trade between two
others.)

The Integration of Production

The CMEA's gradual veering towards a conscious *ex ante*
influencing of production has been the Bloc's functional substitute
for capitalist economies' multilateral trade in competitive markets.
Its beginning was the rather vague allocation of spheres of
specialization as governed by natural resources or historical
development over generations—the allotting, say, of the leading
role in hard-coal and zinc-mining to Poland; in potash and brown-
coal extraction and processing to East Germany; in shipyards to
Poland; and in precision-instrument engineering to East Germany.
The drawing of such broad and established frontiers amounted, as
often as not, to little more than stating the obvious. Subsequently,
formulation of more specific recommendations for potentially
overlapping spheres has become the principal field of the CMEA's
activities, supported by a growing network of specialized technical
coordinating agencies. In particular, catalogues of specialization
were compiled in the 1950's and have been currently revised and
supplemented. The effectiveness of such desiderata has proved,
however, to be extremely limited. We have seen already how little
practical effect was achieved in the intra-Bloc patterning of
engineering and of steel-rolling,[68] a field of coordination with the
longest tradition and experience.

It was discovered before long that fragmentary mutual intra-
Bloc adjustments in selected spheres were not adequate to achieve
a consistently coordinated system. It was increasingly realized that
as often as not they prove unfeasible unless supplemented by deep
adjusting measures all along the line in the inter-connected spheres
and further, that because of their wavelike repercussions throughout modern, tightly interwoven systems, they are likely to become
by themselves—when feasible and implemented—a cause of
wavelike frictions, breakdowns, and bottlenecks in the economies.
Hints have appeared in Soviet economic literature that it is the
economic frontiers that are the root cause of insufficient specialization; that they create the obstacle of national balances of

[68] See above, p. 191.

payments and do not allow for advantage to be taken of economies of scale. The setting up in Central European countries of small national car industries was mentioned as a case in point.[69]

The perception of causes of failure of the existing methodology of intra-Bloc adjustments led, towards the end of the 1950's, to the adoption of a set of principles which required the coordinated economic planning to be detailed and comprehensive in scope, and to be dynamic, carried, that is, over expanded time horizons. These new postulates were considered important enough to be given formal endorsement at the 'summit' conference of the Bloc's political leaders, held in Moscow in May 1958, and subsequently formed the basis of attempts to coordinate plans reaching out to 1980.

It is by such broad stages that the Bloc has moved appreciably nearer to the concept of a supranational, very-long-term planning as an international method consistent with its logic. In discussing the fundamentals of rational planning Professor Oskar Lange argued that economic rationality in a socialist society could and did grow by stages, first via national and later via international plans.[70] A logical step in this direction would be the setting up of a joint planning body, as suggested by the USSR at the end of 1962.

Yet the stronger the emphasis on the international interlocking of national plans, the clearer the obstacles on several planes. First, in techniques. As has been pointed out, price systems of individual Bloc countries fail to reflect opportunity costs. They cannot serve as a reliable guide for patterning outputs on the Bloc-scale as a whole. A CMEA agency has been engaged for some time in formulating criteria and devising basic tools for intra-Bloc decision-making. It is working in particular on methods for comparing efficiency of prime factors in similar sectors of production in different member-countries, it is inquiring into such questions as comparative capital/output ratios, labour productivity, and over-all cost per output unit.[71] Such indicators, expressed in physical-term units (say, output in tons per HP installed or per-man-hour) are expected to yield at least a first approximation and frag-mentary picture of relative efficiencies. The CMEA has been stated to be relying increasingly on the methodology of 'material

---

[69] O. Bogomolov and Yu. Pekshev, in *Plan. Khoz.*, no. 8, 1962.

[70] Lange, *Ekonomia Polityczna—Zagadnienia Ogolne* (Warsaw, 1959), p. 158.

[71] Bogomolov, in *Mirovaya Ekonomika i Mezhdunarodnye Otnosheniya*, no. 4, 1959, p. 32.

balances of output and use of individual products, for the world socialist system as a whole and, first of all, for the member countries of the CMEA'.[72] (It is noteworthy that, on the whole, the CMEA has been somewhat more successful in promoting international specialization in raw materials than in manufactures; compiling a material balance of some manufactures, such as products of engineering, is no doubt beyond the capabilities of the CMEA planners.) We have already pointed out the flaws in this method of national planning. The CMEA apparently contemplates resorting to more sophisticated programming methods and computational techniques: the use of supranational input-output matrices and linear programming was advocated at the Warsaw 1959 session of its Permanent Economic Commission. There is every reason to think that in principle mathematical instruments and techniques of choice-making should be no less effective in selecting an optimal programme on an international, than on the national scale. But the adoption of such methodologies for dynamic supranational planning inevitably, and more than proportionately, multiplies the formidable practical problems and pitfalls it encounters when attempted in less ambitious dimensions of time and space. To sum up this point, as matters stand now, the *ex ante* mapping out of intra-Bloc output pattern based on comparative advantage—though an imperative necessity—is a problem to which no technical solution has been found, at least as yet.

Not only do the techniques of planning raise awkward problems for the intra-Bloc coordinators. To begin with, the very concept of international comparative advantage[73]—of international optimality—is still far from any precise definition in regard to a group of socialist economies. In any case it is obvious that efficient harmonization can only be achieved by conscious shaping of economic destinies over a very long period. Incidentally this may explain the paradoxical fact that as coordination of current plans proved difficult, the CMEA undertook the technically still more difficult task of coordinating the twenty-years' programmes. Patently such long-term shaping cuts deeply into the basic elements of national

---

[72] Ibid.
[73] There is an excellent discussion of the 'schizophrenic existence' of the Ricardo–Mill theory of comparative cost in Marxist theoretical thinking—in an illuminating paper by Dr Frederic Pryor published since this book was written (*Sov. Stud.*, July 1962, p. 50).

economic strategies. Various factors contribute to the difficulty of reconciling them.

One of these factors is the disparity of levels of economic development. Late-comers to industrialization may find themselves handicapped in trying to catch up with the more advanced countries; on this count Central Europeans would on the whole score as against East Europeans. (One has to bear in mind that national income per head in Czechoslovakia and East Germany is roughly half again as large as in the Soviet Union.) On the other hand there are differences in the size and endowment of national economies. On this count on the whole it is the Soviet Union that has the overwhelming advantage over anybody else in the Bloc. Moreover, considering that capital/output ratios are high in primary industries—and in fact more than proportionately so where such industries have to make do with inferior natural wealth—the less fortunate nations of the Bloc would increasingly suffer from the drag of heavy capital absorption in primary as against secondary industries.

The problem is connected with that of remuneration of factors which would underlie the supranational planning. It may be noted that in a Polish discussion of the subject a school of thought[74] argued that in this planning the rent element should be eliminated from the price of raw material. The other question to be borne in mind under this heading is the difference in the national level of real wages. In particular, living standards in the USSR are lower than in the raw-material-importing countries of Central Europe, and are likely to remain so for quite a time. It is indeed one of the 'contradictions' of the Soviet orbit that its leader secures a powerful capital formation rate at the price of keeping real wages below the level existing in some member countries whose growth the USSR is expected to support. The XXII Congress of the Communist Party of the Soviet Union set as a goal the eventual basing of the intra-orbit cost-calculation on 'socially necessary labour'. Still to-day, more than a quarter of a century since the establishment of socialism in the USSR, she has not found it feasible to implement this Marxian precept of socialist economic accounting. One cannot, therefore, see how this will-o'-the-wisp concept could possibly be adopted on the intra-CMEA scale.

[74] See contributions by Rakowski, in *Gosp. Plan.*, no. 6, 1958, pp. 8ff; Bodnar, ibid. no. 8, 1958, pp. 19ff.; S. Polaczek, ibid. no. 8, 1958, pp. 24ff.; and O. Czarnocki, ibid. no. 9, 1958, pp. 43ff.

Conceptually the supranational planner could secure for his system of economies the kind of benefits which are usually thought of as the customs-union effect in regard to market economies. This implies adjusting flows of factors.[75] One wonders whether, under existing conditions, such large-scale intra-Bloc flows of capital are a realistic assumption. Nor does intra-Bloc mobility of labour seem to be any more practicable. A lesson from the past is significant: in an earlier chapter we have pointed to the Bloc's striking inability to redistribute its manpower resources; while deficits of manpower seriously handicap the growth of some member economies, others are no less handicapped by redundant labour.

To sum up: supranational planning involves strategic problems of growth of the component economies, of capital formation and welfare, of distribution of the burden and benefits of development. These matters ultimately impinge on the nation's life far beyond the sphere of economy: indeed the problems involved are ultimately extra-economic. The question arises whether and how far they can be decided supranationally without the intervention of some supranational policy-making and policy-implementing organization with sovereign powers.

The experience of Western European integration has shown that, even within the framework of a free-enterprise market system, economic and political integration mutually condition each other. Yet Professor Viner is probably still right in surmising that it is even more difficult to integrate socialist than capitalist economies without the loss of national identities.[76] One may suspect that there is a conflict in the Bloc between the postulate of economically efficient integration and political feasibility.

[75] See for formal proof in the context of market economies, e.g. J. E. Meade, *Trade and Welfare*, vol. 2 of *Theory of International Economic Policy* (London, 1955), pp. 502ff. See also Professor Meade's *Problems of Economic Union* (Chicago, 1953), especially chapter iii, p. 14.

[76] Jacob Viner, *Am. Econ. R.*, xxxiv/i (Mar, 1944), suppl., p. 328.

INDEX OF NAMES

SUBJECT INDEX